BRITISH COLUMBIA

BRITISH COLUMBIA

A NATURAL HISTORY OF ITS ORIGINS, ECOLOGY, AND DIVERSITY WITH A NEW LOOK AT CLIMATE CHANGE

REVISED AND EXPANDED THIRD EDITION

RICHARD CANNINGS AND SYDNEY CANNINGS

GREYSTONE BOOKS

VANCOUVER / BERKELEY

Greystone Books Ltd.
www.greystonebooks.com

Cataloguing data available from Library and Archives Canada
ISBN 978-1-77164-073-2 (pbk.)
ISBN 978-1-77164-074-9 (epub)

Editing by Nancy Flight and Catherine Plear
Cover and text design by Ingrid Paulson
Cover photograph by Stuart Westmorland/DesignPics/GetStock
Maps on pp. 14, 17, 18, 19, and 30 by Maurice Colpron. Maps on pp.
    35, 40, 44, 52, 63, 68, 69, 70, 71, 88, 104, 106, 112, and 354 by Eric
    Leinberger. Maps on p. 110 by Tongli Wang, Andreas Hamann,
    and David Spittlehouse.
Some of this material was previously published in *Geology of British
    Columbia* and *The New B.C. Roadside Naturalist.*
Printed and bound in China by 1010 Printing International Ltd.
Distributed in the U.S. by Publishers Group West

We gratefully acknowledge the financial support of the Canada
Council for the Arts, the British Columbia Arts Council, the Province
of British Columbia through the Book Publishing Tax Credit and
the Government of Canada through the Canada Book Fund for our
publishing activities.

Greystone Books is committed to reducing the consumption of
old-growth forests in the books it publishes. This book is one step
towards that goal.

Page ii: Sagebrush Mariposa Lily.
Right: These colourfully oxidized rocks above the Bonaparte River
    were formed by ancient hot springs.
Pages vi-vii: Sunrise on the Coast Mountains above Duffey Lake.

CONTENTS

PREFACE

Wᴏᴏ HEN WE WROTE *British Columbia: A Natural History* in 1996, we left many stories unwritten, and many that we had written were edited out for space considerations. In 1998 and 1999 we expanded and rewrote seven chapters to create four smaller books (*Mountains and Northern Forests, The World of Fresh Water, Geology of British Columbia, Life in the Pacific Ocean*) that addressed some of these shortfalls. Much of that material was incorporated into the second edition in 2004. *Geology of British Columbia* was extensively revised in 2011. This revised third edition adds new information and images throughout the volume, including the revisions from *Geology* and material regarding climate change and how it is expected to affect the ecosystems of British Columbia.

British Columbia is a large, diverse province, and the natural history of British Columbia is correspondingly immense; it is simply too big a subject for one book to cover in depth. This book, therefore, is neither an exhaustive collection of facts about the natural history of British Columbia nor a species-by-species guide to the plants and animals of the province. Rather, it is intended to provide an introduction to the ecosystems of the province and to tempt readers to learn and explore more by offering a few intriguing, in-depth stories about life in those ecosystems.

We have used English names of plants and animals wherever possible, and the names of distinct species are capitalized throughout for clarity. The scientific names of all species mentioned are provided in the index.

Each chapter was written predominantly by one of us. Richard wrote most of Chapters 2, 4, 5, 6 and 8, and Sydney wrote most of Chapters 1, 3, 7, 9 and 10. The personal anecdotes contained in each chapter are those of the major author of the chapter. Some of the new material added to Chapters 1, 4 and 10 was written in collaboration with JoAnne Nelson, Marja de Jong Westman and Robert Cannings, respectively.

Each chapter stands on its own; thus, you need not read the chapters in order. However you choose to read the book, we hope that it will help you understand and appreciate the richness and diversity of our province.

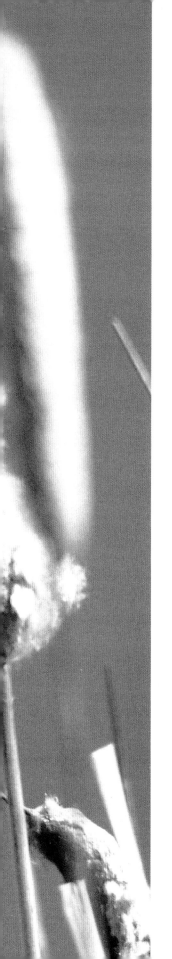

ACKNOWLEDGEMENTS

THIS BOOK WAS inspired by many years of conversations along forest trails, around campfires and in university coffee rooms and government offices. The naturalist tradition in British Columbia is largely an oral tradition, and many knowledgeable people have freely shared their stories with us. We could not have begun to write this book without them.

In particular, we would like to thank Trevor Goward, who provided inspiration and insightful comments on all parts of the book. Chapter 1 was written in collaboration with JoAnne Nelson, and the best prose of that section is hers. Similarly, portions of Chapters 4 and 10 were written in collaboration with Marja de Jong Westman.

Margaret Holm, Leah Ramsay, Douglas Leighton, Nancy Baron, David Stirling, Deanna McLeod, Robert Cannings and Bette Cannings all gave valuable suggestions on the content and style of the original manuscript.

Others that gave freely of their knowledge were Bruce Archibald, Jack Bowling, Tom Carefoot, Maurice Colpron, Dennis Demarchi, Ray Demarchi, Doug van Dine, Graham Gillespie, Carlo Giovanella, Dave Green, Mike Hawkes, Richard Hebda, Catherine Hickson, Darren Irwin, Gail Kenner, Rick Kool, Ken Lertzman, Al Lewis, Don McPhail, Sandra Millen, Jim Monger, Judy Myers, Bill Neill, Tom Northcote, Laurence Packer, Don Reid, June Ryder, Geoff Scudder, Tony Sinclair, Terry Taylor, Howard Tipper, Tongli Wang, Marja de Jong Westman and Grant Zazula. Their comments and suggestions greatly improved the depth and accuracy of the book. Any remaining errors, however, are ours alone.

We truly appreciate the work of Donald Gunn, whose line drawings are a major part of this book. Gerald Straley and Tom Carefoot provided other sets of illustrations, as did Hannah Nadel, Robert Cannings, Tim Parsons, Nola Johnston, Briony Penn, Alex Peden, Wilf Schofield and Bob Carveth. Many photographers freely offered their images as well, but we would especially like to thank Douglas Leighton, Steve Cannings, Chris Harris, Mark Hobson, Al Grass, Graham Osborne and Elaine Humphrey for their help in that regard. Rolf Ludvigsen and UBC Press kindly gave permission to use photographs of fossils from their fine book *Life in Stone*; the photographs were originally provided by the authors of the chapters of the book: Mark Wilson, James Basinger, Ruth Stockey and Wesley Wehr.

A NATURAL HISTORY

INTRODUCTION

INTRODUCTION

WE SPENT A fortunate childhood in the Okanagan Valley, rambling almost every day across wide grasslands and climbing rolling hills covered with flowers and fragrant pines. We took the natural world for granted then; it was literally our backyard. Only later, after exploring more of British Columbia and the world, did we realize how lucky we were to have had parents who encouraged us to love the natural world and learn its ways and how lucky we were to have grown up in British Columbia.

British Columbia is a marvellous place for anyone who is curious about nature. Whether you are strolling in a neighbourhood wood lot, kayaking on the salt chuck, hiking over an alpine pass or driving along a northern highway, the stunning natural scenery lures you on. But British Columbia is more than scenery. For the naturalist, British Columbia is wonderful because it is wonderfully diverse: one province encompassing ten ecological provinces, each with a multitude of natural communities.

Over the millennia, unimaginably powerful tectonic forces have pushed and piled up mountains and plateaus, and ages of rain and glacial ice have carved them into complex systems of valleys, canyons, benches, hills, basins and floodplains. Standing on the western edge of the continent, facing the westerly winds, British Columbia's mountain ranges divide this intricate landscape into climatic stripes of cold and hot, wet and dry.

The complex interaction of geology, topography and climate has produced a tremendous variety of natural communities where animals and plants flourish. The West Coast offers the rich Pacific Ocean and its fringing kelp forests, eel-grass beds and big, sandy bays filled with clams; temperate rain forests of spruce, cedar, hemlock and fir draping steep-walled fiords, with Grizzly Bears fishing for salmon in clear, green rivers; dozens of small islands where oak, juniper and arbutus grow on the sandstone shelves and eagles and sea ducks are drawn to spawning herring.

Warm oceanic winds flow up and over ice-capped mountains; meadows are laden with deep snow in winter and blaze with flowers in summer. Aromatic pine and fir forests cloak the eastern slopes where chipmunks chatter and cicadas whine. Hot, sunny grasslands are awash with the smell of sage after a rainstorm; scorpions and rattlesnakes hide in the warm rocks.

In the deep river valleys filled with marshes, Muskrat, Beaver and Moose move through still waters. Endless plateaus are dotted with lakes, where loons dive for trout. In the big northern spruce forests, Lynx and Snowshoe Hares crouch in thickets of wild rose, Highbush-cranberry and Fireweed.

Pages x–1: An autumn evening at the south end of Okanagan Lake, a landscape shaped by the advance and retreat of Pleistocene glaciers.

Below: Zanardi Rapids, south of Prince Rupert. Canada's richest tidal waters flow past its wettest forests along British Columbia's west coast.

BRITISH COLUMBIA'S BIOLOGICAL DIVERSITY

British Columbia has more species of living things than any other Canadian province (Table 1). But the diversity goes further, since the mountain and water barriers that divide British Columbia have isolated populations of animals and plants from their relatives. Over the millennia, many of these populations have gone their own genetic ways, creating genetic diversity within each species.

Although the reasons for the existence of this rich assemblage of species can be attributed largely to topographic and climatic diversity, other factors are in British Columbia's favour as well. The fact that British Columbia's western border is a major ocean adds many species to the provincial list, and the fact that its eastern border traverses the Rocky Mountains adds a bundle of Great Plains and eastern forest species as well.

The intricate topography of the province juxtaposes mountains, plateaus, valleys and coastal plains with their associated lakes, rivers and wetlands to form a myriad of complex and varied ecosystems. Their plant and animal inhabitants tie all these habitats together to form a cohesive and exciting network of ecosystems that awaits discovery by the curious naturalist.

Some species of animals and plants are endemic to British Columbia, meaning that they are not known to occur anywhere else in the world. On the insect level, 168 species are endemic to British Columbia, and more are discovered every year. Six plant species, most of them restricted to the coast, are endemic as well.

For many other species, British Columbia is home to most of the world population. About 80 per cent of all Cassin's Auklets nest on the British Columbia coast, a million of them on Triangle Island alone. Most Trumpeter Swans nest in Alaska, but more than half spend the winter on British Columbian estuaries. Considering the amount of steep rock habitat in British Columbia, it is not surprising that 60 per cent of the world's Mountain Goats are found there; other impressive tallies for the province include 30 per cent of all Bald Eagles and 25 per cent of all Grizzly Bears.

TABLE 1: NUMBER OF SPECIES OF SELECTED GROUPS OF PLANTS AND ANIMALS

Note: Freshwater and marine fish totals include species that are found in both environments.

	B.C.	Canada
Fungi	10,000	15,000
Mosses	758	1002
Vascular plants	2127	3859
Insects	35,000	55,000
Mites	7000	10,000
Amphibians	22	47
Reptiles	19	48
Mammals	149	218
Birds	509	664
Freshwater fish	99	206
Marine fish	436	1311

LEARNING THE LANGUAGE OF NATURAL HISTORY

How does a curiosity about nature begin? With a high school biology project? A hike in the mountains? Or the birds visiting your backyard bird feeder?

Naturalists fall into the study of natural history in many ways. Most of us start as casual observers of nature, enjoying the outdoors without regard to the names, addresses and occupations of its inhabitants— but then one or two questions about a bird or flower will start to open up a whole world of questions.

But the very diversity that makes the natural world fascinating can also make it an intimidating subject to study. A curious person, setting out with eyes and ears wide open, can learn a lot on his or her own, but by far the easiest way to make a start is to find a friend or acquaintance who shares your interest. Studying natural history is also a lot like learning a foreign language. A few guidebooks are necessary to act as dictionaries, frequent practice is a good idea, and it really helps to have friends who are fluent in the subject.

Many people balk at learning names. Although you can certainly enjoy a walk through a forest without knowing the name of a single tree, it helps to learn the names of at least the common trees and shrubs if you want to understand the forest's basic ecology. And it's fun to learn names—because once you've learned them, you will find old friends in new places. Moreover, knowing the names leads to other discoveries. First, your books will be able to tell you about animal and plant acquaintances. And then you will realize that some species are almost always found together in a natural community and that they like their neighbourhood shady or hot or humid—and you will be well on your way to becoming an ecologist. Don't worry that if you learn the scientific name of a plant, you may no longer be able to appreciate it aesthetically—you will find that learning names only enhances the sense of joy and wonder you experience on your explorations of nature.

After you can answer the simple "What is it?" questions on your explorations of nature, you are ready to go on to the much more interesting questions of where, how, why and when. You are ready to read the landscape, meaning that you keep your eyes and the rest of your senses open for patterns and continually ask yourself questions. Why are all the big trees here Ponderosa Pines but all the seedlings Douglas-firs? Why is this patch of flowers still blooming when all the other ones have gone to seed? Why is this pond ringed with Cattails and that one completely bare of vegetation? Reading

A female Barrow's Goldeneye leaves its nest hole near Riske Creek on the Chilcotin Plateau. Sixty to 90 per cent of the world population of this duck lives in British Columbia, breeding on Interior lakes and wintering on protected coastal inlets.

A crab spider, *Misumena vatia*, waits for an unwary fly on a thistle flower. There are more than six hundred species of spiders in British Columbia, all important predators on insects, yet we know surprisingly little about their distribution and ecology.

the landscape means you can never get bored outside again—it turns every hike and drive into a learning adventure.

THE NEED TO KNOW MORE

The *Birds of British Columbia,* a four-volume set published between 1990 and 2002, was written using a database of over two million bird sightings (most of them supplied by amateur naturalists) and a bibliography of some 4700 books and articles. Although these volumes are an up-to-date synthesis of all that is known about British Columbia birds, the more one uses these books, the more one realizes that they say just as much about what we don't know as what we do know. Vast areas of northern British Columbia have never been visited by a bird-watcher. The distribution and abundance of many species that are restricted to the far northeast or northwest of the province are known only vaguely. We don't know whether they are common and widespread or breed only in one or two valleys.

But our ignorance lies not only in the remote north. Five hundred thousand Ancient Murrelets, about three-quarters of the world population, nest around the Haida Gwaii. These birds move south along the coast in the fall and early winter, then largely disappear, reappearing in spring at the breeding colonies. They probably winter at sea, but where is still a mystery. Thousands of Harlequin Ducks breed in British Columbia, a significant proportion of the world population, but only five nests have ever been found in the province.

Thousands of Sandhill Cranes fly over British Columbia every spring and fall. These are primarily Arctic-nesting populations, whose migration routes are relatively well known. But how many cranes breed in British Columbia? Even though cranes are large, striking birds, they prefer to nest in remote marshes and bogs, and we simply don't know how many nest here. Although we have a vague idea of their breeding range, we really don't know in detail where they nest either. Cranes that nest south of the Arctic can be categorized into two or more subspecies—but we don't know which subspecies breed where in British Columbia. All these questions are important ones if we want to make rational decisions about the management of cranes.

Birds are probably the best-known group of organisms. If you wanted to find where rare wildflowers are known to bloom, you would have to rely on a few decades-old specimens with vague locality labels. And what about mice or bats? Spotted Bats were discovered for the first time in British Columbia in the south Okanagan Valley in 1979, but after a few naturalists learned what they sounded like, they have been heard up through the dry Interior as far north as Williams Lake. But we still don't know what Spotted Bats do in the winter. In fact, we know very little about the hibernation or migration of any of British Columbia's bat species, even the common ones. And our knowledge of invertebrates and fungi, with their awesome diversity, is on a different plane of ignorance altogether.

> HOW DO YOU PLACE A VALUE ON INSPIRATION?
> HOW DO YOU QUANTIFY THE WILDNESS OF BIRDS WHEN, FOR
> THE MOST PART, THEY LEAD SECRET AND ANONYMOUS LIVES?
> Terry Tempest Williams, *Refuge*

We live in times of tremendous environmental change. The grasslands and pinewoods we walked through as boys are filling with walled cities of retirement homes; the south Okanagan natural landscape is considered one of the most endangered ecosystems in Canada. Ancient coastal forests have been reduced to a few remnant valleys; deep, clear fiords are closed to shellfish harvesting because of chemical contaminants. Being a naturalist opens your eyes to these daily differences around you. Knowing more about the natural world helps you listen objectively to conflicting media reports about forestry practices, new housing developments and vanishing species. All of us need to know more about this world. We hope this book will provide a little of this knowledge and, more important, pass on an enthusiasm and a love for the natural world.

ORIGINS

ORIGINS

N BRITISH COLUMBIA, it is hard to ignore geology. Most of us may not understand the rocks around us as well as we would like, but we are well acquainted with them—they stare at us from mountain cliffs and rugged shorelines every day.

If you were to take a flight across the province—say, from Jasper, Alberta, to Port Hardy on Vancouver Island—you would see a jaw-dropping variety of geological features. First come the sedimentary rocks of the glistening Rockies, rising abruptly above the forested plains. Next, the snowy peaks of the Cariboo Mountains rise up across the Rocky Mountain Trench, their crystalline rocks tortured by the heat and pressure of unimaginable forces beneath the surface of the earth. Now the broad Interior plateau comes into view, with its flat surface of poured lava surrounding the eroded valleys and canyons of the Fraser and Chilcotin Rivers. And finally, the shining white ice of Mount Waddington rises ahead, towering over the Coast Mountains' choppy sea of granite. A more diverse flight can hardly be imagined, and this one has ignored the myriad of British Columbia's geological wonders to the north and south.

In more ways than one, geology is the foundation of natural history.

Geological formations not only form the physical base of terrestrial life and control the climate around it but also tell the temporal history of nature. Geology tells us how things came to be the way they are. Moving continents, rising and falling mountain barriers, vast volcanic eruptions and continental ice sheets all have played an essential role in creating the diversity of life in British Columbia today. Without a basic knowledge of geology, it is difficult to make sense of this diversity.

THE BUILDING OF BRITISH COLUMBIA: PLATE TECTONICS

British Columbia is part of the North American Cordillera—the mighty set of mountain ranges that stretch from northern Alaska to southern Mexico. This mountainous landscape arose through plate tectonic processes. Plate tectonics is how the earth works. Its crust and underlying relatively stiff upper mantle form a carapace of plates like the bones of a baby's skull before they suture and lock together. The plates are constantly moving—some growing, some shrinking—at about the speed a fingernail grows. The key to the Cordillera is a long history of interactions between the western edge of the continent, the plates that make up the floor of the Pacific Ocean, and the small, mobile pieces of crust in between that have been created, that have evolved and that have shifted between ocean and land.

Our planet is unique in having plate tectonics. The constant swirling and recycling of the ocean's rocky floor requires that the planet's interior—like Goldilocks's bowl of porridge—must be just right, not too hot and not too cold. Plate tectonics results from a balance between subduction—the sinking of oceanic plates at trenches like the modern Cascadia subduction zone off British Columbia's west coast—and spreading at ocean ridges, where new crust is created by the rise of hot material in the earth's mantle, as is happening at the Juan de Fuca Ridge a little farther west (Figure 1.1). The process of plate tectonics as we know it began sometime in Precambrian time. Exactly when is a matter of current discussion. But geologists agree that before then, the young earth was too hot and the plates were too buoyant to sink deep into the mantle. Eventually, the planet will cool to the point that the upward rise of mantle and melting of basalt to supply the ridges will fail—but we have billions of years left before that time. Meanwhile, the plates shift constantly, slowly, inexorably, building mountains while we sleep, only rumbling their intentions with earthquakes from time to time.

The modern North American continent is constructed like a chocolate-covered nut. At its core is an ancient continent, or craton, called Laurentia. Laurentia holds the record for the oldest rocks yet dated on earth, announced by Quebec researchers in 2008 as 4.28 billion years old. Compared with the craton, the rocks that make up the outer continent margin—including those of the Cordillera—are much younger, generally less than 700 million years.

Pages 8–9: The red volcanic rocks of the Rainbow Range in Tweedsmuir Provincial Park, the product of a hot spot in the earth's mantle, are a testament to the dynamic nature of British Columbia's geology.

All of them have been added to the original continent. There are piles of sedimentary rock that once lay at its outskirts but rode up over it during periodic collisions. There are also continental fragments that had split from the continent but were later pushed back against it, parts of the margin that were dragged sideways by the motion of offshore oceanic plates. Some of the added pieces are actually crustal wanderers that crossed oceans to reach the western reach of the growing continent, and they play their role in building mountains there.

Not that Laurentia simply sat there, waiting for all this to happen. Its story, too, is that of a wanderer. It has been part of two supercontinents, and probably others before them, in the endless flamenco of approach and spurn, touch and turn away that has marked the earth's rocky carapace ever since it formed. The breaking up of the Precambrian supercontinent Rodinia 750 to 550 million years ago did not create our Cordillera—that was many eons later—but it made the Cordillera possible. Without that breakup, Laurentia would have lain serenely within a vast continental interior: a prairie, perhaps, or a vast plain of lakes and wetlands, its smooth, low surface unbroken by even a dream of mountains.

But as it happened, towards the end of Precambrian time, a rift formed in what is now southern British Columbia, one of the many that fragmented the world continent Rodinia into many pieces. Whatever was on the other side of that rift—Australia, Antarctica and Siberia each has its advocates—moved slowly and stately away to the west. The Pacific Ocean was born, and the whole tectonic drama of Cordilleran evolution could begin.

The Cordilleran terranes are pieces of once-mobile crust that make up much of the Cordillera, extending west to the Pacific Ocean from an eastern edge in the Omineca Mountains. On Map 1 (page 14) you see them divided into realms, according to their origins. The peri-Laurentian terranes lie between the Omineca Mountains and the western Coast Mountains and underlie the Intermontane region in between. They once were the bedrock of arc-shaped chains of volcanic islands and small oceans that lay west of the old continent, in a complex and evolving geography comparable with the other side of the Pacific Ocean basin today. Think of Japan, perhaps, or the Philippines. One of the ancient island arcs is named Quesnellia, after the town of Quesnel. It runs from there north to the Yukon border east of Teslin Lake and south past Princeton. The other old island arc, Stikinia, spans western British Columbia from Bella Coola to Atlin. Island arcs form above subduction zones. Their volcanoes build from lavas and explosive volcanic deposits that originate as melts of the subducted plate as it plunges down into hotter and hotter mantle.

Parts of these volcanic island chains were founded on rifted fragments of Laurentia (to imagine a rifted fragment, think of California west of the San

FIGURE 1.1

The plate tectonic setting off the coast of British Columbia today. Magma from the earth's mantle rises upward along the Juan de Fuca Ridge, cooling to form new ocean floor. The walls of the ridge are pulled apart by the same convection currents, and the Pacific Plate and the Juan de Fuca Plate grow symmetrically on either side of the ridge. Where the latter plate encounters westward-moving North America, it slides beneath the continental shelf and descends into the mantle. When it reaches depths of 150 to 100 kilometres, the plate partly melts again, and the resulting magma rises up to reappear as the volcanoes of the Cascade-Garibaldi Arc—among them Mount Meager, Mount Garibaldi, Mount Baker, Mount Rainier and Mount St. Helens. Adapted from C. J. Yorath, *Where Terranes Collide*, p. 123.

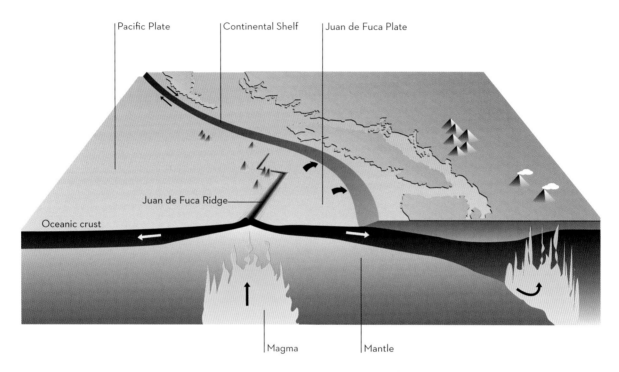

Andreas Fault—this piece of the continent is being pushed inexorably north and will eventually sail past the west coast of British Columbia). The Slide Mountain terrane is the Late Paleozoic seafloor of a minor ocean that grew between one of these rifted chunks and the mother continent. It is spectacularly exposed in the Cassiar Mountains of far northern British Columbia, forming dark peaks of basalt and deep-water sediments where it now rests atop the pearl-grey limestones of western Laurentia. It is as if the floor of today's Sea of Japan, a small ocean that for the last 20 million years or so has been widening between Japan and mainland Asia, were to be shoved back up on top of Korea, and then the whole pile uplifted and carved into mountains.

Compared with the relatively local peri-Laurentian terranes, those of the Tethyan and Arctic realms have travelled astounding distances to arrive in their present Cordilleran berths. Among the many lines of evidence for their

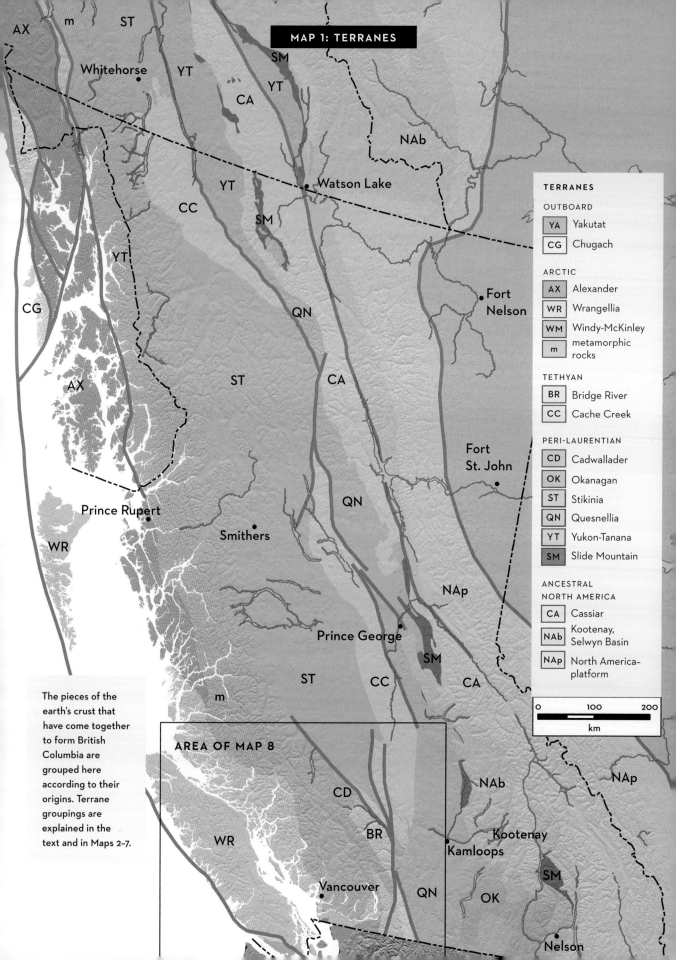

MAP 1: TERRANES

The pieces of the earth's crust that have come together to form British Columbia are grouped here according to their origins. Terrane groupings are explained in the text and in Maps 2–7.

AREA OF MAP 8

TERRANES

OUTBOARD
YA Yakutat
CG Chugach

ARCTIC
AX Alexander
WR Wrangellia
WM Windy-McKinley
m   metamorphic rocks

TETHYAN
BR Bridge River
CC Cache Creek

PERI-LAURENTIAN
CD Cadwallader
OK Okanagan
ST Stikinia
QN Quesnellia
YT Yukon-Tanana
SM Slide Mountain

ANCESTRAL NORTH AMERICA
CA   Cassiar
NAb Kootenay, Selwyn Basin
NAp North America–platform

0   100   200
km

exotic origins, fossils are one of the most compelling. The Cache Creek terrane forms a discontinuous strip in the British Columbia Interior, surrounded
to the east, north and west by more local peri-Laurentian terranes. Its southern exposures can be seen around Cache Creek and Clinton and as far west
as the white limestone bluffs of Marble Canyon. On the drive north of Cache
Creek on Highway 97, some of the nearby low hills are made of curiously
bare, crumbly, dark green to blue-green scree. This is serpentinite, a rock that
once made up the deep mantle underpinnings of oceanic crust. Serpentine is
a stone that grows little moss, and still less complex forms of vegetation.
Compared with continental crust, which has benefited from the distillation of
nutrients in generations of magmas and of sedimentary cycles, mantle is a poverty-
stricken substrate composed of silica, magnesium, iron, nickel, cobalt and
precious little else. Few plants can survive in its nutrient-poor soils. But its
presence here delights the geologist, because its exhumation from deep mantle to grassland demonstrates a powerful process of planet-scale plate motion
and, more specifically, a dramatic collision of an oceanic plate with the
continent.

If you were to look closely at the limestones around Marble Canyon you
would find, along with corals, some unassuming little fossils that look like fat
grains of wheat. They are fusulinids, a now-extinct family of foraminifera
(shelled amoeboid organisms) that flourished in warm Late Paleozoic seas.
The youngest Marble Canyon fusulinids are Late Permian, and some are of
the genus *Yabeina*. These small foreign creatures have no known relatives in
or near Laurentia, but they and all their cousins can be found in their billions
in the Permian limestones of China and Japan. In Permian time, long before
the continental collisions that drove the Alps and Himalayas skyward, a bend
of ocean called the Tethys lay surrounded by Europe, Siberia, Africa, India
and Antarctica, with the continental fragments that now make up China on
its east. *Yabeina* grew prolifically there. The Marble Canyon limestones are
thought to have been reefs built on an ocean island somewhere on that side
of the Pacific. After that, the island must have become entrained in an
eastward-moving oceanic plate, reeled towards the Laurentian margin by
rapid subduction under its fringing island arcs, Stikinia and Quesnellia.

Outside and west of the peri-Laurentian terranes in British Columbia lie
the Insular terranes, Wrangellia and the Alexander terrane—the bedrock of
Vancouver Island, Haida Gwaii (the Queen Charlotte Islands) and the islands
of the Inside Passage. These rocks are also exotic but probably with an
entirely different origin than that of the Cache Creek terrane: they once were
part of the Arctic realm. Their older parts formed and evolved somewhere
near northern Scandinavia and eastern Siberia until in mid-Paleozoic time,
when they were propelled westward through the Arctic Ocean and into the
Pacific. Again, some of the key evidence is fossils. For instance, some unusual

early Paleozoic sponges (480 to 420 million years ago) are found in the Alexander terrane on Prince of Wales Island in southeastern Alaska just north of Prince Rupert. Other than the Alexander terrane, these particular sponges are found only in terranes of northwestern Alaska and Oregon, and in the southern Ural Mountains.

The transport of the Arctic and Insular crustal fragments westward across the Arctic seaway left its traces in glancing mid-Paleozoic collisions recorded in the rocks of the Canadian Arctic Islands and the Brooks Range of northern Alaska. Unlike the ocean floor that ferried the Cache Creek oceanic islands towards the Laurentian margin under traction from its subduction zones, the Arctic terranes were fragments of volcanic island arc and continental origin that might have transited between northern Laurentia and Siberia by a mechanism like the recent history of the Caribbean ocean (Maps 2–7). In the Caribbean, an island arc that once lay next to the Pacific Ocean reformed into a giant, bulging loop that surged over a thousand kilometres across to the Atlantic side, its ends colliding with the Bahama Banks to the north and Venezuela to the south. This incredible journey is well documented by geological observations. It has taken about 60 million years to accomplish, and is still happening, with the eastward migration of the Lesser Antilles island chain. The tragic earthquake in Haiti in 2010 was a catastrophic release of pent-up strain on the Enriquillo-Plaintain Fault, one of the great faults that separates the eastward-moving Caribbean plate from westward-moving North America.

The "loopiness" of island arc chains in general—think of the graceful festoons of the Aleutians, Kuriles and Marianas around the north and west of the Pacific—is caused by the oceanward advance of island arcs towards their subduction zones. The shorter the total length of the arc, the faster its advance because the easier it is for mantle to flow around its ends and into the gap behind it, where a new little ocean opens wider with time. Short arcs clock high rates of forward migration—1.8 centimetres a year for the Lesser Antilles, 5.7 centimetres a year for the Scotia arc southeast of Tierra del Fuego and 6.8 centimetres a year for the Calabrian arc, a tiny obscure feature of the Mediterranean Sea. By contrast, the centre of the 4000- kilometre-long Andean arc is thought to be actually retreating at 0.7 centimetres per year. With this in mind, it is easy to imagine that the short arc segment between Laurentia and Siberia would have been a prime bet as a fast forward traveller.

The evolution of marine faunas in the Insular terranes attests to the terranes' westward migration. By Late Paleozoic time, instead of eastern Arctic forms, fossils in them are typical of northern Pacific waters. They were not yet interacting directly with anything on the western Laurentian margin, but they were getting close enough to play their part in the events to come.

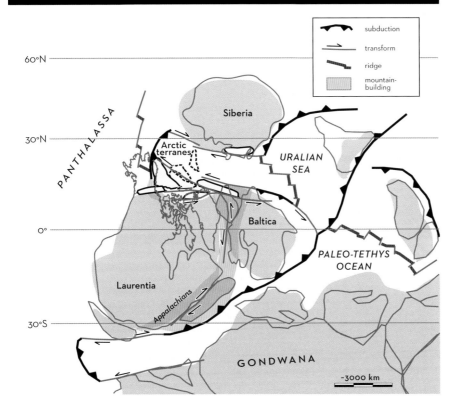

MAP 2: SILURIAN (425 MILLION YEARS AGO)

~3000 km

60°N

PANTHALASSA

Siberia

30°N

Arctic
terranes

PALEO-TETHYS
OCEAN

0°

Baltica

Laurentia

Appalachians

30°S

MAP 3: EARLY DEVONIAN (395 MILLION YEARS AGO)

	subduction
	transform
	ridge
	mountain-building

60°N

Siberia

PANTHALASSA

30°N

Arctic
terranes

URALIAN
SEA

0°

Baltica

Laurentia

PALEO-TETHYS
OCEAN

Appalachians

30°S

GONDWANA

~3000 km

The tectonic evolution of western North America (pages 17–19). The assembling of the west coast of North America is a complex story, and this series of maps serves as a visual guide to the wanderings of terranes. An approximate outline of the present continent is in blue, and the inferred extent of continent through time is shown by grey shading. Orange shading shows active mountain belts.

Top: The Arctic terranes (yellow) that now occupy coastal B.C. and part of Alaska probably originated near the northern end of the Caledonian mountain belt, between the continents of Laurentia, Siberia and Baltica.

Bottom: The westward travel of the Arctic terranes towards Panthalassa (the precursor to the Pacific Ocean) is believed to have been propelled by a Caribbean-style subduction zone. This subduction zone, its island arcs and continental fragments travelled rapidly along a Paleozoic Northwest Passage.

Top: The northward shift of Euramerica (the now-combined Laurentia and Baltica), during its collision with Gondwana, results in the formation of a subduction zone along the West Coast. This subduction begins from the small Caribbean-type zone and moves some of the Arctic terranes southward. The hot upwelling beneath the subduction zone causes a rift in Laurentia, giving birth to the first of the peri-Laurentian arc terranes along the West Coast, including the Yukon-Tanana terrane (blue-green).

Bottom: Westward retreat of the subduction zone leads to widespread island arc volcanism (green) that develops on fragments of western Laurentia (blue-green) and on some of the Arctic terranes (yellow) that had recently arrived. These new arc terranes include the early expressions of Stikinia and Quesnellia. The Slide Mountain Ocean develops between the island arc and the continental margin in the wake of the westward migration of the arc, mirroring what is happening in the present-day Sea of Japan. The Insular terranes of coastal B.C. (Alexander and Wrangellia) come together far out in Panthalassa. Alexander is one of the Arctic terranes with northern European origins.

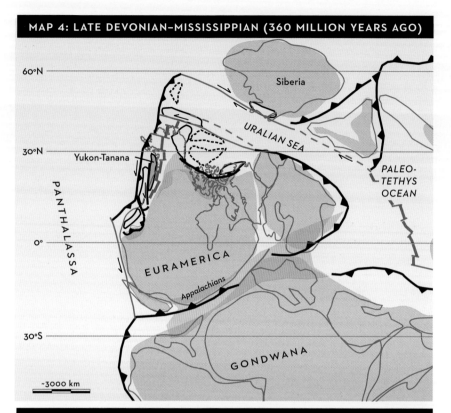

MAP 4: LATE DEVONIAN–MISSISSIPPIAN (360 MILLION YEARS AGO)

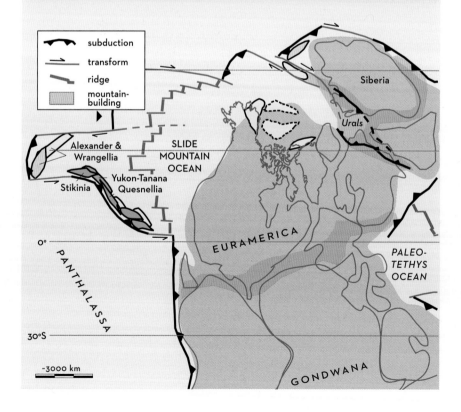

MAP 5: PENNSYLVANIAN–EARLY PERMIAN (300 TO 285 MILLION YEARS AGO)

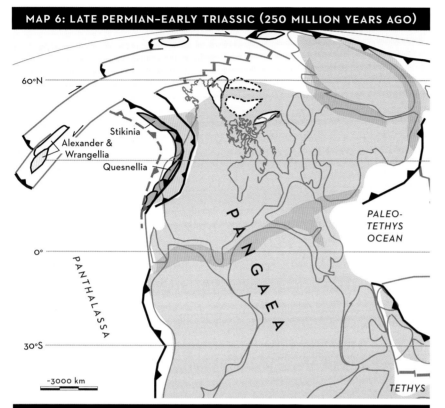

MAP 6: LATE PERMIAN–EARLY TRIASSIC (250 MILLION YEARS AGO)

60°N

Stikinia

Alexander & Wrangellia

Quesnellia

P A N G A E A

P A N T H A L A S S A

0°

30°S

PALEO-TETHYS OCEAN

TETHYS

~3000 km

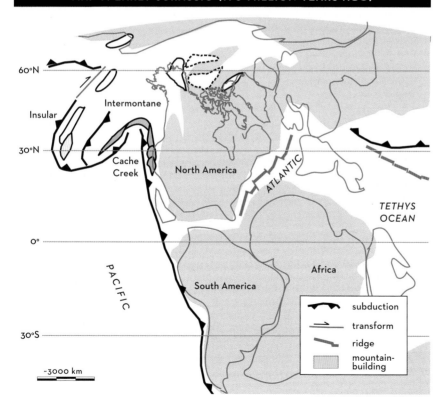

MAP 7: EARLY JURASSIC (190 MILLION YEARS AGO)

60°N

Insular

Intermontane

Cache Creek

North America

30°N

ATLANTIC

TETHYS OCEAN

0°

PACIFIC

South America

Africa

30°S

~3000 km

subduction	
transform	
ridge	
mountain-building	

Top: All major continental masses have converged to form the supercontinent Pangaea. Along its west coast, subduction has reversed to consume the Slide Mountain Ocean, returning the peri-Laurentian arc terranes (green) to near the continental margin. Later in Triassic time, subduction flips once more (dashed grey line), and arc volcanism flourishes again on Quesnellia and Stikinia. Alexander and Wrangellia remain at large in Panthalassa.

Bottom: The Atlantic Ocean is born, growing in the rift between North America, Africa and part of Europe, and propelling North America westward. Buckling of the peri-Laurentian (Intermontane) terranes traps part of the ancient Pacific Ocean floor that was brought to North America by the subduction conveyor belt from far reaches—the Cache Creek terrane. At the same time, the westward-moving North America is on a collision course with the Insular terranes lying offshore in the Pacific. The ultimate collision will build the mountains of western North America and shape the final terrane patchwork.

COLLISIONS AND UPHEAVALS: THE CONTINENT GROWS WEST

The mid-Jurassic, about 185 to 170 million years ago, was a time of crisis and profound change in the Cordillera. Before then, the peri-Laurentian terranes formed a dynamic, shape-shifting zone west of Laurentia. Farther west, the Insular terranes shifted and rifted, still all on their own. After the mid-Jurassic, all of these massive crustal blocks came together to collide and coalesce, heave and pile, thrust and thicken, creating the Cordilleran mountains that we know now.

THE BURGESS SHALE: BRITISH COLUMBIA'S EARLIEST ANIMALS

About 530 million years ago, where today the Rockies tower over the small community of Field, an underwater escarpment perhaps 200 metres high snaked along the ocean floor west of the continental shore. Known as the Cathedral Escarpment, it was the wall of a limestone reef built by calcareous algae—which are seaweeds encrusted with calcium carbonate—for corals had not yet evolved. At the base of this wall, a thriving community of animals lived on, in and above the muddy sediments that drifted down from above.

Periodic mudslides buried these animals in fine silts, which hardened over the millennia to form shale. Today this site is known as the Burgess Shale, named for the pass that is traversed to reach it, and it is the most remarkable fossil bed in the world. Few sites can boast such finely detailed fossils, and few preserve animals of this age. The Burgess fauna lived only geological moments after the Cambrian explosion, the great diversification of complex animal life, and the Burgess Shale provides the sharpest picture we have of that extraordinary period. It also provides an extensive picture, with over 73,000 specimens of 140 species recovered to date. In recent years, more fossil sites bearing Burgess Shale fauna have been found along the Cathedral Escarpment in Kootenay National Park, as well as near Cranbrook, British Columbia, and Jasper, Alberta.

Perhaps the most amazing feature of the Burgess fauna is its diversity, not in the sense of numbers of species, for today's oceans are undoubtedly richer in species, but in the anatomical designs for life. Steven Jay Gould, in his book *Wonderful Life* (a fascinatingly thorough account of the Burgess Shale), uses the term *disparity* to describe this richness of body plans.

The disparity in the Burgess Shale fauna reaches across all levels of classification. At the upper level, at least seven anatomical designs occur that do not fit into any previously known phylum, the highest grouping in the animal kingdom. There are oddities such as *Opabinia,* a segmented creature with five eyes and a clawed, frontal nozzle, and *Anomalocaris,* a large (about 50 centimetres long) swimmer with stalked eyes, a mouth that looks like a pineapple ring and a series of lobed fins. At a lower level, within the phylum

WHY IS *OPABINIA,* KEY ANIMAL IN A NEW VIEW OF LIFE, NOT A HOUSEHOLD NAME IN ALL DOMICILES THAT CARE ABOUT THE RIDDLES OF EXISTENCE?
Steven Jay Gould, *Wonderful Life*

Arthropoda, at least twenty animals are not closely related to other major arthropod groups, living or extinct.

What happened?

The key is in the timing. The Insular terranes collided with the outer margin of the peri-Laurentian terranes, in what is now the western Coast Mountains, in the mid-Jurassic. In southeastern British Columbia, in the Goat Range near New Denver, the peri-Laurentian terranes were first thrust up on the sedimentary apron of the continent—in the mid-Jurassic. The youngest ocean-bottom deposits in the Cache Creek terrane that represent the end of the terrane's existence as an open ocean are from the late Early Jurassic. The volcanoes of Stikinia and Quesnellia all shut down in the mid-Jurassic, signifying the death

What does this disparity mean? It means that early in the evolution of multicellular animal life, there was a much greater variety in basic body plans than there is today. Life did not evolve as a cone of ever increasing diversity; rather, there was a great flourishing of possibilities at the beginning, followed by a great decimation. The loss of many anatomical possibilities has resulted in today's pattern; the vast majority of animal life is contained within a handful of phyla, each with a standard body plan—the arthropods, mollusks, echinoderms, annelid worms, roundworms, cnidarians and chordates.

Why did this great decimation of animal possibilities occur? The textbook answer would be that a few of the body plans were more efficient and successful than the others; they prevailed while others vanished. But if you compared the "failures" with their contemporaries, the early representatives of modern groups, you would find that there is no way to predict why one would prevail and another disappear. Evolution at the phylum level might be more related to historical accidents than to evolutionary "fitness." As Gould puts it, if we rewound the tape of life and let it play again, we would get an entirely different world.

Anomalocaris

A final note: within the animal community preserved in the Burgess Shale is a rare, small, wormlike creature called *Pikaia gracilens*. Named after nearby Mount Pika, it is believed to be the world's first known chordate. Gould sums up his thesis of disparity followed by decimation using this oldest of our chordate relatives as an example:

And so, if you wish to ask the question of the ages—why do humans exist?—a major part of the answer, touching those aspects of the issue that science can treat at all, must be: because Pikaia survived the Burgess decimation.

This response does not cite a single law of nature; it embodies no statement about predictable evolutionary pathways, no calculation of probabilities based on general rules of anatomy or ecology. The survival of Pikaia was a contingency of "just history." I do not think that any "higher" answer can be given, and I cannot imagine that any resolution could be more fascinating.

CACHE CREEK MÉLANGE

Cache Creek has given its name to a piece of crust that forms a slender stripe through the B.C. Interior (see map of geological terranes, p. 14). It appears as though it is the glue that binds Stikinia to the west and Quesnellia to the east— but these two terranes are "local" chunks of crust that rifted from ancient North America and formed island arcs just offshore, whereas the Cache Creek Terrane had its origins in the far-off Tethys Sea, an ancient ocean that once lay south and west of China. How did it find itself between Stikinia and Quesnellia? Recent geological reconstruction has proposed a remarkable explanation. First, it was reeled across the ancient Pacific by rapid subduction under Stikinia and Quesnellia. Then, as it came into contact with the island arcs, they began to buckle in the middle, and the north piece, Stikinia, was pulled down to the west, eventually closing in behind Cache Creek, giving it a big geological hug. During the squeezing, some of these rocks were crushed into a wild mixture—a "mélange" in geological terms—samples of which are visible as blackish, messy rocks behind buildings west of the highway at the south end of Cache Creek.

of the subduction zones that had fed them. Whatever triggered these sweeping and simultaneous changes must have been at a scale vaster than all the terranes taken together.

The likely cause lies in global plate tectonics. In Middle to Late Paleozoic time, Laurentia had become incorporated into the supercontinent Pangaea, by collisions with Europe and South America that built the Appalachians. But supercontinents, like empires, carry the seeds of their own demise. Like Rodinia before it, Pangaea began to break up in the Early Jurassic. The North Atlantic began to open about 180 million years ago—first a crack, then a seaway, and then, by the mid-Jurassic, a nascent ocean. A new continent, North America, with old Laurentia in its core, started to move ponderously westward. The once-independent terranes of the Cordillera simply got in the way.

The result was our mountains—low ones at first, with the initial collisions, but as the continent continued its inexorable course, sedimentary strata at its margin piled up like snow in front of a vast, majestic snowplow, riding up and over eastward to make the shingled stack that later would be sculpted into the modern Rockies. The physiography of British Columbia— its twin backbones of the Coast Mountains and the Ominecas and Rockies separated by the more subdued Intermontane belt—is the result of the two slow-motion, simultaneous collisions. Where the Intermontane terranes piled up onto the old continental margin, the Omineca and Rocky Mountains rose. Where the Insular terranes collided with the outer edge of the Intermontane terranes, the Coast Mountains were born.

THE OMINECA-ROCKY MOUNTAIN COLLISION ZONE

As North America drove under its western neighbours during the Middle Jurassic, large pieces of Quesnellia and the Slide Mountain terrane began to peel off the oceanic plate. Some slices up to 25 kilometres thick overrode the continental margin, becoming stacked like pancakes on top of it. This stacking makes it difficult to say precisely where the old edge of North America lies today. The rocks of the terranes and the old continental shelf were squeezed and folded to form the Columbia, Omineca and Cassiar Mountains. In some areas the intense compression and consequent heating recrystallized the rocks into the metamorphic rocks of the Omineca and Monashee Mountains and the Quesnel and Shuswap Highlands. Partial melting in some regions gave rise to local intrusive igneous rocks.

Compression continued, and the thick layers of sedimentary rocks covering the continental core were pushed ever eastward in front of the colliding wedge and were squeezed, folded and telescoped (Figure 1.2).

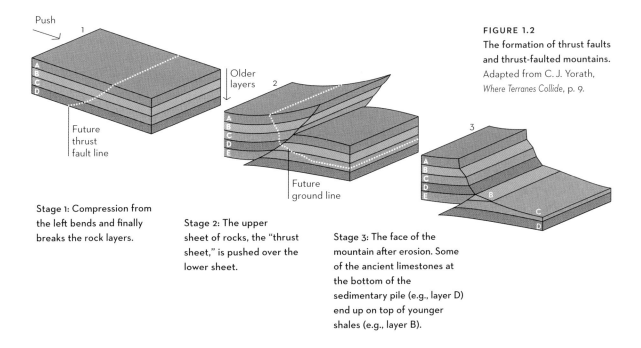

FIGURE 1.2
The formation of thrust faults and thrust-faulted mountains. Adapted from C. J. Yorath, *Where Terranes Collide*, p. 9.

Stage 1: Compression from the left bends and finally breaks the rock layers.

Stage 2: The upper sheet of rocks, the "thrust sheet," is pushed over the lower sheet.

Stage 3: The face of the mountain after erosion. Some of the ancient limestones at the bottom of the sedimentary pile (e.g., layer D) end up on top of younger shales (e.g., layer B).

Treadmill Ridge, looking south along the Continental Divide between Jasper National Park and Mount Robson Provincial Park. These gently sloping mountains end in abrupt cliffs to the east, which mark today's eroded edge of a thrust sheet (see Figure 1.2).

The sedimentary layers first were deformed into waves like those in a carpet being pushed. But the strong, resistant limestone layers broke when folded and became stacked up one on top of another in gently sloping piles. These breaks are called thrust faults, and the blocks of rocks above the break are called thrust sheets. By 120 million years ago, the western ranges of the Rockies were stacking up. A deep depression, the Rocky Mountain Trough (not Trench) formed east of the mountain-building wave, the result of the tremendous weight building up on the edge of the continent. The rapid uplift caused massive erosion of the new mountains, and sediments soon piled up in the trough's inland sea, forming thick deposits of mudstone and shale.

The mountain-building wave in the Rockies continued to move eastward. The main ranges were rising about 100 million years ago and, by the time the pushing stopped about 60 million years ago, the eastern ranges and foothills had been created. When all was said and done, the thrust sheets (Figure 1.2) had been telescoped and shoved up to 250 kilometres eastward from their original position—the rocks of Mount Rundle, at Banff, were originally laid down somewhere around Revelstoke. As the thrust sheets moved to the east and stacked on top of one another, the Rocky Mountain Trough moved eastward ahead of them. But the thrust sheets overtook the shales that had been deposited in the trough's earlier position, and layers of these soft shales were caught between the sheets. The shales erode much more easily than the resistant limestones, and this difference results in a pattern that is seen over and over again in the Rockies—hard, limestone cliffs towering over soft, shale-bottomed valleys (Figure 1.2, page 23).

THE COAST MOUNTAINS COLLISION ZONE

As the Insular terranes ran into the Intermontane terranes, a new subduction zone formed to the west near the present continental margin, and a new belt of continental magmatism replaced the old island arcs along the line of the present Coast Mountains. Many separate but coalescing igneous intrusions rose up in a succession of pulses from 170 to 50 million years ago, creating the Coast Mountains batholith, one of the largest bodies of granite and granitoid rocks on the planet.

The heat of all that intrusion softened and weakened the earth's crust and created a second, outboard zone of crustal thickening between the advancing new continental margin and the subduction zone. If you drive from Terrace west along the Skeena River towards Prince Rupert, you can see the gneisses that make up the roots of these mountains. Some of them have experienced conditions of pressure and temperature that could only have occurred at 25 kilometres below the surface, showing the amount of uplift that has made, and made again and over again, this maritime mountain range over the years.

The huge volume of granites in the Coast Mountains, as well as the intensity of deformation at later stages in their geological evolution, has made the early history of this mountain range particularly hard to decipher. Crustal thickening and metamorphism 100 to 80 million years ago produced such profound changes that evidence for the initial collision between the Insular and Intermontane terranes has been nearly wiped off the record. Another key structural event that was mostly overwritten by the frenzied later Cretaceous is a series of older faults that can help us understand the geological puzzles posed by the southernmost Coast Mountains and North Cascades.

TERRANES OF THE SOUTHERN COASTAL BELT

The southern Coast Mountains and the North Cascades, so accessible to hikers and skiers from Vancouver, actually contain some of the most perplexing geology to be found anywhere in the province. Instead of a few big terranes, they are made up of a whole structural stack of little ones (Map 8). Some of these, the Bridge River, Methow and Cadwallader terranes, represent an ocean like the Cache Creek, except that instead of closing in mid-Jurassic time, it did no such thing until halfway through the Cretaceous. Other terranes, like the Chilliwack and Harrison Lake, resemble parts of Stikinia. Then

Right: The rocks of the Skeena Mountains originated as sediments eroded from an older range of the Cache Creek Terrane and were then squished upward after colliding with the Insular Superterrane.

Below: The Stawamus Chief, an impressive outcrop of the Coast Plutonic Complex, is a big monolith carved in granodiorite that cooled beneath the ceiling of the early Coast Mountains.

Opposite page: Basalt columns form when lava cools quickly. They are a common feature of volcanic landscapes in the Interior and the southern Coast Mountains. These columns are in the Precipice, near Anahim Lake.

there are piles of little terranes in northern Washington State that represent nothing else in British Columbia and in fact have no known equivalents north of the Klamath Mountains of California. A satisfying solution to this puzzle is finally emerging, thanks to Jim Monger and his colleagues. They point out that the late closure of the Bridge River ocean means that, somehow, Stikinia and the Insular terrane were not even there until about 100 million years ago, unlike farther north where they were well in place 70 million years earlier. Also, the stack of little terranes in Washington was thrust up from the south—from neither the northeast nor the southwest, as is the usual case in the main thrust belts of the Coast Mountains or Rockies. These geological anomalies can be explained if you imagine that the outer part of the Coast Mountains, along with the Insular belt, moved southward between mid-Jurassic and mid-Cretaceous time, closing off the Bridge River ocean as it went, and eventually rammed into the western Klamaths of northern California. The faults that this happened along have only recently been found. One of them lies under Grenville Channel, that long, narrow, straight stretch of water that marks the Inside Passage south of Prince Rupert.

Nowadays, we take for granted northward motion of the Pacific plate relative to North America. This movement is what gives us great modern faults like the San Andreas and Denali, and older ones like the Tintina, the Fraser and the Cassiar. But oceanic plates are fickle and evanescent compared with the long-term existence of continents. It seems that in Jurassic up to mid-Cretaceous time, some plate was out there, charging south with respect to North America and dragging the outer part of British Columbia along with it. It only vanished about 100 million years ago, and other north-travelling plates coupled with the Cordilleran margin and dragged the outer parts of it back up—some might say—where it belongs.

Slipping and Sliding

About 85 million years ago, the Farallon Plate under the Pacific Ocean rifted in two (Figure 1.3). The northern plate, named the Kula Plate, began spreading in a much more northerly direction than before. Because the North American Plate was still moving west, the new continental margin was now not only squeezed and foreshortened but smeared to the northwest. The crust had to give, and it slid north along faults like the Northern Rocky Mountain Trench and the Fraser and Queen Charlotte–Fairweather Faults. Along the Northern Rocky Mountain Trench, the land to the west moved certainly 450 kilometres, and possibly up to 750 kilometres northward relative to the Rockies to the east. Faults that separate laterally moving surfaces are called strike-slip faults; the San Andreas Fault in California is probably the best-known example of such a fault. The resulting pattern from all this faulting and sliding is one of elongate, northwestward-trending terranes, as shown in Map 1. But the strike-slip faults do not necessarily mark the edges of foreign terranes—the Northern Rocky Mountain Trench, for example, is 50 to 100 kilometres east of the continental margin. The land displaced to the west of it, although originally part of North America, is called the Cassiar Terrane.

This squeezing and slipping along the coast of North America continues today—Baja California and all of California west of the San Andreas Fault are sliding slowly northward and will probably collide with Alaska in 50 million years or so. Off the British Columbia coast, the Queen Charlotte–Fairweather Fault separates similarly sliding chunks of crust.

Relaxation

By 60 million years ago, the Rocky Mountains were a wide band of magnificent high plateaus and towering mountains probably over 4000 metres in elevation. But then the pushing stopped. The Kula Plate found a new subduction route beneath the new continental margin, and the tectonic pressure eased. The compressed crust relaxed and pieces of it began to slide off the thick pile. Along the western wall of the Rockies from the Robson Valley south, the Southern

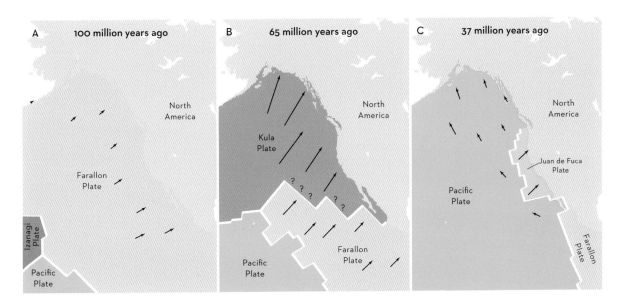

FIGURE 1.3
Speculated plate history in the Pacific Ocean. Successive plates are born, grow and are then consumed. North America is presented as a fixed entity to give a stable reference point, and arrows give relative directions of oceanic plate movement. The lengths of the arrows are proportional to the plates' velocities. In (A), the Farallon Plate dominates the floor of the eastern Pacific Ocean 100 million years ago. At 65 million years ago (B), the Farallon Plate has rifted in two, creating the Kula Plate to the north. By 37 million years ago (C), the Pacific Plate dominates the ocean floor; the Kula Plate has gone and the Farallon Plate is fragmented, creating the small northern Juan de Fuca Plate.
Adapted from H. Gabrielse and C. J. Yorath, eds., *Geology of the Cordilleran Orogen in Canada*, Fig. 3.3.

Rocky Mountain Trench formed. There, the crust foundered and the western block fell up to 1000 metres relative to the mountains on the east. This same faulting process has created valleys like the Elk, Flathead and Okanagan.

In the south Okanagan, beginning about 50 million years ago, a large piece of Quesnellia slid off about 90 kilometres to the west, exposing the basement rocks of the old continental margin. These ancient rocks can be seen along the east side of Skaha Lake, on both sides of Vaseux Lake and, most spectacularly, in the vertical wall of McIntyre Bluff, just south of Vaseux Lake.

The Latest Collisions

About 55 million years ago, the relative direction of the Kula Plate changed, and it began to slide more northward along a fault similar to today's San Andreas Fault in California. Since the Olympic Peninsula did not yet exist, Vancouver Island projected out into the Pacific and formed a trap for northwesterly

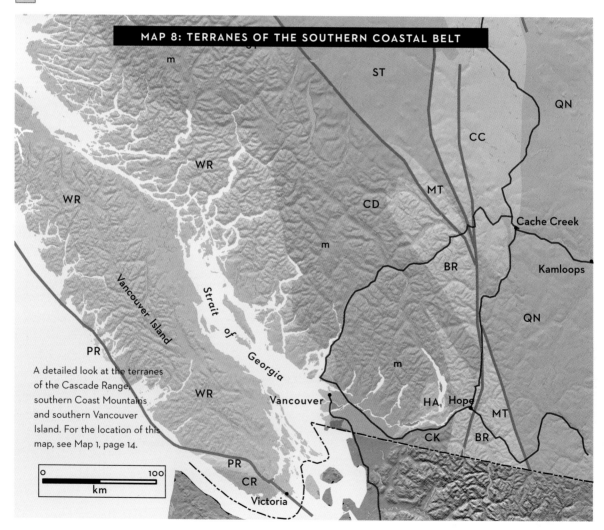

MAP 8: TERRANES OF THE SOUTHERN COASTAL BELT

A detailed look at the terranes of the Cascade Range, southern Coast Mountains and southern Vancouver Island. For the location of this map, see Map 1, page 14.

slipping terranes. During this period, two terranes were brought up the coast on the Kula Plate and pushed into southern Vancouver Island. The Pacific Rim Terrane, which arrived about 55 million years ago, consists of sedimentary and volcanic rocks that now form the southwest coast of the island (Map 8). After it made contact, the fault between the Kula Plate and North America jammed and a new fault formed slightly farther out in the Pacific. The Crescent Terrane, made up of former marine volcanoes that had formed along the fault, was brought alongside some time later, but before 40 million

TRACKING DINOSAURS

The climate was warm 125 million years ago, and dinosaurs roamed through the river deltas in the area that is now the east arm of Williston Lake, west of Hudson's Hope. Along rivers thick with sediments from the young Rocky Mountains, humid floodplain forests of tree ferns, cycads, ginkgos and conifers flourished. As dinosaurs strolled along the calm oxbow ponds beside the rivers, they left footprints in the undisturbed mud. Soon floodwaters brought more silt that covered the tracks. For ten thousand to fifteen thousand years, about 4 centimetres of sediments were laid down every year, and many generations of dinosaurs left signs of their daily activities in layer after layer of mud, silt and sand. These layers, buried under the growing Rocky Mountains, were eventually compressed into sedimentary rocks.

Millions of years later, the Peace River cut through these layers of rock and revealed the tracks of its long-vanished fauna. Although first reported in 1922, the dinosaur trackways were not studied intensively until the site was about to be flooded by the W. A. C. Bennett Dam. Scientists, working quickly over four summers, located over seventeen hundred tracks, took casts of about two hundred and collected ninety individual footprints. They discovered that the tracks record the existence of at least seven species of dinosaurs and, even more fascinating, tracks of an ancient shorebird

and one of the earliest marsupial mammals.

With only a little imagination, we can visualize the stories told by some of the trackways. For example, tracks show that a herd of herbivorous dinosaurs walking south along the riverbank spotted a pack of carnivorous dinosaurs. After quickly turning to the east, they were followed by the carnivores—we don't know the end of the story, since the tracks disappear.

However, the tracks lie deep under the waters of Williston Lake. In 2000, two boys from Tumbler Ridge discovered tracks of an ankylosaur along Flatbed Creek, southeast of Hudson's Hope, and subsequent searches revealed over two hundred tracks of three types of dinosaurs, as well as Canada's oldest dinosaur fossils.

Cast of duck-billed dinosaur (*Amblydactylus gethingi*), Royal British Columbia Museum.

The Okanagan Valley, known as a place to relax, was formed by crustal relaxation. These cliffs of granitic gneiss beside Vaseux Lake are part of the basement of the original continental margin that was exposed when Quesnellia slid off to the west after tectonic pressures were relaxed about 50 million years ago.

Opposite page: The Southern Rocky Mountain Trench—seen here near Golden—is a big crack in the earth's crust formed as the crust stretched after the compression of the Insular Superterrane collision ended.

years ago. In British Columbia, the Crescent Terrane's oceanic lavas form the rocks of Victoria's Western Communities; to the south, they make up the Coast Mountains of Washington and Oregon (the rocks of the Olympic Mountains came later). The Crescent Terrane is separated from the Pacific Rim Terrane by a fault along Loss Creek. The force of this collision did not create big mountain ranges in British Columbia, but it did fold and thrust-fault the sedimentary rocks along the Strait of Georgia to form the ridges and bays of the Gulf Islands.

> WE HAVE STOOD ATOP WINDSWEPT PEAKS AND
> WATCHED CONTINENTS IN COLLISION . . . WE HAVE
> TRAVELLED TO WHERE TERRANES COLLIDE.
>
> C. J. Yorath, *Where Terranes Collide*

Over the millennia, the westward-moving North American Plate steadily consumed the Farallon and Kula Plates. About 40 million years ago, the Kula Plate disappeared and any compression between it and North America ceased. Today only a remnant of the once great Farallon Plate remains—the small Juan de Fuca Plate is being formed by the emergence of lava along oceanic ridges west of Vancouver Island (see Figure 1.1). The crust is pulled eastward by the underlying convection currents and is then subducted beneath the continental shelf of British Columbia.

But one terrane collision is occurring even as you read this. In the St. Elias Mountains, where British Columbia, Yukon and Alaska meet, the Yakutat Terrane is crunching into the Chugach Terrane. There some of North America's highest and most spectacular mountains rise virtually from the seacoast, and the force of the impact continues to push them up at the remarkable rate of 4 centimetres a year.

Volcanic Belts

One of the most obvious results of plate movements is volcanic activity, and British Columbia has had its share of eruptions ever since Pacific plates began actively subducting beneath the continental margin. Many of the terranes that were added to the B.C. coast brought substantial volcanic material with them, but much has happened since the collisions as well.

As compression from colliding terranes ended and the crust relaxed and thinned or was pulled northward by tectonic forces, a period of intense volcanic eruptions began. From about 55 to 36 million years ago, lava flows filled deep basins all the way from Yellowstone to the central Yukon. Examples of these rocks can be seen along the northern shore of Kamloops Lake, where 1450 metres of volcanic sediments and lava are exposed in the Tranquille area, and in the south Okanagan, where 2400 metres of sedimentary and volcanic deposits are laid down in the White Lake basin.

From about 21 to 6.8 million years ago, vulcanism was common along the Pemberton Volcanic Belt from the Coquihalla valley through to Pemberton. Behind this belt of volcanoes, there was an effusion of lava from a multitude of vents in the Chilcotin area from 15 to 2 million years ago. In fact, the immense amount of lava that flowed over the landscape filled in all the low-lying areas and created the flat plateaus of the Cariboo and Chilcotin—all 50,000 square kilometres of them.

Meanwhile, in the Chilcotin, the continental crust was moving westward over a particularly hot spot in the mantle. So a series of shield volcanoes—broad, rounded volcanoes built up by successive outpourings of very fluid lava—formed over the hot spot. As one volcano formed, the crust would carry it to the west and a new volcano would emerge over the hot spot. First the Rainbow Range was formed, followed by the Itchas and the Ilgachuz Range near Anahim Lake and, finally, some very recent cones near Nazko, in the northeastern Chilcotin. Another volcanic chain that is probably related to a mantle hot spot runs from the Brooks Peninsula across northern Vancouver Island to Alert Bay.

TEPHRA: FOLLOW THE WHITE LINES

Some volcanoes erupt quietly and ooze fluid lava; others—those with magma higher in silica—can erupt explosively, as Mount St. Helens did on May 18, 1980. Explosive eruptions produce immense amounts of ash—called tephra by geologists—that is blown high into the atmosphere and carried over long distances on the prevailing winds. In the 1980 Mount St. Helens blast, central Washington was smothered in tephra; in British Columbia only a tiny dusting of the greyish-white powder fell in the Okanagan, but more fell in the southern Kootenay region.

Although we can easily see the lava flows produced by volcanoes, most people miss the ash layers that are evidence of the big bangs of the local volcanic world. In British Columbia, there are at least five important layers from such eruptions in the last 10,000 years. The oldest—and still the largest in the region—came from the eruption of Mount Mazama in Oregon about 7300 years ago. Mount Mazama doesn't exist on maps anymore—Crater Lake lies in the caldera produced when the mountain collapsed following the big explosion. Mazama ash covered a broad swath of southern British Columbia (Map 9).

This line of white volcanic ash in the Similkameen Valley marks the land's surface 7300 years ago, when Mount Mazama erupted and created Crater Lake, Oregon.

From about 3.5 million years ago to recent times, volcanic eruptions and lava flows have changed the face of the Wells Gray Park area. The visitor to this park can see all sorts of volcanic features, but the most spectacular and popular sight is Helmcken Falls, where the Murtle River cascades over the 142-metre headwall of a canyon carved in a 500,000-year-old lava flow. The origin of the falls can be traced to nearby Pyramid Mountain, which is an 11,000-year-old tuya, or sub-glacial volcano. A short hike to the top of the glass-walled cone produces a magnificent view that reveals how the volcano diverted the Murtle River from its pre-glacial course and sent it over the rim of the canyon. And thus a park is born. The volcanic activity of Wells Gray is related to faults along the eastern edge of Quesnellia, probably caused by shear forces as the terrane is shifted northward.

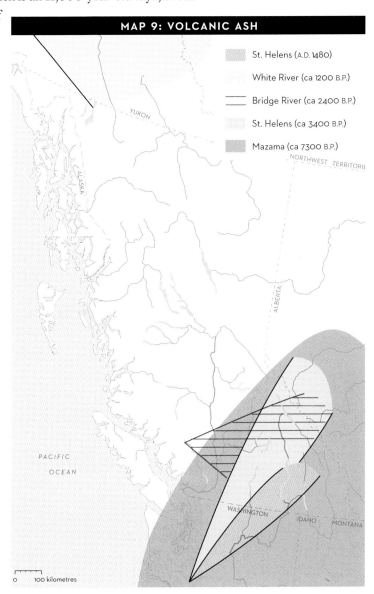

MAP 9: VOLCANIC ASH

St. Helens (A.D. 1480)

White River (ca 1200 B.P.)

Bridge River (ca 2400 B.P.)

St. Helens (ca 3400 B.P.)

Mazama (ca 7300 B.P.)

Mount St. Helens erupted 3400 years ago and again 500 years ago, and each time the winds blew significant amounts of ash northeast into southeastern British Columbia. About 2350 years ago, Mount Meager in the southern Coast Range erupted and the ash—known as the Bridge River ash—blew east as far as the Rockies. In the far north, a volcano in the St. Elias Mountains erupted twice—once 1500 to 1900 years ago and again about 1200 years ago. Ash from the later eruption blew east, and some reached the Atlin district of British Columbia.

These ash layers can be seen as distinct white stripes in road cuts and river banks wherever they occur. They are used by geologists to date the sediments that lie immediately below them.

Paleoecologists find them especially valuable in dating ancient pollen layers in the peat of bogs and bottom muds of ponds (see the box entitled "Pollen: Dust of the Ages," page 102).

Layers of volcanic ash in British Columbia.
Adapted from H. Gabrielse and C. J. Yorath, eds., *Geology of the Cordilleran Orogen in Canada*, Fig. 21.2.

THE EOCENE SCENE

At the dawn of the Eocene Epoch about 50 to 55 million years ago, the earth's climate wasn't as changeable as we experience it today. There weren't the extreme temperature differences between the poles and the equator that exist today, and the seasons at temperate latitudes weren't as pronounced. On the southwest coast of British Columbia, at sea level, the climate was subtropical, with forests containing tree ferns, but up in the highlands of the Interior, the scene was more temperate, with an annual mean temperature perhaps similar to that of Vancouver today.

Sediments gathered in the abundant swamps and lakes of the Interior and preserved many fossils in exquisite detail, giving us a rare glimpse of upland environments of that time. In British Columbia, Eocene fossil sites are known from Smithers south to Princeton, with the richest site being the McAbee shales near Cache Creek. Together, these sites are globally significant, offering a historical record comparable in importance to that of the Cambrian Burgess Shale in British Columbia's Rockies (see box entitled "The Burgess Shale," page 20).

At moderate elevations (perhaps similar to those of the modern Cariboo Plateau), the forests were diverse, far richer in species than modern ones. They were dominated by deciduous conifers—dawn redwoods, swamp cypresses, golden larches, katsuras and maidenhair trees, most of which are also found today only in east Asia.

The ancestors of modern conifers were also present, having recently descended from the cooler highlands—pines, spruces, true firs, sequoias, redcedars, yellow cedars, yews and hemlocks. But the forests had a southern Appalachian touch of broad-leaf trees as well—sycamores, elms, walnuts, beeches, oaks, alders, birches, dogwoods,

The deciduous dawn redwood was a dominant tree of swampy areas in the British Columbia Interior 45 million years ago. These fossil twiglets are from beds in the White Lake area near Penticton.

cherries, magnolias and maples were intermixed with the conifers. Even a small palm (*Uhlia*) was present. And familiar shrubs such as roses, myrtles, grapes, sumacs, elderberries, saskatoons, currants and raspberries formed the rich understorey. So modern naturalists would feel very much at home walking the game trails of British Columbia 50 million years ago, although they might guess they were in the Carolinas.

The lakes themselves were rich in plant, fish and insect life. Waterlilies (*Allenbya*) and mats of water ferns (*Azolla*) floated on the surface and swamp willows (*Decodon allenbyensis*) lined the shoreline. Bowfins (similar to the Bowfin of the Mississippi today) and early relatives of the Goldeye were present, but perhaps the most interesting fish was *Eosalmo driftwoodensis*. This fascinating species was a member of the salmon family, but in a group of fishes ancestral to both the salmon-trout group and the grayling group. Because there is a full size range of *Eosalmo* fossils from fresh water, we can infer that it was not anadromous—that is, it did not migrate to the sea. Fishes missing from this fauna include perches, sticklebacks and sculpins—all yet to evolve.

The insects left remarkable fossils. Caddisflies built cases out of small leaves, mayfly larvae fishtailed through the water, and above them, water striders skated about on the surface. A modern species of water strider from British Columbia is virtually identical to these ancient water striders, differing only in the length of the terminal antennal segment of the male. In contrast, scorpionflies from a now-extinct family graced the Eocene forests. Termites, closely related to some living today only in Australia, burrowed in rotting wood, and aphids infested flower heads.

Bruce Archibald of Simon Fraser University has recently examined hundreds of the best-preserved insect fossils from these beds and made a remarkable discovery: the species diversity was astoundingly high. Archibald postulates that even though these were temperate ecosystems, the Eocene's reduced seasonality allowed species to specialize in narrower ecological niches and to diverge from their geographical neighbours, from valley to valley.

Eosalmo driftwoodensis fossil from the Smithers area.

Fossil saskatoon leaf.

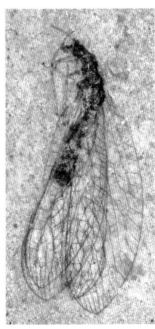

A remarkably preserved green lacewing (*Pseudochrysopa harveyi*) from Driftwood Canyon, near Smithers.

The most recent activity in the province has occurred in the Stikine Volcanic Belt of the northwest. In about 1750, an eruption dammed the Tseax River in the Nass country, impounding Lava Lake and destroying villages of the Nisga'a people. The cinder cone of Hoodoo Mountain, near the southern end of the Alaska panhandle, is another volcano believed to be merely biding its time before erupting once more.

The Cascade Volcanic Arc and the Rebirth of the Coast Mountains

The compression that built the original Coast Mountains ended about 45 million years ago, and for the next 40 million years they lay quiescent, gradually eroding down to perhaps a low chain of hills. By 10 million years ago, they were so low that there was no rainshadow behind them; the Interior was cloaked in lush vegetation. Then, beginning 5 million years ago, the subduction zone of the Juan de Fuca and Explorer Plates steepened, bringing the subterranean mass of molten rock that had created the Pemberton Volcanic Belt directly beneath the huge batholithic belt created by the collision of Wrangellia millions of years earlier.

In the south, this change gave birth to the Cascade Volcanic Arc, a series of impressive volcanoes that range from California's Mount Shasta in the south to Mount Garibaldi and Mount Meager in the north. In the Garibaldi-Bridge River area, there are actually thirty former volcanic cones extending along a 120-kilometre band.

The heat of the subduction zone not only created volcanoes but also heated the thick crust along the B.C. coast. As the crust warmed up, it expanded. Geologists calculate that this thermal expansion alone would result in a 2-kilometre uplift of the Coast Mountains. They have, in fact, risen about this much in the last 5 million years—and they continue to rise today.

Eve Cone, a postglacial cinder cone on the plateau of Mount Edziza in the Stikine Volcanic Belt. This one of the most recent eruptions of the complex that formed over the past 8 million years, as tension along the edge of the northward-moving Pacific Plate cause rifting inland.

Earthquakes: Waiting for the Big One

At 10:00 on Sunday morning, June 23, 1946, the residents of Courtenay were shaken by a tremendous earthquake, registering 7.3 on the Richter scale. The shock was felt as far away as the Lower Mainland, and on the east coast of Vancouver Island rock walls broke, chimneys fell, landslides swept down hills, and the seashore subsided. Just three years later, the largest recorded earthquake in Canada—magnitude 8.1—occurred off the northwestern corner

The west face of Mount Garibaldi. The greatest volcanic activity in the Garibaldi region occurred while most of the surrounding land was covered in the great ice sheets of the last glacial age. Mount Garibaldi was born about twenty thousand years ago, as the Ice Age was beginning to wane. The peak rose quickly through the surrounding ice in a series of explosive eruptions and soon became a gently sloping cone of fragmented dacite lava more than 6 cubic kilometres in volume. But to the west, its flank significantly overlapped the glacier, and as the supporting ice melted away, the mountain's entire west face—about 3 cubic kilometres of rock—collapsed into the Cheekye Valley below. In the volcano's last stage of activity, lava flowed gently out of a vent to the north of the previous plug and formed the now slightly higher northern summit.

of the Haida Gwaii. In 2012, Canada's second-largest recorded earthquake—magnitude 7.8—shook the Haida Gwaii, with the epicentre just 135 km from the 1949 quake.

Earthquakes are an inevitable accompaniment to tectonic plate movement, and British Columbia is no stranger to them. And not all are small, insignificant events—an average of two quakes greater than 6.5 on the Richter scale occur in western Canada each decade. As might be expected, most quakes are directly associated with the Queen Charlotte–Fairweather Fault system, where the Pacific Plate slides northward relative to North America (Map 10). The southern Strait of Georgia is also seismically active; the earthquakes here are probably related to the subduction of the small Juan de Fuca Plate beneath North America.

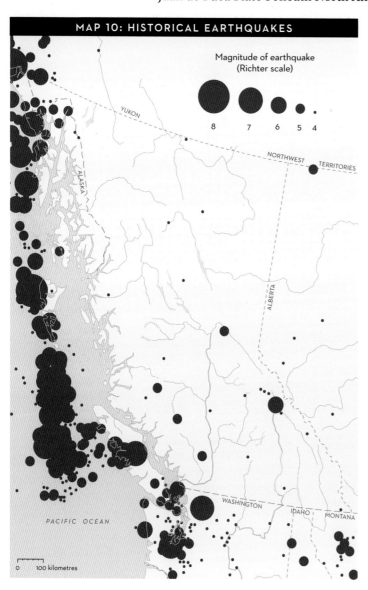

MAP 10: HISTORICAL EARTHQUAKES

Magnitude of earthquake
(Richter scale)

8 7 6 5 4

YUKON

NORTHWEST TERRITORIES

ALASKA

ALBERTA

WASHINGTON IDAHO MONTANA

PACIFIC OCEAN

0   100 kilometres

Recent surveys by researchers from the Pacific Geoscience Centre in Sidney, British Columbia, indicate that the oceanic crust is no longer sliding smoothly beneath us and that the crust of Vancouver Island is being strained. Mountains are rising and being squeezed closer together. Over the past few years geologists have noticed that the earth's crust in central Vancouver Island is being squeezed at different rates. These changes may very well be the early warning signals of a future earthquake—perhaps the Big One!

TWO HUNDRED MILLION YEARS of plate movement, mountain building, relaxation of the crust, volcanic eruptions and earthquakes has created the diverse landscapes of British Columbia. Map 11 shows the six major regions formed by all of this geological activity.

THE SCULPTING OF BRITISH COLUMBIA: GLACIATION

After 200 million years of building and shaping by tectonic movements and water erosion, the stage was set for the sculpting of British Columbia. Great mountain ranges and broad plateaus lay along southeast-northwest lines. The mountains were high but more rounded than today, and they were separated by angular valleys with few lakes and waterfalls.

Glacial Cycles and Drifting Continents

Then, about two million years ago, the age of the great glaciers—the Pleistocene Epoch—began. What caused the ice to come? In several ways, drifting continents had led to a cooling of the earth's climate. First, plate movements had brought the northern continents far enough north that colder climatic periods resulted in the growth of glacial ice. Second, tropical ocean currents were obstructed by the northward drift of Australia and New Guinea and the closing of the gap between Central and South America at Panama. Finally, barriers to polar currents around Antarctica were eliminated.

But the Pleistocene Epoch has not been all cold. It has had a series of climatic ups and downs, of moderate climates alternating with distinctly cooler periods. In the last 800,000 years alone there have been twelve of these cycles.

The colder periods were times of extensive glaciation in northern North America. The glaciers sculpted British Columbia by grinding the mountains, by changing the course of rivers and impounding huge lakes, and by depositing immense amounts of sediments. Over the last two million years glaciers have changed British Columbia and created the face of the province we see today.

At the beginning of each glacial age, either the summer temperature dropped slightly or the precipitation increased or both. In the high country it didn't take much to tip the balance towards the growth of glaciers. Slightly longer, snowier winters produced thicker snowpacks, or slightly cooler summers reduced the melt—both resulted in the persistence of snow from one winter to the next.

So the snow began to accumulate—especially in the high basins of the Coast, Columbia and Rocky Mountains, which remain among the snowiest places on earth today. The snow soon built up into small glaciers, which subsequently grew into great valley glaciers flowing onto the surrounding plateaus and lowlands. Eventually, the centre of the province was covered by ice up to 2 kilometres thick. This was the great Cordilleran Ice Sheet, which met the continental Laurentide Ice Sheet east of the Rocky Mountains. Along the border of the Cordilleran Ice Sheet, glaciers in mountains such as the Queen Charlotte Mountains were largely independent of the main ice cap.

Glacial periods ended when the climate became warmer; this climatic change seems to have usually occurred rather suddenly. In the mountains, glaciers retreated back up the valleys, but in the lowlands and on the plateaus, great glaciers were stranded and died in place, melting from the top down.

THE PLEISTOCENE SCENE: BIG ICE, BIG MAMMALS

The Pleistocene glaciations totally reworked the surface of British Columbia and, in doing so, destroyed most traces of the animals that lived here during the warm periods—a number of them tens of thousands of years long—between ice advances. But a few fossils of large mammals have been found that can give us a glimpse into British Columbia between the ice advances. The Pleistocene wasn't all that long ago in geological terms—glaciations began about two million years ago and have come and gone until about twelve thousand years ago—but a mammal watcher would notice big differences, even towards the end of the Pleistocene.

There would have been many familiar species, such as Bighorn Sheep, Mountain Goat, Mule Deer, Moose, Black Bear, Grizzly Bear and, along the coast, Northern Sea Lion and Walrus. But they would have been seen with some excitingly different creatures. American Mastodons, twig-eating denizens of marshy areas and open spruce forests, browsed alongside grazers such as Helmeted Muskoxen and Western Bison in open parkland. Imperial Mammoths, standing about 4 metres tall with their immense upward-curving tusks, ruled the tundra world, along with the only slightly smaller Columbian Mammoths. Small horses and Giant Bison also grazed in herds on the grassy tundra. The latter were grandiose animals with a horncore span of over 2 metres. The horncore is the smaller bone inside the horns of animals such as bison—the Giant Bison's horns themselves were not preserved as fossils, so we don't know how large they really were. Hunting the big grazers were huge, lanky Short-faced Bears, which stood 1.5 metres at the shoulder and 3.4 metres on their hind legs. Jefferson's Ground Sloth, a long-haired immigrant from South America that arrived in the Northwest during the last interglacial period, was the size of a modern bear and, like its tropical stay-at-home cousins, stripped leaves from trees for a living. It was first described by Thomas Jefferson, the American president, who was also one of the continent's first paleontologists.

The common characteristic of many of these fossil mammals is bigness—mammoth mammoths, large muskoxen, giant bison,

Short-faced Bear

Jefferson's Ground Sloth

huge bears, big sloths and, at least in the ice-free areas of Yukon and Alaska, giant beavers and even giant pikas. They are often referred to as the Pleistocene megafauna.

When did the megafauna disappear? Even though Imperial and Columbia Mammoths thundered across the ice-free tundra in southwestern British Columbia as late as 17,000 years ago, and Mastodons roamed with Helmeted Muskoxen as late as 12,000 years ago, recent genetic work on Pleistocene bones suggests that most of these large mammals were in decline through much of the last 30,000 years.

Why did they disappear? No one really knows for sure. One theory that has been put forward is that humans with new technology and hunting techniques hunted the large herds of grazing animals to extinction quickly, especially as the climate changed and the cold steppe and tundra shrank. And after the big grazers went, the big predators that preyed upon them disappeared as well. But there is no evidence for wide-scale killing and, as we have just learned, the big herds were declining through the last ice advance as well as during its rapid retreat. Perhaps all we can say is that the ice ages have been a time of constant change, and extinction is part of that change.

Bison, of course, survived the Pleistocene extinctions, but it was believed until recently that most of its diverse Pleistocene forms had disappeared by 12,000 years ago. Some 350-year-old Bison bones found in the southern Yukon have, however, changed this story radically—when they were analyzed genetically, they turned out to be Steppe Bison bones! This large, long-horned form was the dominant type in unglaciated Beringia at the end of the Pleistocene, but they obviously did not disappear with the glaciers.

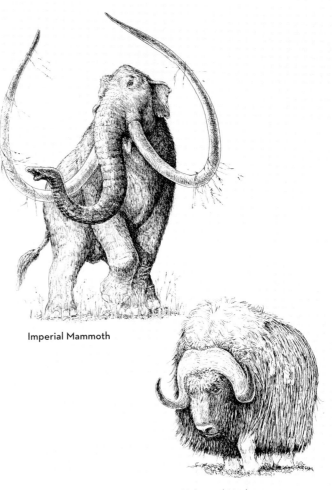

Imperial Mammoth

Helmeted Muskox

Giant Bison

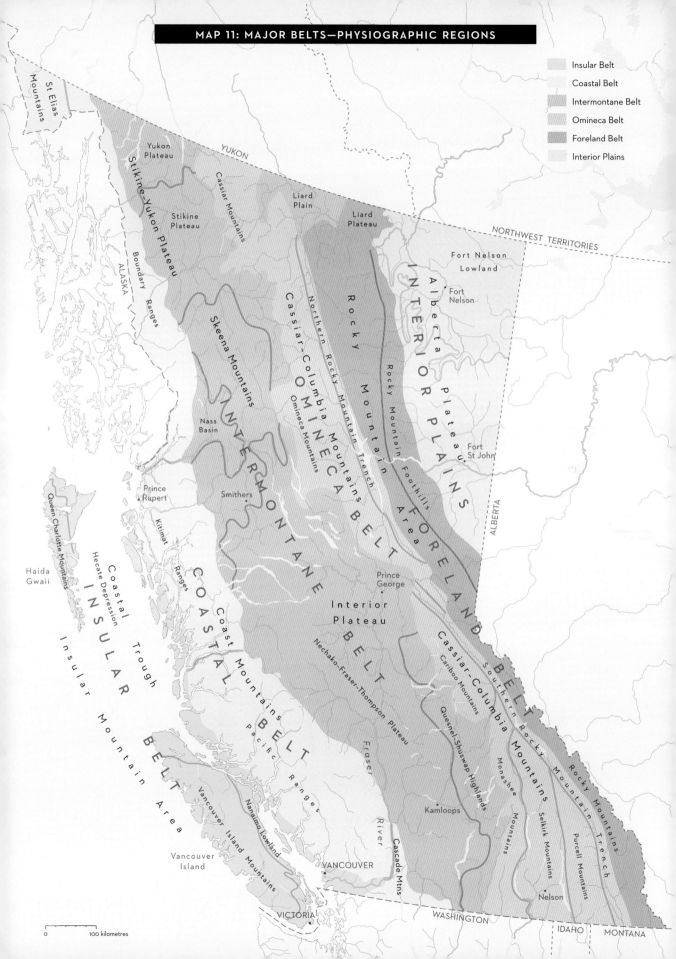

Insular Belt
Coastal Belt
Intermontane Belt
Omineca Belt
Foreland Belt
Interior Plains

St Elias
Mountains

Yukon
Plateau

YUKON

Liard
Plain

Liard
Plateau

NORTHWEST TERRITORIES

Stikine-Yukon Plateau

Cassiar Mountains

Stikine
Plateau

ALASKA

Boundary Ranges

Skeena Mountains

Nass
Basin

Prince
Rupert

Kitimat

Smithers

Cassiar-Columbia Mountains

Northern Rocky Mountain Trench

Omineca Mountains

OMINECA BELT

Rocky Mountain Area

Fort Nelson
Lowland

Fort
Nelson

Alberta Plateaus

Rocky Mountain Foothills

INTERIOR PLAINS

Fort
St John

ALBERTA

FORELAND BELT

Queen Charlotte Mountains

Haida
Gwaii

Coastal Trough

Hecate Depression

INSULAR

Insular Mountain Belt

Coast Mountains

Coast Ranges

INTERMONTANE BELT

Prince
George

Interior
Plateau

Nechako-Fraser-Thompson Plateau

Cassiar-Columbia Mountains

Cariboo Mountains

Quesnel-Shuswap Highlands

Southern Rocky Mountains

Rocky Mountain Trench

COASTAL BELT

Pacific Ranges

Fraser

Monashee Mountains

Kamloops

Nanaimo Lowland

Vancouver Island Mountains

Vancouver
Island

VANCOUVER

River

Cascade Mtns

Selkirk Mountains

Purcell Mountains

Nelson

Insular Mountain Area

VICTORIA

WASHINGTON

IDAHO

MONTANA

0   100 kilometres

Between glacial advances, ice-free periods often lasted for a considerable length of time—several lasted 20,000 to 60,000 years. During these periods glaciers were confined to the mountains, as they are today, and the valleys and plateaus were recolonized by animals and plants from unglaciated refuges to the south and north (see Chapter 3). The last major glaciation left the lowlands of British Columbia about 10,000 to 13,000 years ago— we are living in the latest of what could very well be a continuing series of interglacial periods.

Because the more recent glaciers destroyed or reworked the landscape so completely, geologists know little about the earlier glaciations of the Pleistocene. Evidence of one of these glacial advances can be found at the Murtle River bridge in Wells Gray Park—glaciers covering the Clearwater Valley perhaps about 400,000 years ago left behind sediments that were subsequently covered by lava from a volcanic eruption 200,000 years ago.

Geologists do know, however, that there have been two major ice advances in the last 100,000 years. Because it is older than the limit of radiocarbon dating, the age of the earlier one is not precisely known, but it is definitely older than 59,000 years. Sediments from this glaciation can be seen beneath younger glacial sediments in the Vernon and Okanagan Centre area of the Okanagan and in the lower Fraser Valley. Since its sediments are found beyond the limits of the later glaciation in the central Yukon, we know that the earlier advance was the larger of the two.

After an interglacial period of at least 30,000 years, the last major glaciation began about 25,000 to 30,000 years ago. The glaciers grew slowly at first, and some areas remained ice-free until after 17,000 years ago. The Cordilleran Ice Sheet reached its maximum extent 14,000 years ago but soon began to shrink and, by 10,000 years ago, had vanished, leaving only a few mountain ice fields and glaciers.

Opposite page: The result of 200 million years of geological activity is the diverse landscapes of British Columbia, which can be differentiated into six elongate regions parallel to the continental margin.
(1) The Interior Plains consist of undeformed sediments lying on top of the ancient crystalline core of the North American continent.
(2) The Foreland Belt is a region where the Rocky Mountains have been built as sheets of sedimentary rock folded, broke and stacked up on one another.
(3) The Omineca Belt is the weld between the old continental margin and the Intermontane Superterrane— mountains and highlands of intensely deformed and metamorphosed rocks.
(4) The Intermontane Belt is made up of plateaus, valleys and mountains formed from the various rocks of the Intermontane Superterrane.
(5) The Coastal Belt is the mountainous west coast of British Columbia, dominated by rock that was melted and recrystallized into immense granitic masses during the collision of the Insular Superterrane with North America.
(6) The Insular Belt is the outlying region of the island mountains of Wrangellia and the Alexander Terrane, the Insular Superterrane.
Adapted from C. J. Yorath, *Where Terranes Collide*, p. 102, and from A. L. Farley, *Atlas of British Columbia*, Map 14.

Since this last major glaciation ended, there have been several smaller advances. In fact, the coolest period in the last ten thousand years occurred in the last few hundred years—the Little Ice Age, or, as it is known to local glaciologists, the Cavell Advance, named after Mount Edith Cavell in Jasper National Park. This advance was essentially over by the late 1800s. Since the turn of the century, the Rockies and the Columbia Mountains have lost about a third of their glacial ice and most glaciers in the Coast and St. Elias Mountains have retreated.

What Did Glaciation Do to the Landscape?

As the ice built up and flowed out through the valleys, it altered the land in a number of ways (Figure 1.4). The massive, flowing ice removed the soft bottom sediments of the valleys, and rocky debris held within it carved out the bedrock floors and side walls. In this way, the valleys were deepened, bends were straightened, and the valleys were changed from V shaped to U shaped. This valley carving has made it easier for humans to develop transportation routes through mountain ranges in glaciated country. The spectacular fiords along the coast of British Columbia are valleys that were carved below sea level by major valley glaciers. Many of the province's lakes occupy valleys

Opposite page: Robson Glacier flows in front of Lynx Mountain in Mount Robson Provincial Park. Like many other glaciers in the Rockies, Robson Glacier has shrunk considerably since the turn of the century.

PLANETARY CYCLES, CLIMATIC CYCLES

Climatic fluctuations are caused by cyclical changes in the earth's orbit and tilt. Three cycles are involved. First, there is a 105,000-year cycle as the earth's orbit changes from a strong ellipse to a more circular shape. Second, there is a 41,000-year cycle in the tilt of the earth's axis—that is, the earth wobbles in space like a top. Third, there is a 21,000-year cycle in which the timing of the earth's closest approach to the sun moves through the year (right now the earth is closest to the sun in January).

The primary effect of these three cycles is to alter the contrast in heat between the tropical and the polar regions. When the contrast is great, a strong south-north circulation develops and warm air from the tropics brings moisture to the cold north, which falls as snow, and glaciers grow. When the contrast is less, the dominant circulation is east-west and precipitation declines.

These three cycles also influence the contrast between summer and winter. When summers are relatively cool and winters are moderate, there is not enough heat in the summer to melt the snows of winter and glaciers grow. When summers are hot and winters are extremely cold, the heat wins out and mountain snowpacks melt away before they can accumulate into ice.

Where are we in these cycles now? According to some scientists, a long-term cooling trend began about 7000 years ago. There have been shorter-term warm and cool periods within this trend, but the long-term trend was predicted to reach its coolest point 23,000 years from now. But now predictions have to take into account global warming from increased atmospheric carbon dioxide, a trend that could possibly overwhelm the effects of the natural cycles.

that were similarly deepened where the ice erosion was relatively intense. In fact, Quesnel Lake, at 530 metres deep, is the deepest such lake in the world.

The small side valleys in the mountains were often left "hanging" by the deepening effect of the main valley glacier. These side valleys usually originate in steep-walled mountain bowls called cirques. Cirques are most abundant on the cool north and northeast faces of mountains, where snow accumulates into glaciers that scour the rock at the base and pluck at the walls. The scene is a trademark of British Columbia's mountains—a turquoise mountain tarn lies in the bottom of the cirque's hollow and flows out through an icy stream that plummets out of the hanging valley in a postcard waterfall.

Where cirques are carved out on several sides of a peak, they create a steep, spectacular mountain called a horn—Mount Assiniboine is a classic example. The knife-edged ridges left between side-by-side cirques are called arêtes.

FIGURE 1.4
An imaginary British Columbia landscape reveals the signature of glacial ice on the land.

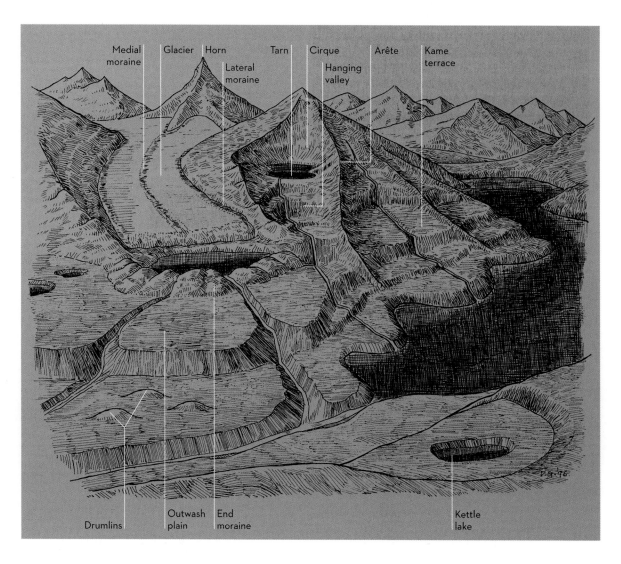

Often where glaciers override bedrock, the debris within the ice scours scratches and smooth troughs in the underlying rock—glacial striations and grooves that show us the direction of the glacier's flow. Look for these whenever you are hiking in the mountains, but the easiest places for many British Columbians to see them are in the rocks of Lighthouse Park in West Vancouver or below the sea cliffs at Dallas Road in Victoria. A plaque highlights a good example at the Centennial Fountain just west of the Legislative Buildings in Victoria.

The tremendous erosive power of glaciers produced a great deal of sediment during the Pleistocene, and evidence of this erosion is everywhere around us. As glaciers move forward over the landscape they act like conveyor belts, carrying within them a great deal of rock and rock debris. This material appears in many forms but is generally referred to as glacial drift. When the glacier stops advancing, the debris builds up at its toe into a ridge called an end moraine. If the toe of a glacier remains relatively stationary for some time, the glacier continues to dump more and more material at the end moraine as it melts each summer. When a glacier begins to retreat, it leaves behind the farthest end moraine, or the terminal moraine. Smaller moraines behind the terminal moraine are formed when the glacier pauses occasionally as it retreats. These are termed recessional moraines.

As the glacier melts back, rocks within it are also dropped along its sides, creating lateral moraines. When several valley glaciers merge to form one large one, the inner lateral moraines of each merge to form medial moraines, giving the large glacier its typical stripy appearance.

At the beginning of a glacial period, the growing glacier ice eroded soft valley floor sediments, and water from the summer melt flushed out huge volumes of sediments that were redeposited downstream in larger valleys, lakes and fiords. Some glaciers dammed tributary valleys and impounded lakes behind ice dams, in which large quantities of finer sediments—silts and clays—settled out. When the ice cap was at its maximum, most of these sediments were scoured away, but in some areas glaciers overrode them without removing them, and significant older sediments remain.

At the close of a glacial period, more erosion ensued as meltwaters carried off the rocks and sediments loosed by the glaciers. After the ice had gone and forests had returned to the land, the supply of sediment was greatly reduced. Rivers, especially those on steep gradients, quickly cut deeply into the sediments deposited earlier, and present floodplain levels were reached within several thousand years of the glaciers' retreat.

Where big glaciers languished in the valley bottoms, outwash from the surrounding streams deposited thick beds of gravel and sand against the ice, leaving outwash plains, or flat benches of stratified drift built up against the melting glacier, and kame terraces, or short ridges of stratified drift from the melting glaciers. These terraces are often the only relatively flat land in the narrower valleys of British Columbia and are now prime real estate for either urban development or agriculture.

Where the ice dammed the valley's outlet, meltwater accumulated against the decaying glacier and formed silty lakes on either side of it. The silt slowly settled out onto the lake bottoms. When the glacier finally disappeared and the lakes drained, the silty lake bottoms remained as flat benches on either side of the valley. As their faces erode today, they create the scenic silt cliffs characteristic of the South Thompson, Okanagan and other glacial valleys.

The ponds at the north end of Alleyne Lake between Princeton and Merritt are kettles—depressions left when large blocks of ice are left stranded in glacial gravel deposits.

Huge lobes of ice occasionally dammed major rivers, impounding large lakes and forcing meltwaters to empty out through adjacent river systems. At times, the upper Thompson and Nicola Rivers emptied out through the Columbia via the Okanagan system, the headwaters of the Skeena (including Babine Lake) flowed through the Nechako into the Fraser, and some upper Fraser tributaries flowed through the Peace into the Mackenzie (Map 12). The ice-dammed lakes, despite their size, were often ephemeral entities, draining catastrophically when the lake became deep enough to float the ice slightly.

Temporary glacial lakes can still be seen today in the glacier-filled ranges of the St. Elias and northern Coast Mountains. The Alsek River has been dammed repeatedly by advances of the Lowell and Tweedsmuir Glaciers—as late as the mid-1800s, the Lowell backed up the Alsek's waters as far as Haines Junction, Yukon, before the lake suddenly drained, destroying Native villages at the river's mouth in Dry Bay, Alaska. Where the Stikine River slices through the Coast Mountains, the aptly named Flood Glacier dams a tributary of the Flood River and creates Flood Lake. On a smaller scale, the famous Bear River Glacier along the high-

way to Stewart created an ice-dammed lake (Strohn Lake) at its terminus five times between 1958 and 1962; each time the lake drained, the floods wreaked havoc all the way down the Bear River valley.

The Ice and the Sea

The great ice sheets of the Pleistocene contained so much of the earth's water that the sea level was at least 100 metres lower than it is today. Much of the coast was covered in ice, of course, but large parts of the continental shelf

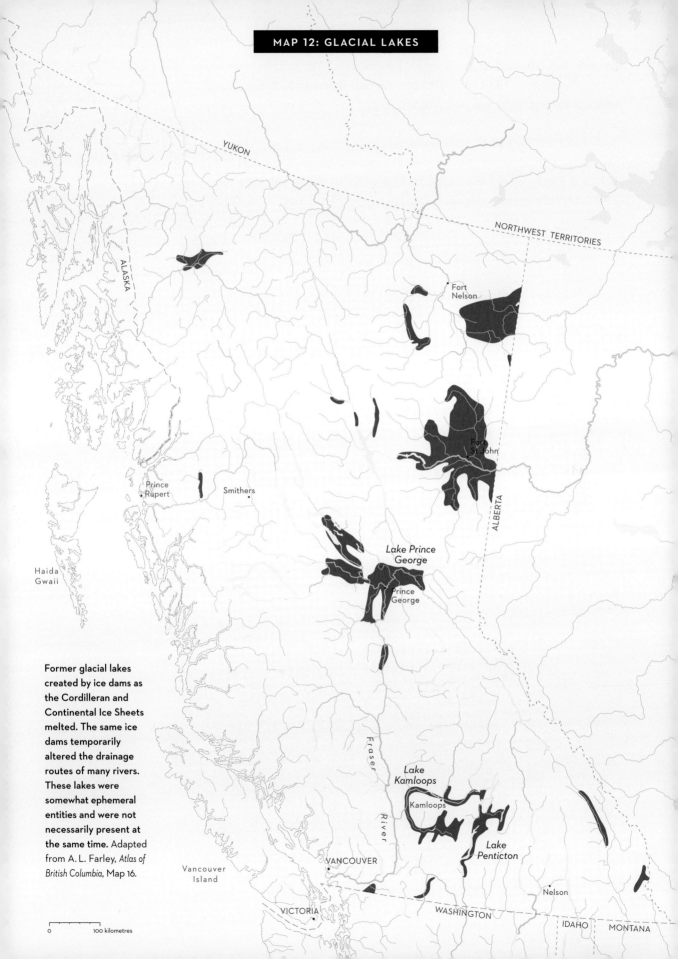

YUKON

NORTHWEST TERRITORIES

ALASKA

Fort
Nelson

Fort
St John

ALBERTA

Prince
Rupert

Smithers

Haida
Gwaii

Lake Prince
George

Prince
George

Former glacial lakes
created by ice dams as
the Cordilleran and
Continental Ice Sheets
melted. The same ice
dams temporarily
altered the drainage
routes of many rivers.
These lakes were
somewhat ephemeral
entities and were not
necessarily present at
the same time. Adapted
from A. L. Farley, *Atlas of
British Columbia*, Map 16.

Fraser

River

Lake
Kamloops

Kamloops

Lake
Penticton

Nelson

Vancouver
Island

VANCOUVER

VICTORIA

WASHINGTON

IDAHO

MONTANA

0   100 kilometres

were exposed during at least the earlier and later periods of the last glaciation. Up to thirteen thousand years ago the eastern coastal waters of the southern Haida Gwaii were dry land and extended more than halfway across what is now Hecate Strait.

But the immense glaciers that covered the British Columbia mainland coast also weighed so much that they depressed the land beneath them as much as 250 metres or more. As they melted, the ocean invaded the depressed coastal lowlands vacated by the retreating glaciers. All but the highest points of the Gulf Islands were covered by the sea, as was the entire coastal plain of eastern Vancouver Island. In the Fraser Valley marine inlets reached from Boundary Bay to at least Pitt Lake and from Bellingham Bay to Agassiz. On the north coast, Pacific fiords occupied the Skeena Valley as far inland as Terrace and the Kitsumkalum Valley almost to Kitsumkalum Lake.

Freed from its icy burden, though, the land began to spring back and the sea level fell correspondingly to its present position relatively quickly— in one or two thousand years. Simultaneously, large amounts of sediment were carried into the valleys from the recently released mountains and plateaus. In the Fraser Valley these two events resulted in the early disappearance of the marine bays, and the Fraser began to build the delta we know today, filling in the shallow bay between Vancouver and Surrey and the island of Point Roberts.

Erosion and Sedimentation Today

"The mighty, muddy Fraser" is a phrase often attached to British Columbia's largest river—and it is an apt one, since each year the Fraser carries about 20 million tonnes of sand, silt and mud from the mountains and plateaus of the Interior and dumps them into the Strait of Georgia. The sediment load of all streams like the Fraser is the result of a myriad of erosional processes— from glaciation to rock-breaking frosts to winter rains to spring floods—that are at work making British Columbia a flatter place.

Studies of the sediment load of rivers on the east slope of the Rockies indicate that these mountains are wearing away at a rate of 6 millimetres every 100 years. From this fact, Ben Gadd, in his *Handbook of the Canadian Rockies,* calculates that Mount Robson will lie at the elevation of Edmonton in exactly 54,766,666 years and 8 months!

Although sediments are not piling up as fast as they did immediately following the retreat of the Pleistocene ice sheets, they still can be a substantial force in creating new landscapes in British Columbia. For example, if it weren't for human interference, the sediments of the Capilano River would someday close off Burrard Inlet and Indian Arm at the Lions Gate Bridge, creating a huge lake in upper Burrard Inlet. But humans have altered the deposition of sediments from Capilano, just as we have for most of the province's major streams. Dams—like the Cleveland Dam on the Capilano—allow sediments to fall out of rivers into the reservoirs, reducing sedimentation at their mouths. Sedimentation in reservoirs is a real problem, of course, since it will eventually fill the reservoir and render the dam useless.

The Capilano's estuary has also been greatly altered. The river has been diked and its mouth moved to the west of the Lions Gate Bridge footing. When rivers are diked, sediments are no longer spread out over estuaries and floodplains in the annual spring floods—they instead go right out to sea and are dumped at the edge of their deltas. On the floodplain and delta of the Fraser River, 530 kilometres of dikes have been constructed and 70,000 hectares of marshland and floodplain have been converted into agricultural and urban land.

To keep channels open for large boats, rivers must be dredged—every year, 2 to 4 million tonnes of sediments are removed from the mouth of the Fraser. The removal of sand from the Fraser and engineering work around the Point Grey cliffs has affected the beaches of Greater Vancouver in a very direct way, since it has resulted in a shortage of sand feeding onto Spanish Banks.

Opposite page: **These elegant white silt bluffs along the Elk River are the bottom sediments of a large glacial lake that occupied this valley at the end of the ice ages.**

ROCKS AND DIRT: THE FOUNDATION OF LIFE

Soil is a product of the climate above it, the plants within it and the rock below it. The bedrock or sediments below are the raw materials that the vegetation and climate work on to produce, over time, productive soil. As different types of rocks weather, they produce different types of soils and, ultimately, different types of vegetation.

Although most soils in British Columbia are derived from glacial drift and sediments, observant naturalists can often see the effect of bedrock on soils and vegetation in the mountains. Soils over volcanic rocks are usually deep and rich in nutrients. Shale weathers into muds and silts, which make up the valuable soils of river floodplains and deltas. Granitic rocks, which make up most of the Coast Mountains, weather into poor, acidic soil. Serpentine rocks, which are rich in toxic metals, produce soils that only a few plants—some of which are unique to these sites—can tolerate.

Limestone, which is primarily made up of calcium carbonate, weathers by dissolving almost completely and so tends to accumulate a soil mantle very slowly. But because the carbonate neutralizes acids, distinctive plant communities grow on limestone bedrock. The next time you are hiking in limestone-rich mountains such as the Rockies, take a look at the boundary between limestone and shale formations. The shale produces acidic soil covered by dwarf shrubs such as Crowberries and Mountain-heathers, whereas the limestone tundra is dominated by grasses and sedges.

The colder and wetter the climate, the less influence that underlying geology has on the soils above, since the water tends to leach all the nutrients away and leave an acidic, nutrient-poor soil.

Millions of years ago	TABLE 1.1: BRITISH COLUMBIA GEOLOGICAL TIMELINE	ERA	PERIOD
570	The diversification of complex life marks the beginning of the Paleozoic Era.	PALEOZOIC	
530	The Burgess Shale fauna lives along the western shelf of North America, near the present site of Field in the western Rockies.		
400	Oldest rocks of Stikinia and Quesnellia formed.		
245	Ninety-six per cent of all marine species become extinct, bringing the Paleozoic Era to an abrupt end.		
200	Stikinia and Quesnellia lie far off the West Coast.	MESOZOIC	
181 to 170	Intermontane terranes dock; the Rockies begin to build.		
115	Dinosaur trackways are preserved along the present Peace River.		
120	Western ranges of the Rockies are stacking up.		
175 to 100	Insular terranes dock; renewed subduction after the collision creates the granitic rocks of the present Coast Mountains beneath the new continental margin.		
100	Main ranges of Rockies are forming. Small terranes of the western Cascades and southern Coast Mountains merge, still well south of the British Columbia coast.		
85	Farallon Plate rifts; Kula Plate spreads north, smearing the continental margin to the northwest.		
65	The dinosaurs and many other life forms become extinct, bringing the end of the Mesozoic Era. Tertiary Period begins.	CENOZOIC	TERTIARY
60	Pressure eases and mountain building in the Rockies stops. The crust stretches and thins, and the land to the west of the Rockies breaks away and drops, beginning to create the Southern Rocky Mountain Trench.		
55	Change in plate movement brings Pacific Rim terrane to the southwest coast of Vancouver Island. Crescent terrane arrives sometime later (before 40 million years ago), forming the southwestern tip of the island.		

THE LIVING LAND

Although the land around us appears stable and fixed, it has changed remarkably over the eons and continues to change today (see Table 1.1). With every minor earthquake, with every landslide and with every spring freshet, the land alters. In a sense the land is living; continents move, ocean floors are swallowed up, and

Millions of years ago		ERA	PERIOD
55	(continued. . .) The compression of the Kula Plate against the North American Plate creates the linear folds and faults of the Gulf Islands.		
50	Relaxation in tectonic pressure opens the Okanagan Valley.		
45	Kula Plate is consumed by subduction underneath the North American Plate, and the compression that had built the original Coast Mountains ceases.		
55 to 36	Lava flows fill many basins in the Interior (e.g., Kamloops Lake area, White Lake in south Okanagan).	CENOZOIC	
10	Original Coast Mountains have eroded to a lower range than today.		
21 to 6.8	Vulcanism is common along a belt from the Coquihalla River through to Pemberton.		TERTIARY
5	Change in the subduction zone of offshore plates gives birth to the Cascade Volcanic Arc and heats and expands crust beneath the Coast Mountains, beginning a 2-kilometre uplift that continues today.		
15 to 2	A multitude of lava flows lays down the plateaus of the Cariboo and Chilcotin.		
Years ago			
2 to 1.6 million	Beginning of the ice ages.		
20,000	Mount Garibaldi is born.		
14,000	Maximum extent of Cordilleran Ice Sheet is reached in the last glaciation in the south.	CENOZOIC	QUATERNARY
13,000	Parts of southwestern coastal lowlands are ice-free.		
10,000	Glacial ice has left all the lowlands.		
7300	Mount Mazama erupts, creating Crater Lake, Oregon, and covering southern British Columbia in volcanic ash.		
250	The last volcanic eruption in British Columbia: lava from a volcanic eruption in the Nass Valley dams the Tseax River and destroys Nisga'a villages.		

TABLE 1.1: BRITISH COLUMBIA GEOLOGICAL TIMELINE

mountain ranges rise and fall. It is difficult to perceive the change over a human lifetime, but the evidence of the moving land is in the rocks we stand on. This grand geological history is the foundation for the natural world of British Columbia, and our enjoyment and appreciation of nature is increased immeasurably by understanding it.

THE PACIFIC PROVINCE

THE PACIFIC PROVINCE

THE EARTH IS TRULY MISNAMED, for it is water that covers most of this planet, and the waters coursing through the huge ocean basins shape the patterns of life found on all continents. British Columbia sits on the eastern edge of the largest mass of water in the world, the Pacific Ocean, and it is the primary force designing the tapestry of life in the province. Great geological forces have created the giant canvas we call British Columbia, but it is painted by the Pacific.

There are patterns within these Pacific waters, patterns of waves and currents, temperature and salinity, light and darkness. These patterns shape a massive food chain, channelling energy from tiny plants through shrimp and fish and birds, onto the shore and into the rivers and mountains. The warmth and moisture of this great ocean, warmth and moisture needed by all living things, are carried by westerly winds and waves to coastal forests, over ice-covered mountains and into Interior valleys. The events in the atmosphere above—storms lashing the coast with rain, Arctic air flooding the Interior plateaus—are the actions of weather. The seasonal patterns of weather, patterns of hot and cold, warm and dry, cloud and sun, are the stuff of climate.

THE OCEAN

British Columbia meets the Pacific Ocean along a rugged outer coast, a windward coast where dark rock walls meet green waves and white foam before sinking into the sea. The rocky floor slopes down to a depth of 200 metres or so to form the continental shelf, a mosaic of sunken headlands and river-borne debris. The shelf extends 40 to 90 kilometres offshore before it too slopes steeply down to the proverbial bottom of the sea almost 2 kilometres below the waves. The continental shelf is widest along the southwestern edge of Vancouver Island, narrowing to the north, and is almost nonexistent off the Haida Gwaii, where the Pacific is already 2.5 kilometres deep only 30 kilometres from shore.

Inshore Waters

The mainland coast of British Columbia is protected along its length by a myriad of islands and narrow inlets. This inner coast is much calmer than the outer shores of the islands. Surface waters are often rather fresh, fed from Pacific storms slamming into immovable mountains and from summer glacial melt. The Strait of Georgia is the largest body of protected salt water on the coast, the submerged part of the Georgia Depression between the metamorphic rocks of Vancouver Island and the granitic Coast Mountains. Other inshore waters along the coast are mostly long, narrow inlets. These inlets are fiords, valleys plowed out by glaciers spilling through the mountains from Interior ice fields and then left to the sea as the ice pack dwindled and disappeared.

The glaciers scoured out the floors of these fiords to depths of 600 metres or so—three times that of the continental shelf—and left almost vertical valley walls. Fiords are not known for their sandy beaches; their shores plunge directly into the sea. Each glacier also left at least one terminal moraine in its fiord, a massive wall of rubble pushed ahead of the glacier and marking its farthest advance. These submerged moraines are called sills, barriers that separate the deep inner zone of the fiord from the outer seafloor. Sill floors are shallow, sunlit and vibrant with undersea life, nurtured by strong tidal currents pouring in and out of the fiord twice a day. The deep inner waters, isolated from the open ocean and the oxygen-rich surface, are often stagnant and relatively lifeless (Figure 2.1).

Pages 58–59: Like most channels and inlets along the British Columbia coast, Princess Royal Channel is a fiord—a submerged, glacier-carved valley.

FIGURE 2.1
Cross-section of an estuary and fiord. The fresh river discharge flows out to sea on the surface, drawing the upper layer of sea water with it. This layer is replaced from below by a deep countercurrent, a process called entrainment. Adapted from R. E. Thomson, *Oceanography of the British Columbia Coast*, Fig. 2.7.

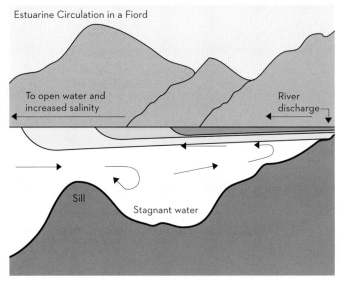

Estuarine Circulation in a Fiord

To open water and increased salinity

River discharge

Sill

Stagnant water

Estuaries: Where Rivers Meet the Sea

The Pacific meets the British Columbia coast against rain-lashed mountains, and the fresh water pouring out of these mountains plays an important part in the coastal marine environment. The flow of large rivers is especially important; at maximum flow in early June, the Fraser can turn the surface layer of the entire Strait of Georgia into a large, brackish lake.

EL NIÑO

Peruvian mariners gave this name—which means "The Child" in Spanish—to a current that often appears around Christmas along the Pacific coast of South America. Normally, easterly trade winds carry tropical waters away from the South American coast. Occasionally these winds fail, and the equatorial waters piled up in the western Pacific slosh back to the shores of South America as El Niño. A strong El Niño current can bring warm, clear, blue tropical waters north to British Columbia, radically affecting local marine life. The water is clear because it has almost no nutrients and therefore little life, forcing subtropical marine animals north in a desperate search for food. At this time, Brown Pelicans dive for fish off Race Rocks in the Juan de Fuca Strait, huge Leatherback Sea Turtles glide through Active Pass, and large, disk-shaped sunfish bask on their sides off Cape Scott. Local fish are forced north as well, and seabirds that normally feed on the rich schools of fish and shrimp west of Vancouver Island disperse to avoid starvation. El Niño also affects climate; the warm air and water intensify the Aleutian low-pressure zone, bringing stronger winter storms to British Columbia.

Brown Pelican

Besides water, rivers and creeks also carry nutrient-laden silt into the sea. Many of these nutrients are trapped and held in the estuary at the mouth of the river, making the deltas jewels of life embedded in an already rich coastline. As the fresh water of a river meets the sea, it flows out on top of the heavier salt water in a thick wedge, thicker near the river mouth, thinner out to sea. As it flows over the salt water, it pulls the upper layers of the heavier water along with it, a process called entrainment. This water is replaced from below, creating a deep countercurrent of saline water in the estuary. Most silt and detritus sinking into the salt water below the brackish wedge is thus carried back towards the river mouth and deposited on the bottom. The Fraser alone adds 20 million tonnes of silt to its delta each year.

Oceanic Currents

Oceanic currents are sections of huge gyres—immense eddies of water driven by prevailing winds. Since the prevailing winds at the latitude of British Columbia are westerlies, most of the surface flow in the Pacific Ocean at that latitude is westerly as well (Map 13). It is a steady but slow flow; at a speed of 4 to 8 kilometres a day, a parcel of water off the coast of Japan could take two to five years to cross the Pacific to British Columbia. This westerly flow is divided into the Subarctic and North Pacific Currents, separated by the Subarctic Boundary, a line where precipitation matches evaporation. The balance between precipitation and evaporation is of critical importance to surface salinity. South of the Subarctic Boundary, evaporation removes water

Surface currents in the North Pacific Ocean. Double arrows indicate a stronger current. Adapted from R. E. Thomson, *Oceanography of the British Columbia Coast,* Fig. 13.17.

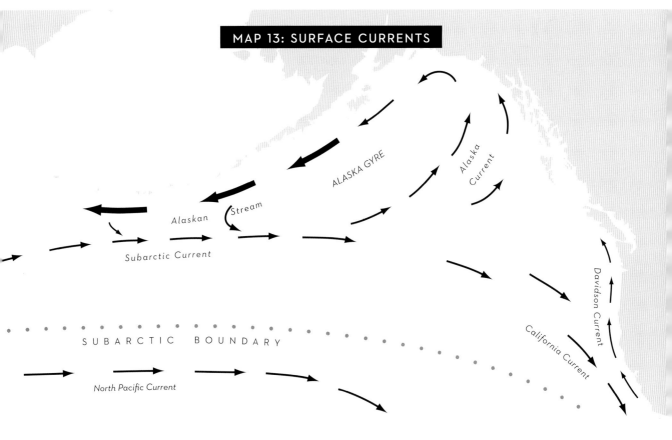

MAP 13: SURFACE CURRENTS

ALASKA GYRE

Alaska Current

Alaskan Stream

Subarctic Current

Davidson Current

California Current

S U B A R C T I C   B O U N D A R Y

North Pacific Current

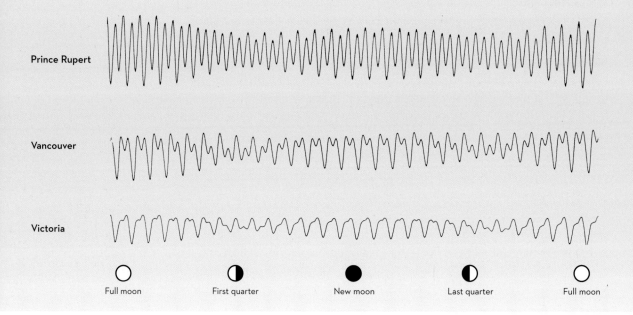

Prince Rupert

Vancouver

Victoria

Full moon   First quarter   New moon   Last quarter   Full moon

FIGURE 2.2
Tidal cycles at Prince Rupert, Vancouver and Victoria.
Adapted from R.E. Thomson, *Oceanography of the British Columbia Coast*, Fig. 3.5.

from the surface faster than precipitation can replace it. Since the salts are retained, the surface water becomes more saline. North of the boundary, precipitation adds water to the salt solution, diluting it and lowering the salinity. This abrupt change in salinity at the Subarctic Boundary acts as a very real barrier between the two currents. It is also a barrier to fish movements—tuna prefer to stay in the warm waters south of the boundary, while salmon remain in the cold, rich waters to the north (see box entitled "El Niño," page 62).

Off the coast of North America the Subarctic Current splits in two, forming the Alaska Current flowing north and the California Current flowing south. The Alaska Current flows north along the coast of British Columbia and then west along southern Alaska to form the Alaska Gyre. This current is especially strong in winter, when the prevailing winds are southwesterly along the British Columbia coast. A second northerly current develops in winter as well, the coast-hugging Davidson Current bringing water up from California.

In summer, most of the winds are northwesterly, weakening the Alaska Current and eliminating the Davidson Current. Summer is thus a season of variable currents off British Columbia.

Tides

Perhaps the most important aspect of water movement to people working and vacationing along the coast is the rise and fall of the tides. This daily, predictable fluctuation sets the time for almost every coastal activity—boating, shore walking at low tide, watching shorebirds forced off mud flats by high tide and fishing at slack tide. Figure 2.2 shows that although tidal patterns vary greatly along the British Columbia coast, most have a semidiurnal—twice daily—fluctuation. Often one of the fluctuations is much smaller than the other, especially at low tide. At Victoria this second tide is so small for much of the month that the tides are essentially diurnal—one fluctuation per day.

Since tides are a direct result of gravity, it is perhaps not surprising that they were first figured out by Sir Isaac Newton. His *Equilibrium Theory of the Tides,* published in 1687, was a remarkably accurate treatise on the cause of tides. In its simplest form, it says that the water on the side of the earth nearest the moon is pulled towards the moon by gravity, causing one of the daily tides. The second tide occurs because the earth on the side opposite the moon is pulled towards the moon more strongly than the water, allowing the water to bulge away from the earth there as well. The moon's involvement explains why the tides shift almost an hour later each day, since the lunar day (moonrise to moonrise) is twenty-four hours and fifty minutes long.

Anything affecting the gravitational forces on the waters off our coast will alter the tides. The strongest of these effects is the period of the moon. At the time of new and full moons, the sun and the moon are aligned, and the gravitational attraction from the sun, added to that of the moon, produces the highest tides of the month—the spring tides. The smallest tidal fluctuations are the neap tides, which occur at the first quarter and the last quarter of the moon, when the sun is acting in opposition to the moon.

So what causes the differences between the two daily tides? Because the earth is tilted in relation to the plane of the moon's orbit, the moon is only over the equator for two short periods each month. The tides at this time are roughly equal and are called equatorial tides. At other times the moon is closer to the Northern Hemisphere (and therefore to British Columbia) for half the day and closer to the Southern Hemisphere for the other half. This inequality produces two daily tides of different height—the tropic tides. The tilt of the earth also produces annual tidal effects. Tidal fluctuations are greatest near the summer and winter solstices, when the sun is over the Tropics of Cancer and Capricorn, and least when it is over the equator at the equinoxes.

These factors affect various parts of the British Columbia coast differently. Declinational effects—how high the sun and moon are above the equator—are strongest in the Juan de Fuca Strait and the Strait of Georgia, producing the mixed, almost diurnal tides there (Figure 2.2). Effects due to the phase of the moon are strongest along the outer coast, producing more or less pure semidiurnal tides.

The elliptical orbits of the moon and earth also affect tidal heights, since the moon is closer to the earth and the earth is closer to the sun at varying times. All of these tidal effects have different cyclic periods, resulting in the incredibly complex tidal patterns we see on tide tables.

Pages 66-67: Although they look calm when viewed from above, the waters of Active Pass between Galiano and Mayne Islands churn with each change of the tides. Strong rip currents and upwelling domes bring cold, nutrient-filled bottom water to the surface, creating a rich food chain made visible on the surface by flocks of Pacific Loons, Brandt's Cormorants and Bonaparte's Gulls feasting on the fish and shrimp below.

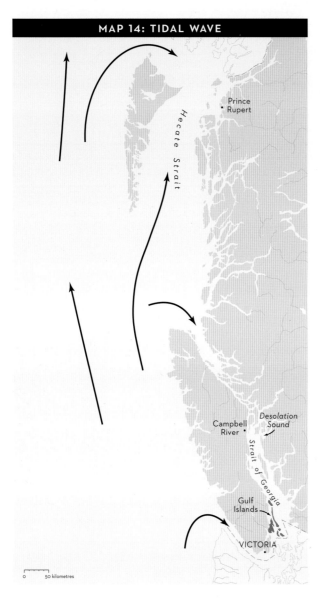

Prince
Rupert

Hecate Strait

Campbell
River

Desolation
Sound

Strait of Georgia

Gulf
Islands

VICTORIA

0   50 kilometres

The tidal wave along the coast of British Columbia. Adapted from R. E. Thomson, *Oceanography of the British Columbia Coast,* Fig. 3.19.

The wave generated by the tides—a true tidal wave, unlike the tsunamis created by earthquakes—races northward up the west coast of North America at a speed of 740 kilometres per hour, slowing down in shallower waters (Map 14). Tides occur almost simultaneously along the outer coast of Vancouver Island and about thirty minutes later on the Haida Gwaii. The tidal range increases as the wave travels through narrow inlets and shallow passages such as Hecate Strait. Victoria has an average tidal range of only about 2 metres, whereas Prince Rupert, at the north end of Hecate Strait, has a range of over 7 metres.

The timing of tides in the Strait of Georgia is greatly affected by the many narrow passages the tidal wave must pass through to reach the main basin. It takes two to four hours for the tidal wave to travel the length of Juan de Fuca Strait to the first of the Gulf Islands. The narrow passages there slow the wave considerably, and it takes another hour for it to reach the open expanse of the Strait of Georgia. The tidal wave moving south from Cape Scott along the inner coast of Vancouver Island is slowed even more by the narrow straits and passages along that route and takes two hours longer to reach Campbell River than the wave coming from the south. The meeting of the two tidal waves results in confused tidal patterns and weak tidal currents in the northern Strait of Georgia. These weak currents allow surface waters in places such as Desolation Sound to warm up to a comfortable swimming temperature in the summer.

The many narrow channels along the British Columbia coast are well known for their strong tidal currents. Tidal streams flowing into one end of the channel are so restricted by the narrow passes between the islands that the tide rises more quickly there than on the other end and so the sea can be as much as one metre higher on one side than the other. This difference creates riverlike currents raging through the channel with each change of the tides. There are many such sites along the coast, but perhaps some of the best known are Active and Porlier Passes at Galiano Island and Seymour Narrows at Quadra Island. The strongest currents are at Nakwakto Rapids at the north end of Vancouver Island and Skookumchuck Rapids at Sechelt Inlet, where current speeds of up to 16 knots are common.

As tidal streams encounter shallower water at the entrance to channels, the cold, deeper waters are forced upwards, seen on the surface as smooth upwelling domes. Upwelling currents bring cold, nutrient-rich water from the bottom to the surface of the sea. In addition, these strong tidal streams continue out the other end of the channel as strong jets of fast-moving water, with eddies and whirlpools at their edges and chaotic tidal rips where they meet oncoming tidal and wind-borne currents. This strong mixing also recycles nutrients that would otherwise have been lost to the sediments on the seafloor. These narrow passes are therefore very rich in marine life and often are home to remarkable concentrations of fish, mammals and birds—Bald Eagles wheeling over masses of herring, flocks of dainty Bonaparte's Gulls feasting on shrimp, rafts of Pacific Loons and Brandt's Cormorants and herds

Twelve different ecosections comprise the diverse marine habitats of the British Columbia coast. Courtesy of Mark Zacharias.

of barking sea lions harvesting fish of all sorts. The shallow floors of the channels themselves are cloaked with an amazing array of undersea life taking advantage of the rain of nutrients that comes with each tide.

Large-scale upwelling occurs along the Pacific coast of North America each summer, driven by the northwest winds. These winds create drift currents down the coast. These currents in turn are deflected offshore by the Coriolis effect caused by the earth's rotation. As the surface water moves away from the coast, cold water from the bottom is forced up to replace it. This effect is particularly strong along the coasts of northern California and Oregon but is irregular off Vancouver Island. Summer water temperatures are therefore lower and fog is more common off San Francisco than off Tofino.

The various combinations of seafloor type, currents, salinity and

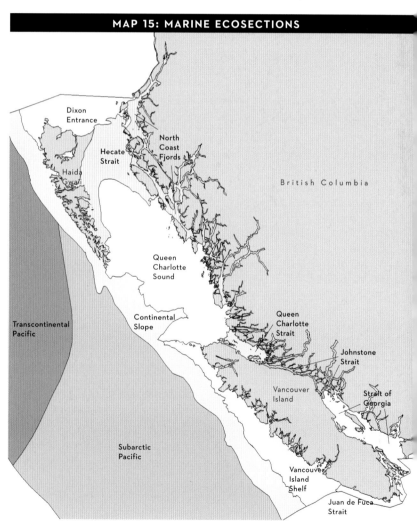

MAP 15: MARINE ECOSECTIONS

Dixon Entrance

North Coast Fjords

Hecate Strait

Haida Gwaii

British Columbia

Queen Charlotte Sound

Continental Slope

Transcontinental Pacific

Queen Charlotte Strait

Johnstone Strait

Vancouver Island

Strait of Georgia

Subarctic Pacific

Vancouver Island Shelf

Juan de Fuca Strait

other oceanographic properties have resulted in a diverse array of marine habitats along the British Columbia coast. To complement the terrestrial ecosystem classification in British Columbia, twelve different ecosections have been designated to encompass these marine habitats (Map 15.) The marine ecosections include the Strait of Georgia, an important nursery area for salmon and herring with abundant shellfish habitat; Johnstone Strait, a vital migration corridor for salmon and whales, and famous for the rich invertebrate communities on its rocky floor; the Continental Slope, with its nutrient-rich upwellings and highly productive plankton communities; and the Subarctic Pacific, a crucial summer feeding ground for salmon.

CLIMATE

The climate in British Columbia is a panoply of extremes. The combination of high mountain ranges, deep valleys and westerly winds off a large ocean produces some of the rainiest, snowiest, driest, hottest, coldest and windiest climates in Canada (Table 2.1 and Maps 16, 17, 18 and 19).

The British Columbia coast is famous for its rain. The west coasts of Vancouver Island and the Haida Gwaii are inundated each winter with the heaviest rainfalls in North America. This winter rain turns to snow as you

Climate summaries for British Columbia. Map 16 adapted from map of the biogeoclimatic zones of British Columbia 1992, B.C. Ministry of Forests. Maps 17-19 adapted from A. L. Farley, *Atlas of British Columbia*, Maps 20, 21 and 22.

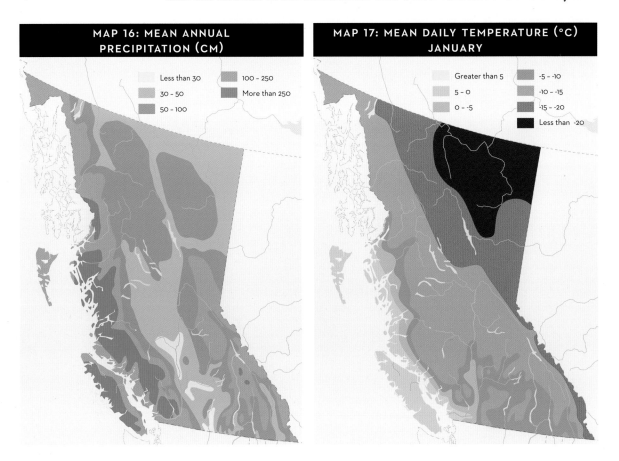

MAP 16: MEAN ANNUAL PRECIPITATION (CM)

Less than 30
30 – 50
50 – 100
100 – 250
More than 250

MAP 17: MEAN DAILY TEMPERATURE (°C) JANUARY

Greater than 5
5 – 0
0 – -5
-5 – -10
-10 – -15
-15 – -20
Less than -20

climb the mountains, so the Coast and Columbia Mountains record some of the deepest snow in the world. In contrast, locations nestled in the lee of the Coast Mountains, some only 100 or 200 kilometres from the wet coast, receive so little precipitation that they can almost be considered deserts.

> THE TRAVELLER WHO LANDS AT VANCOUVER . . . FROM THE EAST KNOWS AT ONCE THAT HE HAS STEPPED INTO A DIFFERENT WORLD: COOL AND LESS HUMID IN SUMMER; MILD, CLOUDY, AND WET IN WINTER. NOTHING LIKE THESE PACIFIC CLIMATES EXIST IN THE REST OF THE COUNTRY . . .
> F. Kenneth Hare and Morley K. Thomas, *Climate Canada*

Temperatures along the open coast are moderated by the massive waters of the Pacific Ocean, rarely dipping below freezing in winter and rarely exceeding 25°C in summer. Sites east of the coastal ranges are cut off from the moderating influence of the ocean, and annual temperatures there can fluctuate widely. This effect is especially apparent in the north, where long summer days produce highs above 35°C and frigid Arctic fronts bring winter lows down to –50°C or worse.

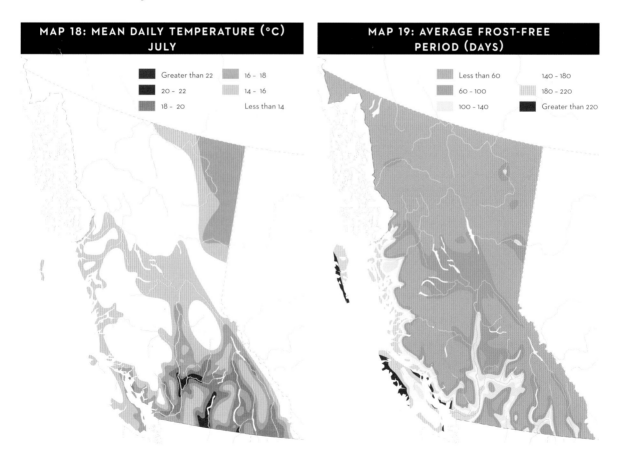

MAP 18: MEAN DAILY TEMPERATURE (°C) JULY

Greater than 22	16 – 18
20 – 22	14 – 16
18 – 20	Less than 14

MAP 19: AVERAGE FROST-FREE PERIOD (DAYS)

Less than 60	140 – 180
60 – 100	180 – 220
100 – 140	Greater than 220

TABLE 2.1: BRITISH COLUMBIA CLIMATE FACTS

Precipitation

Most in one year	Henderson Lake	8123 millimetres (1931)
Least in one year	Ashcroft	71 millimetres (1938)
Most rain in one day	Ucluelet	489 millimetres
Longest period of rainfall	Cape Scott	66 days
Most snow in one winter	Mount Copeland	24.47 metres (1971-72)

Temperature

Lowest	Smith River	-58.9°C
Highest	Lytton	44.4°C
Longest frost-free period	Victoria	685 days (1925-26)

Wind

Greatest wind speed	Bonilla Island	143 kilometres per hour
Winds reported most often	Cape St. James	99 per cent of the time
Gales reported most often	Cape St. James	every third day

Sunshine

Highest annual average	Cranbrook	2244 hours
Lowest annual average	Prince Rupert	985 hours
Highest annual	Victoria	2426 hours (1970)

It is impossible to treat the climate of British Columbia as a single entity, but the forces that create all the climates in the province are essentially the same. The processes that bring British Columbia its famous weather and climate begin far, far away. The equatorial regions, where the sun is directly overhead all year, receive far more energy from the sun each day than they can lose overnight. The atmosphere and the oceans absorb this excess heat and move it towards the poles.

As the equatorial air heats up, it rises into the stratosphere and then spreads out and begins to move towards the poles, gradually cooling as it goes. By the time it reaches about 30°N, it has become cooler than surface air, and since cool air is denser and heavier than warm air, it begins to sink. The sinking air creates large high-pressure zones, usually over cool areas—over oceans in summer and over continents in winter. The North Pacific High, the closest one of these zones to British Columbia, is usually about 1000 kilometres west of San Francisco. The tropical air, still relatively warm, is forced out of the high-pressure centre as air continues to sink into it. Some moves back to the equator, while some moves towards the poles, this time at the surface.

Meanwhile, air near the poles is being cooled, since it usually receives less energy from the sun each day than it radiates away at night, a process enhanced by the highly reflective cover of ice and snow at high latitudes. This cold air is

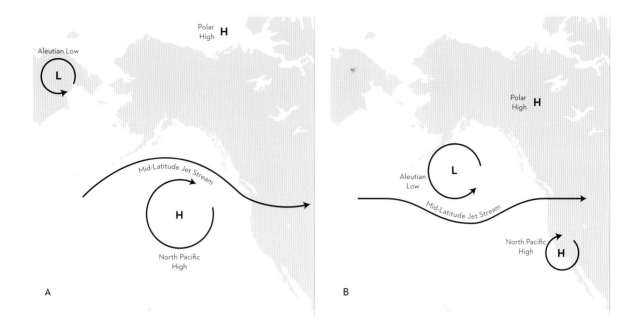

A

B

forced out of the Arctic by both the high-pressure zone and the prevailing winds and moves south to meet the warm, moist tropical air. When these two air masses meet near the Gulf of Alaska, the warmer air rises over the Arctic air, creating a strong low-pressure centre known as the Aleutian Low. Airflows around the southern side of the counterclockwise Aleutian Low and the northern side of the clockwise North Pacific High result in the prevailing westerly airflows over most of Canada (Figure 2.3).

The strongest winds form at the upper limit of the stratosphere, about 10 kilometres above the ground. The core of this airflow is an intense, linear air current travelling about 160 kilometres/hour—the Mid-Latitude Jet Stream. A jet stream is as a rapidly flowing river of air coursing between relatively stationary air masses. At these altitudes, the jet stream is bounded on the north by the Polar Vortex, a large cyclonic feature that spins counterclockwise around the Polar High. The Polar Vortex is strengthened in winter when frigid Arctic temperatures contrast with warmer air farther south.

In winter, the Aleutian Low moves south to cover most of the Gulf of Alaska, bringing a seemingly endless cycle of winter storms to the coast of British Columbia. These winter cyclones form in the western Pacific, near Japan and south China, and are carried to British Columbia on the Mid-Latitude Jet Stream. As they move across the wide Pacific, they deepen and intensify, spiralling counterclockwise, sending off frontal systems like the vanes of a giant pinwheel before dying in the Gulf of Alaska, buried in the Aleutian Low. The frontal systems are generally aligned from the southwest when they reach British Columbia, bringing rain and relatively warm southerly winds—the "Pineapple Express"—sometimes at less than two-day

FIGURE 2.3
Positions of the Mid-Latitude Jet Stream, North Pacific and Polar Highs and Aleutian Low in summer (A) and winter (B). Circular arrows show the direction of winds around the two strongest low- and high-pressure centres, respectively. The Polar High is simply a shallow dome of cold air and has essentially no winds associated with it.

intervals. The pinwheel vanes disappear over North America, broken by collisions with mountain ranges and cold Arctic air.

In summer, this whole system moves north with the sun as Arctic regions warm up and the Polar High weakens. The Aleutian Low shrinks and retreats into eastern Siberia, while the North Pacific High drifts north to dominate the weather off the B.C. coast. The Mid-Latitude Jet Stream also shifts north and weakens to about half of its winter strength. The result is predominantly northwest winds and long periods of fine weather over most of the province as the storm tracks target Alaska and Yukon.

Mountains and Valleys, Rain Forests and Rain Shadows

Although the basic ingredients of the British Columbia climate are Pacific cyclones, a westerly jet stream and seasonal masses of Arctic air, this mixture is shaped and portioned out by the rugged land itself. First, there is the physical barrier of the mountains themselves. Moist air carried by storms off the Pacific is immediately confronted by the almost impenetrable wall of coastal mountains. As the air is forced to rise over the mountains, it cools and the water vapour in it condenses to fall as rain or snow. The mountain slopes, therefore, receive more precipitation than the narrow coastal plains. This phenomenon is of vital importance to coastal ecosystems. It puts the rain into rain forest, creating towering cathedrals of Douglas-fir, Western Hemlock, Western Redcedar and Sitka Spruce. It also has important effects on local

Opposite page: **The magnificent mountain ranges of British Columbia not only affect the movement of Pacific storms and Arctic air masses but can also create weather of their own. High winds carrying moist air pass over the peak of Mount Robson, drawing up cool air from the glaciers on the lee side. The ice-cooled mountain air condenses the moisture to form the banner cloud.**

THE CHINOOK

The eastern slopes of the Alberta Rockies are famous for their chinooks—warm, dry winds that can turn the most frigid winter day into spring in a matter of minutes. These winds come to British Columbia as well, affecting the Interior valleys just east of the high coastal mountains. A rancher near Kamloops at the turn of the century wrote :

After having a cold snap of zero weather, with a foot of snow... there comes a change; heavy dark clouds loom up from the west and southwest, accompanied by a very strong wind—at times one might call it a gale... within a few minutes the air becomes balmy as spring—by contrast it
seems hot. I have known the thermometer to rise 59°F in five minutes. When we have this wind, one can read in the daily papers of shipping disasters and storms off the Vancouver Island and Washington coasts... one foot of snow [is] sucked up from off the ground (the ground being frozen to the depth of several inches). In three or four hours not a vestige of snow may remain, and yet not a trickle of water crosses the road... So when we have a heavy fall of snow and zero weather our sole ambition is for a chinook.

[From R. T. Grassham, 1907, "The 'Dry' Chinook in British Columbia," *Monthly Weather Review* 35:176.]

precipitation. Annual rainfall in the Greater Vancouver area, for instance, increases from about 0.8 metres in Tsawwassen to 1.2 metres at Point Grey, 1.5 metres along the West Vancouver shoreline and over 2 metres in the North Shore mountains.

By the time the moist air crests the coastal mountains and begins the descent into the Interior valleys, it has lost much of its moisture. As the air descends, it warms up and can hold more moisture than before. The rain stops, the moisture often evaporating before it reaches the valley floor. A few grey clouds drift east over golden grasslands and grey sagebrush. The

driest valleys in the province—the lower Thompson and Similkameen—are tucked in right behind the Coast Mountains and Cascade Range.

The warm, dry air picks up more moisture as it moves over the lakes and rivers of the South Thompson and Okanagan Valleys and then runs smack into another series of high ranges—the Cariboos, Monashees and Selkirks. The process repeats itself, and towns like Revelstoke and Nelson on the windward slopes of these mountains are drenched with rain and buried in snow before the air descends into the Rocky Mountain Trench.

In midwinter, the sunny Okanagan is often dark and gloomy under a layer of valley cloud, which forms when cold Arctic air meets warmer, moist air over the unfrozen lakes.

Arctic air flowing into British Columbia from the northeast has a completely different character from the warm, moist air from the Pacific. This is frigid air, and because it is cold, it is heavy. It fills the valleys, often leaving the mountaintops surrounded by warmer local air. If the cold air at ground level cannot be warmed enough during the day, as in winter, when the ground is covered with cold snow and ice, and if there is little or no wind, this lower cold layer is trapped beneath warm upper layers, creating an inversion.

You can easily spot an inversion in an urban area, where trapped smog forms a brown haze. Inversions are harder to detect in the wilderness, but strong winter inversions can be felt as a distinct rise in temperature as you ascend a mountain, as opposed to the usual cooling that occurs with increasing elevation.

You can also see the effects that winter inversions have on plant communities. Red bands of dying trees are occasionally seen in mountain valleys. Called winter kill, this phenomenon occurs when warm, drying winds enter the valley, flowing over cold ponding air in the valley bottom. The layer of warm air thaws the frozen dormant trees at middle elevations; these trees lose water through transpiration but cannot replace it through their still-frozen roots. A longer-term effect of winter inversions can be seen in far northern valleys, where a band of trees cloaks the mountain slopes while the valley floor is covered in a shrub tundra community of willows and birches. These valleys are periodically filled with frigid air in winter, killing most conifer seedlings in the valley bottom.

Lakes can also have a dramatic effect on mountain weather. Large lakes are great heat sinks in the summer, moderating air temperatures around them. Thus, the midsummer high temperatures in the province come from southern valleys away from lakes, at towns such as Lytton, Spences Bridge and Oliver. The lakes release this stored heat throughout the winter as long as they remain ice-free. During outbreaks of Arctic air, the moisture in the air over large, ice-free lakes such as Okanagan Lake condenses to form a low layer of valley cloud.

Seasons

Winter is a season of successive storms along the coast; it is the wettest time of the year for southern sites such as Vancouver and Victoria. If you step outside during a Vancouver winter, chances are one in three it will be raining. These disturbances are often swept inland, bringing heavy snowfalls to the mountains and flurries to Interior plateaus and valleys.

A dome of very cold Arctic air centred on the Mackenzie River sends frigid air south into British Columbia. The edge of this air mass, the Arctic Front, usually reaches Prince George by early November, but its progress is slowed by mountain ranges and the flow of Pacific air over the southern half of the province. It is often late December before the air mass reaches southern valleys such as the Okanagan and the Kootenays. The arrival of this polar air mass signals the start of real winter weather in the Interior—bitterly cold weather and long-term snow cover.

Occasionally, blocking high-pressure ridges form along the coast in winter. These ridges deflect the flow of Pacific air northward to Alaska and allow the frigid Arctic air to sweep south and fill the Interior. The cold, heavy air flows through the coastal passes at ground level and pours onto the coast as strong outflow winds. Perhaps the best known of these winds on the south coast is the Squamish wind that howls down Howe Sound and across the Strait of Georgia to Nanaimo. Heavy, prolonged snowfall can occur where the moist Pacific and cold Arctic air masses meet, turning the Gulf Islands into a winter wonderland and paralyzing traffic in Vancouver. Coastal locations in the path of cold outflow winds get more than their share of snow; Nanaimo's annual snowfall is almost eight times that of Victoria, only 90 kilometres to the south.

> FOR MOST CANADIANS, SEASONAL CONTRAST MEANS A BITTERLY COLD WINTER AND A WARM, OFTEN HUMID SUMMER. FOR COASTAL BRITISH COLUMBIA, THE TERM MEANS THE DIFFERENCE BETWEEN A DRY, BRILLIANT SUMMER AND THE GLOOMY, WET WINTER.
>
> F. Kenneth Hare and Morley R. Thomas, *Climate Canada*

As the sun moves north in spring, the westerly flow becomes weaker and Pacific storms hit the coast less frequently. Although Victoria will always boast of its January flowers, the south coast really blossoms with the prolonged sunny, warm periods of early April.

Spring in the Interior is marked by an eastward shift of the Arctic air stream, bringing blizzards to the prairies and eastern Canada but allowing warm maritime air to fill British Columbia. Spring therefore arrives more quickly in the Interior of British Columbia and has fewer setbacks than in areas east of the Rocky Mountains. The thaw moves north into southern valleys in late February, central regions by the third week of March (when it is arriving in Toronto, far to the south) and reaches the Yukon border by the middle of April. April showers may bring May flowers, but spring is usually the driest season of the year throughout the Interior. Higher elevations, still cloaked in deep snow, can remain cool and cloudy through spring, and May snowfalls are not unheard of.

As the sun nears its highest point in the sky in June, increased daily heating and other factors cause unstable moist air to bring clouds and showers to most of the province. "Cold-low" storms sweep across the province, putting a damper on early summer picnics. June is the wettest month of the year in the southern Interior. As the North Pacific High begins to dominate the south coast in July, Pacific flows are often blocked for weeks on end, deflecting westerly storm tracks to the north coast and Alaska. July is the driest month on the southern coast, but the north coast can be cloudy and cool most of the summer. Prince Rupert has the cloudiest summers in Canada, seeing the sun for only 110 hours. July is also the wettest month of the year in northern Interior sites such as Fort St. John and Fort Nelson. The southern Interior basks under clear, hot skies for much of the summer, interrupted by occasional heavy thundershowers. Some of these thunderstorms can douse a local area with a tenth of the total annual precipitation in a single hour.

As the Aleutian Low builds and slips southward, the westerly flow increases again and Pacific cyclones arrive with increasing frequency. The north coast is hit earliest and hardest as the jet stream slips southward; October is the wettest month of the year in Prince Rupert. Unhindered by Arctic air, these storms move inland easily at this time of year. The flow of warm Pacific air into the Interior slows the influx of cold polar air, and so freeze-up moves southward more slowly than the thaw moves northward in spring. With each passing cyclone, however, cold polar air is drawn farther south, heralding the beginning of winter in the northern Interior.

CLIMATE CHANGE

Half of the world is always bathed in sunlight. This light provides essentially all the energy that supports life on our planet, warming the atmosphere and driving the chemical cycles that produce food for every living thing. At night, on the dark side of the earth, this absorbed energy is radiated away as infrared light. Most of it leaks away into the black vacuum of space, but some of these photons bump into certain types of molecules in the atmosphere that absorb the energy, then release it again as infrared light. The energy these molecules release can go in any direction, but by chance about half is sent back down to earth. It is this process that keeps the world at just the right temperature for life as we know it, but it is a delicate balance, and that balance depends on the right concentration of these molecules. Because they act like the glass in a greenhouse—transparent to visible light but absorbing infrared light—these chemicals are known as greenhouse gases. The commonest greenhouse gas in our atmosphere is carbon dioxide.

One of the most dramatic effects of human civilization on British Columbia's ecosystems over the next century will be a significant change in climate due to increased carbon dioxide and other greenhouse gases in the atmosphere. British Columbia's climate has changed almost continuously over its millions of years of existence, but what makes the predicted changes remarkable is their speed and magnitude—and the fact that humankind is responsible for them.

The latest report from the Intergovernmental Panel on Climate Change states unequivocally that the cause of this changing climate is the rising levels of carbon dioxide and other greenhouse gases in the atmosphere. The same report places the blame for rising greenhouse gas levels squarely on the human addiction to burning fossil fuels.

Carbon dioxide is definitely increasing in the atmosphere. From 1975 to 2001, measurements taken along the British Columbia coast at Cape St. James and Estevan Point ballooned 40 parts per million to 372 parts per million. Not only are these concentrations already significantly higher than they ever have been over the past 800,000 years, but they are expected to double within the next few decades. And even if we reduce our carbon dioxide output around the world, those concentrations will stay high for centuries.

Not surprisingly, the world is warming quickly. The five warmest years since temperature measurements began in the mid-nineteenth century have all occurred since 2005, and the last three decades have, in turn, each been the warmest. The rate of this change is greater than at any other time in the last ten thousand years. In British Columbia, mean annual temperatures are expected to rise at least 2°C by the end of the century. Mean winter temperatures have already risen by 2°C since 1900, while summer temperatures have risen by 1°C over the same time period. This warming, especially that in winter, will be strongest in the northeast corner of British Columbia. Summer warming will be more equally distributed across the province. The annual frost-free period has increased by three to four weeks over the last century, and this trend will continue, particularly in western British Columbia.

Precipitation patterns will also change, although with less predictability; most models suggest an increase in precipitation in northern British Columbia and a decrease on the southern coast. The interaction between changing seasonal patterns of temperature and precipitation will mean significant changes in patterns of river flow. In most British Columbian rivers, these patterns are driven by snowmelt, resulting in strong peaks of discharge from June through early July. Warmer springs will produce broader peaks of flow in May, followed by very low flows during longer, drier summers.

The oceans play a huge role in the story of carbon dioxide and a warming world. The oceans hold about fifty times as much inorganic carbon as the atmosphere and continually absorb about one-third of the carbon dioxide released into the atmosphere. The oceans are thus an important sink for carbon dioxide. There is some evidence that this absorption is slowing—and may have even stopped in parts of the southern oceans—as the surface layers of the water are warmed and become saturated with carbon dioxide, but the situation is highly complex.

When carbon dioxide is absorbed by water, it forms carbonic acid. Normally, some of this acid reacts with dissolved carbonates and is neutralized, but the rate at which carbon dioxide is entering the water is outstripping the natural production of dissolved carbonates through the weathering of rocks. It is not surprising, then, that the oceans are becoming more acidic every year. Acid concentrations in the oceans have risen by about 30 per cent over the past 250 years, a rate ten times faster than at any other period in the earth's history.

The melting of polar ice, particularly in the vast ice sheets of Greenland and Antarctica, is also filling the world's oceans with more liquid water, and sea levels are rising. Sea levels have already risen more than 20 centimetres over the past century, and are predicted to rise a further 40 to 80 centimetres by the end of this century. In addition, the warming atmosphere heats the surface of the ocean, causing the water to expand, pushing sea levels even higher. Rising sea levels then hasten the melting of the over-sea ice sheets in Antarctica, one of the many positive feedback loops fuelling rapid climate change.

Of course, ice is not only melting in the Arctic, but in the mountains of British Columbia as well. In 1898, Mary Vaux, a pioneer glaciologist, reported that the Illecillewaet Glacier in Glacier National Park had retreated significantly since she first visited the area in 1887. That park has since lost more than 25 cubic kilometres of ice, including much of the Illecillewaet Glacier; in a few decades, it might be Glacier National Park in name only. And as the glaciers disappear, the mountain rivers that take their summer meltwaters to the ocean will shrink dramatically too.

Rather than global warming, many now call the phenomenon "global weirding." The rising temperatures in the atmosphere and oceans are causing a complex cascade of effects. An example of this is the loss of ice in the Arctic Ocean. While this loss obviously directly affects the marine ecosystem there, it also has an indirect, but substantial, effect on weather throughout the Northern Hemisphere. When the Arctic Ocean is covered with ice and snow, much of the summer sunlight there is reflected back into the sky, and polar air temperatures remain cold. But if that ice melts away in summer—as it has increasingly done so over the past decade—the dark water absorbs heat from sunlight and moderates air temperatures throughout the Arctic. The Polar Vortex and the Mid-Latitude Jet Stream are fed by temperature differences between air masses in the Arctic and adjacent temperate regions, so both weaken when Arctic air warms. As the jet stream slows, it begins to meander like a river slowed by flat land, tracing huge looping curves across the continent. In winter, the north-bending loops can bring unseasonably warm weather to northern British Columbia, and the south-bending loops can bring frigid air south from the Polar Vortex. These looping patterns often stall in place, causing tremendous rainfall on one side of the loop and unseasonable drought on the other. That's one example of global weirding—an increase in the frequency of extreme events such as floods, droughts, gales and heat waves.

Climate change means an uncertain future for many of British Columbia's ecosystems. Some of the predicted effects—from fires to insect plagues, disappearing tundra to increasing grasslands—will be discussed in the following chapters of this book.

THE LEGACY OF THE ICE AGE

THE LEGACY OF
THE ICE AGE

T ODAY THE GREAT ICE SHEETS of the Pleistocene are gone, but their legacy remains. Their advances and retreats not only changed the physical landscape utterly but also shaped the plant and animal communities that followed them.

POST-GLACIAL IMMIGRATION

Most of the plants and animals of British Columbia are descendants of immigrants that colonized British Columbia after the retreat of the Pleistocene ice sheets only ten thousand years ago. How they populated the landscape left bare by the shrinking ice is a complex, fascinating story. Although all of the province's species have particular ecological needs that determine where they *can* live, where they *do* live relates just as much to where their forebears lived during the Pleistocene, the immigration routes that their forebears used following the glaciers' retreat and their ability to disperse. For some species, colonization continues today.

The Role of Glacial Refuges

During the glacial advances of the Pleistocene, there were four primary ice-free areas where species from British Columbia survived: (1) the forests, grasslands and shoreline habitats of coastal California, Oregon and southern Washington; (2) the tundra, forests and grasslands of the interior southwestern United States; (3) the forests and grasslands of the southeastern United States; and (4) the tundra and cold steppes of central and northern Yukon and Alaska (Map 20). As they followed the retreat of the glaciers, some species spread across British Columbia, but many were thwarted by barriers of mountain ranges, ice caps and wide rivers. The more restricted distribution of these species today can be directly related to their home during the ice ages. For example, some songbirds, such as the Cape May Warbler, emigrated from the southeastern United States but never managed to cross the Rocky Mountains—in British Columbia, species such as this one are found only in the Dawson Creek and Fort Nelson areas.

Species that were widespread in northern North America were split apart by the Pleistocene ice sheets, and this separation had profound effects on their evolution. Not only were major eastern and western groups separated from each other, but many populations in the west were fragmented into still smaller groups by mountain ranges and desert basins.

In a small, isolated population, random genetic changes that begin in an individual can become firmly established throughout the population over relatively few generations, even without the pressures of adaptation and natural selection. This means that *chance* differences in characteristics such as appearance can evolve rapidly. And because the isolated populations are living in

Pages 84–85: Near Ashcroft, the Thompson River flows through a channel carved in a thick mantle of glacial sediments and glacial drift.

Below: The all-white Dall sheep survived the Pleistocene glaciations in the ice-free mountains of northern Alaska and Yukon.

Ice-free refuges for British Columbian animal and plant species during maximum glacial periods of the Pleistocene. Recolonization routes following the retreat of the ice sheets are shown by arrows. Also shown are biological suture zones entering British Columbia: (A) Northeast-Southwest; (B) Coastal-Interior; (C) Beringia-Cordillera. Each of these zones represents the coming together of many formerly separated populations of animals and plants. Adapted from H. Danks, ed., *Canada and Its Insect Fauna* (Ottawa: Entomological Society of Canada, 1979), Fig. 3.45.

different places, their appearance, behaviour and ecological requirements often change through *adaptation* to new habitats or climates as well.

For example, the ranges of species of the northern forests, such as the White Spruce, were split in two during glacial periods. Forced south by the advancing ice sheets, eastern and western populations were separated by inhospitable, treeless plains. Over the centuries, they evolved different appearances and, to some extent, different ecological strategies. Examples of east-west pairs abound in British Columbia (Table 3.1). Jason Weir and Dolph Schluter of the University of British Columbia studied a number of species pairs of boreal forest birds, and using a standard genetic-mutation "clock," they confirmed that all these northern pairs diverged during the Pleistocene ice ages.

With few exceptions (the Jack and Lodgepole Pine pair being one), the "eastern" member of these pairs is today the northern member and the "western" member is really the southern, mountain one. The eastern Yellow-shafted Flicker, for example, is found right across northern British Columbia and, in Alaska, extends much farther west than the western Red-shafted Flicker. This fascinating, consistent pattern is the result of the timing of deglaciation in different parts of the Canadian west. As the Pleistocene ice sheets melted, the first corridor to open up the north and connect ice-free southern North America with ice-free Yukon and Alaska was probably along the thin edge of the continental sheet on the east slope of the Rocky Mountains. This corridor was invaded early by White Spruce and its eastern companions. As the ice continued to melt, these species moved through the low passes in the northern Rockies and colonized northern British Columbia. Their western siblings, however, were isolated from the north by huge ice domes that persisted in central British Columbia. These populations remain south of Prince George even today—an ecological case of first come, first served.

MAP 20: ICE-FREE REFUGES

4
C
B
A
1
2
3
grasslands
Ice cover
1 - 4 Ice-free refuges
A - C Suture zones
0 500 kilometres

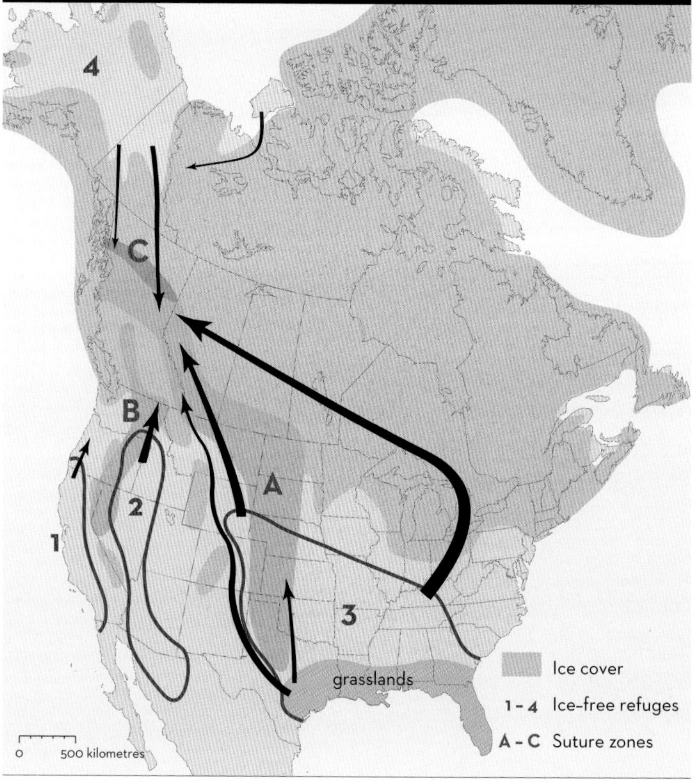

West of the Rocky Mountains, many forest animals and plants were separated into coastal and Interior populations by harsh, dry conditions in the Interior northwest during the Pleistocene glaciations; today these groups come

MIXED-UP FLICKERS

A glance at an old field guide for birds will reveal one of the classic east-west species pairs: the Yellow-shafted Flicker of the east and the Red-shafted Flicker of the west. The plumages of these two ground-feeding woodpeckers are very different: eastern birds have bright yellow under-wings and tail, a brown face and grey crown and a red crescent on the back of the head, and the males have black whiskers; western birds have salmon-red underwings and tail, a grey face and brown crown and no crescent on the back of the head, and the males have red whiskers. Because they look so different, one might expect that the eastern and western birds would shun each other completely. But perhaps because feeding behaviour and mating displays are essentially identical between eastern and western populations, flickers from one population do not hesitate to mate with members of the other population. Hybrids are very common across central British Columbia, where the two populations meet, and birders in southern British Columbia often encounter them in winter. These confusing birds have yellow-orange wings (or both red and yellow feathers), black and red

whiskers and other mixed-up characteristics in all imaginable combinations. Do not expect these garbled characters to spread out of the central plateaus; the large pool of pure flickers in northern and southern British Columbia will keep the hybrid zone stable for millennia.

into contact along the crest of the Cascade and Coast Mountains. Examples include the Interior and coastal subspecies of Douglas-fir, Red and Douglas' Squirrels, Red-naped and Red-breasted Sapsuckers, and Cordilleran and Pacific-slope Flycatchers. In some species, these groups exist but are not obvious to the average observer. Genetic analysis of Black Bear, American Marten and Montane Shrew all reveal coastal and Interior populations that

TABLE 3.1: EAST-WEST PAIRS OF PLANTS AND ANIMALS OF THE NORTHERN FOREST

Note: Subspecies names are in parentheses.

EAST	WEST
White Spruce	Engelmann Spruce
Jack Pine	Lodgepole Pine
Balsam Poplar	Black Cottonwood
Yellow-bellied Sapsucker	Red-naped/Red-breasted Sapsuckers
Northern (Yellow-shafted) Flicker	Northern (Red-shafted) Flicker
Yellow-rumped (Myrtle) Warbler	Yellow-rumped (Audubon's) Warbler
Rose-breasted Grosbeak	Black-headed Grosbeak
Dark-eyed (Slate-coloured) Junco	Dark-eyed (Oregon) Junco
Baltimore Oriole	Bullock's Oriole

The Stone's Sheep in the northern Rockies are a product of ancient hybridization between Thinhorn and Bighorn Sheep. Even though their less robust form and slender, flaring horns speak of their Thinhorn ancestry, their mitochondrial DNA (which records maternal lineage) reveals an even closer relationship to the Bighorns of the southern Rockies. Stone's Sheep probably survived glaciation in a shifting archipelago of ice-free refuges on the eastern slopes of the Rocky Mountains.

have diverged genetically but not, to our untrained eyes, in appearance.

Some coastal-Interior species pairs, such as the sapsuckers mentioned above and the Hermit and Townsend's Warblers (see the Genetic Genocide sidebar on p. 95), also have an eastern sibling. In these cases, the two western species diverged from their eastern sibling first—perhaps a million years ago according to Weir and Schluter's DNA clock—and subsequently diverged from each other later in the Pleistocene.

To the north, another group of animals and plants flourished in the cool but ice-free lands of Yukon, Alaska and eastern Asia. During the height of glaciation, so much of the world's water was tied up in ice that sea level was about 100 metres lower than it is now. The unglaciated portion of Alaska and Yukon was broadly connected by the Bering land bridge to eastern Siberia. Totally isolated from the rest of North America by immense glaciers, this area (termed Beringia by geographers) was biologically more Asian than North American during the Pleistocene.

The plants and animals that lived in Beringia were citizens of the tundra and Arctic steppe, and when the intervening glaciers melted, many species dispersed down the alpine spines of the Rockies and the Coast Mountains. The White Marsh-marigold, Mountain Monkshood, Partridge-foot, Mountain Harebell and Golden Saxifrage probably all populated British Columbia's mountains from the north—although some may have survived in high mountain refuges within British Columbia. Grizzly Bears swept out of Beringia to populate all of western North America.

Just as some species were divided east and west by glaciation, others were split into populations north and south of the ice sheets. In British Columbia, some Beringian species are still confined to the far northwest. Examples of Beringian-southern pairs include Harlan's and Red-tailed Hawks, Collared and American Pikas, Arctic and Columbian Ground Squirrels, and Thinhorn (Dall's) and Bighorn sheep. Even spawning populations of salmon were separated; Chinook salmon diverged into a stream-type fish—which enters fresh water in the spring—north of the glaciers and an ocean-type fish—which enters fresh water in the fall—to the south.

Several populations meet and hybridize along an east-west zone stretching through Prince George. This is a textbook suture zone—a narrow band that marks the meeting of two biotas, or areas of different types of flora and fauna, that were once separated but are now in contact again. Such zones provide vital biological field laboratories for studying the great changes that have occurred over the last 100,000 years.

A number of suture zones snake across North America; three make their way into British Columbia (Map 20). The longest is the zone mentioned above, where northern and eastern populations meet their western counterparts. This zone follows the 100th meridian north along the boundary of the humid eastern woodlands and the dry western plains and then swings west to the crest of the Rockies, continuing north before swinging west through central British Columbia. Another zone follows the crest of the Cascade and Coast Mountains, and a third zone marks where plants and animals of the far northwest meet their siblings of the southern mountains.

Some species pairs hybridize extensively in suture zones; others hybridize much less readily or do not even come into contact. Whether or not these pairs are new, separate species is a matter of some debate and depends on the individual circumstances as well as the various specialists' concept of what a species is. For example, Yellow-shafted and Red-shafted Flickers hybridize so widely that ornithologists generally agree that they are only well-marked, geographic subspecies.

THE DIVERSITY OF LIFE FORMS, SO NUMEROUS
THAT WE HAVE YET TO IDENTIFY MOST OF THEM,
IS THE GREATEST WONDER OF THIS PLANET.
Edward O. Wilson, ed., *Biodiversity*

White and Engelmann Spruce hybridize widely, but many botanists still treat them as separate species, calling most spruce in central British Columbia merely hybrid spruce. Myrtle and Audubon's (collectively Yellow-rumped) Warblers also meet near Prince George, but there is only a very narrow zone where hybrids occur. Baltimore Orioles and Rose-breasted Grosbeaks range into the Peace River district, but their western counterparts, Bullock's Orioles and Black-headed Grosbeaks, do not extend that far north. Thus, the two groups fail to meet there, though there has been a single report of hybrid grosbeaks in the Northern Rocky Mountain trench near McBride.

Although most of British Columbia was completely overrun with ice during the Pleistocene, there is considerable evidence that a number of small areas in British Columbia remained ice-free during the last glacial advance.

Along the outer coast, especially on the outer coasts of Vancouver Island and the Haida Gwaii, there were a number of hospitable refuges. Where the cordilleran glaciers tapered off into ice shelves, even modestly elevated ridges were exposed above the ice surface. And between the tongues of large

Baltimore Oriole

Bullock's Oriole

Red-breasted (left) and Red-naped (right) Sapsuckers meet along the crest of the Cascade and southern Coast Mountains. A good place to look for hybrids is Allison Pass, along Highway 3 in Manning Provincial Park.

glaciers, steep, west-facing seaside slopes often escaped the icy advance and supported thriving communities of plant and animal life. Because sea level was considerably lower during maximum glaciation, these seaside refuges could have been significantly larger than is apparent today. They would be even more extensive farther out on the present continental shelf, where the ice was thin and the land had not been depressed as much by the ice.

Evidence for the existence of these refuges comes largely from endemic species. Endemics are species that are confined to small areas and are found nowhere else in the world. There is a group of wildflower species, for example, that is found only on the ridges of Moresby Island in the Haida Gwaii and on the rugged spine of the Brooks Peninsula on northwestern Vancouver Island. Flowers such as Taylor's Saxifrage and Newcombe's Butterweed appear to be remnants of a much more widespread coastal flora eliminated elsewhere by glaciation. These species, which obviously have not dispersed very far in the last ten thousand years, are biological markers that record the areas that survived glaciation. Another, similar pattern occurs in some alpine plants that are restricted to the mountains of Vancouver Island and the Olympic Peninsula of Washington State.

There are no endemic species of vertebrates on the Haida Gwaii, but a number of endemic subspecies tell the same story as the plants. Non-migratory birds such as the Northern Saw-whet Owl, Hairy Woodpecker, Steller's Jay and Pine Grosbeak are represented by endemic subspecies on the islands, each with a distinctive genetic signature. Coho Salmon spawning on the islands show genetic evidence of a late glacial refuge there, too.

Other endemic species of plants—and beetles as well—are restricted to gravelly or rocky seaside habitats along the east coast of the Haida Gwaii. This pattern points to refuges at sea level, and there is direct evidence of alpine communities in plant remains held in sea cliff exposures on Graham Island that have been dated at sixteen thousand to thirteen thousand years ago. Half of Hecate Strait was once dry land with tundra-like meadows, but these in fact may have been post-glacial.

These refuges must have been ephemeral, however, since these shores of the islands show evidence of being covered with ice at some point during the last ice advance. But at any one time, there was probably a chain of ice-free refuges along the outer west coast of North America. Although they came and went, these refuges acted as stepping stones for animals and plant species moving up and down the coast.

Just as fascinating as the stories from the Haida Gwaii and the north coast are recent revelations that there must have been a number of small ice-free refuges in the mountains of British Columbia's dry northern interior (for example, the area around Iskut and on the eastern slopes of the Rockies). Genetic

Newcombe's Butterweed, a wildflower found only on the Haida Gwaii.

evidence from Mountain Goats, Stone's Sheep and Mountain Sorrel shows that alpine ecosystems persisted in those regions through the last ice advance, and that the animals and plants that lived there subsequently dispersed across the north and down the mountains as the glaciers receded. The biological evidence seems contrary to the glaciological evidence; it seems that the simple stories of recolonization from large refuges to the north and south are just that—too simple.

Evolution of Rivers and the Fish Invasion

How did freshwater fish repopulate drainages like the Fraser and the Skeena, which were totally glaciated only fourteen thousand years ago? Anadromous fish like salmon, steelhead and White Sturgeon had no problems—they moved in from the ocean, swimming up the young, silt-laden rivers to find new pools and new spawning gravels. Fish entirely restricted to fresh water, however, had to immigrate from river systems that had remained at least partly ice free during the Pleistocene glaciations—systems such as the Chehalis, the Columbia, the Missouri-Mississippi and the Yukon.

Fish can't normally cross passes between watersheds—but they had to move across several divides to populate the Skeena from the Columbia. How did they do it? The answer lies in the complex interaction of evolving river systems and the retreats and advances of glaciers at the close of the Pleistocene. In simple terms, the rivers acted as canals—as local glaciers advanced, they closed and flooded the rivers' locks, sending the water from one drainage into the neighbouring one over now elevated divides.While glaciers covered British Columbia and Puget Sound, a unique fish fauna—closely related to that in the Columbia—developed in the isolated Chehalis River at the base of the Olympic Peninsula. As the massive ice lobe melted back up Puget Sound, large lakes formed along its margin. The Chehalis fish entered these lakes and followed their meltwater streams north into the Fraser Lowlands. But the Fraser Canyon was blocked by ice until about 11,500 years ago, so the Chehalis fish were able to establish themselves there before any fish came down the Fraser from the north.

The two fish that represent this interesting fauna in British Columbia are the Salish Sucker and the Nooksack Dace, both now restricted to a handful of small streams in the lower Fraser Valley and both gravely threatened by urban and agricultural development.

THE ONLY SOLID PIECE OF SCIENTIFIC TRUTH
ABOUT WHICH I FEEL TOTALLY CONFIDENT IS THAT
WE ARE PROFOUNDLY IGNORANT ABOUT NATURE.
Lewis Thomas, *The Lives of a Cell*

Large lakes were also dammed by glaciers retreating from the valleys of the southern Interior (Map 12). For a time, the upper Thompson and Nicola Rivers drained through the big lakes in the Thompson, Shuswap and Okanagan systems and into the Columbia. So the fish in the Columbia system easily entered the waters of the Fraser system, as soon as the ice melted.

A little later, an ice advance dammed some upper tributaries of the Fraser and forced them to drain north over the pass at Summit Lake and into the Peace system. The connection was brief, but it did allow some Columbia River fish to enter the Peace River.

Around the same time, the Skeena Valley was blocked by glaciers flowing out of the Coast Mountains, and the upper Skeena, including the Babine River, drained east into the Nechako and upper Fraser system. In this way, some species of Columbia fish colonized the Skeena.

The continental ice sheet left the eastern foothills of the Rockies relatively early, and as it did, a complex of large lakes covered much of the Peace River country. At different times, these lakes drained either south into the Missouri-Mississippi system or north into the Mackenzie system, allowing Missouri River fish to colonize most of northeastern British Columbia.

GENETIC GENOCIDE

Genetic research by Sievert Rohwer of the University of Washington has uncovered a fascinating story of recolonization and genetic genocide in a pair of wood warblers.

The Townsend's Warbler is one of the commonest warblers in the coniferous forests of British Columbia's Coast and Interior Mountains. Although it is brightly coloured, it prefers to live in the treetops and is usually detectable only by its high, wheezy song. The closest relative of the Townsend's Warbler is the Hermit Warbler, which lives to the south of British Columbia—in the Coast, Cascade and Sierra Mountains of California, Oregon and southern Washington. The ancestor of these two species was apparently split from the wide-ranging, boreal stock of the eastern Black-throated Green Warbler during one of the glacial advances of the ice ages.

Today these species meet and hybridize in southern Washington, especially in the neighbourhood of Mount Rainier. Closer examination of birds around the contact zone indicated that genes of the Townsend's Warbler infiltrate the populations of Hermit Warbler to the south, but the reverse is not true: there is no evidence of Hermit Warbler genes in Townsend's Warblers north of the contact zone. Sievert Rohwer decided to investigate this hybrid zone by looking at the mitochondrial DNA of the warblers. Mitochondrial DNA (mtDNA) is not involved directly in sexual reproduction, but is passed on from mother to offspring in minute intracellular organelles within the egg. It is therefore a good marker of maternal lineages.

Rohwer's studies revealed a remarkable pattern. The Townsend's Warblers of the Rockies had "pure" Townsend's mtDNA and the Hermit Warblers of the Sierras had "pure" Hermit mtDNA, just as predicted, but the Townsend's of the British Columbia coast had a good portion of Hermit Warbler DNA in their mitochondria! Even more remarkable, the Townsend's of the Haida Gwaii and the Alexander Archipelago (of the Alaska panhandle) had 100 per cent Hermit Warbler mtDNA!

This tells us that at one time, Hermit Warblers inhabited the entire west coast of British Columbia—and that they have been subsequently genetically overrun by Townsend's Warblers. It seems that the ancestors of Townsend's and Hermit Warblers were separated from each other during glaciation, just as they were both separated from their boreal counterparts. They were isolated by the unfriendly, desert habitat of the Great Basin, and the Rocky Mountain group evolved into the Townsend's Warbler and the coastal group evolved into the Hermit Warbler.

As the glaciers retreated, Townsend's Warblers moved up the Rockies into the Interior of British Columbia but were blocked from the coast by the still-extensive ice dome of the central Interior. Hermit Warblers colonized the newly created temperate coniferous forests of the coast, reaching well into coastal Alaska. But when the ice finally retreated into the highest mountain peaks and coniferous forests moved through the large valleys, Townsend's Warblers descended on the coast and began hybridizing with Hermit Warblers. For some reason, the Townsend's Warbler genes dominated those of Hermit Warblers, and the hybrid zone moved south down the Cascade Mountains—and is presumably still doing so.

Townsend's Warblers

SPECIES-CRAZY STICKLEBACKS

Until recently, students were taught that evolution occurs gradually over the grand scale of geologic time and that the origin of a new species spans several million years. Recent discoveries have swept those ideas aside, however, and there is no better example of fast-tracked evolution than the Threespine Stickleback and its colonization of the west coast of British Columbia.

The Threespine Stickleback is a spiny little fish that is common along the coasts of the North Pacific and North Atlantic Oceans. It feeds on plankton in shallow marine waters but also invades creeks. Along the glaciated coast of British Columbia and Alaska, many lowland lakes contain stickleback populations.

In six lakes on the Gulf Islands and Vancouver Island, however, a curious event has occurred. In each of these lakes (Spectacle, Paxton, Priest and Emily Lakes on Texada Island; Hadley Lake on Lasqueti Island; and Enos Lake on Vancouver Island), there are two species of Threespine Stickleback. One lives around the edge of the lake, feeding on invertebrates in the weeds and mud of the lake bottom; the other is a fish of open water, feeding on the plankton in the water column. But though each pair shares its lake in a similar ecological way, there are differences between the species, implying that they have evolved separately.

What does glaciation have to do with this phenomenon? Since all these lakes were covered with ice during the last glaciation, these species must have evolved in the last twelve thousand years. The simplest explanation of this phenomenon involves the intriguing events that followed the melting of the glaciers along the coast.

As explained in Chapter 1, the immense ice sheets that covered the Strait of Georgia and Vancouver Island depressed the land beneath them as much as 250 metres or more. As they melted, the salt water invaded the low-lying land exposed by the retreating glaciers. All but the highest points of the Gulf Islands were covered by the sea, as was the entire coastal plain of eastern Vancouver Island. The sticklebacks came along with the invading sea and populated the new inlets and basins. Then, freed from its icy burden, the land sprang back and the sea level quickly fell correspondingly to its present position.

As the sea level fell, populations of sticklebacks were left behind in new lakes and were isolated from their seagoing rela-tives by waterfalls and rapids on the new coastal creeks. In big, steep-walled, fiordlike lakes, the sticklebacks remained general plankton feeders like their ancestors. And they remained similar in appearance, too—slim, with small mouths and long gill rakers. But in lakes with broad, shallow, warm edges rich in food, they began to exploit the inverte-brate life on the muddy, weedy bottom. This successful shift in feeding strategy

White Sucker

Before about ten thousand years ago, a lake briefly covered the Peace River Canyon, which before had been a serious barrier to fish movement. This lake allowed some Missouri fish to enter the upper Peace and later, via the Summit Lake connection near Prince George, allowed two Great Plains species—the White Sucker and Brassy Minnow—to colonize the Fraser.

The most fascinating story about fish in British Columbia is the rapid evolution of new forms following deglaciation. The stickleback story (see the box entitled "Species-Crazy Sticklebacks") is perhaps the best example, but it selected for individuals with a noticeably different form from that of other stickle-backs, and populations of stocky, wide-mouthed fish with short gill rakers soon evolved.

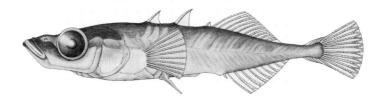

Open-water species

Then, a thousand to two thousand years after the sea level had fallen, it rose again, although only to about 50 metres above its present level. This rise was enough, however, to carry marine sticklebacks over some of the barriers separating them from the lowland lakes. Some of them reached the lakes colonized many generations before, but when they got to lakes with bottom-feeding stickle-backs present, the immigrant fish found that they couldn't compete with the residents. They could only coexist with residents if the lake was relatively large and deep—that is, if it had a well-developed open-water zone with enough plankton for the new arrivals to live on.

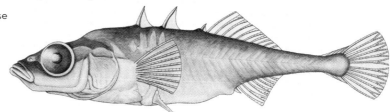

Bottom-feeding species

As the sea level fell once more, the lakes again became isolated from marine sticklebacks. Even though the two popula-tions in each lake were closely related and could produce fertile hybrid offspring, they rarely interbred—and the differences between them were maintained genera-tion after generation. They had essentially become new, separate species—in less than two thousand years.

It turns out that this phenomenon occurred in only a handful of lakes in the

Strait of Georgia area. These lakes were all low enough to be colonized by two consecutive immigrant invasions, high enough to become isolated from the ocean by waterfalls or other barriers and large enough to have a substantial open-water zone, and they had broad, sloping edges that were shallow enough to sup-port a rich littoral, or shoreline, zone.

Who needs to go to the tropics to look for exotic stories of evolution in action when we have such superb examples right here in British Columbia? These little sticklebacks are biological treasures—and we should treat them with the care due to unique creatures. Tragically, we have already lost one pair of species—predatory catfish were introduced into Hadley Lake and have apparently caused the extinction of the sticklebacks there.

is only one of a number that could be given. Two things are needed for rapid evolution—geographical isolation and ecological opportunities—and for freshwater fish, post-glacial British Columbia was an evolutionary paradise.

Fish entered various river systems through huge but ephemeral lakes and were subsequently isolated from their parent populations. The fish com-munities in the new lakes and rivers did not have to cope with the diversity of species that their ancestors had coped with south of the ice, so there was a variety of new ecological opportunities available.

Pages 98-99: Mountain goats apparently made it to Vancouver Island soon after the ice left, but they didn't stay.

New forms of fish appeared quite quickly—a tiny deep-water sculpin in Cultus Lake, landlocked smelts in Pitt and Harrison Lakes, "giant" Pygmy Whitefish in McLeese and Tyhee Lakes, an unusual Largescale Sucker in the upper Kettle River, a lamprey that never leaves Cowichan Lake and a species pair of whitefish that existed in Dragon Lake before the fish were poisoned so that trout could be introduced. And the list could be a lot longer. Our knowledge of fish evolution and taxonomy in British Columbia is limited, and more detailed studies will undoubtedly come up with many more such cases.

Island-Hopping

The coast of British Columbia contains one of the great archipelagos of the world: thousands of islands, ranging in size from the great Vancouver Island to small rocky islets that barely make it onto the marine charts. Most of these islands were glaciated up to twelve thousand years ago, but now they abound with life. A closer look reveals that their plant and animal communities are not the same as those on the mainland.

Consider Vancouver Island. It was likely revegetated quickly with wind-borne seeds, and most birds made the flight over from the mainland in a matter of geological minutes (although one species, the familiar Black-capped Chickadee, is absent to this day). Mammals, however, have had a harder time of it. Of the sixty or so species on the mainland coast, only twenty-seven occur on Vancouver Island. The list of absentees is full of familiar faces: Snowshoe Hares, Coast Moles, chipmunks, Porcupines, Coyotes, Red Foxes and Grizzly Bears, to name a few.

Many species that did manage to colonize Vancouver Island and the Haida Gwaii have evolved in isolation from their mainland populations long enough to be recognizably different. A few are now considered separate species, including the Vancouver Island Marmot. Most, however, have not crossed the species boundary and are classed as subspecies. The Haida Gwaii is home to so many of these unique island forms that it has been called the Canadian Galápagos.

Perhaps the most interesting and complex example of island-hopping is that of the Deer Mice. These big-eyed, big-eared mice are one of the commonest species of mammals throughout the province and are found on all but the tiniest coastal islands. Ian McTaggart-Cowan and other biologists exploring the small islands off Vancouver Island and the Haida Gwaii noticed a strange pattern. There seemed to be two types of Deer Mice on these islands: a large, long-tailed type and a smaller, shorter-tailed type. The two types were never found together on the same small island. On some islands, such as Triangle Island, the mice were almost three times the weight of mainland Deer Mice. Subsequent genetic studies have unravelled much of the mystery. There are two species, and both are found on the mainland as well as the islands. The big island mice are apparently Keen's Mice, a long-tailed species found high in the Coast Mountains and the Cascade Range and at lower elevations along the northern coast. Smaller island mice are the same species as the Deer Mice of lower elevations along the southern coast.

But why is there only one species on each small island, and how did they get there? The best guess is that the mice rafted from the mainland on large pieces of debris brought down the mountain slopes and into the sea by landslides. The first species to arrive on and populate any particular island could then exclude the other species by sheer weight of numbers.

AFTER THE ICE AGE: CLIMATE AND ECOSYSTEM CHANGE

You have seen how post-glacial immigration has shaped the distribution of many plant and animal species in British Columbia. But climate also plays an important role in the distribution of species—some like it hot, some like it cold, some like it dripping wet, and some can withstand months of drought. And climate is always changing. When most of us think of climate change, we think of the recent phenomenon of rapid, human-induced change, but, over the long term, the earth's climate has never been static. And along with changes in climate come changes in the distribution of plants and animals. The range maps shown in bird and flower guides are not permanent and fixed but are always shifting.

Twelve thousand years ago, after the glaciers receded, the climate of the southern mainland was colder and drier than it is today; the coast received about 600 millimetres less rainfall annually than it does today. On the dry east side of Vancouver Island and the Gulf Islands, large bison (from a now extinct species) roamed through an open landscape dotted with aspen groves.

Lodgepole Pine dominated the first forests to invade the southern mainland after the glaciers left. This species prevailed for about two thousand years, even as the climate became moister. But about ten thousand years ago, as the climate rapidly became warmer, Douglas-fir swept up the coast—even as far north as northern Vancouver Island—to replace the pine. At this time, Sitka Spruce was also more common than it is today, but Western Hemlock played only a minor role; Western Redcedar was especially sparse.

In the southern Interior, cold steppe with sagebrush and grasses dominated, but scattered populations of Whitebark Pine, Western White Pine, fir and spruce imply that the climate was cooler than today.

But the glaciers were shrinking from British Columbia because the Northern Hemisphere had entered a warm interval. Summer solar radiation reached a peak between nine thousand and ten thousand years ago, when it was 8 per cent greater than today; winter solar radiation, in contrast, was 10 per cent less than it is today (see the box entitled "Planetary Cycles, Climatic Cycles" on page 46). With increased summer sunshine, the east Pacific subtropical high-pressure system expanded, intensifying summer drought. But the huge ice age glaciers continued to affect regional climate until they dwindled away, so the warmest period of the present interglacial period followed about two thousand years after the peak in solar radiation.

As a result, Interior summers eight thousand years ago were much hotter and drier than they are today, and thus grasslands were much more extensive. East of the Coast Mountains, grass covered many south-facing mountain slopes, even in the far north. The lower timberline stood at around 1300 metres in the south, compared with about 500 metres today. The distribution of some Prairie and Great Basin plants and animals extended from Osoyoos all the way to central Yukon.

Conversely, wetlands and alpine areas were much less extensive than they are today. Many modern lake basins were dry or only held water ephemerally during the spring. Alpine tundra, so widespread in the mountains south of the ice during the glacial advances, dwindled and, on the lower, more isolated mountains, disappeared completely.

Between 4000 and 7000 years ago, the climate became moister and cooler. Along the southern coast, Western Hemlocks and then Western

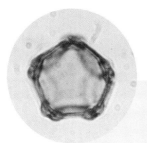  

Pollen grains of (from left) alder, spruce and pine.

POLLEN: DUST OF THE AGES

How do we know what the climate was like thousands of years ago? Paleoecologists use a variety of clues to piece together the ancient landscape, but the most often used evidence comes from a very familiar source—pollen. Every spring and summer the pollen from a host of plants drifts on the warm breezes—giving some of us hay fever—and settles to the ground as a fine, dusty film. When pollen lands on a lake or bog, it sinks into the mud or peat on the bottom (have you noticed the golden rings of pine pollen around drying mud puddles?), where it is soon entombed by this year's sediments and debris. Preserved in this oxygen-poor environment, the pollen grains turn into millions of microscopic fossils, each of which can be identified. Summer after summer the pollen layers build up, continually recording the ecosystem around the pond or bog.

The translation of this record—which falls to a branch of science called palynology—is a difficult task and is often plagued by lack of information. Few lakes and bogs have been sampled and analyzed and, as Richard Hebda of the Royal British Columbia Museum writes, "Every lake tells a story—and adds another piece to the puzzle of the environmental history of British Columbia."

Redcedars expanded at the expense of Douglas-fir and Sitka Spruce. On southern Vancouver Island, Garry Oaks appeared and prospered—by 6000 years ago, they formed a continuous forest or woodland in the vicinity of Saanich Inlet. In the Interior, forests expanded and reclaimed most of the grasslands area. By 3000 to 4500 years ago grasslands had decreased to their minimum extent, and relatively modern conditions prevailed. But even today you can see reminders of that warmer, drier time 8000 years ago—for example, relict grasslands on steep, south-facing slopes in northern British Columbia and a Douglas-fir stand on the slopes overlooking Stuart Lake, a lonely outpost of southern forest in the land of spruce.

The chronology outlined thus far is the story of southern British Columbia. The details of northern plant communities are less well known but can be inferred from two or three sites. In the far northwest, shrub tundra prevailed immediately following the retreat of the glaciers about 9250 years ago but quickly gave way to spruce woodland. There was a general increase in warmth and moisture until about 6100 years ago. Following a trend to a more semi-arid climate about 4100 years ago, Subalpine Fir and then Lodgepole Pine joined the spruce forest about 3200 years ago.

In British Columbia, the last four millennia have been dominated by the coolest climate since the glaciers left. During this interval cool summers and moist winters caused the expansion of mountain ice fields and established the mature rain forests along the West Coast. This interval culminated in the coolest period—sometimes called the Little Ice Age—which began in about 1650 and ended with a warming trend that started around 1850 and, with a minor decline in the middle of the twentieth century, continues to this day.

MAPPING TODAY'S PATTERNS

The patterns of living communities in British Columbia today are the product of interactions between geology, topography, climate, glaciation, colonization and the competition among species for space. Although these patterns may seem hopelessly complex—and, at finer levels, they may be—ecological zones that help make sense of British Columbia's biological diversity can be identified.

There have been several attempts to identify and map British Columbia's ecological zones, but only two systems are widely used today. Vladimir Krajina, a plant ecologist who worked at the University of British Columbia, developed a system of "biogeoclimatic zones," which are areas characterized by climatic factors and defined according to the tree species that dominate in climax forests (or grass species in climax grasslands, in nonforested areas) on average sites within them. These zones can be subdivided into subzones and subzone variants according to climate and vegetation.

Since biogeoclimatic zones help predict what plants will grow in certain areas and how much trees will grow, the provincial Ministry of Forests

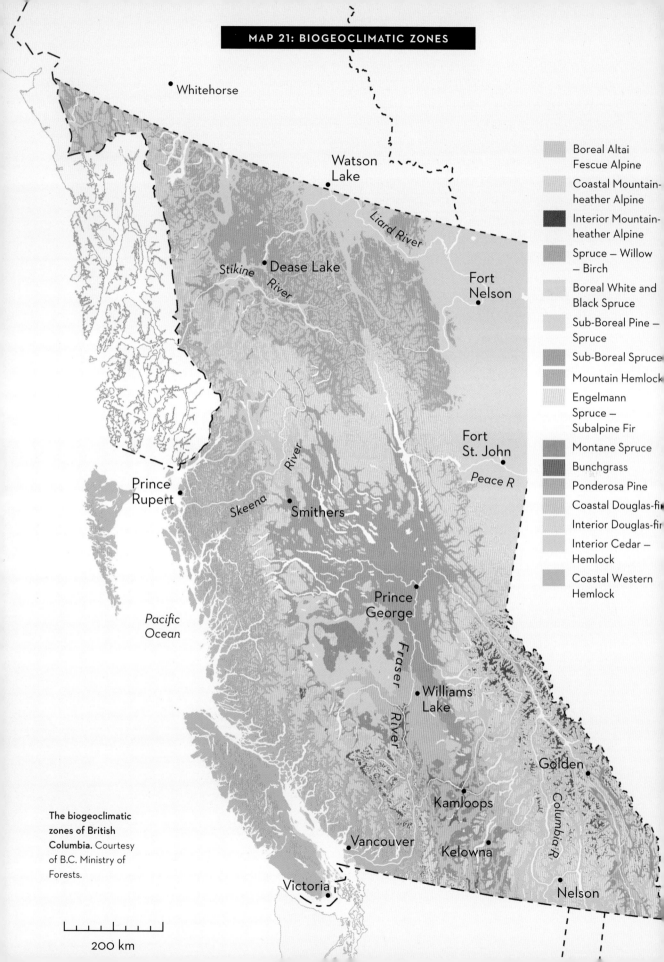

MAP 21: BIOGEOCLIMATIC ZONES

Whitehorse

Watson Lake

Liard River

Stikine River Dease Lake

Fort Nelson

Fort St. John

Peace R

Prince Rupert

River

Skeena Smithers

Pacific Ocean

Prince George

Fraser River

Williams Lake

Golden

Columbia R

Kamloops

Vancouver

Kelowna

Nelson

Victoria

Boreal Altai Fescue Alpine

Coastal Mountain-heather Alpine

Interior Mountain-heather Alpine

Spruce — Willow — Birch

Boreal White and Black Spruce

Sub-Boreal Pine — Spruce

Sub-Boreal Spruce

Mountain Hemlock

Engelmann Spruce — Subalpine Fir

Montane Spruce

Bunchgrass

Ponderosa Pine

Coastal Douglas-fir

Interior Douglas-fir

Interior Cedar — Hemlock

Coastal Western Hemlock

The biogeoclimatic zones of British Columbia. Courtesy of B.C. Ministry of Forests.

200 km

adopted and refined Krajina's system and mapped the province at the sub-zone variant level. Sixteen major zones are now described (Map 21).

Dennis Demarchi of the provincial Wildlife Branch took a different approach from Krajina's. He recognized a shortcoming of biogeoclimatic zones—in mountainous country they become complex, sinuous strips following the contour lines along the fingerlike ridges. But animal and plant populations do not necessarily experience the landscape in narrow, zonal bands; they often use several zones. For example, Western Redcedars in the southern Interior can live quite happily in the Bunchgrass Zone, as long as they are beside a creek in a cool, dark canyon, and they will also grow along the same creek in the Interior Douglas-fir and Montane Spruce Zones upstream. In one day a Grizzly Bear could traverse several biogeoclimatic zones while moving from salmon stream to berry patch to ground squirrel colony. A band of California Bighorn Sheep may depend on a snow-free slope of grass in the Bunchgrass Zone for winter forage, a series of rock bluffs in the Ponderosa Pine Zone for escape terrain and moist grasslands in the Interior Douglas-fir Zone for summer pasture.

Demarchi wanted to map ecosystems the way an animal would experience them. At the most general level, his "ecoregion" classification begins as Krajina's does—dividing the province into broad climatic areas—but then it subdivides these areas according to major physiographic units (such as plateaus, mountain ranges and major valleys) as well as climate. There are five levels of organization in the ecoregion classification: the first two—ecodomains and ecodivisions—place British Columbia in a global context, whereas the next three—ecoprovinces (Map 22, overleaf), ecoregions and ecosections—relate portions of the province to the rest of North America or to other ecological areas within the province. Ecosection and ecoregion boundaries are primarily geographical barriers such as rivers or lakes or the edges of different physiographic features, but the system also uses the boundaries of biogeoclimatic zones—for example, to separate highland areas from adjacent valleys.

British Columbia is far ahead of most other jurisdictions in North America in having its complex ecological regions described and mapped in such detail. And there is great advantage in having two different approaches to ecological classification—they can be tied together in a complementary way to produce a powerful, detailed method of describing the ecology of this province.

THE TEMPORARY NATURE OF NATURE

Even though the regions of British Columbia can be described and mapped, the ecological map of the province is far from static. Although large-scale changes may not be readily apparent on human time scales, change is happening all the time—map boundaries are constantly shifting. Probably the

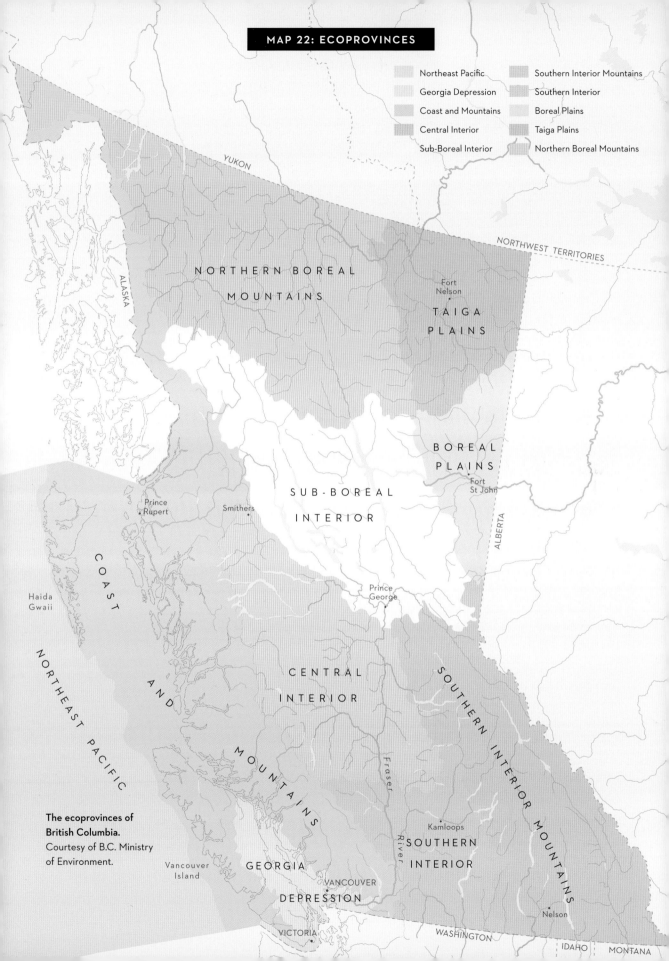

MAP 22: ECOPROVINCES

Northeast Pacific
Georgia Depression
Coast and Mountains
Central Interior
Sub-Boreal Interior

Southern Interior Mountains
Southern Interior
Boreal Plains
Taiga Plains
Northern Boreal Mountains

YUKON

NORTHWEST TERRITORIES

ALASKA

NORTHERN BOREAL
MOUNTAINS

Fort
Nelson

TAIGA
PLAINS

BOREAL
PLAINS

Fort
St John

ALBERTA

Prince
Rupert

Smithers

SUB-BOREAL
INTERIOR

Haida
Gwaii

C
O
A
S
T

A
N
D

M
O
U
N
T
A
I
N
S

Prince
George

CENTRAL
INTERIOR

SOUTHERN
INTERIOR
MOUNTAINS

N
O
R
T
H
E
A
S
T

P
A
C
I
F
I
C

Fraser

Kamloops

River

SOUTHERN
INTERIOR

**The ecoprovinces of
British Columbia.**
Courtesy of B.C. Ministry
of Environment.

Vancouver
Island

GEORGIA

VANCOUVER

DEPRESSION

VICTORIA

Nelson

WASHINGTON

IDAHO   MONTANA

most obvious changes humans can see in their lifetime are the great range expansions of some birds. Some of this avian immigration may be related to the climatic warming following the end of the Little Ice Age. As flying animals, birds can disperse widely and quickly and so offer the best examples of recent changes. For some birds, the extension of ranges northward over the last century has been remarkable.

The Wilson's Phalarope was first recorded in the province in 1922—just across the 49th parallel in the south Okanagan—but by the 1980s it had reached the marshes of the far northeast of British Columbia and the southern Yukon Territory. White-throated Swifts also put in their first historical appearance in British Columbia in the south Okanagan—in 1907. Now they careen around rock bluffs as far north as Williams Lake and the Clearwater River canyon. Most recently, Gray Flycatchers expanded northward from Oregon through the Ponderosa Pine forests of Washington State in the 1970s and reached the south Okanagan in the mid 1980s—where they are now a locally common species.

Conversely, some birds have spread west and south from the northeast. The Barred Owl was first recorded from the province along the Liard River in 1943, reaching the southern Interior (Wells Gray Park) by 1958 and the southern coast by 1966. We didn't see our first Barred Owls until the 1970s—but they are now found throughout the province and are one of the most dependable species to put on a loud hooting show on a spring night of owling.

The question may be asked: if birds can fly anywhere they want, why don't all bird species

The Barred Owl has moved into British Columbia during this century, reaching southern forests in the late 1950s and becoming commonplace there in the 1970s.

TABLE 3.2: TIMELINE: CHANGING CLIMATE

Years ago	Events
16,000 to 13,000	Glaciers cover most of British Columbia. Tundra-like ecosystems along parts of the east coast of the Haida Gwaii.
13,000	Glaciers leave lowlands of southern mainland.
12,000	Climate is cooler and drier than it is today. Forests in southern mainland dominated by Lodgepole Pine; the east side of Vancouver Island open country with scattered aspen groves.
10,000	Glaciers have left all the lowlands. Climate has become moister and now becomes rapidly warmer. Douglas-fir sweeps up the coast and replaces Lodgepole Pine; Sitka Spruce common, but Western Hemlock and Western Redcedar sparse. In the southern Interior, cold steppe with sagebrush and grass dominates; presence of subalpine trees implies that climate is cooler than at present.
10,000 to 9000	Summer solar radiation reaches peak—8 per cent greater than today, but huge glaciers still affect regional climate.
9250	Shrub tundra prevails in north, but spruce woodland dominates soon after.
8000	Warmest period of present interglacial period. Interior summers hotter and drier than at present. Grasslands much more extensive, but wetlands and alpine ecosystems much less extensive than today.
7000 to 4000	Climate becomes moister and cooler. Western Hemlocks and then Western Redcedars expand at the expense of Douglas-fir and Sitka Spruce.
6000	On southern Vancouver Island, Garry Oaks are more widespread than today.
4500 to 3000	Interior grasslands reach minimum extent; relatively modern conditions prevail there.
3200	Subalpine Fir and then Lodgepole Pine join spruce forest in north.
350 to 150	Climate cools, mountain glaciers expand during Little Ice Age.
150	Present warming trend begins.

immediately move into habitats they can make use of? One reason is that birds are quite conservative animals and resist moving into entirely new habitats. Gray Flycatchers, for instance, were formerly restricted to the sagebrush-juniper deserts of the Great Basin of the United States. In the late 1960s, a population of Gray Flycatchers took a liking to Ponderosa Pine forests along the east slope of the Oregon Cascades, perhaps because pine forests that have been selectively logged mimic the juniper woodland that the flycatchers are wired to look for. These flycatchers found the pine forests empty of fly-catching competition and quickly spread north.

Another question is whether the glaciers will return. Although they left the lowlands 12,000 years ago, there is no evidence that we are out of the Ice Age. The last two million years have been times of almost constant change, and if past patterns are any indication, we may only be living in a short interval of warmth amid a long period of ice. Looking at the past 200,000 years as a whole, many of the plant and animal species of southern British Columbia are more correctly seen as residents of California and Oregon visiting here temporarily during the warm season.

Table 3.2 summarizes the climate changes of the last sixteen thousand years.

MAPPING TOMORROW'S PATTERNS

There is no doubt that the climate is warming and changing, and that habitats are shifting. But what will British Columbia's natural world look like in fifty or a hundred years? This was the question that Tongli Wang of the University of British Columbia asked when he described the "climate niche" of each of the province's ecosystems, and set out to predict where those niches would move to, based on the consensus of twenty climate change models. The results of Dr. Wang's and his colleagues' work are presented in Map 23, and in Table 3.3. To be clear, we are talking about the climate of these ecological zones, not their vegetation. For example, the climate of the present-day Interior Douglas-fir Zone will move upslope and northward, but the Douglas-firs and their associates may lag considerably behind.

The first conclusion that jumps out of the models is that the climate of British Columbia has already shifted substantially in the thirty or so years since the zones were first mapped—23 per cent of the province's land is now in the climate envelope of a different biogeoclimatic zone. By the end of this century, the shift is predicted to be far more dramatic. As might be expected, subalpine, alpine and sub-boreal zones are among the most vulnerable— the Boreal Altai Fescue Alpine, Interior Mountain-heather Alpine, Montane Spruce, and Sub-boreal Pine-Spruce Zones are projected to lose more than 80 per cent of their climate area by the end of the century. Similarly, the Sub-boreal Spruce and Spruce-Willow Birch Zones are projected to lose 44 per cent of their climate area. In more extreme climate-models, the alpine zones virtually disappear. In contrast, grasslands and the warm forests of the Interior are predicted to expand—in Wang's consensus projection, the Bunchgrass Zone more than doubles in size, whereas the Interior Cedar-Hemlock Zone grows three-fold and becomes the most widespread climate type in the province.

The cause of these contractions and expansions, of course, are the climate shifts upslope and to the north—in the consensus prediction, zones moved an average of 209 metres upslope and 84 kilometres to the north. The greatest movement uphill comes on the coast; the Coastal Western Hemlock and Mountain Hemlock Zones climb the mountains 323 and 455 metres respectively. The Engelmann Spruce-Subalpine Fir Zone moves the farthest north—278 kilometres. But there are zones that are more stay-at-home than others. The Coastal Douglas-fir Zone, for example, shifts northward only

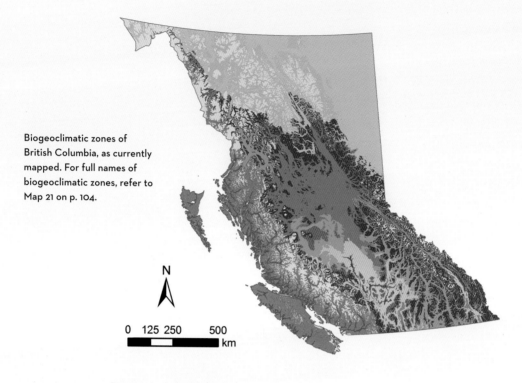

Biogeoclimatic zones of
British Columbia, as currently
mapped. For full names of
biogeoclimatic zones, refer to
Map 21 on p. 104.

N

0 125 250   500
                km

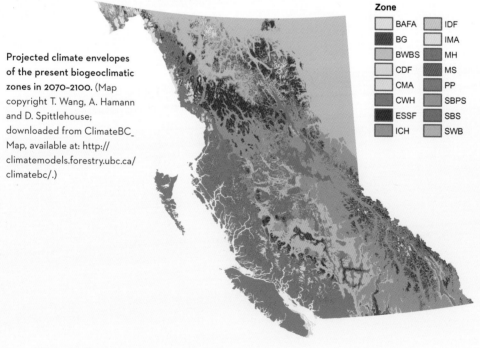

Projected climate envelopes
of the present biogeoclimatic
zones in 2070–2100. (Map
copyright T. Wang, A. Hamann
and D. Spittlehouse;
downloaded from ClimateBC_
Map, available at: http://
climatemodels.forestry.ubc.ca/
climatebc/.)

Zone

BAFA	IDF
BG	IMA
BWBS	MH
CDF	MS
CMA	PP
CWH	SBPS
ESSF	SBS
ICH	SWB

10 kilometres and, on the Chilcotin Plateau, the Sub-boreal Pine-Spruce Zone simply shrinks in place.

How confident are the researchers in their predictions? When the twenty different climate scenarios are run, the projections become somewhat less certain as they look farther into the future—by 2085, they agree only 51 per cent of the time for a given point in the province. Another example of uncertainty focuses on the northeast: there, the consensus projection maintains the Boreal White and Black Spruce Zone as the dominant ecosystem of the region, but other, North America–wide studies predict an expansion of prairie grassland ecosystems there. Still, these models provide a powerful tool to visualize a future British Columbia and make us realize that change, however unpredictable, is already here.

TABLE 3.3: THE PROJECTED CHANGE IN CLIMATE ENVELOPES FOR BRITISH COLUMBIA'S BIOGEOCLIMATIC ZONES, FROM 1960-90 TO 2070-2100.			
BIOGEOCLIMATIC ZONE	CHANGE OF ELEVATION (M)	CLIMATE ZONE SHIFT (%)	NORTHWARD SHIFT (KM)
Boreal Altai Fescue Alpine	–81	170	95
Bunchgrass	128	186	14
Boreal White and Black Spruce	11	70	18
Coastal Douglas-fir	19	128	10
Coastal Mountain-heather Alpine	–45	208	138
Coastal Western Hemlock	69	323	69
Engelmann Spruce-Subalpine Fir	–33	123	278
Interior Cedar Hemlock	325	260	127
Interior Douglas-fir	91	72	126
Interior Mountain-heather Alpine	–81	246	38
Mountain Hemlock	–12	455	75
Montane Spruce	–88	312	105
Ponderosa Pine	211	235	77
Sub-boreal Pine-Spruce	–85	190	–2
Sub-boreal Spruce	–44	154	145
Spruce-Willow-Birch	–44	212	23

(Adapted from T. Wang et al. 2012. Projecting future distributions of ecosystem climate niches: uncertainties and management applications. *Forest Ecology and Management* 279 [2012].)

TIME AND CHANGE

I often recall the June day I hiked into Berg Lake at the base of Mount Robson's north face. It was an overcast day and the mountain was hidden by clouds that threatened snow in this high part of the Rockies. We tramped through forests clogged with last winter's snow on the steep face beside Emperor Falls. But upon emerging from the forests into the hanging valley south of the lake, I was awestruck—I suddenly felt I had stepped back twelve thousand years to the end of the Pleistocene glaciations. Tumbling Glacier hung suspended from the low clouds, and the river flats lay in front of us—a great expanse of gravel, Yellow Mountain Avens and scattered conifers. It felt as though the glaciers had just left, and I honestly expected to see a small group of Woolly Mammoths amble away into the mists.

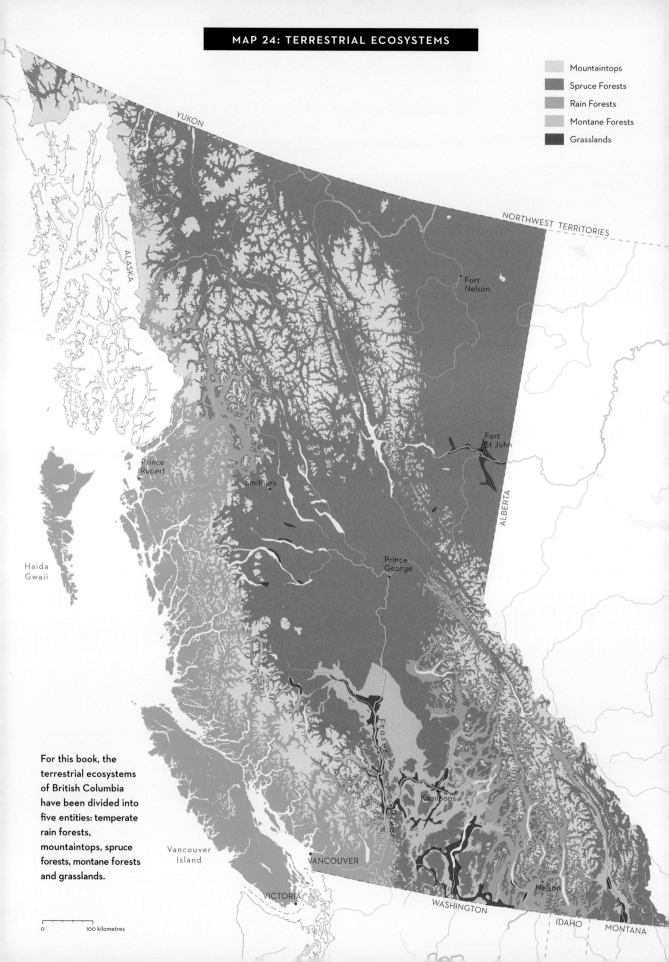

Mountaintops
Spruce Forests
Rain Forests
Montane Forests
Grasslands

YUKON

NORTHWEST TERRITORIES

ALASKA

Fort Nelson

Fort St John

Prince Rupert

Smithers

ALBERTA

Haida Gwaii

Prince George

Fraser River

Kamloops

For this book, the terrestrial ecosystems of British Columbia have been divided into five entities: temperate rain forests, mountaintops, spruce forests, montane forests and grasslands.

Vancouver Island

VANCOUVER

Nelson

VICTORIA

WASHINGTON

IDAHO   MONTANA

0   100 kilometres

We do not often personally experience the profound changes that have taken place in our familiar landscapes over geological or even ecological time. With our short lifetimes and even shorter memories, we tend to view the world as static. Continents and mountain ranges stay put and islands remain offshore. We are not even aware of the movement of glaciers. Every once in a while a volcano erupts or an earthquake shakes us, but the landscape on a grand scale looks much the same. And on the time scale of years, living things seem static, too. Polar Bears stay in the Arctic and sloths stay in the tropics. Sitka Spruce forests don't leave the coast and sagebrush steppes don't stray from the Interior. Seasons may come and go, but they seem to do so

THE EVER-WHIRLING WHEEL OF CHANGE;
THE WHICH ALL MORTAL THINGS DOTH SWAY.

Edmund Spenser, *The Faerie Queene*

in a predictable fashion. Some Julys are hotter than others, but we can compare all of them with a reasonable average.

But continents are moving and mountains are growing every day— at 4 centimetres per year, the St. Elias Range has been uplifted 4 metres in the last 100 years. The Rockies and the Columbia Mountains have lost a third of their glacial ice in the same time. In the past fifty years, a third of the Kootenay's grasslands have become forested and Barred Owls moved in from the northeast to occupy the entire province. Change is the only real constant in our world—British Columbia is being transformed in front of our eyes.

The first three chapters of this book have set the historical and physical scene in British Columbia. The remaining chapters discuss the broad natural regions or ecosystems of the province, which are roughly based on the biogeoclimatic zones mentioned earlier in this chapter. The aquatic systems—marine and fresh water—are covered in Chapters 4 and 10, respectively. The terrestrial ecosystems (Map 24) are described in Chapters 5 to 9 and include the rain forests (comprising the Coastal Western Hemlock, Coastal Douglas-fir, Mountain Hemlock and Interior Cedar-Hemlock Zones), mountaintops (comprising the Alpine Tundra and Spruce-Willow-Birch Zones and the higher parkland portions of the various subalpine zones), spruce forests (comprising the Engelmann Spruce–Subalpine Fir, Montane Spruce, Sub-boreal Spruce, Sub-boreal Pine-Spruce, and Boreal White and Black Spruce Zones), montane forests (comprising the Interior Douglas-fir and Ponderosa Pine Zones) and grasslands (comprising the Bunchgrass Zone and drier parts of the Ponderosa Pine and Interior Douglas-fir Zones and several other zones).

CHAPTER FOUR

LIFE IN THE PACIFIC

LIFE IN THE PACIFIC

A TRIP TO THE FISHING BANKS west of Vancouver Island is an unforgettable experience for any landlubber naturalist. The little boat leaves the coastline behind, bearing southwest from Ucluelet in 3-metre swells, and you try to hold onto the railing and your breakfast as best you can. For the first hour or two, the waters are almost deserted of birds, mammals and boats. Then, about 30 kilometres out, with the mountains of Vancouver Island fading on the misty horizon, small flocks of birds begin to fly by, leading to a scattering of fishing boats ahead. This is La Pérouse Bank, an undersea plateau on the edge of the continental shelf. It teems with life. Huge clouds of gulls, shearwaters, fulmars and albatrosses wheel behind rusty Russian trawlers like mosquitoes on a Moose; rafts of murres and puffins dive into the depths, coming up with silvery fish in their beaks. Occasionally a huge Humpback Whale rockets out of the water and crashes down in an explosion of spray.

La Pérouse Bank is part of the leading edge of British Columbia, the first place to receive the currents, wind and weather of the Pacific Ocean. Although most British Columbians live on the edge of the Pacific, few have spent enough time on the outer coast to appreciate its vastness, the immensity of that long, flat horizon. But the Pacific Ocean is more than just a western boundary to British Columbia and the source of its winter rains and howling gales. Its waters teem with plants and animals. Along a coastline choked with islands, cold, turbulent waters surge through narrow passages, constantly bringing nutrients to an amazing assemblage of species. From kelp to Killer Whales, from octopus to sea stars, the marine life of British Columbia is among the most diverse in the world, and British Columbia is one of the best places on earth to study marine organisms.

Life began in the sea, and the diversity of basic life forms, or phyla, in the oceans is still greater than that on land. Although the diversity of species is greater on land, thanks largely to the beetles, the number of plant and animal phyla is far greater in the sea. We think of all plants as being green because all land plants are green—trees, grass, moss and ferns all belong to the Chlorophyta, the green plant phylum. But marine plants belong to more than seven phyla and come in a rainbow of colours and forms. Besides the green algae (also in the Chlorophyta), there are brown algae, red algae, golden diatoms, orange dinoflagellates and more, all as different from each other as they are from the green plants. Only one of the thirty-three animal

Pages 114-15: A luxuriant growth of marine algae and surf-grass clothes the intertidal zone on Spring Island, Kyoquot Sound.

Below: Killer Whales are the top predators in the food chain of British Columbia's productive inshore waters.

phyla (an obscure parasitic group) has totally forsaken the sea, and fifteen have never ventured out of salt water. The echinoderms—such as sea stars, sea urchins and sea cucumbers—are perhaps the best-known exclusively marine animal group, but several other familiar groups, such as sponges, corals and jellyfish, are almost totally restricted to marine waters.

> FOR WHATEVER WE LOSE (LIKE A YOU OR A ME) IT'S ALWAYS
> OURSELVES WE FIND IN THE SEA.
>
> e. e. cummings, "maggie and milly and molly and may"

The watery world of the sea is not our world, and observing the life there has always been difficult. The intertidal zone—the narrow band of shoreline between the high-tide and low-tide lines—provides a rich and fascinating window on marine life. But for years, marine biologists attempting to unravel the mysteries of the open ocean and the dark sea bottom were restricted to glimpses obtained through various instruments, bottles, nets and dredges lowered from ships on long cables. The invention of scuba equipment has provided the opportunity to watch marine life in its own environment, but there are still many secrets held beneath the surface of the oceans.

NEAR THE SURFACE

Just as life on land stays close to the ground, bound by the need for nutrients and water tied up in the soil, so life in the oceans is concentrated near the surface of the water. Plants need three things to live: water, light and nutrients. Water is, of course, freely available in the sea, but light is found only near the surface. Water absorbs light at such a rate that below 40 metres it is too dim for plants to photosynthesize; below 600 metres it is as black as a moonless night. Plants, and the animals that eat them, must therefore live near the surface in the zone of light, called the photic zone.

Life in the dark depths below the photic zone is given over to a food chain based on the consumption of detritus, the nutrient-rich rain of dead plants and animals that constantly falls from the sunlit waters above. This rain of detritus continually removes that third requirement for plant life—nutrients—from the photic zone. Marine life can only flourish where these nutrients are recycled to the surface by upwelling currents or where they are replaced by nutrients in the outflow of rivers.

These conditions are met along many coastlines of the world. More than half of the plant biomass in the oceans is in seaweeds anchored to intertidal and subtidal rocks. Most of the world's fisheries are concentrated in small areas of rich coastal upwellings such as La Pérouse Banks. Beyond the continental shelves, nutrient levels are usually so low that the open oceans are biological deserts.

Plants on land are always battling for the essentials in life, their roots spreading outward seeking water and nutrients, their branches reaching skyward to find light. Over millennia, these battles for sunlight have bred the huge trees of the world, including the titanic conifers of the British Columbia coast. Marine plants have little need to be large. Giant kelp will grow from spores settling 30 or 40 metres or so below the surface, but below that it is too dark for growth. Along the shore, the pounding surf makes being small a distinct advantage, but it is in the open ocean where smallness is truly a big thing. There, 90 per cent of the biomass is of plants and animals so small they cannot swim against the slow oceanic currents. These creatures, drifting at the whim of the currents, are the plankton (singular, *plankter*). The plant-like drifters are the phytoplankton; the animals are the zooplankton.

Phytoplankton

Phytoplankters carry smallness to an extreme; most consist of a single cell. Some of the phytoplankton, collectively called flagellates, have whiplike flagellae that give them some ability to move around. Others, including most of the common species, have no means of locomotion at all and are truly adrift at sea. How do they stay afloat near the sunlit surface? First, at their tiny scale water is very viscous, so they sink very slowly. Some species slow this sinking further by growing long spines or forming chains of cells to increase their surface area. Finally, many phytoplankters store their photosynthetic products as droplets of oil rather than starch. These oil storage droplets can take up much of the cell and, being lighter than water, act as a lifejacket to keep the cell up in the sunlight. This oil has proved useful to humans as well, for all the oil reserves in the world formed in rich marine sediments where tiny, oil-filled cells drifted to the mud bottom. The remains of ancient terrestrial plants produced our other fossil fuel, coal.

Plankton shows remarkable bursts of productivity, called blooms, at certain times of the year. Most important are the diatom (see box entitled "Diatoms," overleaf) blooms of spring, triggered by the lengthening days of February and early March. The calmer spring weather and increased sunshine produces a stable layer of warmer water at the surface of coastal waters. Such waters are said to be stratified, and they are a perfect environment for plankton. By March, each cell is splitting in two every twenty-four hours or so; with this exponential growth a single cell can produce a million offspring in twenty days. Within a month or two the coastal waters are a soup of diatoms. Diatom concentrations peak in March in some protected waters, April in the Strait of Georgia and May along the outer coast.

The Strait of Georgia becomes stratified sooner than the outer coast not only because it is calmer but also because the Fraser River enters the strait. The huge volume of water released by the Fraser River spreads over the strait as a plume of fresher water that floats on top of the salt water, rapidly stratifying the surface. With increased runoff from the mountains, the plume builds through the spring and early summer and the entire Strait of Georgia becomes a brackish lake.

There are several distinct diatom blooms in spring, each including a slightly different suite of species. This production of billions of cells uses nutrients, however. By summer the levels of nitrates in coastal waters begin to drop below optimal levels. In addition, zooplankton consume diatoms, and by June the diatom soup begins to thin.

As nutrient levels fall and zooplankton consume more and more diatoms, another group of phytoplankton begins to dominate the brackish waters of the Strait of Georgia. *Heterosigma akashiro* is a tiny flagellate that can move just enough to get around the problems faced by non-motile diatoms. Swimming a metre per hour, *Heterosigma* can spend the night in the nutrient-rich waters below the surface layer, thus avoiding some of the zooplankton predators that feed at the surface during the night, and then wiggle 5 metres or so to the surface to bask in the sunlight all day. *Heterosigma* densities can become so high that they are toxic to fish constrained in aquaculture pens.

Another major group of phytoplankton is the dinoflagellates. These are strange creatures. Some obtain food by ingesting other plankton; others, like

DIATOMS

Diatoms are the foundation of life throughout most of the oceans. Through a microscope, these single-celled plants look like exquisitely crafted crystal wheels or lenses, each golden cell enclosed in a pair of intricately patterned silica glass shells called frustules. The frustules fit one inside the other and are sculpted and pitted in marvellous symmetrical designs.

When diatoms reproduce in the normal way, which is simply by splitting in two, new frustules are formed inside the old ones. The cells therefore become smaller and smaller and can only revert to their larger size when they reproduce sexually by producing male and female gametes. Spring phytoplankton blooms are dominated by large diatoms such as *Skeletonema*, *Chaetoceros* and *Thalassiosira*.

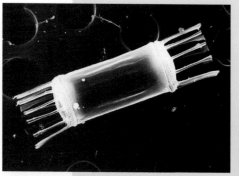
Skeletonema

Chaetoceros

Thalassiosira

good plants, make their own through photosynthesis, and still others do both. Dinoflagellates grow best in the warm, strongly stratified waters of summer, and their blooms can be spectacular. Concentrations of up to nine million cells per litre can turn the ocean red, orange, burgundy or milky white—popularly called red tides.

Among the most spectacular phytoplankton blooms in British Columbia waters are those of *Noctiluca* (Latin for "night light"), which literally light up the sea. This "bioluminescence"

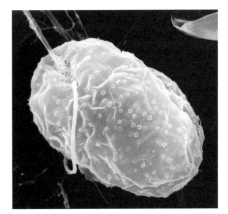

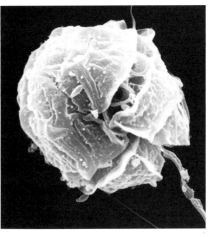

RED TIDE

On June 16, 1793, a group of sailors under the command of George Vancouver were surveying an inlet east of Klemtu, deep in what is now known as the Great Bear Rainforest. Stopping for breakfast in a small bay, they gathered mussels and roasted them over a fire. An hour later, four of them noticed their lips, hands and feet going numb; shortly after noon one of them—John Carter—was dead. Vancouver named the channel Mussel Inlet; the small bay, Poison Cove; and the site where the unfortunate sailor was buried, Carter Bay. The incident became the world's first published account of paralytic shellfish poisoning.

The cause of paralytic shellfish poisoning is a dinoflagellate, *Alexandrium*. *Alexandrium* looks like a golden top, spun through the water by a whiplike flagellum around its grooved waist while another vertical flagellum controls its movement. This tiny cell produces a chemical called saxitoxin that blocks the transfer of impulses in animal nerve cells. Saxitoxin is extremely deadly, ten thousand times more deadly than cyanide, and a dose of less than a milligram can kill a human in twenty minutes.

Normally *Alexandrium* is found in concentrations that are low enough to be safe, but in summer, especially in warm bays, its numbers can build to dangerous levels. The dinoflagellates are filtered out of the water by clams and other mollusks, which are for some reason unaffected by the toxin. Clams concentrate the toxin in the tips of their siphons, perhaps as a defence against fish, which often nip the siphon tips off. Butter Clams (*Saxidomus*, which gave the toxin its name) can hold the toxin for a year or more.

Anyone eating an affected clam will first notice a tingling in the lips as the nerves shut down, followed by general paralysis that will kill by asphyxiation unless artificial respiration is administered immediately. Patients lucky enough to get to a hospital in time will recover after a number of days on a respirator. While paralyzed they are fully aware of everything going on around them, but they are completely unable to move, breathe or speak.

Although humans cannot taste the difference between affected and unaffected clams, gulls often regurgitate poisoned prey. Kills of wild animals are rare, but a paralytic shellfish poisoning in Pacific Rim National Park in late August 1989 killed thousands of Pacific Sand Lance and more than 250 seabirds that ate the poisoned fish.

Heterosigma (top) **and** *Alexandrium* (bottom)

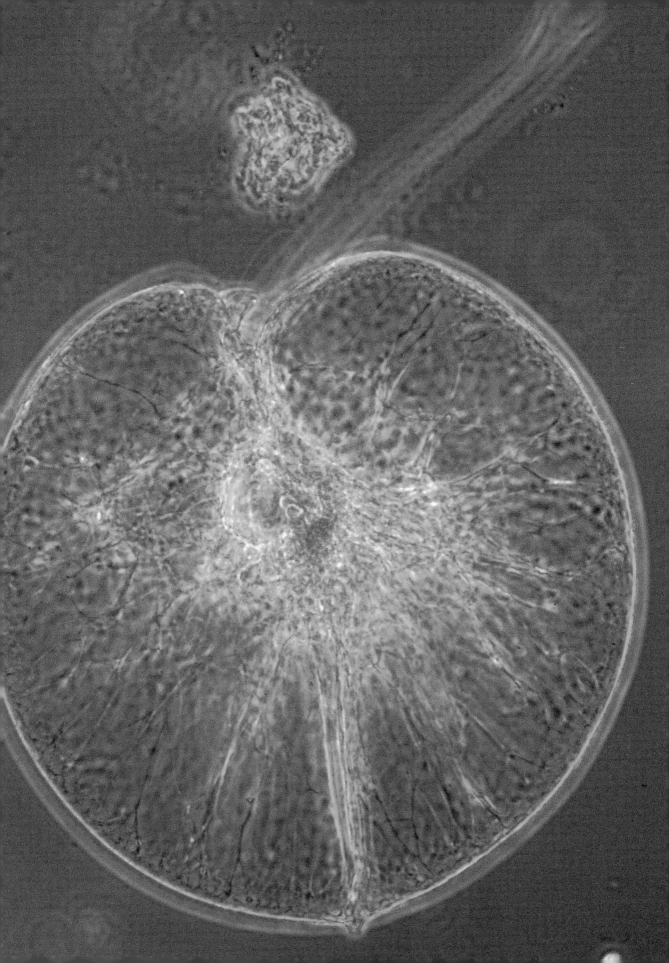

is produced by the chemical luciferin, triggered by the enzyme luciferase. It is not restricted to *Noctiluca*; several other species of plankton and bacteria and many of the animals that eat them also glow in a dark sea. Some jellyfish glow with the light of a different chemical reaction, stimulated by the release of calcium. Sea pens glow when touched, and many deep-sea fishes concentrate luminescent bacteria in spots along their bodies to act as signal lights in the dark depths.

Biologists are still unsure why bacteria and dinoflagellates light up, but the effect is spectacular. On one memorable, moonless night I was kayaking in a luminescent bay in the Haida Gwaii. The bow of the kayak glowed eerily, and each paddle stroke exploded in a new universe of underwater stars. To top it off, the water was filled with Ancient Murrelet chicks, balls of fluff paddling out to sea for the first time, each shining like a tiny comet in the black bay.

To sustain growth, upwelling or wind-driven currents must mix the warm upper water with the cold, nutrient-laden deeper waters. Mixing not only brings nutrients to the surface but also carries the plankton down into the murky depths where they cannot grow. Occasional mixing is best for growth— it brings nutrients to surface waters while providing some stability to allow blooms to take place. Increased winds in the late summer and fall boost nutrient levels in upper waters and trigger a series of minor plankton blooms.

Winter weather is an anathema to phytoplankton growth. Light levels are low, days are short, the water is cold, and wind-driven currents too often send the phytoplankton to the dark bottom. Many diatoms and other planktonic species form cystlike resting stages that wait out the winter on the seafloor, but they can only do this in the relatively shallow waters along the coast. Open-ocean species could never return from the abyssal depths and so must constantly stay near the surface. Winter phytoplankton communities along the coast are dominated by very tiny flagellates—cells less than a fiftieth of a millimetre across. These species can apparently stay up in the water column by constantly swimming towards the light and can grow more efficiently than diatoms under the cloudy skies and in the short days of winter.

Zooplankton

If members of the phytoplankton look strangely beautiful to human eyes, many zooplankters look simply strange. From tiny jelly balls with waving tentacles to vaguely shrimplike creatures with incredible spines to animals that look like lunar landing craft, the zooplankton is a bestiary that is beyond imagination.

Although most members of the phytoplankton are permanent fixtures of the drifting community, many zooplankters are there only temporarily. About 80 per cent of marine invertebrate species, including crabs, shrimp, clams, barnacles, sea anemones, sea stars, worms and sea squirts, have planktonic

Opposite page: **The dinoflagellate** *Noctiluca* **is one of the many micro-organisms that set the sea sparkling with bioluminescence on summer nights.**

Most marine invertebrates begin their lives as planktonic larvae. This is the first larval stage of a crab—a zoea larva—from English Bay, Vancouver.

larvae that spend time floating in the photic zone before settling down to an adult life.

The most abundant members of the zooplankton in British Columbia—and the commonest animals in the sea—are tiny crustaceans called copepods. In spring and early summer one species of copepod—*Neocalanus plumchrus*—dominates the zooplankton in the Strait of Georgia. *Neocalanus* feasts on the burgeoning spring diatom populations, growing larger and larger. In July, when diatom numbers begin to fall, *Neocalanus* stops feeding, bails out of the photic zone and begins to move into the dark depths; by September it is 300 metres down, and by early winter it is below 400 metres. It matures throughout the winter and breeds near the bottom in February and March, producing billions of larvae. The larvae then swim to the surface, arriving just in time for the spring phytoplankton blooms. *Neocalanus plumchrus* thus has the best of both worlds: the lush spring production of the photic zone and the relatively predator-free safety of the depths.

Many other successful zooplankters share this strategy. Although fish are not generally thought of as members of the zooplankton, many fish larvae most certainly are. Pacific Herring spawn in March so that their newly hatched larvae, only 7 millimetres long and lacking gills and a true mouth, can join the plankton during the spring feast. By the time the plankton stocks begin to dwindle in early summer, herring larvae have matured on their diet of copepods and are mobile enough to swim off in schools to search for rich patches of food. Rockfish give birth to live larvae in spring that drop out of the plankton in late July to begin lives near the bottom.

Euphausiid shrimp, or krill, concentrate at the surface during the day only to mate. They must mate at the surface so that the sinking eggs can hatch before they hit the seafloor, but why they do it during the day is still a mystery to biologists. Herring schools rip through euphausiid mating swarms from below, while screaming flocks of gulls advertise them to other seabirds. Thousands of dainty Bonaparte's Gulls, resplendent in their black-headed breeding plumage, gather in Active Pass between Mayne and Galiano Islands in April and early May to feed on the euphausiid *Thysanoessa raschii*.

The largest of the plankton, jellyfish, put a twist on this strategy. Jellyfish and their relatives, the sea anemones and corals, are members of the phylum

Cnidaria, identified by stinging cells in their tentacles. In the summer, bays along the coast are often choked with jellyfish, but these animals are extremely rare in winter; they too have disappeared into the depths. In late summer, jellyfish breed and the larvae descend to the bottom. There they settle down on one end, sprout tentacles from the other and spend the winter as tiny anemone-like hydroids. In spring tiny jellyfish, or medusae, bud off the hydroid and swim to the surface to join the plankton.

Another common zooplankter with a migrating habit is *Euphausia pacifica*. This shrimplike animal spends the daylight hours more than 100 metres

Hydroid medusae resemble jellyfish but are usually smaller and possess a fine membrane called a velum under the bell. Their tentacles, however, are equally well endowed with stinging cells. Specialized sensory cells around the edge of the bell provide both balance and light detection.

below the surface, presumably to avoid being eaten by arrowworms, larval fish or other predators in the crowded photic zone above. But as night falls, *Euphausia* swims up to the surface to feed on phytoplankton, then retreats before dawn.

Fish and Fish Eaters

The wheeling flocks of gulls are a reminder that despite the abundance and importance of the plankton, it is the plankton eaters that attract the most attention from naturalists. Most of the natural attractions of the open ocean are fish and the animals that eat fish: seals, whales and seabirds.

There are more than 325 species of marine fishes on the British Columbia coast, most hugging the bottom at shallow to moderate depths. Those that feed in open water naturally focus on the plankton-based community near the surface. Many species familiar to British Columbians, such as salmon (see Chapter 10) and herring, share this strategy.

Not surprisingly, many fish follow the common strategy of resting in the dark depths during the day and then rising close to the surface to feed at night. For some species this means vertical migrations of between 200 and 500 metres. These deep-water fish typically have long, narrow bodies, large heads, long teeth and light-producing organs called photophores along their sides. Lanternfish, named for their bright photophores, often dominate these communities. The photophores function to attract both other lanternfish of the same species and the zooplankton that make up the bulk of the fishes' diet. One deep-water species, the Pacific Viperfish, lures prey with a luminescent fin ray that dangles over its large, fanged mouth.

An even stranger group of fish in the abyssal depths is the dreamers. Like Viperfish, they have a "fishing lure" organ attached to their foreheads, but perhaps the strangest thing about the dreamers is their bizarre sex life. The males are tiny, degenerate fish without eyes or teeth and lead parasitic lives attached by their mouth to the body wall of a female. One light-studded fish species can be quite easily seen by the land-based naturalist.

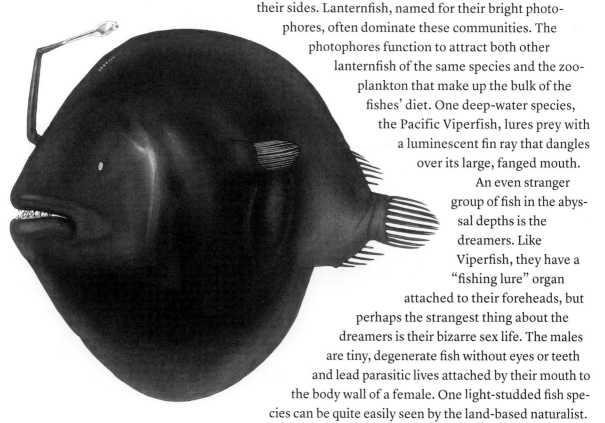

Dreamers, such as this female *Chaenophryne melanorhabdus*, are members of the often bizarre deep-water fish community.

The Plainfin Midshipman leaves the depths to mate and lay its eggs in bouldery intertidal habitats. This species is also called the singing fish—it can create a honking sound by squeezing air in its gasbladder over a diaphragm. If you ever hear a curious *oonk!* coming from beneath a large intertidal rock, carefully tilt it back and you may see a male guarding a mass of eggs attached to the bottom of the rock.

One of the most spectacular natural events in British Columbia happens in March, when huge schools of Pacific Herring spawn in sheltered bays along the coast. Each female lays twenty thousand or more pearl-like eggs. The eggs become very sticky on contact with sea water and are literally glued to whatever is on the bottom, often seaweed and eel-grass. Birds and mammals quickly fill the bays, attracted by the bounty. The air is filled with the barking and splashing of hundreds of California Sea Lions and the low roars of Northern Sea Lions. Flocks of Bald Eagles gather, swooping down to snatch herring from the surface. Gulls are always there, ready to pick up any floating egg masses or spent herring. Huge rafts of ducks such as scoters, scaup and goldeneyes, sometimes ten thousand or more to a bay, dive to feed on the roe, while loons and cormorants go after the fish.

BASKING SHARKS

Perhaps the most impressive plankton-eating fish off the coast of British Columbia, at least in terms of size, is the Basking Shark. The largest shark of temperate marine waters, the Basking Shark is so called because of its habit of swimming slowly at the ocean surface with just its dorsal fin exposed. They have often been the stuff of sea serpent tales. With their slightly calcified cartilaginous skeletons and long horny gill rakers, dead animals have the overall look of mythical sea monsters.

Like the great baleen whales, these 13-metre-long leviathans cruise open-mouthed through the plankton blooms of spring and summer. They are literally sieving the sea for zooplankton, combing the water with their huge gill rakers. As the plankton populations decline in fall, Basking Sharks largely give up on feeding and may spend the winter inactive at the bottom of the sea. Their numbers off the British Columbia coast have declined dramatically in the past few years, but biologists have no clear answer as to the cause of this decline.

Basking Shark

Perhaps the most important marine fish in British Columbia is the Pacific Sand Lance, a small, slender fish that forms massive schools in a wide range of depths and habitats. It is the staple diet of most British Columbian seabirds and the main prey of many larger fish, including salmon, Pacific Herring, Pacific Cod, Walleye Pollock and Lingcod.

On the outer coast, even Gray Whales come into the bays to feed on herring roe. Gray Whales normally feed on mud-dwelling crustaceans called amphipods, but herring roe is an attractive change. The whales dive to the bottom, turn over on their right sides and then suck mud, seaweed and roe into their toothless mouths. An upward thrust of their big tongues pistons the seawater and mud out through the baleen plate filters, leaving a rich meal of herring roe with a side of seaweed.

Most of the sea lions in British Columbian waters, particularly along the south coast, are nonbreeding male California Sea Lions. They leave their breeding colonies along the coasts of Mexico and California in late summer to spend the winter in northern waters. After fattening on herring in early spring and Eulachon in April, they return to southern shores for the summer. The larger Northern Sea Lion, or Steller's Sea Lion, is paler brown and lacks the abrupt forehead of the California. Local Northern Sea Lions breed in large rookeries on the Scott Island group off the northern tip of Vancouver Island, in the rocks off Cape St. James at the southern end of the Haida Gwaii and on Forrester Island, Alaska.

About twenty species of whales are found along the coast of British Columbia, from the 2-metre Harbor Porpoise to the Blue Whale, the largest of all animals. Most of the great whales suffered a serious decline in population during the whale fisheries of the 1800s and early 1900s. Humpback Whales were a foundation of the Nuu-chah-nulth culture on Vancouver Island and were common in the Strait of Georgia until they were hunted to extirpation by 1909. Humpback numbers seem to be slowly building again, but other species, such as Blue Whales, are still critically endangered.

The British Columbia coast has one of the highest populations of Killer Whales in the world. Thanks to the diligent work of the late Mike Bigg and other biologists, these large dolphins are perhaps the best-known whales in the world. By analyzing thousands of photographs, these biologists found they could identify individual whales by the shape of their dorsal fins, scars and patterns of back coloration. Identifying the whales allowed them not only to get a very accurate census of Killer Whales along the British Columbia coast but also to track groups of whales year after year.

Killer Whales travel in groups called pods. A pod is headed not by one of the huge bulls but by the oldest female, who is the mother or grandmother of all other pod members. Each whale is born into a pod and does not leave it.

New pods can form only if a female separates from her mother's pod, taking her progeny with her.

There are two types of Killer Whales along the coast: residents and transients. Residents travel in large pods of up to eighty whales and eat fish, especially salmon. Despite their name, resident Killer Whales are common along the coast only in summer. They follow the salmon as they enter inside waters in spring and then move to the open ocean in fall after the big salmon runs have disappeared upriver. Transients travel singly or in very small pods and eat marine mammals such as seals, sea lions, dolphins, porpoises and even other large whales. They can be seen any time of year along the coast, but they never stay in one place for long and their visits are impossible to predict. Residents and transients also differ in physical ways, such as the shape

JOURNEY OF THE GIANTS

Each year, more than twenty thousand Gray Whales steam north to Alaska to summer in the rich Bering Sea. Beginning in late February, small groups can be seen off the outer coast, never more than a kilometre from land. Mothers and calves are the last to pass, in late April and May. Gray Whales begin to return in September, led by the pregnant females, with the last stragglers coming through in December, headed for the calving and breeding lagoons of Baja California. The 10,000-kilometre trip takes six to eight weeks.

Whalers of the mid-nineteenth century found this species to be an easy target in the breeding lagoons and in fifty years hunted the 30-tonne giants to the edge of extinction. Few were killed in the first half of the twentieth century, and in 1947 the hunt was completely banned. Gray Whales have made a remarkable comeback in numbers since then, totally regaining their former population.

Herring Gull

California Gull

Ring-billed Gull

Mew Gull

Bonaparte's Gull

Glaucous-winged
Gull

WHEN IS A SEAGULL NOT A SEAGULL?

When it is nesting on the prairies! Half of the ten gull species found in British Columbia spend a lot of time inland. Herring, California and Ring-billed Gulls nest on lakes in the Interior and the Canadian prairies, feeding in freshly mown fields on mice and insects and, of course, scavenging garbage in landfills. Mew and Bonaparte's Gulls breed on small lakes throughout northwestern Canada. The Bonaparte's is unique among Canadian gulls in building its nest in trees. Only the Glaucous-winged Gull regularly nests along the British Columbia coast. Most adult gulls can be identified by bill and wing pattern and by eye colour.

of their dorsal fins, and some biologists have even ventured that they are separate species.

One group of seabirds, the tubenoses, is rarely seen by most British Columbians, even though hundreds of thousands, if not millions, stream up and down the coast each year. To see them, you usually have to be well off-shore on the outer coast, for tubenoses are quintessential marine birds. A large group that includes albatrosses, shearwaters, fulmars and storm-petrels, tubenoses get their name from the tubular nostrils on their bills. These nostrils are unusually sensitive to fishy odours—most birds have almost no sense of smell. Exulting in the ocean winds on long, narrow, stiffly held wings, shearwaters and albatrosses are the ultimate flying machines, capable of crossing the Pacific in a matter of two or three weeks.

Perhaps because most of the world's oceans are in the Southern Hemisphere, most tubenoses breed south of the equator, but several species spend their winters—our summers—in the north. Sooty Shearwaters breed on the islands of southern Chile and then move north up the coast, huge numbers passing British Columbia in May and again in September. Short-tailed and Buller's Shearwaters nest around New Zealand and follow seasonal winds in an incredible figure-eight migration around the Pacific each year, visiting British Columbia in the late fall. The two albatrosses found off the British Columbia coast, the Black-footed and Laysan, breed in more tropical waters, mostly in the western Hawaiian chain.

The only tubenoses that breed in British Columbia are Leach's and Fork-tailed Storm-Petrels, small swallowlike birds that flutter over the waves, picking zooplankton off the surface. They nest by the thousands on small islands along the outer coast, their burrows honeycombing the ground. On these islands they are almost always joined by that other completely marine group of birds, the auks.

The Great Auk is a well-known symbol of extinction, a magnificent flightless bird gone forever because of human greed and thoughtlessness. But its

Triangle Island

ISLAND OF BIRDS

Fifty kilometres west of the northern tip of Vancouver Island lies the most remote island in British Columbia and the jewel in the crown of the province's Ecological Reserve system. Triangle Island is a treeless, 200-metre-high pyramid about 1 kilometre across set in the roughest waters of the Pacific coast. It boasts a large Northern Sea Lion rookery, mice three times the size of those on the mainland and over a million seabirds.

Every inch of the island is tunnelled with nesting burrows, most of them belonging to Cassin's Auklets. Over 500,000 pairs, perhaps 70 per cent of the world's population of this small grey bird, nest on Triangle. The grass-covered rock at the southwestern tip of the island is home to 30,000 pairs of Tufted Puffins and a half-dozen Horned Puffins, while 6000 pairs of Common Murres and a few Thick-billed Murres cling to the cliffs. Thousands of Rhinoceros Auklets, strange puffins with a hornlike projection at the base of their bills, burrow into the steep slopes above the southern bay. Predators are attracted by this bounty; several pairs of Peregrine Falcons nest on the island's cliffs. A pair of Bald Eagles, normally tree nesters, waive this requirement and nest on the ground to be able to cash in on the auklets of Triangle Island.

Tufted Puffins breed on grassy islets along the outer coast, digging nesting burrows up to 5 metres long in the turf. They spend the winter in the open ocean, hundreds of kilometres from shore.

relatives live on, and nowhere in such abundance and diversity as the North Pacific Ocean. There are no less than twenty species of auks in the North Pacific, nine of which breed in British Columbia. Largely black and white, most look and act like the northern equivalent of penguins. In fact, the word *penguin* is the Gaelic name for the Great Auk and was only later transferred to the tuxedoed birds of the Southern Hemisphere. Despite the outward similarity, auks are not related to penguins but to gulls, terns, sandpipers and plovers.

Auks are highly adapted for swimming and diving but are not great at flying. Their small wings, like those of penguins, are better adapted for flying underwater, propelling the birds to depths of over 100 metres.

Auks are an excellent example of how a group of closely related species can live in the same area by using different feeding and nesting strategies. The larger species feed on fish such as sand lance, herring, sauries and juvenile rockfish, whereas the tiny Cassin's Auklets go for large plankton such as euphausiid shrimp. Most auks nest in large colonies, usually on small, remote islands, safe from predators. Puffins, auklets and Ancient Murrelets nest in long burrows dug into the turf, whereas murres choose ledges on sheer rock cliffs. Pigeon Guillemots nest singly in rock crevices or under large pieces of driftwood on rocky beaches. Marbled Murrelets are unique among seabirds in placing their single egg on a mossy branch high in an old-growth conifer.

Cassin's Auklet

ON THE BOTTOM

Life on the bottom of the sea is very different from life in the plankton-based food chain at the surface. Many plants and animals of the seafloor begin life as spores or larvae in the plankton; this is the dispersing phase of their lives. Within a set time, however, they must settle to the bottom, and where they settle is critical to their survival. If a larva of the rock-dwelling Plumose Anemone finds itself drifting down onto the kilometres of mud at the bottom of the Strait of Georgia it will almost certainly die, but one lucky enough to hit a slender telephone cable there will have a long, productive life. Life on the bottom, or in the benthos, can be very long; Geoduck clams can live to be 140 years old, rockfish can live up to a century, and barring accident and environmental change, sea anemones seem to go on forever.

Deep Water

As in the open ocean, the dimness of light below 40 metres changes the life on the seafloor completely. Plants are necessarily absent from the black abyss of deep coastal basins. Life is slow, usually a matter of constantly processing nutrient-rich mud or filtering cold water for small, detritus-feeding animals. Seasons are barely noticeable; often the most powerful signal of annual change is the amount of organic detritus drifting to the bottom.

LIVING FOSSILS

Ratfish

The seafloor is a dark, quiet place where conditions have changed very little since life began. Many of its denizens have long histories on this planet, including two interesting fish species that inhabit the coastal waters of British Columbia, the Pacific Hagfish and the Ratfish.

Hagfish are eellike, eyeless, jawless, scaleless scavengers with only partially developed skulls. Their cartilaginous skeletons have not been preserved as fossils so their origin is shrouded in mystery, but they are doubtless a very primitive group. These 60-centimetre fish have the delightful habit of burrowing into the dead bodies of other fish by way of the mouth or anus, eating the viscera and muscles, and leaving only the skin and bones behind. Four Pacific Hagfish were once found in one Spiny Dogfish! Their main mode of defence is to exude copious amounts of toxic slime when disturbed, hence their other common name, slime-eels. This slime and their primitive metabolism make hagfish popular candidates for medical research.

Dating back some 345 million years, Ratfish look like no other fish in our waters. They are instantly identified by their glowing emerald-green eyes, rabbit-like buck teeth, scaleless skin and large, winglike pectoral fins. Outfitted with a primitive cartilaginous skeleton, Ratfish share an ancient ancestry with skates, rays and sharks. They have a good sense of smell to locate clams, crabs and shrimps from the sandy bottoms of the deep sea. Pairs of adult Ratfish perform elaborate courtship rituals in which the males dramatically change colour. The females then deposit dark leathery egg cases on the bottom mud.

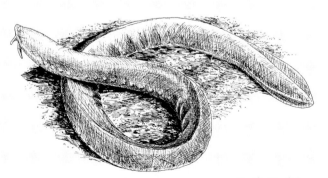

Pacific Hagfish

THERE'S A HOLE IN THE BOTTOM OF THE SEA: HYDROTHERMAL VENTS

More than 1000 metres below the surface of the Pacific Ocean, along the Explorer Ridge, are some of the most bizarre oases of life on earth. The Explorer Ridge is part of the East Pacific Rise, one of the long cracks in the earth's surface where magma rises to create new sea-floor and push continents apart. The seafloor along the ridge is peppered by numerous hot springs called hydrother-mal vents, some spewing water as hot as 300°C. When the scalding water meets the frigid waters of the deep sea, metallic sulfide compounds precipitate to form a dense black smoke that collects to build tall chimneys around the vents.

The most abundant chemical coming out of the hot springs is hydrogen sulfide, extremely poisonous to most life on earth but capable of releasing a great deal of energy when it meets oxygen. Specialized bacteria, however, can use the energy in hydrogen sulfide to produce sugars from carbon dioxide and oxygen, much as plants use the energy in sunlight.

So whereas the seafloor around them is relatively devoid of life, these vents are covered with bacterial mats, limpets and worms, all feasting on a food chain totally disconnected from our sun. Most of the animals found around hydrothermal vents are not found anywhere else on earth. Limpets graze on the bacteria mats, and several remarkable species of worms gather bacteria on their sticky tentacles. Perhaps most amazing are the giant, gutless tubeworms; they get their daily bread by transferring hydrogen sulfide and oxygen to bacteria sequestered in special body tissues. These animals are able to withstand almost unimaginable temperatures. The bacteria grow at tem-peratures above 110°C, and a worm was seen unconcernedly crawling for several seconds on a temperature probe reading 105°C, a temperature that would congeal most animal proteins like a boiled egg.

Most of the animal species found directly associated with deep-sea hydro-thermal vents show primitive characteristics and have probably evolved in isolation for millions of years. For although boiling water choked with hydrogen sulfide may be a dangerous habitat in the short term, hydrothermal vents provide a reliable source of energy coupled with protection from the catastrophic climate changes that have caused major periodic extinctions in the sunlit world above.

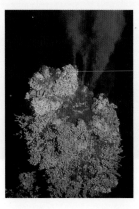

Along the crack where the Pacific and Juan de Fuca Plates split apart, superheated 330°C water laden with metallic sulfides spews out of a chimney.

Although most of the British Columbia coast is rocky, the deep seafloor is generally covered in mud, sand or gravel. There, dense aggregations of slimy, sluglike burrowing cucumbers lie buried up to their mouths in the mud, waving their feathery tentacles to capture small animals and bits of detritus. Meadows of Orange Sea Pens, each a colony of thousands of polyps related to sea anemones, brighten the seafloor in protected waters. These meadows are so extensive that the Orange Sea Pen is likely the most abundant animal by weight in the protected marine waters of British Columbia. Heart Urchins plow across the bottom like miniature Porcupines, while small polychaete worms swim through the mud and sand as fish swim through water. The Sea Plum, a sea cucumber that looks more like a large sweet potato, burrows in the silt, filling itself with mud and sand to extract any digestible material.

Deep rocky bottoms—sides actually—are found along the walls of the many fiords carved into the British Columbia coast. These submarine cliffs can descend 600 metres or more and provide a fascinating opportunity to study the distribution of animals and plants in deep waters. Fiord walls are

Plumose Anemone

Below: China Rockfish, like other species of rockfish, can live up to a century, staying in the same small patch of rich sea bottom throughout their lives.

Serpulid tubeworm

Squat Lobster

covered with incredible animal gardens, with brown cup corals dominating the deepest zone, spectacular soft corals and glass sponges at moderate depths, and serpulid tubeworms, ascidean sea squirts, sea anemones and encrusting sponges in shallower waters. Most of the animals attached to these cliffs are filter or suspension feeders, sieving the cold waters for plankton or detritus. Predators such as sponge-eating sea stars are also common, and Squat Lobsters search for detritus in the glass sponge skeletons.

Shallow Rocky Bottoms

Farther up, in the blue-green glow of sunlight, the combination of readily available nutrients from the bottom and sunlight from above is a recipe for tremendous biological growth. Along rocky shores the macroalgae, or seaweed, form the base of this pyramid of growth.

Red algae often grow deepest. Their photosynthetic pigments absorb the blue light that penetrates the water farthest (and reflect mostly reddish light—hence their colour), and their slow respiration is better adapted to the low light levels. The middle depths are dominated by the kelps, large brown algae, many swaying in the current on long stipes attached to the rocks with strong, tangled rootlike structures called holdfasts.

The shallow subtidal environments along the rocky coast of British Columbia are among the most spectacular marine habitats on the planet. Although tropical coral reefs are hard to top for their colourful diversity, the warm oceans are on the whole rather devoid of life. Cold, upwelling currents, in contrast, are usually saturated with nutrients, and the currents surging through rocky channels on the north Pacific coast are among the richest anywhere. Over six hundred species of seaweed flourish along the British Columbia coast, including thirty-four species found nowhere else. The seaweeds shelter over seventy species of sea stars, the most of any coast in the world. Much of the diversity of coral reefs is in tiny, inconspicuous species, but benthic animals and plants of the North Pacific tend to be large and obvious, including the largest octopus in the world.

Perhaps the most important habitats on the rocky seafloors along the coast are the kelp forests. Like terrestrial forests, these underwater gardens have their dominant plants. The two largest kelps, Giant Kelp and Bull Kelp, create forests complete with undergrowth and canopy. Kelp forests provide food, shelter and a structural diversity attractive to hundreds of animals found nowhere else in the sea.

Beds of Bull Kelp are an integral part of coastal scenery, the thin stipes, round floats and long brown fronds bobbing on the surface of many bays. In winter, windrows of Bull Kelp are cast up on beaches and become food for sandhoppers, for Bull Kelp is an annual species. In late summer each plant produces over a trillion zoospores before dying in the winter. The flagellate zoospores disperse along the coast and then settle to grow into very small plants, invisible to the naked eye. These plants, the gametophytes, are male or female. In spring male gametophytes produce sperm cells, which swim to female gametophytes and fertilize the stay-at-home eggs. This union produces a new kelp plant, the spermatophyte, which grows through the spring and summer to become the world's largest marine plant. Growing up to 60 centimetres each day, a Bull Kelp can reach 20 metres or more—the height of a good-sized tree—in one summer. It is not surprising to learn that kelp forests are among the most productive habitats on earth.

Unlike Bull Kelp, Giant Kelp cannot tolerate the relatively low salinity of the Strait of Georgia and other inside waters and so is restricted to the outer coast. There its forests flash with schools of kelp perch, kelp crabs forage in its fronds, and a host of other species thrive in its dappled shadows. Kelp forests

Bull Kelp

GIANT OCTOPUS

British Columbia has the distinction of being home to the Giant Pacific Octopus, the largest species of octopus in the world. The biggest specimen on record had an arm spread of 9.6 metres and weighed 272 kilograms. These creatures are highly specialized, with a complex brain and a fishlike eye capable of forming images and discerning objects as small as 0.5 cm from a distance of 1 metre. This keen eyesight makes locating prey an easy task. Although they prefer a secretive lifestyle in dark, quiet rocky caves, octopus are very active predators. Their menu is vast—snails, abalones, clams, scallops, shrimps and a variety of fish. Octopus capture prey with eight sucker-filled arms, subdue it with a salivary toxin, break the shells or skin with a parrotlike beak and tear off chunks of tissue using a rodlike tongue called a radula.

Because of their hardiness and capacity to learn, octopus are frequently used as research animals, but little is known about the natural history of this species. They are thought to live up to five years.

Males and females can be told apart by the lack of suction discs on the tip of the third right arm of the male. This part of the arm is used to transfer a package of sperm from the mantle cavity of the male into the mantle cavity of the female. Once the eggs are fertilized, the female will lay them in grapelike clusters in rocky recesses and stay with them for up to seven months until they hatch.

Giant Pacific Octopus

lead a fragile life, however, since their existence depends largely on the interactions between two animals, the Sea Otter and the sea urchin.

Sea Otters are large, seagoing weasels, the only truly marine members of their family. River Otters are common along the British Columbia coast as well, foraging in quiet bays and estuaries, but they make their homes on land. Home to a Sea Otter is a good thick kelp forest, its bed a wrapping of kelp fronds. Sea Otters live, feed, sleep and breed in the cold waters of the North Pacific, but unlike other marine mammals, they lack a thick layer of blubber for insulation. They rely instead on their magnificent pelts of eight hundred million hairs for warmth and spend most of their waking hours grooming their precious fur.

It was the precious fur of the Sea Otter that decimated the kelp forests of the North Pacific. Early Russian, British and American traders found that the lush pelts brought astronomical prices in China. Within a century, a healthy population of a half-million otters was reduced to one or two thousand animals hidden in small bays in California and a few remote islands in Alaska and eastern Siberia.

SOMEDAY, TAKE YOUR BINOCULARS TO A ROCKY
COASTAL SHORE AND WATCH THE WILD SEA OTTERS . . .
AS YOU LOOK THROUGH YOUR FIELD GLASSES,
YOU MIGHT SPOT AN OVERSIZED BROWN POWDER PUFF,
WITH A TINY BLACK NOSE AND TWO VERY BLUE EYES,
CRADLED ON ITS MOTHER'S CHEST IN THE BRIGHT MORNING
SUN. IN THIS TINY ANIMAL, YOU CAN CELEBRATE A VICTORY
OVER HUMAN GREED AND INCREDIBLE ODDS.

Stefani Paine, *The Nature of Sea Otters*

This slaughter was tragic in itself, but how did it destroy the kelp? The answer lies in the food of the otters. Although they eat a variety of animals from the seafloor, Sea Otters are the only serious predator of sea urchins. After the otters were gone, the urchins thrived. Sea urchins are vegetarians, grazing algae, including kelp, on the seafloor. Not only do they eat kelp, but they are messy eaters, chewing at the stipe above the holdfast and destroying the anchor of the huge plant. And like a ship adrift, one kelp plant set free can drag others with it; whole beds can be ripped loose if some of their number lose their grip on the rocks below.

After the kelp disappeared, the rich community of plants and animals it sheltered vanished as well. The forests were replaced by "urchin barrens," large areas of bare rock patrolled by hundreds of urchins, constantly grazing any algae that tried to grow there. This was the situation in 1968, when the provincial government started a program to reintroduce Sea Otters to

the British Columbia coast. Otters were taken from Amchitka Island, one of the Aleutian chain, and released in a remote part of northwestern Vancouver Island. With urchins and other prey in abundance, the Sea Otters thrived and populated other suitable sites along the west coast of Vancouver Island. Giant Kelp beds and the diverse fauna they harbour are expanding as well.

A Sea Otter rests in its favourite blanket of Giant Kelp fronds.

Shallow Sandy Bottoms

Sandy bottoms do not provide a good substrate for the rootless algae; a golden-brown film of diatoms is often the only plant life there. These areas are often studded with Sand Dollars, not lying flat, as their white skeletons, or tests, are found on the beach, but standing upright, half-buried in the sand. These velvety, purple-black cousins of sea urchins pick through grains of sand with their tube feet, selecting certain ones, perhaps those with a good icing of diatoms, for eating. They choose others for their weight; iron oxide grains are eaten and kept in the gut to provide a "weight belt" on one side of the Sand Dollar to help keep it on the bottom of the coastal sea.

Starry Flounders also lie half-hidden in the sand. These flatfish eat a variety of bottom-dwelling animals, including crabs, shrimp, worms and the tips of clam siphons, nipped off where they poke above the sand. Like other flatfish, such as halibut, flounders begin life as planktonic larvae, looking like normal tiny fish. During metamorphosis, the small fish move to the seafloor and begin swimming on one side. The lower eye migrates to the upper surface, which becomes spangled to blend in with the sun-dappled sand.

Meadows in the Sea: Eel-Grass

The eel-grasses are flowering plants that grow below the tides, rooted in mud and gravel. These emigrés from the terrestrial world form waving green meadows in shallow coastal bays, underwater prairies with a unique fauna. Like kelp forests, eel-grass beds are tremendously productive and are critical to the survival of several conspicuous coastal animals.

Freshwater plants bloom at the surface, but eel-grass keeps its inconspicuous flowers beneath the waves. Murky clouds of long, filamentous pollen grains drift with the currents, much as grass, pine or alder pollen is carried by the wind. The seeds are kept on the plants and are only dispersed when the plants are dismembered by winter storms or foraging geese.

Although eel-grass beds may appear uninteresting at first glance, closer inspection reveals a great diversity of life. Because the habitat is so homogeneous, many species mimic the eel-grass and are not easily seen. Penpoint Gunnels, green as grass, dart through the meadows. Slender green skeleton shrimp are almost invisible on the narrow leaf blades, waiting motionless like praying mantises, snatching quickly at any prey floating by. Skeleton shrimp are the main prey of another strange denizen of eel-grass leaves, the Stalked Jellyfish.

Penpoint Gunnel

Skeleton shrimp

Brant

The bird most tightly tied to eel-grass is the Brant, a small, dark goose that nests on coastal Arctic tundra. Like all geese, the Brant is a grazing bird, and its pastures of choice are eel-grass beds. Although a few hundred spend the winter in Boundary Bay on the Fraser Delta and at Sandspit on the Haida Gwaii, most of the Pacific coast population flies directly from Alaska to the coastal lagoons of Baja California. They work their way north in April, when thousands rest and feed on the eel-grass beds of the Fraser Delta and eastern Vancouver Island.

THE INTERTIDAL ZONE

A shoreline is by definition a boundary between water and land, a wall between two worlds. Along seacoasts, tides are like a swinging door in this wall, bringing the sea onto the land and then extending the land into the sea. The zone between the tides offers a fascinating introduction to sea life for the shore-bound observer.

Although spectacular at times, it is a selective window. Only those marine animals and plants able to live out of water for hours or days at a time can survive between the tides, and many of them survive only through closing up shop completely when their watery medium drains away.

Exploring the intertidal zone from top to bottom is a little like studying mountain life from the barren, icy peaks down to the fertile valleys below. Living between the tides is stressful, and as on the mountains, the stress increases with height. Only a few species can withstand the hot, dry days in the high intertidal zone. The upper limits are dominated by huge numbers of very few tolerant species, whereas the lush diversity of the low intertidal zone can take your breath away. For this reason marine biologists often circle the dates of low, low tides on their calendars, even those that occur near midnight in the dead of winter.

Intertidal Zonation

One of the first things the observant naturalist notices about the seashore is that many dominant species of algae, barnacles and mollusks are arranged in

BARNACLE SEX

Sex in the animal world doesn't get much stranger than between barnacles—hermaphroditic crustaceans locked in shells, standing upside down with their heads glued to rocks. How do they do it? With a penis twenty times longer than their body! When a barnacle larva is ready to live the settled life of an adult, it looks not only for a rock surface with good currents for feeding but also for other barnacles. It must have a neighbour within one penis length to be able to breed. The sex of the neighbour doesn't matter, since all barnacles are both male and female.

After the ten thousand or so eggs are fertilized, they are held within the body until the spring phytoplankton bloom and are then released into the water as a cloud of larvae.

horizontal bands. This zonation is not directly caused by the tides; freshwater shorelines show such zonation as well. Tides, however, emphasize and broaden the zones.

On rocky shores, the highest splash zone is marked by the black, encrusting Sea Tar Lichen, one of the few lichens tolerant of high levels of salt. The lichen crust and any algal film is constantly grazed by herds of tiny periwinkle snails. In winter, red laver, a red alga known to sushi aficionados as *nori*, grows in this high splash zone but is killed by the hot spring sun. It survives the summer in its conchocelis phase—tiny filaments living in shells or barnacles in the lower intertidal zone.

Dog Whelk feeding on barnacles

The top of the true intertidal zone lies at the height of the highest spring tides and is marked by the upper limit of barnacles. The highest-growing species, the Small Acorn Barnacle, is extremely tolerant of desiccation. Spring tides occur only once every thirteen days and may immerse the highest barnacles for only four hours each month. Growth is slow when you can only feed and breed twice a month. Common Acorn Barnacles occur lower in this zone. This species cannot tolerate weeks or even days out of water, so it cannot survive higher than the level of high neap tides, which occur at least once a day. Below this level, however, its large size and faster growth crush any Small Acorn Barnacles that try to colonize the lower rocks.

The lower limit of the Common Acorn Barnacle coincides with the upper limit of mussels and Dog Whelks. The mussels crowd out the barnacles and the whelks eat them. These patterns are mirrored by the distribution of many other intertidal organisms: upper limits of intertidal species are set by tolerance to physical factors such as desiccation and heat; lower limits are set by biological factors such as competition and predation.

The largest permanent residents of the lower intertidal zone, and perhaps its most feared predators, are the sea stars. Their hydrostatic skeleton, a network of water-filled tubes, is ideal for life on wave-washed rocks, since it can stiffen to absorb the shock of the surf and then relax as the sea star moves along on hydraulically operated tube feet.

The common sea star of the intertidal zone is the Ochre Star. Like the Sea Otter, which has a tremendous impact on kelp forests through controlling sea urchin predation, the Ochre Star is a keystone species. Ochre Stars prefer to eat mussels and in doing so prevent the mussels from carpeting the rocks in the lower intertidal zone. An Ochre Star can eat eighty big California Mussels per year and live for twenty years, so the potential effect on mussel populations is great. A researcher once removed all Ochre Stars from an area with twenty-five species of plants and animals attached to the rocks and watched the area slowly but surely turn into a monoculture of one species—mussels. Mussels flourish in the middle intertidal zone, which is too high for most sea stars to reach before the tide goes out again.

Other animals besides sea stars depend on a diet of fresh mussels. Surf Scoters and Barrow's Goldeneyes forsake the frozen taiga and plateaus to winter along the coast, preferring protected inlets with substantial mussel beds. When the tide is in, these ducks dive to the rocky bottom and pull the mussels off with their powerful beaks. They swallow the shellfish whole, using their muscular gizzards to grind up their prey.

Several species of wintering shorebirds hunt through mussel beds at low tide. Black Turnstones, Surfbirds and Rock Sandpipers rummage through the shells and seaweed for small invertebrates.

Black Oystercatchers are common and conspicuous residents of the rocky coast, foraging at low tide for limpets and other shellfish.

Turnstones become very attached to good feeding grounds; the same flock will winter on the same headland year after year. The turnstones and sandpipers breed in Arctic Alaska and winter along the Pacific coast of North America, whereas the Surfbirds breed on barren mountain ridges in Yukon and Alaska and winter from southern Alaska to Tierra del Fuego. Biologists don't know how they choose who gets to migrate 500 kilometres and who has to wing it for 10,000 kilometres.

Tidepools

Small tidepools are refuges for animals that cannot tolerate being left high and dry by the tide. It is not all idyllic in these miniature seas, however. Tidepool denizens must put up with soaring water temperatures on hot summer days, followed by an instant chilling when the first wave of the incoming tides splashes in. As anyone who has brought fish home to an aquarium knows, most aquatic creatures are accustomed to very stable temperatures. It takes a special fish to tolerate the drastic temperature fluctuations in a tidepool.

Many of the rocky tidepools along the coast are patterned in green and pink—the coralline algae encrusting the rock like pink icing on a cake, the pink and green tentacles of the Aggregate Anemones waving in the clear water. With their green stems and petal-like tentacles, intertidal sea anemones look for all the world like fat flowers blooming under the sea. Their green colour comes from tiny single-celled algae that the anemone has ingested and

Above: A colourful tidepool on the west coast of Vancouver Island, containing (clockwise from upper left) two colour forms of the Ochre Star, Giant Green Sea Anemones, a Blood Star, a Purple Sea Urchin and coralline red algae.

Opposite page: The Frosted Nudibranch is one of the many beautiful nudibranchs found in British Columbia coastal waters.

stashed in the walls of its gut, which extends up into the tentacles. These cells remain alive, photosynthesizing in the sun, giving the anemone an extra dose of sugars for its daily energy requirements.

When sea anemones find a good spot to live, they take advantage of it by filling it with family. Not through sexual reproduction—which, in sea anemones and most other marine invertebrates, sends larvae drifting in the plankton and settling who knows where—but through binary fission. The fattened anemone simply splits in two, creating a set of identical twins.

Given time, identical Aggregate Anemones can fill a tidepool tentacle to tentacle, a perfect clone. Sea anemones fight off any intruding anemone (they can slowly slither around on their muscular foot) with powerful stinging tentacles, but they do not attack members of their own clone. Clonal boundaries therefore show up as narrow anemone-free zones between two tightly packed clusters.

This self-recognition of anemones has been used by the subtidal Candystripe Shrimp to con the Crimson Anemone into giving it protection.

This Tidepool Sculpin blends in perfectly with the sandy bottom of a tidepool near Bamfield.

By allowing itself to be stung slightly numerous times, the shrimp is gradually coated in anemone mucus. It can then swim into the centre of the tentacles without triggering a response from the large predator and is presumably safe from fish predation there.

Other animals obtain the protection of anemone tentacles by more insidious means—they eat them. Some nudibranchs, or sea slugs, can eat sea anemones without discharging the stinging cells. The stinging cells are then transferred to tentacle-like extensions of the nudibranch's gut that grow out of its back. Thus armed, these nudibranchs warn would-be predators of their arsenal with bright colours, making them some of the most spectacular marine invertebrates.

Mud Flats

Mud flats are probably the least appreciated intertidal habitat. The aversion of adult humans to sticky muck and the lingering odour of hydrogen sulfide are enough to dissuade all but the most avid naturalist from exploring them.

Mud flats don't look all that interesting at low tide either; often the only signs of life are patches of brown slime, limp green algae and a myriad of holes and tiny tracks.

Water and food are easy to come by for mud-dwelling animals. The mud around burrows retains moisture even when exposed at low tide, and the surface ooze is a rich soup of microscopic plants and animals, organic debris and nutrients. The main problem with living in the mud is an almost total lack of oxygen below the top few centimetres of muck. Anaerobic microbes in this lower black mud produce hydrogen sulfide as a metabolic byproduct, giving mud flats their characteristic rotten-egg smell. The hydrogen sulfide reacts with iron oxides in the silt to produce iron sulfide, turning the mud black.

At high tide the gooey bottom comes to life. Diatoms, the brown slime on the surface, are one of the pillars of the food chain on the mud, as they are in the open ocean. Unlike their drifting planktonic relatives, mud-dwelling diatoms can move by using the surface tension between the water and the mud. During the day, the diatoms are at the surface taking in the sunlight, but at night the glassy cells slide a centimetre or so beneath the surface of the mud to avoid the grazing mouths of snails and other intertidal herbivores.

The incoming tide carries a wealth of small animals and organic debris, and many strange creatures emerge from the mud to spread their nets. Green Burrowing Anemones, attached to buried shells or pebbles, bloom like green, pink and white flowers, and Parchment Tubeworms secrete a mucus net to sample the fare. Ghost Shrimp and Mud Shrimp stay down in their burrows, pumping in oxygen-rich water with their abdominal flaps and catching a detritus dinner on their hairy legs. The mud pumped out of Ghost Shrimp burrows forms little volcanoes at the entrances.

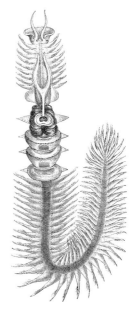

Parchment Tubeworm

Holes with narrow coils of mud around them are the homes of lugworms. These worms live in J-shaped burrows with their back ends at the surface. They gather mud with a sticky proboscis, swallow it and deposit the inedible portions at their doorsteps. In some areas there are up to fifty lugworm burrows per square metre of mud; the total number of burrowing worms of all types runs into the thousands per cubic metre of mud.

With all this life buried in the mud, often the most obvious indication of its presence is the abundance of bird life that gathers to consume it. In spring and late summer, thousands of sandpipers and plovers carpet the intertidal mud flats, gorging on the annual harvest of worms and shrimp to fuel their long migrations. Over twenty species of shorebirds feed on mud flats, each looking for different prey, searching different microhabitats with bills of different sizes. The big Whimbrels use their long, curved bills to probe shrimp burrows, while Black-bellied Plovers pick morsels off the surface with their short beaks. Godwits and dowitchers stab the mud with long, straight, worm-hunting bills, and the tiny sandpipers search for smaller prey near the surface.

WESTERN SANDPIPERS

Motorists racing to catch the Tsawwassen ferry in the evening in early August are likely to drive by one of the most spectacular wildlife spectacles in the province. As the evening tide comes in, covering the vast mud flats of the Fraser Delta and Boundary Bay, flocks of tiny sandpipers are forced into smaller and smaller areas. Small flocks coalesce into larger groups, and as the last flats are covered, wheeling flocks of up to 30,000 birds flash in the last rays of the sun.

Almost all these birds are Western Sandpipers, a species that breeds on the Arctic coast of Alaska and winters on the shores of South America. Weighing only 23 grams and measuring only 15 centimetres long, these birds can fly up to 1500 kilometres between stops. Such flights burn a lot of fat, and the sandpipers must spend about four days refuelling before continuing on. Although they feed on whatever small invertebrates their probing bills find in the mud, recent research has shown that up to one-half of their daily food intake is in the form of biofilm, a mucous-like layer on top of the mud, rich with microbes and nutrient. At the height of spring migration, the birds can consume 20 tonnes of this snot-like material on the Fraser Delta every day.

Almost the entire world population of Western Sandpipers visits the Fraser Delta on their way north in spring and again on their way south in late summer. About a million birds pass through in April, adorned in their fresh, rust-spangled breeding plumage. The first returnees are seen in late June, the rusty feathers fading, to be replaced by grey winter feathers. These early birds are adults, which abandon their young on the breeding grounds as soon as they can fly short distances and fend for themselves. By late July, most of the adults have passed through and the first of the juveniles are arriving.

It is the juveniles that form the huge flocks of late summer. These birds, grey and white except for a fresh, rusty shoulder, have flown all the way from Alaska by themselves. Like most young migrant birds, they are born with an innate sense of which direction to go and how long to keep flying. This simple system gets most of them to South America, where they join the adults.

After leaving the Fraser Delta, some birds go south along the coast, stopping at rich feeding sites such as Gray's Harbor, Washington, and the San Francisco Bay area. Others fly inland over the Cascades and Rocky Mountains to Cheyenne Bottoms, Kansas, a huge wetland in the centre of the continent. By October, most of the world's Western Sandpipers are

ESTUARIES

Rivers not only replenish the water of the oceans, they endow it with nutrients washed from the forests and grasslands of the continental interior. These nutrients are not immediately distributed throughout the ocean but are concentrated and held for long periods at the river's mouth, creating one of the richest environments on earth, the estuary. The nutrients are trapped by a combination of forces, the strongest of which is entrainment. Tidal currents also reverse the seaward flow of rivers, allowing sediments to add to the growth of the delta.

ensconced for the winter on the mud flats along the coast of South America.

The few rich feeding sites along the migration routes of these and other shorebirds are critical to the survival of these species. The Fraser Delta is under constant threat of industrial development and pollution, Cheyenne Bottoms is drying up because of huge irrigation projects, and San Francisco Bay is in the middle of one of the largest urban centres in western North America. These areas and their tremendous biological productivity must be preserved to ensure that the huge flocks of sandpipers will still be visiting them well into the future.

Most of the world's Western Sandpipers, more than a million individuals, rely on the rich mud flats of the Fraser Delta as a refuelling stop on their annual migrations between South America and Arctic Alaska.

Where the fresh water meets the salty sea, a few species of marsh plants edge their way out into the brackish waters. These salt marshes are tremendously productive and are an important habitat for many animals. The most widespread plant of British Columbia salt marshes is Lyngby's Sedge, which forms dense green meadows along the shores of many estuaries. The succulent, cylindrical stems of American Glasswort, now served in trendy restaurants under the more palatable name of sea asparagus, are typical of more saline mud flats.

Although young salmon and a myriad of invertebrates live hidden under the waters of estuaries, some wildlife are conspicuous denizens of the mud flats

and salt marshes of estuaries. Ducks, geese and swans gather each fall to reap the harvest of the deltas, stripping seeds from salt marsh plants, grazing on seaweed and pulling fat roots up from the shallow muddy bottoms. They have come from the Arctic shores of Siberia and Alaska as well as the boreal lakes and prairie ponds of western Canada, drawn by a promise of mild winter weather and a wealth of food.

American Wigeon are perhaps the most abundant waterfowl wintering in British Columbia. Unlike most ducks, they are grazing birds, clipping marsh grasses, eel-grass and seaweed with a short, stubby bill like that of a goose. They are joined by thousands of Northern Pintail, Mallards and Green-winged Teal and a smattering of other ducks in the coastal marshes.

Each summer, about 100,000 Snow Geese return to Wrangel Island off the Arctic coast of eastern Siberia to nest. When the young are ready to fly in late August, they move to the Siberian coast for a final fattening up and then depart for the south. After one or two stopovers in coastal Alaska, they arrive on the Fraser Delta in late September and early October.

Half of the flock moves on to winter in California, but about 50,000 remain to feed on the roots of salt marsh sedges and grasses at the mouth of the Fraser. By mid-December, this food supply becomes depleted, so the birds make a short flight to the mouth of the Skagit River. They return to the Fraser in mid-February for a few more weeks of feeding. Then, on the warm breezes of spring, they rise into the blue April sky, wave after wave of white birds fading into the northwestern horizon.

> WILDEST OF ALL ARE THE SALTINGS AND MUD FLATS
> OF THE COAST. HERE THE SKY IS A MASTER OF THE SCENE . . .
> THE CREEKS WIND SLUGGISHLY FROM THE MARSHES TOWARDS
> THE OPEN SEA, AND AT FLOOD TIDE SEA ITSELF COMES
> WANDERING BACK . . . IN THIS WORLD LIVE THE WILDFOWL.
> Peter Scott, *Wild Chorus*

Opposite page: The Fraser River estuary attracts huge numbers of migrating and wintering birds, including fifty thousand Snow Geese from Wrangel Island, Siberia.

On a cold, foggy January day, I was walking the dike along Nicomen Slough, one of the side branches of the Fraser River near Mission. Suddenly I heard a sonorous honking in the air, and then out of the white fog flew twenty magnificent white swans gliding in for a perfect landing on the dark grey water. These were Trumpeter Swans, the largest waterfowl in the world. Hunted to near extinction, this huge bird has rebounded under strict protection to become a common sight along the British Columbia coast in winter. Indeed, most of the world's ten thousand Trumpeters winter in British Columbia estuaries; the largest concentration is a group of more than a thousand in the Comox Valley. The Comox flock, and others in similar habitats along the southern coast, have adapted to modern agriculture and have added pasture grass and culled potatoes and carrots to their normal diet of sedge roots.

British Columbia's estuaries may be hard hit by rising sea levels over the next few decades. Sea level at the Fraser River Delta is predicted to rise from 50 to more than 100 centimetres by the end of the century. This change will raise the salinity of estuarine waters and could drastically affect the local salt marsh and mud-flat ecosystems.

CHAPTER FIVE

FORESTS OF RAIN

CHAPTER FIVE

FORESTS OF RAIN

WE WERE BORN in the southern Interior of British Columbia and raised on arid air and open grasslands. Each summer we ventured west on the Hope-Princeton Highway to Vancouver for a short holiday on the coast. The road climbed over Allison Pass and then wound down through the cool subalpine forests of the upper Skagit. It always hit us somewhere below Skaist Creek—a wall of humid air filled with the exotic aroma of redcedar and humus.

We had entered a different forest, an entirely different world from the bunchgrass and Ponderosa Pines of Penticton. This was a forest of rain, where curtains of moss hung from branches, ferns sprouted from huge trunks and deer trails struggled through a tangled undergrowth of Devil's Club and Salmonberry. This ancient forest was home to some of the largest trees in the world.

The windward slopes of the Coast Mountains and Cascade Range are cloaked in temperate rain forests, and the temperate rain forests of British Columbia are as extensive and awe-inspiring as any of their kind anywhere.

Elsewhere in the world, temperate rain forests are dominated by deciduous trees, since those areas receive much of their rain in the summer, when deciduous trees are fully leaved. The forests of the Pacific Northwest receive most of their rain from November to March and so are dominated by huge conifers that can photosynthesize and grow through the mild winters. Coastal conifers can achieve up to half of their annual growth from October to April, when the alders and maples are dormant, leafless skeletons. This ability to grow throughout the year makes the temperate rain forests of British Columbia one of the most biologically productive environments on earth. Western Hemlock forests produce about 5 tonnes of plant material per hectare each year, and some very rich sites produce more than 30 tonnes per year.

The temperate rain forests of British Columbia are divided by ecologists into four zones. The first zone, the lowland forests along the Coast Range and western Vancouver Island, are the classic temperate rain forests and collectively are known as the Coastal Western Hemlock Zone. Whereas the drier forests of the Interior are shaped by summer drought and fire, these coastal forests are the product of winter monsoons. From November to March, a seemingly endless series of Pacific storms sweeps in from the west. The sodden clouds are wrung dry as they pass over the Coast Range, and some places receive as much as 5 metres of rain each year.

The second zone, which includes southeastern Vancouver Island and the Gulf Islands, is shielded from this onslaught of precipitation by the Olympic Mountains of Washington and the mountains of Vancouver Island itself; this zone is known as the Coastal Douglas-fir Zone. Like the open coast, this area receives the bulk of its rain in winter but has drier summers and less than a metre of rain annually. These conditions create a forest dominated by Douglas-fir.

At higher elevations along the coast, a third zone occurs where snow accumulates each winter to levels that bury small cabins. These snow forests are dominated by Mountain Hemlock and thus are known as the Mountain Hemlock Zone.

The fourth type of wet forest, known as the Interior Cedar-Hemlock Zone, is found in two parts of the Interior. The Skeena Valley allows winter storms into the northern Interior for a short distance, creating a hybrid forest with both coastal and interior characteristics. In the southern Interior, the dry eastward-moving air picks up moisture over the Interior valleys and loses that water as it rises and cools over the high mountains of southeastern British Columbia. This phenomenon creates another band of wet forests in the West Kootenays, Monashees and Columbia Mountains, often called the Interior Wet Belt. Although these Interior forests receive their precipitation more evenly through the year than those on the coast, their forests are similar in many respects.

Pages 152-53: Massive Western Redcedars tower over a jungle of Devil's Club in the wet lowland forests of the southern Interior.

OLD-GROWTH FORESTS

In contrast to the dry forests of the British Columbia Interior, wildfires are rare in rain forests. Thus, the fast-growing trees can live for centuries and reach immense sizes. Much of the impressive skyline of downtown Vancouver is actually lower today than it was two hundred years ago, when 100-metre-high trees were common along the southern coast of British Columbia. Most of these huge trees were Douglas-firs that were as much as a thousand years old. At higher elevations and along the north coast, where fires are exceedingly rare, the forests can be truly ancient; some Yellow Cedars may be more than two thousand years old and the forests themselves may be centuries older still.

Brown Creepers are commonest in old-growth forests, where they nest behind slabs of peeling bark on snags.

Most biologists consider forests more than 250 years old to be old-growth forests. The most obvious feature of an old-growth rain forest is the sheer

size of the trees. Huge trunks lift a green canopy almost 100 metres above the damp soil. Much of the life in the forest goes on here, unseen by ground observers. Hanging gardens of moss and lichen, gradually accumulated over the centuries, drape the sunlit branches. The high, complex canopy of an old-growth forest acts as a climatic buffer, moderating temperatures and humidity among its branches throughout the year. On hot summer days the canopy microclimate is cooled by evaporation from the needles.

Old forests have a structural diversity that is absent in younger forests. Fifty-year-old forests tend to be monotonous stands of similar-sized trees and little else. Sunlight cannot penetrate the unbroken canopy; the forest floor is dark and relatively lifeless. As a forest matures, some of the large trees fall, creating significant openings in the canopy. Sunlight streams onto the forest floor. Small trees and shrubs, held in check for decades by lack of light, shoot upwards to create a multilayered subcanopy beneath the remaining large trees. A walk through an ancient forest reveals an ever changing mosaic of light and dark, massive trunks and small saplings.

Large dead trees, both as snags and as logs, are another important characteristic of old-growth forests. About one-fifth of the biomass of an old temperate rain forest is dead wood. Although dead in one sense, snags and logs are almost as long-lived as the trees that produced them. A Douglas-fir snag can stand for fifty years or more before falling to the ground, where it remains a recognizable log for more than a hundred years.

Decaying wood not only is a major source of food energy in these forests but also provides homes for many animals. Woodpeckers, nuthatches and chickadees hollow out cavities for themselves, which are used in turn by bumble bees, squirrels, swifts and owls. Rotten logs are important refuges for mice and chipmunks; in summer they provide moist homes for salamanders and insects.

> THIS IS THE TEMPERATE RAINFOREST, NOT JUST BIG TREES,
> BUT LITTLE TREES GROWING ON BIG TREES GROWING ON
> FALLEN TREES LYING ATOP ROTTED TREES, ALL LINKED IN AN
> UNBROKEN CHAIN OF LIFE THOUSANDS OF YEARS LONG.
>
> Randy Stoltmann, *Written by the Wind*

An important ecological factor that often confuses the issue of the importance of old-growth forests is species diversity—most simply defined as the number of species found in a particular area or habitat. The diversity of a three-century-old forest is appreciably greater than that of a fifty-year-old tract. But as many foresters are quick to point out, plants and animals are even more diverse in recently deforested areas, temporarily cloaked in shrubs, grasses, herbs and small trees. The species found in these shrubby habitats are generally the same as those found in rural backyards; however, almost all of them are absent from old-growth forests. Similarly, species common in old-growth forests are usually absent from clearcut shrubbery and are uncommon or rare in young forests (Table 5.1). And for some groups, such as the all-important fungi, species diversity probably increases steadily as forests grow old. The number of species in a mosaic of different-aged forests is therefore much higher than that in a clearcut. To maximize biodiversity, therefore, we must maintain forests of all ages, especially ancient forests, and in significant amounts.

TABLE 5.1: CHARACTERISTIC BIRD SPECIES OF DIFFERENT-AGED COASTAL FORESTS

5-year-old	50-year-old	250-year-old
Orange-crowned Warbler	Swainson's Thrush	Pacific-slope Flycatcher
Song Sparrow	Townsend's Warbler	Brown Creeper
Dark-eyed Junco	Wilson's Warbler	Varied Thrush

Life in the Trees

The relatively constant environment of an old-growth forest is nirvana for lichens. Most arboreal lichens prefer dappled sunlight and regular breezes, but in a young forest a canopy-dwelling lichen is soon overtopped by the fast-growing trees, doomed to a slow death in the dark shadows and stagnant air. Lichens, perhaps more than any other group of organisms, are prime indicators of very old forests. Diversity of lichen species begins to increase when a forest reaches about 150 or 200 years old and doesn't peak until the forest is more than 350 years old.

Although lichens have largely been ignored in forest ecology, recent studies have found that they play important roles in nutrient cycles. Lettuce Lung Lichen is perhaps the most important of these epiphytes, or plants growing on another plant, in old-growth hemlock forests, and not just because it makes up half of the lichen biomass. The cyanobacteria (formerly known as blue-green algae) cells it farms within itself can take atmospheric nitrogen and turn it into the nitrates organisms need, much as bacteria in clover roots do. Lettuce Lung is therefore one of the most important sources of nitrates in this nutrient-poor environment.

One of the most unlikely members of the old-growth rain forest community is a drab, starling-sized seabird called the Marbled Murrelet. It is an alcid—one of the auk family—and alcids usually nest on sheer cliffs or in burrows on small islands to keep their eggs and young safe from mammalian predators. Marbled Murrelets evolved next to the towering conifers of the temperate rain forest and now use these huge trees as relatively safe havens from their ground-based predators. A single egg is laid on a wide, mossy branch 20 to 50 metres off the ground in a tree over 50 metres high. When the nestling is old enough to leave the nest, it must fly well, since it may have more than 50 kilometres to go before it reaches the ocean, and murrelets are

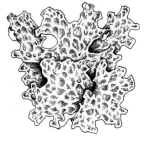

Lettuce Lung Lichen

Opposite page: **An adult Marbled Murrelet perches on a mossy Western Hemlock limb.**

IN THE CARMANAH CANOPY

Very little is known about the masses of tiny invertebrate animals that live in old-growth forests. Neville Winchester of the University of Victoria has been studying invertebrates in the upper Carmanah Valley on Vancouver Island. After collecting 1.4 million specimens, he estimates that the Carmanah is home to between 10,000 and 15,000 species of invertebrates, mostly insects. This is about one-third of the known species total for Canada and includes about 500 species new to science! As many as 5000 species of ichneumonid wasps, parasites of plant-devouring

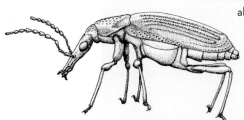

The rove beetle *Tanyrhinus singularis*

caterpillars, may be present in the Carmanah. Many species in the Carmanah study seem to be restricted to old-growth habitats, many of them to the canopies of the giant trees themselves. There, deep moss mats on the huge branches are home to 46 species of soil mites alone, over half of them unknown to science before Winchester's study. *Metrioppia walbranensis* is a soil mite found in fungus-rich soil beneath old-growth redcedar trees. Despite extensive searches for soil mites in coastal British Columbia, this species has been found in the world only in four small areas on southwestern Vancouver Island. Similarly, the rove beetle *Tanyrhinus singularis* is known in Canada only from the old-growth forests of the Carmanah Valley.

unable to take off from the forest floor. As old-growth forests are logged along the coast, more and more nesting habitat for Marbled Murrelets disappears. This factor and others have caused a serious drop in murrelet populations, serious enough that the species is listed as Threatened in Canada. A national recovery strategy offers hope that the decline can be stopped through ongoing retention of old-growth forests.

Life in the Soil

When you are walking through a majestic old-growth forest of towering hemlocks and cedars draped in moss and lichen, it may be hard to think of it as a tough place for plants to live—winters are mild and there is plenty of water. But although water is essential for plant growth, too much of it can cause problems. Constant winter rains leach away nutrients released by decaying forest litter, leaving poor, acidic soils behind. High water tables force trees to spread their roots in a shallow surface mat, leaving the trees susceptible to being blown over by the wind. And moist soils and humid air provide ideal growing conditions for a bewildering array of fungi, many quite capable of killing giant conifers.

Leaching forces trees along the coast to get essentially all of their nutrients directly from the thin layer of organic material at the top of the soil horizon. To do this, they enlist the help of surprising allies, the fungi. Many soil fungi form such intimate associations with trees that the trees could not live without them. Although some of these fungi fruit as conspicuous, often familiar mushrooms, such as russulas and amanitas, most form their fruit underground. The most famous of these fungi are truffles. Most of us know truffles as exquisitely flavoured fungi that are sniffed out by pigs and dogs among the roots of oak trees in France, dug up and sold for outrageous prices. Well, there are truffles in our forests, too. They may not interest gourmets, but their odour is irresistible to many small mammals, such as flying squirrels, chipmunks and mice. The mammals dig up the ripe truffles, eat them and plant the spores elsewhere in their droppings.

How does this help the trees? The vegetative, or food-gathering, part of the fungus is a wide-spreading mat of fine hairs called the mycelium, which spreads through the organic layer at the top of the soil. Everywhere they turn, these fine hairs encounter tree roots, and if the species combination is right, the fungus and root form a remarkable partnership. These partnerships are called mycorrhizae—literally, "fungus root." The fungal side of the deal provides the tree with nutrients that the mycelium can extract from the soil much more efficiently than the roots. Some fungi even provide the roots with more water than they could normally get, helping the tree through summer droughts. The tree in return gives the fungus sugars produced by its leaves.

Opposite page: Luridly beautiful but extremely poisonous, Fly Agaric mushrooms are the fruiting bodies of one of the many soil fungi that are essential to the health of forest trees.

FUNGI AND FLYING SQUIRRELS

One of the most important animals in this forest is the Northern Flying Squirrel. This big-eyed rodent is completely nocturnal, sleeping the days away in tree cavities. This behaviour is normal for most mammals but decidedly unusual in the sun-loving squirrel family. Because they hide away during the day, flying squirrels are rarely seen, even though they are just as common as the more familiar diurnal squirrels in most of our forests. Flying squirrels eat almost nothing but fungi in summer and fall, providing a critical service in spreading the spores to the roots of young trees. They also depend on other types of fungi—those in arboreal lichens. Flying squirrels survive the mushroomless winter by eating arboreal lichens; they also line their nest cavities in snags with a cosy bed of lichens. Both snags and arboreal lichens are common only in mature or old-growth forests. Flying squirrels have a link to another well-known old-growth forest species—they are the main prey of the spotted owl.

Without this partnership, most trees can barely stay alive, let alone grow to towering heights.

Mycorrhizae are not just a phenomenon of the temperate rain forest; most conifers and many other woody plants cannot grow normally without their fungal fix. Orchids are perhaps an extreme example of dependence on mycorrhizae; their seeds will not germinate until they are invaded by the right kind of fungal hyphae, or hairs of the mycelium.

Honey Mushrooms

The fungus-root partnership is amazing enough, but it is actually more complex than this. Most mycorrhizae also contain nitrogen-fixing bacteria (*Azospirillum*) and a yeast culture. The bacteria provide nitrates for both the fungus and the tree, and the yeast apparently stimulates bacterial growth and fungal germination. All these essential elements are neatly packaged in the droppings of rodents that have eaten truffles or underground mushrooms. For whereas above-ground mushrooms spread their spores on the wind, those species that fruit underground are totally dependent on mammals to spread their spores.

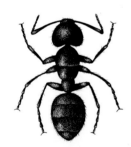

Carpenter ant

In an environment where 98 per cent of the biomass is locked up in wood, it is logical that organisms that can eat wood will prosper. Fungi are the most abundant examples of this lifestyle, and some are not so benign or helpful to the trees as truffles. Honey Mushrooms are common, ordinary-looking mushrooms scattered around the ground on coastal forests. They are the fruits of a large mass of shoestring-like structures called rhizomorphs that grow underground, searching for tree roots to feed from. Honey Mushrooms thrive on the roots of stumps and dead trees but will also invade and kill live trees.

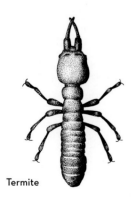

Termite

The big market for fungi in rain forests, though, is in digesting dead wood—logs and snags. Although there is plenty of dead wood to eat in a rain forest, it makes for a monotonous, unbalanced diet—a lot of carbohydrates and very little protein and other nutrients. Fungi have to snack on other items to stay healthy. Many of them consume the nitrogen-fixing bacteria common in decaying logs, first killing them with natural antibiotics (most of the antibiotics we use were first discovered in soil fungi). Others go after slightly larger prey. Luring nematode worms and other small animals with chemical attractants, the fungi catch them with an incredible arsenal of harpoon cells, inflatable nooses and exploding poison sacs, to name a few things in their sinister bags of tricks.

Insects team up with fungi in attacking dead or dying trees. Beetles bring fungi with them, often intentionally, when they cut through the protective bark of dying trees. Tiny ambrosia beetles cannot digest wood, so they farm fungi by collecting fungal spores in special cavities in their bodies and then seeding the spores throughout their galleries in the heartwood of newly fallen trees. The fungi digests the tree, and both the adult and larval beetles eat the growing fungi.

When fungi and bacteria have softened the wood of a dead tree or log, other insects move in. Carpenter ants chew long, elaborate galleries in the wood to provide a home for their colony. Like ambrosia beetles, carpenter ants are farmers, tending herds of aphids that suck the sap from healthy trees nearby and then gathering the honeydew excreted by the tiny bugs. Being good farmers, the ants gather aphid eggs in late fall and shelter them in their colony over winter, then they "plant" them on vegetation in spring.

On the west coast of British Columbia, late summer is termite time, when the warm evening skies are often filled with the fluttering wings of swarming adults. These are young Pacific Damp-wood Termites seeking out new homes in rotting logs and stumps as well as mates to share their homes with.

Damp-wood termites are slow fliers but may travel several hundred metres before settling. Most of the dispersing insects do not make it to their newly chosen homes, however, but are consumed by all sorts of opportunistic predators keying in on the fluttering feast. Along the coast, look for gulls—especially Bonaparte's Gulls—flying erratically as they snap up the airborne tidbits one by one. Robins, Varied Thrushes and Steller's Jays gobble them up on the ground, and even tiny shrews will gorge on termites as they tumble clumsily en masse out of their log homes.

The Indian-pipe, like a number of other parasitic plants of the forest floor, steals its daily needs from the mycorrhizal partnership between fungi and tree roots.

Those that survive their maiden flight shed their wings immediately upon landing. After losing their wings, the females raise the tips of their abdomens to release an attractive scent and wait for males to arrive. When a female finds a mate, she leads the male on a search for a suitable colony site. When the right place is found, she chews a cavity in it (the male sits by idly) and then seals the pair of them in it with a barrier of wood pellets and liquid feces.

Colonies grow slowly at first; after a year, they typically contain the reproductive male and female (the royal pair), one soldier and ten to twenty nymphs. Adults live for about five years, and a colony several years old could number between 2000 and 3500 individuals. Most of the colony is composed of nymphs or winged adults awaiting dispersal; soldiers number about 1 in 50 colony members.

THE COASTAL WESTERN HEMLOCK ZONE

Trees

The windward slopes of the coastal mountains are cloaked in mist, rain and an incredible blanket of giant conifers. The dominant tree of this forest is the Western Hemlock, easily recognized by its drooping leader, finely furrowed bark and feathery foliage—dark green above and silvery below. Hemlocks are supremely adapted to this cool, wet forest. They have no taproot; their roots spread like a mat just beneath the surface of the soil. Since nitrates are all but nonexistent in these leached, acidic soils, hemlocks have developed the ability to use ammonium as a source of protein-building nitrogen. Hemlock seedlings are also very tolerant of shade and are often the only tree species regenerating on the floor of coastal forests.

One of the most interesting things about conifer seedlings in rain forests is that almost all of them—as much as 97 per cent, in fact—are growing on decaying logs, stumps, or even snags. Although these nurse logs are common in many forests, they are usually not nearly as important as they are in temperate rain forests. Why? The answer seems to lie in the moss covering the forest floor; the moss is so thick that it is almost impossible for conifer seeds to germinate there. As long as they have a thin layer of humus, freshly fallen logs offer seeds a much better surface for germination. Mycorrhizal fungi and nitrogen-fixing bacteria in the decaying wood provide nutrients for the seedlings. The logs also retain water much better than the surrounding soil, a vital aid for young seedlings during a summer drought. The few hemlocks that manage to germinate on mossless ground, however—perhaps where the root mass of a fallen tree has exposed mineral soil—appear to survive to maturity much better than those that take root on nurse logs. Ground-rooted trees are perhaps more stable than the products of log nurseries, which can topple as their logs decay.

Western Redcedar is another characteristic tree of wet forests. Since its scalelike needles do not have a waxy coating, redcedar loses water easily

A straight line of young hemlocks marks the nurse log on which they germinated as seedlings.

through transpiration and can only grow where water is readily available year-round. Young trees growing in poorer sites are often flagged with red, dying branchlets in dry summers. Redcedars can tolerate stagnant water tables less than 15 centimetres below the surface of the soil and often dominate the saturated soils of flat valley bottoms. Their heavily buttressed trunks reduce the chances of windthrow. Redcedars growing in open areas often develop multiple tops, which can die back in very old trees to leave bare spike tops, a common sight along the open coast.

Another tree that prefers the rich soils of river valleys, estuaries and the misty spray zone along the coast itself is the Sitka Spruce. This is a very fast-growing species, which can live up to eight hundred years, thus dominating

Western Hemlock

Western Redcedar

Sitka Spruce

Western White Pine

Pacific Yew

Red Alder

Bigleaf Maple

its neighbouring hemlocks, most of which die before they are five hundred years old. Most dense, mixed stands of Sitka Spruce and Western Hemlock are undergrown by hemlock seedlings, but spruce takes over quickly if canopy openings occur.

Several other trees are locally common in wet forests. Western White Pine is easily recognized by its long, grey-green needles and large, banana-shaped cones. Most of the white pines in southwestern British Columbia died in the first half of the century after the accidental introduction of White Pine Blister Rust from Europe. The alternate hosts of this rust are plants in the genus *Ribes*—currants and gooseberries. Several Depression-era programs tried in vain to eradicate the rust by hiring men to destroy as many wild currants and gooseberries as possible.

Pacific Yew is a small, slow-growing, shrubby tree found in the under-storey of wet forests. Its dark green, parallel rows of needles look superficially like those of hemlocks or true firs, but its seeds develop in red, berrylike arils rather than in cones. Once ignored by foresters as useless, yews are now being harvested at an alarming rate to extract taxol, a drug proven useful in the treatment of cancer.

Historically, fire played a minor role in these wet forests in comparison with the dry Interior forests. With the advent of logging, however, opportunities for pioneer species to become established increased spectacularly. On the coast, one tree assumes the role of pioneer that is so abundantly carried out by Lodgepole Pine in the Interior. The Red Alder is the largest member of its genus in British Columbia, growing to heights of over 30 metres while its relatives barely escape classification as shrubs.

Typical of pioneering species, Red Alders grow rapidly and produce huge quantities of tiny winged seeds that can travel long distances on the wind in a lottery to find new cleared habitats. Like other members of the birch family, alders are wind-pollinated. In March, festoons of catkins colour large tracts of alder a dull red, and the spring breezes carry clouds of pollen through the forests.

Often scorned by foresters as a weed species that slows reforestation by more valuable conifers, Red Alder is now known to be important in enriching the poor coastal soils. It accomplishes this task with the help of a nitrogen-fixing bacterium, *Frankia*, which is found in nodules in the alder roots. This ability to use atmospheric nitrogen is almost essential for a species to colonize coastal soils after the organic layer has been stripped off by fire or erosion.

Another deciduous tree that does well in forest openings and cleared areas is the Bigleaf Maple. Its big leaves—up to 25 centimetres across—make it easy to identify. The Bigleaf Maple has furrowed, calcium-rich bark that supports rich moss communities and epiphytic licorice ferns. The maple can actually benefit from all these hangers-on. The thick patches of moss build

up a layer of soil beneath them, and the maple sends adventitious roots from its branches into this soil, where it can get a significant amount of nutrients. Bigleaf Maples can easily live two hundred years or more, and old specimens, draped in moss and ferns, are one of the many beautiful sights in the coastal forest.

Whether a Salmonberry cane bears red or golden berries is genetically controlled by a single gene, with red being dominant.

Shrubs

Although most of the biomass, or living matter, of any forest is found in the trees themselves, coastal rain forests have a diverse shrub layer as well, especially where openings created by fallen trees bring light to the forest floor. Salmonberry forms dense thickets in moist, rich soils. In March its cinnamon-coloured canes, delicate green leaves and bright pink flowers provide one of the first signs of spring after a dull coastal winter. Rufous Hummingbirds synchronize their northward migration with these blooms, and large patches of Salmonberry can support dozens of pugnacious male hummingbirds frantically displaying to feeding females. As the flowers are a sign of spring, so the golden or red berries are a sign of early summer.

On drier sites with poor soils, Salal dominates sunny openings and edges. Beach walkers along the outer coast are often confronted with an impenetrable wall of leathery, evergreen Salal leaves if they try to turn inland. Like many plant species in these cool, wet forests, Salal is in the heath family. Its small, bell-shaped flowers are exquisitely beautiful if viewed closely, and its dark purple berries make an excellent addition to pancakes, especially if picked from plants in a sunny location. In sites with rich soils, Salal is usually restricted to growing on rotting conifer stumps or logs.

On similar soils in shadier situations, Salal is replaced by another shrub from the heath family, the Red Huckleberry. It too is often found growing on old stumps, seeded there through bird droppings. Red Huckleberry takes advantage of the mild coastal winters by keeping some of its leaves. Other understorey plants, such as Salal, Dull Oregon-grape, Evergreen Huckleberry and Sword Fern are evergreen as well, photosynthesizing whenever the weather permits.

Sunlit gaps in dark coastal forests are often brightened by the beautiful Vine Maple, its pale green leaves providing a delicate contrast to the surrounding shadows. In larger openings, October frosts turn the leaves flaming orange and scarlet, a small but spectacular show of fall colour in the evergreen forests.

Extremely wet nutrient-rich sites in coastal forests are often cloaked in the huge leaves of Skunk Cabbage. In early spring, the air around them is filled with a pungent, skunky odour, which attracts tiny rove beetles to the spike of tiny flowers framed by a spectacular yellow bract.

Opposite page: Licorice ferns grace the mossy, calcium-rich bark of a Bigleaf Maple.

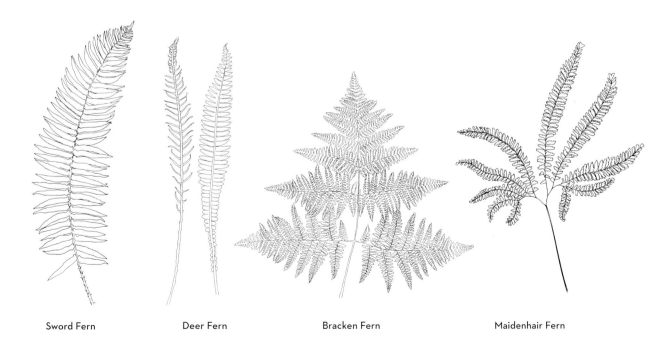

Sword Fern   Deer Fern   Bracken Fern   Maidenhair Fern

The Banana Slug, a common denizen of British Columbia's coastal forests, is one of the world's largest slugs.

Opposite page: The Ensatina Salamander is one of the commonest vertebrates in coastal forests.

Ferns

Perhaps nothing characterizes a rain forest more than the abundance of ferns, their lacy leaves draped over logs and tree trunks or forming waist-high thickets in the understorey. Sword Ferns form rosettes of metre-long fronds in shady forests with rich soils. Deer Ferns are found on poorer soils and produce two markedly different fronds—one vegetative, the other purely for spore production. Bracken Fern, one of the most widespread and abundant plants in the world, is common in disturbed, open areas along the coast and in the southern Interior. Small ferns growing on tree trunks, especially those of Bigleaf Maple, are usually Licorice Ferns. As the name suggests, its rhizomes have a sweet licorice smell. The beautiful Maidenhair Fern, with its elegant black stems and delicate green fronds, is commonly found in hillside seepage areas.

Slugs

Although the southern coast of British Columbia is often called the "banana belt" of Canada, the only bananas growing there are Banana Slugs. These large mollusks reach 26 centimetres in length and are one of the largest slugs in the world. Banana Slugs are voracious herbivores, grinding up leaves and stems with their radula, a rasplike organ in their mouth. Slugs are tremendously important members of the forest environment. There are over a dozen species of them in coastal forests, and they can comprise up to 70 per cent of

the animal biomass. In some areas there are more than 40 kilograms of the slimy creatures per hectare!

Surveying a field of tiny stumps that was once a promising patch of lettuce, many coastal gardeners may well ask how any young plant can survive the annual spring slugfest. Most such garden problems are entirely due to slugs inadvertently imported from Europe. But forest plants on the coast have evolved with the big Banana Slugs and have developed ways of coping with hungry radulas. Wild Ginger, for instance, has two distinct forms. A fast-growing form is favoured in rich, moist soils—its strategy is simply to produce leaves, flowers and seeds as quickly as possible so that it can complete its summer's task before being mowed to the ground. A second form grows much more slowly on drier, poorer soils. Since it cannot outgrow the slugs' grazing, it produces chemicals that slugs find distasteful. Interestingly, Banana Slugs do eat quantities of Bracken Fern, a plant so full of nasty chemicals that most other animals refuse to eat it.

Salamanders

Throughout many of the coast forests of British Columbia, the commonest vertebrates are not mice or small forest birds but some rather unusual sala-manders. These are the plethodonts, or lungless salamanders, represented by three species along the southern coast—the Ensatina Salamander, the

Clouded Salamander and the Western Red-backed Salamander. Each of these species can occur at densities of about two hundred animals per hectare. A fourth species, the Coeur d'Alene Salamander, is a rare resident of the West Kootenays, found along small creeks and in the spray zone around waterfalls.

Lungless salamanders are found only in terrestrial environments where they can keep moist enough to absorb oxygen through their skin alone. Besides lacking lungs, they are extraordinary in other ways. Ordinary amphibians spend much of the summer in aquatic habitats, where the females lay hundreds or thousands of eggs in gelatinous masses in the water. Lungless salamanders don't have to go back to a pond or stream in summer—they lay their eggs in rotten logs or other, similar moist environments. The larvae develop inside the egg and emerge as small salamanders about two months later. To allow this internal development, plethodont eggs must provide more space and food for the growing larvae and are therefore much larger than most amphibian eggs—about 5 millimetres in diameter. Each female can afford to lay only a dozen or so of these big eggs every other year and guards the precious grapelike cluster throughout the summer.

Fertilization is also a little more complicated than the fishlike external fertilization typical of most amphibians. Courtship culminates in a "tail walk," in which the female walks close behind the male, straddling his tail with her forelegs. The male then deposits a packet of sperm on the ground and the female picks it up in her cloaca.

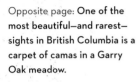

Opposite page: One of the most beautiful—and rarest—sights in British Columbia is a carpet of camas in a Garry Oak meadow.

Mammals

There are three species of moles in British Columbia, all restricted to the Lower Mainland. The largest of the three species, the Townsend's Mole, is found only in wet pastures around Abbotsford. The Coast Mole is common throughout the lower Fraser Valley in a wide variety of habitats. As with the Townsend's Mole, about three-quarters of its diet consists of earthworms. Shrew-moles are the smallest and most agile of the moles. Their forefeet are less adapted for burrowing than those of other moles, and their long tails allow them to indulge in occasional climbing. Shrew-moles do not make extensive tunnels and never make molehills but instead hunt for their prey under the leaf litter of forests and woodlands. Earthworms make up almost half of their food, but isopods such as pillbugs and sowbugs are important as well.

The forests of the Cascade Mountains are home to one of British Columbia's strangest mammals. The Mountain Beaver is the world's most primitive rodent—among other features, it has five toes on its front feet, whereas all other rodents have only four. Unrelated to the beaver, it does clip off small branches and saplings as its namesake does. Mountain Beavers live in underground burrows, with larger chambers for their nest, food storage

Mountain Beaver

and toilet. They stay very close to these nests; most adults rarely venture more than 25 metres in their search for the Sword Ferns and Bracken Ferns that make up most of their diet. Lactating females eat a substantial amount of tree branches as well and are considered pests in some newly replanted forests in western Washington and Oregon.

THE COASTAL DOUGLAS-FIR ZONE

If any Canadian forest could be considered more benign than the Western Hemlock forest, it is the drier forest along the southeastern coast of Vancouver Island and throughout the Gulf Islands. Although its dry, sunny summers are a godsend to residents and tourists alike, they can be stressful for the plants of this area. Douglas-firs do not grow as large in this drier habitat as they do in the coastal Western Hemlock forest, but they dominate the climax forests since it is too dry for hemlocks to survive. On wetter sites with rich soils, Grand Fir is common. Its smooth grey bark and dark green foliage combine to form one of the most elegant trees in the province.

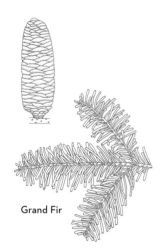

Grand Fir

The shrubby edges of this habitat, where Oceanspray blooms beside Saskatoon and Salal, are the only Canadian home to several species of songbirds. Bushtits, tiny distant relatives of the chickadees, roam the woodlands in frantic flocks, flying leapfrog fashion from bush to bush, egging each other on with their sputtering calls. Bewick's Wrens scold intruders from their thicket hideaways, and Black-throated Gray Warblers sing their wheezy songs while almost invisible in the treetops.

In the driest parts of this zone, especially on south-facing slopes with good drainage, the summer drought creates an open forest, each tree battling with its neighbours for precious water. In the past, First Nations people regularly burned these forests to maintain meadows of camas and other food plants. This savanna-like ecosystem is characterized by two broad-leaved tree species found nowhere else in Canada—the Arbutus and the Garry Oak. It is one of the most endangered ecosystems in the country; most of its former strongholds are recognizable only from scattered trees in the suburban sprawl of southern Vancouver Island.

Garry Oak

The Arbutus is the only evergreen broad-leaved tree in Canada, and its open trunks, covered with smooth, coppery-red, peeling bark, are an integral part of the landscape of southern Vancouver Island and the Gulf Islands. Its clustered white flowers are shaped like tiny bells, a clue that it is in the heath family, along with Salal, Kinnikinnick and many other forest plants in British Columbia. The flowers in turn produce bright red berries, favourites with Pileated Woodpeckers, American Robins, Varied Thrushes, Cedar Waxwings and Band-tailed Pigeons.

The Garry Oak, the only oak native to British Columbia, is another classically beautiful tree. One of the white oaks, Garry Oak produces sweet acorns that attract wheeling flocks of Band-tailed Pigeons in the fall. Its gnarled, deeply furrowed grey trunks are resistant to the grass fires that once raced through the grasslands each summer. Modern fire-suppression practices have largely put an end to these fires, so many of the meadows are being invaded by Douglas-fir seedlings (see Chapter 9 for more about the meadows).

The physical characteristics of this oak woodland—large, thick-barked trees interspersed with meadows and small grasslands—are similar to those of the Ponderosa Pine forests of the southern Interior. Two species of birds otherwise restricted to Ponderosa Pine in British Columbia were found in Garry Oak woodlands as well, at least before this habitat became severely fragmented in the last half of the twentieth century. Lewis's Woodpeckers are great acorn lovers and appreciate the open skies of this woodland for their summer fly-catching forays. Western Bluebirds use natural cavities and woodpecker holes in the oaks for nest sites as well as perches between flights to catch ground-dwelling insects. Both of these birds are essentially gone from the southern coast, hit by a combination of habitat loss and fierce competition for nest sites from the introduced European Starling.

Arbutus

THE MOUNTAIN HEMLOCK ZONE

As the Pacific storms collide with the western slopes of the coastal mountains, the clouds sweep upwards. As they rise, they cool, and as they cool, the water in them condenses to fall as rain. In winter, the sodden clouds cool to the point of producing snow, and the North Cascades and Coast Mountains end up with more snow than anywhere else on earth. This smothering of snow has a marked effect on the vegetation, and these mountain forests are significantly different from those below.

Mountain Hemlock

Western Hemlock, so dominant at lower elevations, is replaced by Mountain Hemlock. Mountain Hemlock exhibits the drooping leader typical of its cousin but has more grey-green foliage and much larger cones. Mountain Hemlocks are supremely adapted to life in the snow and can photosynthesize even when there are several metres of snow on the ground. Amabilis Fir takes the place of the lowland Grand Fir in these high-elevation forests, while Western Redcedar is replaced by Yellow Cedar, superficially similar to the redcedar but not closely related. Its true relatives are the cypresses, as shown by its cubical, berrylike cones.

Amabilis Fir

Yellow Cedars are very resistant to insect attack—no defoliating infestations have ever been reported—and have several antifungal chemicals in their heartwood that delay the inevitable invasion by heartrot fungi. Since Yellow Cedars live in an essentially fire-free environment, these adaptations to repel attacks by insects and fungi allow trees to live to very great ages—one tree on the Sechelt Peninsula's Caren Range was 1824 years old.

Yellow Cedar

SPIRIT BEARS

You would think that an animal called the Black Bear would be black, but brown individuals are common and there is even a population of bears on the British Columbia coast in which pure white Black Bears are found. These coastal bears are considered a separate subspecies—the Kermode Bear—that was isolated from Interior bears for about two hundred thousand years while the coastal mountains were an impenetrable barrier of ice during the Pleistocene. The white bears are a recessive colour phase, somewhat like red-haired people; cubs from a black mother can be white and vice versa.

So most Kermode Bears are black, but on some of the larger coastal islands the proportion of white bears is quite high. About 20 to 30 per cent of the bears on 25-kilometre-long Gribbell Island, for instance, are white, while on 80-kilometre-long Princess Royal Island the ratio is about 10 per cent. On the adjacent mainland, only about 1 per cent of the bears are white.

White bears in a dark forest break one of the cardinal rules of ecology—Gloger's Rule—which states that animals living in humid environments tend to be darker in colour than their relatives found in drier habitats such as grasslands and deserts. How can these white bears persist in an environment where they stand out like a polar bear in a coal pit?

The isolation of the island populations obviously helps the white form to persist, but there must be some advantage that white bears have over their black siblings that ensures the survival of this form. Dr. Tom Reimchen of the University of Victoria is studying these island bears, hoping to find out what this advantage might be. What special factors might be at work on these islands? There seem to be two obvious ones. First, coastal bears rely on the summer and fall salmon runs for much of their annual protein intake. And second, there are no Grizzly Bears on the islands.

Reimchen feels that salmon are the key to this puzzle. Because there are no Grizzly Bears on the islands, the Black Bears there can fish for salmon more freely than Black Bears on the mainland, so salmon are even more important to these bears. One of the possibilities Reimchen and his students are looking into is whether being white makes it easier for bears to catch salmon unawares. If white bears could indeed catch salmon more easily than black bears, that could explain the success of the white form on the islands. On the mainland, the white form is confronted with aggressive Grizzly Bears, and being white would almost certainly be a disadvantage in that case.

Opposite: A white Kermode Bear emerges from a creek on Princess Royal Island with a fresh salmon dinner. Success at salmon fishing might be the key to the persistence of this remarkable colour form of the Black Bear.

Sunlit openings in these snow forests are cloaked in shrubs—False Azalea, White-flowered Rhododendron, Copperbush, blueberries—all members of the Ericaceae, or heath, family. Why is this family so dominant here? Snow forests have cool, moist acidic soils. Acidic soils contain very low concentrations of nitrates, which are essential to protein production in most plants and animals. For this reason, many plants cannot tolerate such soils. But the heath family relishes acid soils, for two reasons. First, heaths can use ammonia, a common compound in acid soils, as a source of nitrogen. Second, heaths seem to require a great deal of iron, which is also easy to obtain in acidic soils but is often chemically bound in neutral to basic soils.

Chestnut-backed Chickadees are common in Western Hemlock forests throughout British Columbia.

THE INTERIOR CEDAR-HEMLOCK ZONE

Although most of the Interior is too dry in summer or too cold in winter to support the lush forests typical of the coast, two regions do have mountains cloaked in hemlock and cedar. Forests in the Columbia and West Kootenay regions and the central Nass and Skeena Valleys are a rich mix of coastal and Interior environments and have the greatest diversity of tree species in British Columbia. One can often count seven or eight species of conifers within a few hundred metres, including Subalpine Fir, Grand Fir, hybrid spruce, Lodgepole Pine, Western White Pine, Western Larch and Douglas-fir as well as the ubiquitous Western Hemlock and Western Redcedar. There is even a small outpost of Yellow Cedar in the West Kootenays.

These are not true rain forests—most of them receive less than a metre of precipitation annually, less than almost all of the coastal forests. So why are the forests so similar? Interior wet forests get up to half of their annual precipitation in the form of snow. Melting snow keeps soils moist in spring, and summer rainfall (three times that of the nearby Ponderosa Pine forests) is

enough to keep them moist through the peak growing season. The combination of very warm summers and moist soils is enough to produce the magnificent forests we see in these valley snow forests.

Golden-crowned Kinglets are among the most common birds in moist coniferous forests, yet they are rarely seen as they forage in the treetops.

The bird communities of these forests are similar to those found on the coast. Chestnut-backed Chickadees replace the Mountain Chickadees found in other Interior forests, and the Red-breasted Sapsuckers replace Red-naped Sapsuckers, at least in the Quesnel Highlands area. Golden-crowned Kinglets, Varied Thrushes and Winter Pacific Wrens, otherwise restricted to the cool forests at higher elevations in the Interior, are commonly heard singing in the moist valley bottoms of this zone.

CHAPTER SIX

MOUNTAINTOPS

MOUNTAINTOPS

MOUNTAINTOPS ARE MAGICAL places. Their wildness, their isolation from the human world and their magnificent vistas evoke strong emotions in all of us. Every hiker has his or her own magical memories— my favourite is of a glorious end-of-summer evening atop Tonquin Hill, an alpine knoll amid some of the most spectacular scenery in the Rocky Mountains. Leaning into a warm west wind, my friends and I surveyed the seemingly endless mountains. From Mount Robson towering above the northern skyline to the headwaters of the Fraser River just below the southern horizon, not one sign of human activity was visible. A small herd of Caribou clattered over the rocks below, and as the sun went down, White-tailed Ptarmigan began to fly into the alpine meadow behind me, cackling to each other as they went to roost.

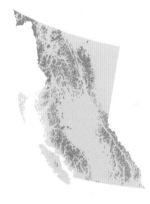

From most places in British Columbia, even from downtown Vancouver, you can see wave upon wave of mountains. But most British Columbians spend little time on mountain peaks, admiring them from below instead. In more ways than one, however, you get an entirely different view of the world from a mountaintop. We normally see British Columbia as a series of valleys framed by postcard peaks, but if you stand atop even a small mountain in the Rockies, Coast Mountains, Cassiars, Selkirks or Purcells, you will always be impressed by the sea of rugged mountains around you and by how small the lush valleys really are.

Entirely different too is the life at your feet, where cushions of Moss Campion huddle behind rocks and fat bumble bees tack against the wind to the next flower. At lower elevations, competition among organisms is rampant—trees battle among themselves to get more and more sunlight and more nutrients from the soil; barnacles and mussels fight on intertidal rocks just to find a place to settle down. Above the timberline, however, most of the competition is between organisms and the harsh environment—plants struggle to grow a few millimetres each summer and maybe even set a few seeds; marmots slip into a deep winter sleep each September, hoping they have put on enough fat to get them through an eight-month fast until the first spring shoots appear in late May.

TIMBERLINE

The natural world is full of boundaries, narrow zones where changes in environmental forces such as moisture or temperature produce a radical shift in the flora and fauna. One of these boundaries, obvious to even the most casual observer, is the timberline, the zone between thick forests and barren tundra. Although at close range it can appear to be a relatively wide zone where forests gradually give way to larger and larger meadows and trees become progressively smaller, from a distance the timberline is usually remarkably abrupt. The timberline zone can be divided into narrower belts by defining three boundaries associated with it: the forest line, where continuous forest is invaded by subalpine meadows; treeline, the upper limit of erect trees; and the krummholz line, the upper limit of stunted mats of conifers (Figure 6.1). Ecologists refer to the region above the treeline as the alpine zone; the forests, woodlands and meadows immediately below the treeline are generally termed subalpine.

> BUT THE SOUL OF THE COUNTRY IS OUT PAST THE TIMBERLINE.
> Murray McLauchlan, "Out Past the Timberline"

What are the forces that produce such a sudden change in the habitat? Cold and snow. It is usually not frigid winter temperatures that govern the elevation of treeline, however. Conifers can withstand temperatures down to -60°C or lower, and winters at treeline in British Columbia are much milder than that, at least in the south. The forces of cold and snow act together in different combinations throughout British Columbia to create three different kinds of timberline: coastal, southern Interior and northern Interior.

Coastal Timberlines

On the moist west slope of the Coast Mountains, where winters consist of a series of Pacific storms, it is the sheer amount of snow that governs the upper limit of tree growth. There, that upper limit is usually around 1650 metres, the lowest treeline in southern British Columbia. The winters are rather short and mild in the coastal mountains, with mean January minimum temperatures of about −5°C and frost-free periods of over 100 days. But this is the snowiest place on earth, with annual snowfalls of more than 15 metres and maximum accumulations of 5 metres or more. The heaviest winter snowfall ever recorded occurred in 1971–72 on Mount Rainier, Washington—27.4 metres; similar snowfalls undoubtedly occur in the British Columbia Coast Mountains, but there are no permanent weather stations to measure them. A weather station that operated for six years at 1625 metres elevation above Kemano on the central coast recorded an average annual snowfall of 19.7 metres, more than the average at Mount Rainier.

These huge snowpacks take so long to melt that the growing season is too short for tree seedlings to germinate. It is often late July or even August before timberline plants emerge from the snow in coastal mountains, especially in protected bowls where heavy, cold air pools on spring and summer nights, slowing melting even further.

On coastal mountains exposed to the full force of Pacific storms, treeline is even lower, since winds of up to 300 kilometres per hour blow any branches away. This is especially evident in the mountains of the Haida Gwaii, where alpine habitats are encountered as low as 1000 metres elevation.

Opposite page: At treeline, conifer branches can only thrive under the winter snowpack, forming dwarfed shrubs called krummholz— German for crooked wood.

FIGURE 6.1
Generalized mountaintop in southern British Columbia showing the relationship between the forest line, treeline and krummholz line. Note that these occur at lower elevations on the shadier north side of the mountain.

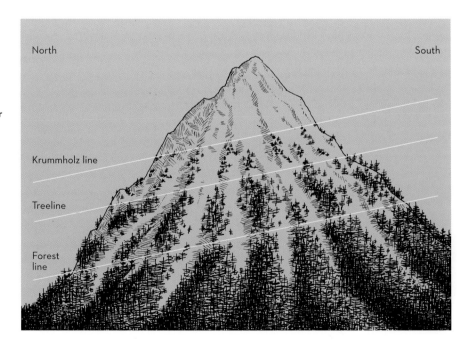

North

South

Krummholz line

Treeline

Forest line

Southern Interior Timberlines

Snowfall in most of the Interior mountains is much less than on the coast, but winter temperatures are still not harsh enough to be the critical factor shaping treeline. A quick look at the stunted patches of krummholz, with their spreading skirts protected under the snow and every attempt at growth above the snow killed back, reveals that it is the winter winds that are bringing the forest to its knees. It is not the cold winds that kill the branches but the warm, drying winds of late winter. These winds melt the branches' thin protective coats of frost and snow and then draw water out of exposed needles. The tree cannot replace this water, since its roots are frozen into the rocky soil. Below timberline, the trees wear thick coats of snow through the winter that protect them from the drying winds.

Freezing temperatures can prune back trees as well, but not usually in winter. Timberlines in the southern Interior experience balmy winters compared with those of northern forests. The real harshness in southern timberlines occurs in summer, which is cool and very short. The mean July temperature at an Interior treeline is less than 10°C, compared with over 16°C in a far northern valley forest. In addition, there are only about 100 frost-free days in a year at this altitude, and usually the longest period between two frosts is a mere three weeks.

Trees at timberline have little time, therefore, to put out new growth, and seeds have little time to germinate. The critical period for new tree growth is in the last half of summer, when an early frost could easily kill the soft, immature needles. Mature needles can withstand all but the lowest winter temperatures imaginable. They have a thick wax layer to prevent water loss and a low water content to minimize the effects of freezing. But even the small amount of water in needles can freeze and do damage to cell structure if bitterly cold weather hits before the tree is prepared. Many trees in northern forests can withstand temperatures as low as -40°C through a process called supercooling. Water won't freeze at 0°C if it has no minute particles or rough edges to initiate crystal formation; if cell walls are smooth, the water in them can supercool to -40°C before ice begins to form. But the hardiest trees—those found in the far north and near treeline on mountains—use a different strategy to survive even more frigid temperatures. It is the formation of ice crystals within cells that quickly kills vegetation by causing cells to rupture and die. Extremely hardy conifer species can move water out of cells and into intracellular spaces where ice can do little damage, a process triggered by increasingly severe frosts. So it is a sudden, hard frost in early August that can affect new twigs. Their water-filled needles, still soft to touch, are quickly killed back.

Simply put, treeline in the southern Interior mountains is at the altitude where the summer is too cool and short for trees to harden new growth and where winter winds are so strong that they dry out exposed twigs. Stunted mats of krummholz can survive at higher elevations because some of their new growth is insulated from the winter winds by the snowpack. The krummholz line, above which no conifers grow at all, marks the altitude where the growing season is too short to allow germination of trees.

Northern Timberlines

Across northern British Columbia, the timberline zone is somewhat different from that of the southern mountains. Instead of flower-filled meadows between clumps of conifers, the area above the forest line is a mosaic of conifers, mostly White Spruce, and a dense growth of willow and birch shrubs. The willows and birches continue upslope above the limit of the conifers, eventually giving way to the treeless alpine zone.

Conifers usually have an advantage over deciduous plants in areas that have short, cool summers. Although their needles are relatively inefficient, they can photosynthesize on any winter day that is warm enough and are fully leaved when spring arrives. At high altitudes in the far north, however, the long summer days apparently favour the production of deciduous leaves, which are more efficient photosythesizers and are shed before the deadly autumn frosts.

Thus, the forest line of northern British Columbia may be governed simply by low temperatures. The spruce grows as far up the mountains as the autumn frosts allow, and the willows and birches continue up to the point where the growing season is too short to allow germination. The transition between the dense willow-birch shrub zone and open alpine meadows (perhaps shrubline would be an appropriate term) is often very abrupt, suggesting that this boundary replaces the krummholz line of southern mountains.

BELOW THE TREELINE:
THE SUBALPINE PARKLAND TRANSITION

The zone between the forest line and treeline is one of the most beautiful forest types in British Columbia, a favourite with hikers for its stunning combinations of dark, fragrant trees, spectacular flower blooms and open vistas of the mountains beyond. These open parklands, like the treeline itself, are the result of several forces. The importance of each force varies with geography and climate.

Tree germination is so difficult and early growth of seedlings so slow at these altitudes that any factor that can clear the forest or further suppress germination can produce meadows in the midst of forests. You can measure the slow growth of small trees yourself next time you are in one of these meadows. Find a small conifer a metre or so high and count the distinct whorls of branches up the trunk. Every year, conifers produce an erect shoot, the "leader," from their terminal bud, as well as a circle of side branches. Small trees in open areas retain most of these side branches for years, so it is relatively simple to count the whorls and come close to the tree's true age in years. Trees near sea level in British Columbia can easily grow a metre in a couple of years, but at the forest line it can take a fir fifty years to reach its first metre and can take another century or two to produce a forest.

The Creation of Subalpine Meadows
In the barren rocks of Castle Peak in the southern Chilcotin, 130 metres above the present-day treeline, a group of weathered stumps bears witness to a time when forests grew higher on these mountains. Local climates are always changing—over millennia, centuries or even mere decades. The warmest period since the glaciers retreated from British Columbia occurred between nine thousand and six thousand years ago. Since then, the climate has been more or less the same as it is today, except for a cold period between 1600 and 1900—the Little Ice Age. Cold winters and heavy snowfalls during the Little Ice Age likely destroyed many timberline forests, their trees already growing at the limit of endurance.

Pages 188-89: Many subalpine meadows in the southern Interior of British Columbia are carved out of the high forest by fire, as the weathered logs on this ridge in the Monashee Mountains suggest.

In the last century, trees have probably been inching their way up the mountains again. This upward progress, like the downward destruction of the Little Ice Age, does not usually proceed in nice horizontal lines. Instead, trees invade meadows in patches—long stringers moving along relatively fertile soils or up snow-free ridges; tree islands forming around hardy pioneering individuals. Thus, some of the subalpine meadows we see today could be remnant alpine tundras now surrounded by forests about a hundred years old.

The present-day climate creates meadows in subalpine forests as well. Just as a heavy accumulation of snow lowers the treeline on coastal mountains, heavy snow accumulation in bowls, in gullies and on the lee side of ridges can make it almost impossible for trees to become established. These snow-created meadows are usually carpeted with mountain-heathers and sedges that tolerate very short growing seasons. Cold air pooling into mountain cirques and northern valleys can also shorten the growing season to the point of excluding trees.

The Role of Fire

One hot July weekend I was hiking with a friend along a subalpine trail in the western end of Manning Park. The flowers were in full bloom—meadows knee-deep in valerian, lupine and paintbrush. Towering clouds built up in the afternoon, and as we reached the last ridge we were suddenly enveloped in a violent thunderstorm. We huddled in a small valley as a series of lightning flashes lit up the dark fog and deafening thunder echoed off the rock walls. An hour later it was over, mist rising off the green meadows, puddles of hail melting in the sun and, here and there, plumes of smoke rising from distant ridges where lightning strikes had ignited trees. It had been an exhilarating and frightening experience of one of the forces that had created the flower meadows we had enjoyed all morning.

Many Interior subalpine meadows are born of fire, the flames of lightning strikes clearing thick forests of spruce and fir. Each meadow is only temporary (on the time scale of a tree's lifetime), slowly regrowing to forests of Subalpine Fir and Engelmann Spruce, but the patchwork of meadows is permanent. In the drier parts of the southern Interior, fires return to any given subalpine forest about once every hundred years, so by the time one meadow begins to disappear beneath the branches of young trees, another is cleared.

Coastal Subalpine Meadows

Subalpine meadows on coastal mountains are almost all snow meadows dominated by heaths and sedges; colourful fields of flowers are generally small and restricted to seepage areas and stream banks. Masses of tiny pink, cream and white heather bells brighten the meadows in summer, and in fall the huckleberry and blueberry leaves turn yellow, orange and scarlet against the dark green heather needles, providing a beautiful backdrop for berry pickers.

As you climb higher in the Coast Mountains, the meadows become larger and the forest is isolated into small islands of Mountain Hemlock, Subalpine Fir and Yellow Cedar. Amabilis Fir, often common in the forests just below the forest line, is rare in this parkland zone. Some meadows show signs of invasion by seedling hemlocks. These small trees germinated during a series of warm, dry years when low snowpacks melted early. They grow exceedingly slowly, but after they reach a critical height their crowns will be above the snow early enough to actually speed snowmelt around them. Because the branches are dark, they readily absorb sunlight and release the energy as heat. This phenomenon significantly increases the growing season for these small trees. It can also save them from serious damage from the snow mould *Herpotrichia juniperi*, which forms black mats on branches that remain under the snow for any length of time in spring.

The change from a moderate coastal climate to a more continental interior climate occurs over a short distance as one travels through the Coast Mountains, and mountain meadows on the eastern slopes are similar to those in Interior mountains. Even as close to the coast as Garibaldi Lake, the heather meadows are broken by wide swaths of lupine, cinquefoil and valerian, and Subalpine Fir is an important member of the high forest.

The inflated air sacs in the neck of a male Sooty Grouse produce deep hoots to attract females.

Sooty Grouse are common in these meadows, the females leading downy chicks that tumble over the heather. The female is sometimes also followed by a male with amorous intentions, its black tail raised and fanned and neck sacs inflated, exposing circular patches of bright yellow skin surrounded by startlingly white feathers—looking for all the world like a pair of fried eggs, one on each side of the neck. This display is accompanied by a series of deep hoots amplified by the inflation of the air sacs. Males usually hoot up in trees, where they

can be almost impossible to find; they are ventriloquists, and Mountain Hemlock foliage is very dense. If a female comes by, though, the male takes to the ground to pursue her. After mating, males take no part in nesting or the care of young but spend all spring and summer hooting and hoping.

One of the rarest mammals on the continent, the Vancouver Island Marmot is found only on a few mountain ridges on central Vancouver Island. Only 350 or so are known to be alive today, but the good news is that this represents a welcome increase from a terrifying low of twenty-one in 2003. Most of the increase has occurred in the southern part of their range; the only thriving colony north of Alberni Inlet is at Mount Washington. A successful captive breeding program designed to rebuild the dwindling wild population was begun in 1997 and has now produced a total of 515 pups. These efforts seem to have brought the wild population up to a point where it is less threatened by chance events.

They live in lush subalpine meadows on steep mountain slopes, where avalanches and snow creep limit tree growth and where food plants such as lupine, Indian-paintbrush, meadowrue, Cow-parsnip and Woolly Eriophyllum thrive.

No one knows how long these marmots have been isolated from their mainland cousins—they may have colonized the island since the glaciers left ten thousand years ago, or they might have survived the Pleistocene ice ages in an ice-free refuge, perhaps along the island's west coast. Marmot bones seven hundred to over nine thousand years old have been found in caves to the north and west of the present range, suggesting that the species may have been more widespread in the past. In fact, the species was first discovered by zoologists on Douglas Peak near Port Alberni, a mountain where no marmots have been seen for over thirty years.

Why is this species so rare? Part of the answer may be that lush mountain meadows are not common on Vancouver Island and are separated by great swaths of dense, dark forests. The colonies that survive in small patches of ridge-top meadows may die out occasionally, and recolonization is chancy across the wide, deep valleys. Young marmots do disperse through these forests, but most do not find good alpine habitat on the other side. They are also easily hunted, and their limited range may have made local populations susceptible to elimination by early hunters.

We don't know for sure what caused the recent, dramatic decline but, as is often the case with endangered species, the story is probably a complex one. Historically, young marmots would disperse through forested valleys to find new, open meadows to colonize, but lately they've shown a distinct preference for clearcut logging slash. But clearcuts are destined to become regenerating forest in a few years, the antithesis of good marmot habitat. In addition, turnover of individuals in clearcuts is very high. More troubling are the results of recent studies that discovered that predation by wolves, cougars and Golden Eagles accounted for 80 per cent of marmot deaths. This high predation rate resulted in big losses at some colonies over just one summer. But predation is a natural phenomenon, so why has it now become

The starchy bulbs of the Yellow Glacier Lily were an important part of the diet of southern Interior Native people. They were gathered in late summer and cooked by steaming, baking or boiling.

Opposite page: Summer in subalpine meadows is a brief but spectacular blaze of colour as Arctic Lupines, Common Red Paintbrushes and other mountain flowers hurry to set seed before the late-summer frosts.

such a problem for marmots? There is always a dance of numbers between predators and their prey, and populations fluctuate over the years. On Vancouver Island, biologists speculate that logging and other landscape changes may have caused the ups and downs of wolves, cougars and deer to become more extreme recently. These circumstances could have forced some predators to shift their gaze from deer towards the rare but locally abundant marmots. Only further research and ongoing conservation efforts will help ensure that this unique British Columbia species once again prospers in the wild mountains of Vancouver Island.

Southern Interior Subalpine Meadows

These subalpine meadows are most famous for their fabulous fields of flowers, blooming synchronously in the short mountaintop summer. These flowers appear in two distinct "bloom waves." The first bloom wave occurs immediately after snowmelt. This wave is usually at its peak in June, depending on the altitude and the year, but its representative flowers can be found later in the summer alongside any late-melting snowbank. These early flowers are species with bulbs or tuberous roots, which allow rapid growth and flower production before leaf growth. The flowers are usually borne on short stalks to avoid the snow-cooled winds and produce a carpet of ankle-high white, cream and yellow blooms.

The showiest species is the Yellow Glacier Lily, which sometimes covers entire mountain ridges in a mantle of gold. Another conspicuous early flower is the Western Anemone, whose large cream flowers grow close to the ground on short, hairy stalks. Anemones are also known as windflowers; *anemos* is the Greek word for wind. After the anemone flowers are pollinated, the stalk grows 20 to 30 centimetres and produces a distinctive moplike seed head, often called a tow-head baby. The long stalk puts the seed head above the taller flowers of late summer so that the wind can spread the long-tasselled seeds.

The third important member of the first bloom wave is the tiny Spring Beauty. Like the lily and anemone, it can also occur in single-species concentrations, covering whole meadows in a pinkish-white mass of flowers. Another name for it is Indian potato, a reference to the small white corms on

BUTTERCUPS VERSUS BUTTERCUP EATERS

The leaves of the Western Anemone and Globeflower, like the leaves of many of their relatives in the buttercup family, contain ranunculin. This is an innocuous chemical itself, but it readily hydrolyzes to form an extremely irritating oil, protoanemonin. This chemical blisters the tongue and throat if eaten, an obvious deterrent to grazing animals. Plants in the buttercup family have long been used in folk medicine to raise hot blisters when applied as poultices. Cultivated mustard, which is also used in poultices, produces similar irritant oils.

White Marsh-marigold

Western Anemone

Globeflower

its roots, which are harvested by the Interior Native people. They are also a favourite of Grizzly Bears, which often dig up large areas of plants with their long claws.

Often the first snow-free areas in mountain meadows are along small brooks overflowing with meltwater. Here White Marsh-marigolds and Globeflowers grow and bloom in the shallow flowing water. Both species have white flowers similar to those of the closely related Western Anemone, but their leaves are quite different.

As the snow melts and the soil surface dries in midsummer, other species of plants grow and mature. By late July, these plants are ready to flower, and the second bloom wave covers the subalpine meadows. This is a much more diverse bloom, both in colour and in form, than the first, including white valerian, red paintbrush, blue lupine, yellow arnica, avens and ragwort, and purple daisies and asters.

Take a close look at the paintbrush flowers—the red or orange "petals" aren't petals at all, but brightly coloured leaves. The true flowers are the green shoots coming out at the bases of the leaves. The red or orange colour is a clue that paintbrush is a hummingbird flower—one that is pollinated almost exclusively by hummingbirds rather than bees or flies. The long, tubular flowers are the right shape to accommodate hummingbird bills; no honey bees and few other insects have tongues long enough to get at the nectar at the base of paintbrush flowers.

In seepage areas the large leaves of Indian Hellebore are distinctive. Although the small green flowers of the hellebore aren't striking to look at, their delicate watermelon fragrance is worth sniffing. Don't be tempted to add the leaves to a wilderness salad; the entire plant is extremely poisonous.

Although many of the trees found at timberline in the mountains of the southern Interior are also found below in the subalpine forests, two conifer species are more or less restricted to timberline itself—the Whitebark Pine and the Alpine Larch.

Rufous Hummingbirds use the flower-laden mountain ridges as their migration highways en route to their winter quarters in the Sierra Madre of western Mexico.

HUMMINGBIRD MIGRATION

By the time the subalpine flower meadows are in full bloom in late July, male hummingbirds are moving south. They need to refuel regularly, and one of their favourite fuels is paintbrush nectar. An old wives' tale has it that hummingbirds migrate south on the backs of geese, but that story has two fatal flaws. One is that hummingbirds migrate before the geese—even females and young have left by early September, whereas geese don't pass through southern British Columbia until early October. Another is that geese migrate to the central and southern United States, settling in for winter well north of the Mexican winter home of the hummingbirds.

Whitebark Pine is easily identified by its upsweeping branches, often multi-trunked form, bright green needles clustered five to a bunch (compared with two in the Lodgepole Pine, a related species occasionally growing near timberline), smooth grey bark and spineless, purplish cones. This species is common on relatively warm, often south-facing slopes in open parkland and can be found as close to the Pacific as Garibaldi Lake in the Coast Mountains.

Whitebark Pine

Alpine Larches are often the last trees one encounters on a hike up a mountainside in southern British Columbia. Their deciduous habit likely gives them the advantage over evergreens in surviving bitter frosts in late fall, but they need full sun in summer to get the energy to make all those new needles. Alpine Larches can only germinate in cool conditions, though, and are therefore commonest on open, north-facing slopes, nicely complementing the Whitebark Pines growing on south-facing slopes. Alpine Larches grow in such harsh conditions that successful seed production and germination is rare; it is an uncommon event to find a young seedling.

Alpine Larch

Whitebark Pines and Alpine Larches are often the pioneer members of tree islands. These clumps of trees form in alpine meadows after one individual grows tall enough to shelter the growth of new seedlings. These islands can gradually grow outward as more trees germinate around their circumference. The pioneer tree may eventually die, leaving a hollow centre in the island. As more central trees die and new ones grow outward, the island can become a doughnut-shaped "tree atoll."

If the pioneer tree of a tree island was a Subalpine Fir, the younger trees are likely genetically identical copies of it—clones—since this species often

Pocket gophers remain active all winter, packing excavated dirt into snow tunnels on the surface of the ground. These dirt-filled tunnels are evident in summer as raised, miniature highways of earth running through the meadows.

Northern Pocket Gopher

CLARK'S NUTCRACKERS AND WHITEBARK PINES

Like its crow and jay cousins, the Clark's Nutcracker is an opportunistic feeder with a predilection for robbing other birds' nests to feed its own young. And like the Gray Jay, it can become quite a panhandler for food, especially in mountain parks such as Manning and Cathedral Provincial

Parks, and throughout much of the Rocky Mountains. But in late summer and early autumn, the Clark's Nutcracker switches to eating large pine seeds, which it finds in the cones of Ponderosa and Whitebark Pines. Its mountaintop relationship with Whitebark Pine is nothing short of remarkable.

The Whitebark Pine is not an ordinary pine. Most pines have thick cones armed with nasty spines or a heavy coating of pitch to deter squirrels and other animals from eating the seeds, which are usually small with large wings so that they can fly far on the fall winds. Whitebark cones, in contrast, have no spines or heavy pitch and look like dark purple flowers on the ends of branches. The seeds are very large and wingless, and the cones do not open fully to release the seeds when mature—if the cones did release the seeds, they would just fall to the ground and grow up competing with the parent tree. Instead, Whitebark Pines rely almost entirely on Clark's Nutcrackers to open their cones and gather, disperse and plant their seeds.

The nutcrackers have a throat pouch with space to store up to a hundred pine seeds. When it is full, the birds fly off, sometimes for several kilometres, to a suitable place to cache the seeds for winter food. A suitable place is usually a windswept southern exposure with sandy soil, allowing the birds easy access all winter to their supply of seeds. It is no coincidence that this habitat is also ideal for Whitebark Pines. The birds land on the ground and bury the seeds in groups of five or six under a couple of centimetres of soft soil; then they take off and harvest more. An adult nutcracker will cache 30,000 to 100,000 seeds in this manner each fall.

How do they find them again? Studies have shown that Clark's Nutcrackers have remarkable spatial memories and outperform zoology graduate students time and time again in tests of finding buried seeds. They don't find all 30,000 or so seeds, of course, and come summer the hillsides are dotted with clusters of tiny pine seedlings, a half-dozen or so in each group, depending on how many seeds the nutcracker planted. Some of these clusters survive to grow into the many-trunked form that is typical of Whitebark Pine.

reproduces by layering. In this process the lowest branches, when pressed to the ground by the spring snowpack, put down roots and send up trunks of their own, which eventually become separate trees.

Many of the small mammals of subalpine meadows spend much of their lives underground, for the most part to escape predators and the rigours of the mountain climate. The ground squirrels and marmots, for example, sleep underground most of the year, coming above to feed only on summer days. One animal that you rarely see above ground in daylight is the Northern Pocket Gopher, a curious rodent that tunnels like a mole. Unlike moles, however, it eats plants instead of worms and insects. If you see "molehills" in the British Columbia Interior, they are the work of pocket gophers; molehills on south coast lawns are the real thing. Although they have a bad reputation in Interior vegetable gardens and alfalfa fields, pocket gophers provide valuable rototilling service to subalpine meadows, aerating the soil and increasing water absorption so that the surface runoff doesn't all disappear downhill. North of the Thompson-Shuswap valley, this service is provided to some extent by other rodents, including lemmings, voles and ground squirrels.

Northern Timberline: The Shrub Tundra

The subalpine zone in northern British Columbia (north of Williston Lake) is characterized by tall willow and birch shrubs. Although these shrubs can be difficult to walk through, hikers resting in small openings in the cover are rewarded with flowers typical of the spruce forests below, such as Tall Bluebells, ragwort, larkspur, monkshood and shootingstars. As you break out into the open alpine zone, the ground is carpeted with blueberries and Alpine Bearberries. In late summer and fall the bearberry leaves turn colour and paint the mountainsides a brilliant crimson. This biogeoclimatic zone, the Spruce-Willow-Birch zone, is threatened by climate change. As temperatures warm through this century, almost half of the province's shrub tundra is projected to be replaced by boreal forest moving upslope and by the southern subalpine zone—the Engelmann Spruce–Subalpine Fir Zone—moving north.

Brown Lemming

Northern subalpine valleys often have two timberlines—one on the mountain ridges and another just above the valley bottom. These lower timberlines are found in wide valleys where heavy, frigid air collects in the bottomlands. This ponding of cold air significantly lowers temperatures throughout the year and can often result in permafrost conditions in the valleys. Such valleys are filled with shrubs, grasslands and fens and provide the only breeding habitat in the province for Gray-cheeked Thrushes and Smith's Longspurs.

Snowshoe Hares don't often venture beyond the cover of the spruce forest, but Arctic Groundsquirrels are common in the alpine meadows of the far northwest and the runways of Tundra Voles and Brown Lemmings can easily

be found in grassy swales. Almost everyone is familiar with the story of lemmings—how entire populations go on crazy migrations, eventually committing suicide by jumping off cliffs into the sea. That's the Walt Disney version, though; the real story is somewhat less dramatic but no less fascinating.

Lemmings are large, tundra-dwelling mice with short legs, short ears and almost no tail. There are several species around the Northern Hemisphere; the one in British Columbia is the Brown Lemming, distinguished by its orange backside. It is found in the high mountain tundras of the northwestern quarter, coming as far south as Tweedsmuir Provincial Park.

Most lemming populations, as well as those of their close relatives, the voles, or meadow mice, undergo tremendous peaks and crashes, usually at three- to five-year intervals. These population cycles have puzzled ecologists for over fifty years, and the cause of these cycles is still somewhat of a mystery. The following is a simplified account of what seems to happen.

During the low phase, lemmings are very hard to find. Over the next year or two, lemming predators—owls, hawks, foxes and weasels—are forced to disperse from the tundra and switch to other prey species if they can. The stage is now set for the increase phase. Given a deep, insulating blanket of snow, lemmings can breed throughout the winter as well as in the summer, increasing their numbers tremendously in one year. Soon their populations are in plague proportions, and their aggressive instincts take over.

Lemmings are highly territorial, and at high population densities young animals are constantly being driven out of adult territories. At this point lemmings appear to be everywhere, and young animals are seen dispersing through unsuitable habitats such as forests. And yes, they can even be seen attempting to swim across large lakes, desperately trying to find a place where their rear ends aren't being constantly bitten by bigger lemmings.

Back on the tundra, predator numbers are up, hawks and owls taking advantage of the lemming feast by producing large, healthy families. The adult lemmings, perhaps distracted by all that aggression, produce fewer and fewer young and begin to die of old age themselves. Within a year, the lemming population has all but disappeared.

THE ALPINE TUNDRA

As you approach treeline, the krummholz skirts of trees grow larger and the erect trunks shorter. The last trunks are mere krummholz flags: short poles with a tuft of branchlets near the top on the leeward side of the trunk. The lower branches above the snowpack are scoured off each winter by blowing ice. Finally, you reach an altitude where there are no trunks at all, only krummholz mats huddled behind rocks. In this cold, wind-lashed environment, plants cannot grow large enough to create more favourable microclimates, as the forest does a few hundred metres downhill. Rocks and natural hollows are often the only sites that offer enough protection from the wind to allow plants to germinate. Krummholz trees growing behind rocks often spread gradually leeward, new growth surviving only in the wind shadow of the tree itself.

Although the alpine regions of British Columbia are united by their lack of trees and by cool, short summers, three quite different zones can be recognized, differing both in climate and vegetation.

The Coastal Mountain-heather Alpine Zone occupies the windward ranges of Vancouver Island, Haida Gwaii and the Coast Mountains, where deep and prolonged snow cover lowers treeline by as much as 900 metres relative to that in the drier mountains to the east. Although the vegetation can be lush, much of this zone is occupied by glaciers or recently exposed bare rock.

The Interior Mountain-heather Alpine Zone occupies the lee side of the Coast and Cascade Mountains and the ranges of the southern and central Interior. Because it begins at higher elevations than the other two alpine zones (2500 metres in the dry south to 1800 metres in the north), this is the smallest of the three zones in area. Summers are warm relative to the coast and northern zones.

The Boreal Altai Fescue Alpine Zone ranges along the spines of the northern mountains and the lee side of the Coast Mountains as far south as the Chilcotin. Much of this zone is occupied by well-vegetated tundra. The cool summers have very long days, and frost-churning features are common.

Opposite page: Afternoon sun along the Haines road highlights thickets of willow and birch shrubs, which dominate the subalpine zone of northern British Columbia.

Alpine Plant Life

Tundra plants reward close inspection; you almost have to get down on your knees to appreciate them at all. Dwarf willows lie flat against the gravel except for their upright, down-jacketed catkins. A hurrying hiker could mistake Spotted Saxifrage for a moss with tiny white flowers; a face-to-face look reveals the exquisite scarlet and gold spots on the petals. Alpine Forget-me-nots reflect the blue mountain sky with their tiny flowers. Like the forget-me-nots, many of the tall herbs of the subalpine meadows are replaced by prostrate relatives above treeline—the catchflies by Moss Campion, Arctic Lupine by Dwarf Mountain Lupine, Subalpine Daisies by the tiny Golden Fleabane.

The tundra biomes of British Columbia are among those most threatened by climate change. Moderate projections of recent temperature increases indicate that upslope treeline advance could eliminate between 45 per cent of coastal alpine and over 80 per cent of interior alpine by the end of the century.

It may be hard to think of alpine meadows as deserts, but after the snowpack is gone, water is very hard to come by on high, rocky ridges. Summer rainwater disappears quickly into the shallow, well-drained soil, and the intense sunshine and dry winds quickly desiccate leaves. Alpine plants therefore share many characteristics with desert plants. Some, such as stonecrop, are succulent and fleshy, enabling them to store water through the summer drought. Others, such as Sulfur Buckwheat, locoweed, pussytoes and Dwarf Mountain Lupine, have leaves encased in grey, woolly hairs to reduce evaporation.

Many alpine rocks are colourfully patterned with living patches of bright orange or vivid yellow-green and black, crusts of life covering the stones.

THE COST OF SEX

Alpine plants live in an uncompromising environment where any extra costs could mean the difference between surviving and perishing, and one of the most metabolically expensive practices in plants and animals is sex. The cost of producing a new plant through sexual reproduction—which requires flowers, pollination, seed production and seed survival—is about ten thousand times that of producing a copy through a runner, as strawberries or buttercups often do. That's why lawns are often overrun with highly successful buttercups. It's not surprising that many alpine plants choose this method of copying themselves.

Sex does have great advantages, though, so most species practise both methods of reproduction. The Alpine Bistort produces a flower stalk with small white flowers at the top and what look like green flower buds below. The buds are actually vegetative bulbils, which can also grow into new plants after they drop off the stem. Other species make sex more efficient by being dioecious—producing the male and female flowers on separate plants. Some of the most successful alpine plants fall into this category—the willows, Moss Campion, Mountain Sorrel and Cloudberry.

Alpine Bistort

These are lichens, and they can tell much about the area they grow in. The circles of Rock Orange Lichen, for instance, grow only where there is a source of calcium or nitrates, often from bird droppings or mammal urine. These brightly coloured rocks therefore indicate favourite lookout sites for pikas, cliff nest sites of hawks and eagles or song posts of Horned Larks. The dark brown mats of Blistered Rock Tripe and black tufts of Velcro Lichen grow on acid rocks. Some colonies of crustose lichens grow slowly—only a few centimetres a century—but live so long that they can be used to date ancient gravesites or the movements of glaciers.

Gravelly ridges on mountaintops are often covered in White Mountain-avens; the cream flowers appear shortly after snowmelt, replaced in late summer by a carpet of tasselled seed heads.

> THE ALPINE TUNDRA IS A LAND OF CONTRAST AND INCREDIBLE INTENSITY, WHERE THE SKY IS THE SIZE OF FOREVER AND THE FLOWERS THE SIZE OF A MILLISECOND.
>
> Ann. H. Zwinger, *Land above the Trees*

At first glance, the alpine tundra flower communities of British Columbia seem to violate one of the tenets of ecology, that species diversity decreases as you get closer to the poles. Yet alpine flower communities on mountains in southern British Columbia have fewer species than those in the north. The same pattern holds true for alpine butterflies. This odd situation is easy to understand if you picture the alpine habitats of the south as increasingly small, isolated islands of tundra in a sea of forest.

The alpine meadows of northern British Columbia are much larger islands, all close to other alpine meadows and closer to the huge Arctic tundra that was the source of the alpine species. The farther away from the source populations the southern tundra islands are, the fewer Arctic emigrants there are that have been able to reach them.

When species disappear from small, isolated islands for one reason or another, they are rarely replaced by new ones, since the source populations are so far away. And the smaller the island, the smaller its plant and animal populations, making it all the more likely that these populations will disappear. In the north, species don't often disappear from the large tundra islands, and seeds can easily blow or butterflies fly from one mountain ridge to another, providing a constant supply of species to replace any that disappear.

Insect Singles Bars and More

Have you ever hiked up a mountain on a fine summer morning and plunked down at the top, relaxing on the warm rocks, beaming with accomplishment—and found yourself surrounded by buzzing flies? I don't mean the biting kind, just all sorts of flies: big ones and small ones, yellow ones and black ones, hovering ones and crawling ones. If you don't remember such an event, look closely the next time you are on a mountain or hilltop. For a moment, take your eyes off the magnificent landscapes below and focus on the rocks around you. If there is a cairn on top, watch that. If it is warm and sunny, you will see the singles bar of the insect world!

Sarcophagid fly

Most male insects go about finding mates in conventional ways—they hang around the place they were born, they sniff the air for a particular perfume, they check out the best local flowers, or they search the places where females may want to raise a family. Some insects, however, have come across a simple but ingenious way of getting together. These are generally widely dispersed but strong-flying insects, primarily true flies and some butterflies and moths. Finding each other in the big, wide forest may be a challenge for these insects, so they have evolved an intuitive understanding—"Let's meet at the top of the hill." All they have to do is fly uphill until there is no more uphill to fly.

Tachinid fly

Generally speaking, males fly to hilltops and stay there, waiting for females. The females fly up for brief visits only—they quickly find a mate and then journey back down to their particular habitat on the hillside or in the valley, where they lay their eggs. Watch quietly from your hilltop resting spot and you will see bristly tachinid flies zooming around in frenetic haste; flower flies, sarcophagid flies and blow flies maintaining their watch from the warm rocks; and swallowtail butterflies flying rapidly over the ridge and down the other side a ways before resuming their upward flight. Hilltops are also just about the only place you will ever see a male horse fly. You can distinguish males from their female counterparts in two ways: by their extra-large eyes that meet across the top of their heads and by the fact that they totally ignore you!

Some insects, especially some ladybird beetles, meet on the tops of mountains to gather into large hibernation groups. In the late summer, they can be seen swarming over mountaintop boulders before they crawl beneath them to spend the winter in a mass of friendly red bodies. In the British Columbia Rockies, bear biologists have discovered that some Grizzlies abandon good berry crops on the slopes to go to the peaks and fatten up on beetles and moths.

Dead insects can be surprisingly numerous on the vast snow fields of the higher mountains. These are unlucky members of the aerial plankton, insects that disperse by flying high into the atmosphere and letting the wind take them away from their birthplaces. The wind currents rise up over the mountains and then are cooled by the altitude, ice and snow; the resulting downdrafts deposit the insects on barren rock and chilling snow. Most are flying ants, whose presence over the mountaintops can be detected by flocks of chattering Black Swifts. These large, swallow-like birds specialize in consuming swarms of ants, flying long distances to the mountain peaks each day from their nest sites, usually located in moist canyons far below.

Black Swift

Birds and Mammals

I once led an autumn field trip for university students into the Cascade Mountains to study the animals of the treeline. One of our objectives was to find White-tailed Ptarmigan, the small grouse of alpine habitats in western North America. When we paused for lunch, a student handed me a small white feather. "Ptarmigan?" he asked. I nodded encouragingly. "Is that ptarmigan poop?" he asked again, pointing at a pile of toothpaste-shaped droppings. I nodded again. "Are those ptarmigan?" he continued, indicating a dozen lichen-coloured grouse just now getting to their feet and trying to walk out of the lunch circle without being noticed. I had long known how easily you could walk by a well-camouflaged ptarmigan, but to half finish my lunch within a few feet from a dozen was too much!

There are actually three species of ptarmigan in the world, all of them found in British Columbia. They are distinguished from other grouse by their heavily feathered feet and white winter plumage, both adaptations to their life in the snow. The largest is the Willow Ptarmigan, found throughout the willow shrub tundra of northern British Columbia. The Rock Ptarmigan is a moderate-sized species found in grassy alpine habitats in the north and throughout the Coast Mountains. The White-tailed is the smallest and most widespread species, found in rocky alpine areas throughout the province.

In fall, ptarmigan moult into their white winter plumage, Willow and Rock retaining their black tails (usually hidden under long white covert feathers) and White-tailed turning totally white except for black eyes and beak. The white plumage not only makes them hard to see against the snow but also keeps the birds warmer. White feathers (and white hairs for that matter) are hollow and empty of pigment and are significantly better insulators than coloured feathers.

In late fall, young ptarmigan often leave their mountaintop homes to find new ridges to colonize and occasionally turn up in very odd places. A friend of ours was surprised one November afternoon to see a White-tailed Ptarmigan strolling across the postage-stamp-sized lawn of her townhouse on the Fraser Delta.

Come spring, the females moult back into their cryptic summer plumage, but the males delay the moult for a month or so to perform their courtship rituals in white winter dress. Willow Ptarmigan males actually regain their reddish-brown head and neck and then stop the moult to jump and cackle in a startling two-tone spring outfit.

The barren ridges above the treeline attract a small but distinctive songbird community. Alpine tundras in the far northwestern corner of the province are the summer home of the Snow Bunting, a handsome white sparrow with black trim, known to other areas of British Columbia only as a winter visitor. Elsewhere in the province, there are really only three species of songbirds that nest above treeline. Steep slopes, especially those with lush growth around seepages, are habitat for American Pipits, and the ridges themselves are inhabited by Horned Larks. Both the larks and the pipits sing their territorial songs while in flight, a habit common among birds of treeless environments. The third songbird species here is the Gray-crowned Rosy Finch, a chocolate-brown bird with bright pink wings and rump found in the rocky cliffs and ice

Opposite page: Probably the best time of year to look for White-tailed Ptarmigan is in August and September, when the lichen-coloured birds are in family groups, making it less likely they can slip by unnoticed. Listen for the clucking calls of the females to their chicks.

MIGRATING HAWKS AND SONGBIRDS

The next time you are hiking along a windswept mountain ridge in August or September, look up! Chances are a hawk or eagle will be somewhere in view, sailing along on the updrafts created by the prevailing winds deflected upward by the ridge. These birds are on their way south, like a lot of birds at that time of year, and are using the ridges as expressways. In parts of the world where mountain ridges are not as common as in British Columbia, remarkable concentrations of hawks and eagles are seen in spring and fall. The largest concentrations of this sort in British Columbia are along the headlands west of Victoria, where the south-bound birds run out of mountain ridges and are forced to wait for good soaring weather before crossing the Strait of Juan de Fuca.

Cypress Provincial Park is a good subalpine site near Vancouver, as is the Three Brothers area of Manning Park, but almost any good ridge will provide some action. Try looking on days when there is a steady wind out of the north or northwest.

Mountain ridges are also used by songbirds on their southward migration. They are perhaps also attracted by the prospect of a good tail wind but are certainly taking advantage of the end-of-summer feast of berries and insects available. Songbirds avoid high mountains during spring migration if at all possible—the deep snow hides any food source and could prove fatal if the weather changes quickly.

Horned Larks almost always tuck their nests into the lee of a rock or small alpine plant. The bright orange mouths of the nestlings, conspicuously spotted with black, provide a clear target for the adults at feeding time.

fields of the highest mountains. Rosy finches can often be seen in summer foraging on the permanent snow fields, picking up windblown insects and seeds.

Almost all the birds of the alpine tundra abandon the mountaintops in winter for milder climates. Larks fly off to southern grasslands, pipits to temperate coastal mud flats and Gray-crowned Rosy Finches to gravel banks of intermontane valleys. Only the ptarmigan stay, huddled under the snow for up to 80 per cent of the day, feeding on seeds on the windswept ridges.

The less mobile mammals, however, are forced to stay and deal with the long, frigid nights and short, hungry days. To survive, mammals use a variety of strategies, most of which involve lying low and using as little energy as possible. The extreme form of this strategy is hibernation, exemplified by the ground squirrels and marmots. These mammals gorge themselves all summer on grasses, flowers and other plants, putting on a thick layer of fat. At summer's end they go into their burrows to a special hibernation den, curl up and fall into a deep sleep. This deep sleep is called torpor, and in it the animal's body temperature falls to near that of the surrounding air. In this way the hibernator can save a large amount of energy, since it doesn't have to burn very much fat to keep up its temperature.

Some of the smaller rodents can get through the winter by foraging under the cover of snow, eating dried grasses and herbs. The Heather Vole leaves behind evidence of its subnivean lifestyle when the snow melts in summer, exposing a cosy little grass nest close to a large pile of tiny droppings—the mouse's winter outhouse.

VANISHING ISLANDS: CLIMATE CHANGE MEETS ALPINE TUNDRA

While many aspects of climate change and its effect on British Columbia's ecosystems may be difficult to tease out of complex models, one result is self-evident. As the climate warms over the next century, treeline will rise—and as it rises, it will flood the mountaintop islands of alpine meadow and rock with a sea of trees. In the southern Interior, alpine plants such as Dwarf Mountain Lupine, Moss Campion and Golden Fleabane will have nowhere to go. In the north, their island homes will become much, much smaller. Detailed modelling by Tongli Wang and his colleagues at the University of British Columbia predicts an overall rise of treeline by 170 metres to 246 metres between about 1975 and 2085, and a loss of 45 per cent of the coastal alpine zone from British Columbia during the same time (Map 23, page 110).

PIKAS: CANARIES OF CLIMATE CHANGE

Pikas are small, unreasonably cute relatives of rabbits that inhabit talus slopes and boulder fields of the mountainous west. There are two species in British Columbia: American Pikas range through the southern mountains, whereas their Beringian cousins, Collared Pikas, live in the far northwest. Although they are small and rock-coloured, they can often be seen after their alarm call—a nasal *enk!*—gives their location away. Instead of storing winter food as fat, the pikas exemplify the saying "Make hay while the sun shines." They forage on grass, herbs and flowers growing adjacent to their bouldery homes, and put hay piles aside for winter forage, since they don't hibernate. When their hay is cured, pikas move it under the cover of large, flat rocks for use during the long winter.

Pikas are the poster bunnies of climate change because they can die if they are forced to spend more than two hours above 25°C, and they require open mountain meadows with abundant herbaceous plants to eat. So as the summers get hotter and the tundra meadows close in with

American Pika

shrubs and trees, their numbers are expected to dwindle and local populations may vanish. Pikas are also sensitive to heavy snowfalls in spring, which lengthen the time that snow covers new forage at a time when their hay piles are exhausted. Although this may be counterintuitive, the warmer, wetter winters predicted for our changing climate often result in more snow than usual in the alpine, not less. Some populations may be able to adapt, however. Pikas living in low-elevation talus slopes in Oregon survive hot temperatures by eating more moss than any other mammal—this low-calorie, high-fibre diet allows them to stay within the cool confines of their rocky backyards. These individuals also don't need to store as much food for the winter, since winters are much shorter there.

CHAPTER SEVEN

THE SPRUCE KINGDOM

CHAPTER SEVEN

THE SPRUCE KINGDOM

MOST BRITISH COLUMBIANS live along the coast or in the southern valleys and thus like to think of the province as a temperate place: the "banana belt" of Canada. The vast majority of the province, however, is relatively isolated from the moderating influence of the Pacific Ocean. The Interior mountains and plateaus have long, Canadian winters; they are the land of the spruce, the realm of Moose and mosquitoes. When the words *wilderness* and *camping* are mentioned, this is the country Canadians usually think of. Most of our large parks are predominantly spruce forests, where Common Loons cry from clear lakes, Hermit Thrushes sing their flutelike songs from fragrant, swaying fir trees, and Lynx wait in ambush for Snowshoe Hares.

Ecologists describe these forests as boreal, from the Greek *boreas,* the north wind; they are part of the great band of spruce forests that rings the Northern Hemisphere. The scale of these forests is immense, and to ground-based humans they often appear monotonous and almost featureless. But patterns are everywhere in the spruce forests: spatial patterns caused by fire, frost and water, and the temporal patterns of a continental climate and of dramatic, decade-long population cycles in the animals that inhabit them.

On a provincial scale, the mountain and northern forests of British Columbia have been divided into a number of ecological zones based on climate and dominant trees (see Chapter 3). Although there are differences among these forest zones, they do share many common features and thus are grouped in one chapter in this book.

> THE BOREAL FOREST IS A FORMIDABLE ENVIRONMENT
> THAT CHALLENGES ALL THOSE WHO VENTURE INTO IT,
> AND THAT IS ITS TRUE FASCINATION.
> Cameron Young, *The Forests of British Columbia*

It should be mentioned, however, that in a strict sense, boreal forests are forests of the northern plateaus. Differences in climate and dominant tree species separate them from the similar subalpine forests of the southern mountains. Although both regions have long winters, the plateaus have a more continental climate, a climate of extremes. The plateaus are enveloped in frigid, Arctic air for weeks at a time each winter but enjoy long, hot summer days. Winters in the southern mountains are milder, influenced more strongly by Pacific air masses, whereas summer days there are shorter and cooler than on the northern plateaus.

FORESTS OF SPRUCE AND FIR

White and Engelmann Spruce

The northern and mountain forests of British Columbia are dominated by two species of spruce—those prickly-needled, scaly-barked conifers that thrive in cold climates. White Spruce and Engelmann Spruce are sibling species—closely related species that have evolved from a common ancestor only recently. These spruce apparently diverged when they were separated by the glaciers of the Pleistocene ice ages; White Spruce now dominates the eastern and northern boreal forests, and Engelmann Spruce is common in the high forests of the Western Cordillera. The two species mingle and hybridize on the mid-mountain slopes of southern British Columbia and across its broad, central plateaus, where it can be difficult to find a pure tree of either type. Even experts label them simply as hybrid spruce. In those areas, spruces above 1500 metres elevation can generally be safely identified as Engelmann, whereas those below 900 metres are usually White Spruce. The keen naturalist can try to verify this rule by examining spruce cones: Engelmann's are papery and flexible, with wavy-edged and more pointed scales; those of White Spruce are stiffer, with rounded, smooth-edged scales.

White Spruce
Engelmann Spruce

Many spruce trees have compact tangles of small branches called yellow witches' broom, the result of an infection by Spruce Broom Rust. The stunted needles on the branchlets are bright gold instead of grey-green and are shed in fall. When the rust matures, a strong, musky smell wafts through the forest and flecks of orange spores cover the needles. Most rusts (like most gall aphids) alternate between unrelated hosts such as Subalpine Fir and Fireweed, Lodgepole Pine and aster, spruce and Labrador Tea. The spores of Spruce Broom Rust blow through the forest, infecting its other host, Kinnikinnick.

Subalpine Fir

Subalpine Fir

The other conifer sharing the spotlight with spruce in the cold forests of British Columbia is Subalpine Fir. Subalpine Fir is called balsam by foresters, but the real Balsam Fir is a close relative confined to eastern North America. The smell of Subalpine Fir's foliage is the smell of the British Columbia mountains, and a brief hint of its fragrance on a cool breeze can transport you back to memories of past mountain adventures. When I am driving through the mountains, I roll down the window at the top of the pass to relive those memories. From a car, you can also identify Subalpine Firs visually by their tidy, symmetrical appearance and their flat, tiered whorls of branches.

The cones of the Subalpine Fir and other species in the "true fir" genus *Abies* are distinctive in a couple of ways. First, they stand erect along the

CONELIKE GALLS

When checking cones, you will probably notice that some at the tips of spruce branches aren't cones at all. These conelike structures are the abandoned homes of the Cooley Gall Aphid, and if you look closely, the scales are really swollen, dried needles. This effect of the aphids superbly illustrates the fact that cones themselves evolved from simpler structures at branch tips. If you break a gall apart, you will see small chambers at the base of each needle. Each of these chambers held several aphids when the gall was fresh. These

aphids started as parthenogenetic eggs—unfertilized but viable, and all female—laid on the soft new twig. The young aphids suck plant juices from the stem, exuding chemicals that stimulate the growth of the gall around them. They later mature into winged adults that emerge through cracks in the dry gall and fly off to found a new generation of woolly aphids on Douglas-fir trees. This generation produces no galls. The cycle is complete when the progeny of those aphids return to the spruce forests. Cooley Gall Aphids are therefore found only in mountain forests where Douglas-firs are growing nearby. Other species form galls in northern British Columbia, but they either stick to spruce throughout their life cycles or alternate with larch or pine hosts.

upper branches of the tree, and second, they do not harden and drop off the branches when mature but disintegrate while they are still attached. After the bracts have fallen and the seeds have flown away on the winds, the central cores remain, standing like slender candles atop a Christmas tree.

Throughout much of the boreal forests, the trees are draped with blackish horsehair lichens. To many people, the lichens make the trees look damaged, sick or even burnt, but they actually do little or no harm. The lichens are merely using the trees as a support to hang in the breeze, absorbing water and nutrients from the air. Like all lichens, they are fungi that have discovered

HAIR LICHENS

Two types of lichens commonly drape themselves on coniferous trees in this region—the cream-coloured witch's hair lichen and the dark brown horsehair lichen. Both are important winter food for Caribou, and both are indicators of old forests. They are also common; some old-growth forests support up to 3300 kilograms of hair lichen per hectare. Horsehair lichens break apart easily and spread from tree to tree on the strong mountain winds; snow fields often look like the floor of a barber shop hundreds of metres from the nearest source of lichens. They cannot tolerate being wet for long, though, and only grow well on open branches typical of older trees; there the wind can dry them quickly after misty rain or snow. Witch's hair lichens are much stronger and don't break so easily. They therefore spread into new forests more slowly than horsehair lichens, especially at lower elevations where winds are not as strong.

Although hair lichens grow well in cool, moist forests, they are intolerant of prolonged dampness. The abrupt lower line of these common witch's hair lichens on the Mountain Hemlock trunks marks the winter snow depth.

greenhouse agriculture—they farm algae within their own bodies. The fungi provide a moist, nutrient-rich environment for the algae, while the algae use their chlorophyll to turn sunlight, air and water into sugar. When deep snow blankets the ground, Caribou in the mountains of southern British Columbia depend on these tree lichens for their winter sustenance.

Shrubs and Flowers

A forest, of course, is much more than a collection of trees, and spruce forests are home to many other plants. The understorey of the forest can tell you a lot about the local conditions. The commonest shrubs of the boreal forest are Highbush-Cranberry and Prickly Rose; in moist, rich sites these are joined by jungles of Black Twinberry and Red Swamp Currant. Northern woodland flowers are abundant in mature, open forests—look for carpets of the rounded leaves of Twinflower and get down on your hands and knees to smell the delicate, bell-like flowers. Bunchberries indicate areas of nitrogen-poor soil, whereas the delicate runners of Trailing Raspberry indicate moist, nitrogen-rich sites.

In the mountain forests of southern British Columbia Black Huckleberry, White-flowered Rhododendron and False Azalea are important parts of the understorey. The rhododendron's branches sweep downhill to lie flat under the heavy burden of winter snow, but to any hiker trying to bushwhack uphill in the summer they can be an impenetrable tangle, giving this shrub its alternate name, mountain misery. False Azalea has the loose whorls of leaves

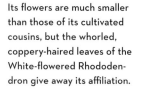

Its flowers are much smaller than those of its cultivated cousins, but the whorled, coppery-haired leaves of the White-flowered Rhododendron give away its affiliation.

OF MOOSE AND MOSS

One of the most remarkable plant-animal interactions in the boreal forest involves a strange group of mosses in the genus *Splachnum*. In an environment where nutrients are hard to find, these plants have come up with a novel solution—they grow almost exclusively on Moose droppings! Most mosses produce small, rather inconspicuous sporophytes—stalks bearing a capsule full of dustlike spores. The spores are shaken out of the capsule like salt out of a salt shaker and then blown through the forest on the wind. That works fine if the moss isn't too choosey about where it grows.

Splachnum has come up with another adaptation that helps ensure that its spores land on Moose dung. Its capsules are expanded outwards like small parasols, which are attractive landing pads for flies attracted to the Moose dung. *Splachnum* also has sticky spores that get stuck on the feet of the flies and are transported to the next pile of droppings. A closely related genus, *Tetraplodon,* lacks the parasol landing pad but does have the sticky spores. *Tetraplodon* is usually found on carnivore dung or old carcasses of small mammals.

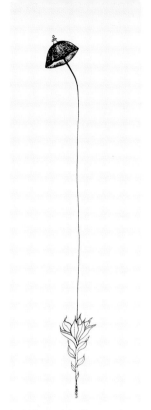

Splachnum

of the rhododendron-azalea group, but its flowers are tiny and bell shaped, like those of blueberries, and are an unusual copper colour.

The floor of dry, open, mountain forests is carpeted with the delicate green foliage of Grouseberry, Mountain Arnica and Western Meadowrue. In wetter areas, Oak Fern, Knight's Plume Moss, leafy mosses, Queen's Cup, Sitka Valerian and Rosy and Clasping Twistedstalks predominate.

Oak Fern

MUSKEG FORESTS OF THE NORTH

Trees

Black Spruce always looks like the poor cousin of the spruce family. This is the scrawny conifer of northern muskegs, generally growing thin and straight, with a clubbed top. It is found as far south as Blue River in the Monashees and Quesnel on the Fraser Plateau. Although it is generally associated with peatlands, in the north it often grows on well-drained areas, as Lodgepole Pine does. Black spruce has small, tough cones that squirrels find difficult to deal with. In addition to producing seed-bearing cones, this species can also reproduce by layering. As the lower, live branches become covered by moss, they put down roots and become trees of their own.

Black Spruce

Living with Black Spruce in the northern wetlands is Tamarack. Tamaracks, like other larches, are deciduous conifers; they lose their needles each fall. In the spring new, soft, light green needles reappear, adding a delicate touch to the muskegs. Despite usually living in cool, wet places, Tamaracks demand sunshine and do not grow in shady woods. They share this habit with Lodgepole Pine and, indeed, both trees are common post-fire colonists on sunny, sandy and gravelly soils.

Tamarack

Biting Flies

Nothing links humans with the insect world more effectively than a cloud of black flies—except perhaps a single, whining mosquito in a bedroom at the first light of dawn, or maybe a gigantic horse fly circling a canoe. Our link with these flies is their desire to sip on our blood. Female black flies, mosquitoes, horse flies and biting midges all require blood meals to maximize their egg production; males do not need blood and are not attracted to humans.

After mating, the female mosquito begins her search for a blood meal, a search that may take her a number of kilometres from her birthplace. Carbon dioxide is the first clue she seeks, since all animals exhale it in quantity. Flying towards increasing concentrations of carbon dioxide, she then detects heat at relatively close range if the victim is warm-blooded, and finally she sees you. The most effective mosquito repellant, DEET, interferes with her detection of body heat.

After doubling or even tripling her own weight with a blood meal, the female retires to a sheltered place to allow her eggs to develop. When she has laid her eggs, she immediately seeks out another blood meal—and the cycle continues. In southern British Columbia, mosquitoes may be able to complete up to five egg-laying cycles in a season.

Mosquito

The larval stages of all these biting flies are associated with water. Mosquitoes prefer standing water, and depending on the species (there are forty-five in British Columbia), larval "wrigglers" can be found in a variety of ponds, marshes, bogs and even tree holes.

Black flies are smaller but chunkier than mosquitoes; they are usually grey or black, but one common group is bright orange. After they land, they scurry around looking for a good place to feed and usually settle on areas with thin skin that are somewhat protected, such as under a collar or at the base of a bushy beard. Because black flies use a "slash and lap" method of feeding and employ an effective anticoagulant, their bites are often very messy events, with blood flowing freely.

Black fly

Larval black flies develop in running water, explaining why a cloud of adult females may descend on you as you take a hiking break beside a clear mountain stream. In the stream the larvae glue themselves to rocks and use large brushes on their heads to filter out the tiny plankton rushing by.

The tiny flies known to most of us as no-see-ums are biting ceratopogonid midges. The adults are large enough to see but small enough to scramble through regular mosquito netting. Their bites are fiery and out of all proportion with the biter's size. The larvae are small, clear worms that live in a variety of aquatic habitats.

Horse fly

Horse flies and deer flies are at the large end of the scale of biting flies. These two closely related groups can be distinguished in several ways. Horse flies are larger, have clear wings and usually have iridescent stripes through their eyes. Deer flies are smaller, have dark marks on their wings and have iridescent spots on their eyes. Unlike mosquitoes, which prefer the warm, humid early morning and evening hours, horse flies and deer flies thrive in the hot sunshine of midday.

FORESTS OF FIRE

Drifting in on a warm evening breeze, the sweet, soft smell of a forest fire is one of the scents of summer in the Interior of British Columbia. Spectacular summer thunderstorms are common, and the lightning bolts flashing out of the sky start thousands of fires each year. Most of these conflagrations remain small, but some grow to a considerable size, burning thousands of hectares; all do their part to create a complex and dynamic forest. In fact, old-growth spruce forest in the Interior can be scattered and rare, and the fire succession forests of Lodgepole Pine and Trembling Aspen are much more common.

In the early part of this century, fires swept unchecked through the cold forests of British Columbia at an unnaturally high rate—fires accidentally set along new railway lines or started by prospectors to find patches of bedrock hidden by the forest. Vast tracts of old spruce and fir were vaporized and replaced by young Lodgepole Pine forests. Although most of these pine forests would eventually grow back over the centuries into spruce and fir, modern logging practices have changed the natural order of succession. And although the old spruce forests and the young forests of fire are adapted to the same harsh winters, they are very different forests.

Lodgepole Pine

Lodgepole Pine is well equipped to take advantage of a fire, since many of its cones are sealed with resin, remaining tightly closed until they are opened by intense heat. After the fire roars through the forest, a rain of tiny, spinning pine seeds floats to the ground, which has just been conveniently fertilized with ash and cleared of brush, grass and other competitors. If a fire doesn't occur, the sealed cones remain on the tree's branches, and some are eventually enveloped by the bark and wood of the growing tree. The seeds in these embedded, sealed cones can remain viable for at least 150 years. Lodgepole Pines also produce cones that open as soon as they mature, so the species can also colonize open areas where fire has not occurred.

In the bright sunlight of the fire meadows, the young pines grow quickly. If too many seedlings grow up, however, they form an amazingly thick forest of straight, skinny trees—called a dog's hair forest—and their growth can be slowed and stunted. Sometimes trees a little over a metre tall can be seventy years old. Over the years, most of these trees are shaded out by faster-growing individuals and die and fall, creating a tangle resembling a pick-up-sticks game. The surviving pines are tall and slim—they can be 15 metres tall but

Lodgepole Pine

only 15 centimetres in diameter! Between the slender logs, spruce and fir seedlings grow quietly in the cool, humid shade and after a couple of hundred years overtop and replace the sun-loving pines.

In the dry, western Chilcotin Plateau, in the rain shadow of the Coast Mountains, only a minor amount of spruce regeneration occurs, and older Lodgepole Pines form open, sunny forests. The forest floor there is blanketed with the shiny evergreen leaves and bright red berries of Kinnikinnick, a soft cushion of haircap mosses and feathermosses, and a lush mat of lichens, particularly Reindeer Lichen. In some areas, Soopolallie bushes provide abundant fall food for bears and other berry-loving animals.

Lodgepole Pine has two common parasites, which often catch the eye of naturalists. The most obvious are the large galls found on the trunks of young pines or the branches of older trees. Like the witches' broom on spruce, these are caused by a rust fungus, the Western Gall Rust. The galls take two to four years to mature, after which orange spores appear on the surface of the gall. The spores are blown by the wind through the forest and, unlike most other rusts, which require an alternate host, directly infect other pines. Western Gall Rust rarely kills the pine, but galls on the trunk are a major source of weakness and the trunk often snaps at this point before the tree reaches maturity.

A less obvious parasite, but one with a greater impact on the health and growth of the pine, is the Western Dwarf Mistletoe, a tiny, yellow-green leafless plant growing on the pine branches. The mistletoe roots burrow into the branch to steal sugars, water and other essential nutrients from the host tree, reducing its vigour, but they usually do not kill the tree. Mistletoes are flowering plants that produce berries with sticky seeds. Dwarf mistletoes disperse their seeds in an unusual way. When the single-seeded "berries" are mature they drop from the stalk, and at the same instant the skin around the seed splits open and contracts violently. This propels the seed at speeds of up to 80 kilometres an hour, much as a moist orange seed or cherry pit will if squeezed between the fingertips. In this manner seeds can infect branches up to 10 metres away. You can see that mistletoe can spread much more easily in young, dense stands of pine than in thinned stands where trees are much farther apart.

One of the most important forces directing the logging industry on the plateaus of central British Columbia for the last twenty years has not been catastrophic fires or the near extinction of old-growth forest but a tiny insect named the Mountain Pine Beetle. Although its scientific name suggests that it enjoys Ponderosa Pines as well, this beetle really thrives on the vast monocultures of Lodgepole Pine carpeting the province's Interior. It also thrives on climate change, since it booms in long, hot summers and is checked only by bitterly cold winter weather.

Opposite page: **Young Subalpine Firs and Engelmann Spruces grow among the straight trunks of a Lodgepole Pine pioneer forest.**

Adult beetles go on the attack in July and August, searching out mature pines, preferably greater than 25 centimetres in diameter. They bore through the thin outer bark into the nutritious cambium beneath. The tree immediately fights back by exuding copious pitch, but only the most vigorous of trees growing in ideal conditions can withstand a concerted attack by many beetles. Infested trees show pitchy holes by late summer and reddening foliage by spring. As the beetles chew out egg chambers in the cambium, they bring with them spores of Bluestain Fungi, and the combination of voracious beetle larvae and fungal infection girdles and kills the tree. Next summer, the larvae mature and emerge as adults, which fly off to look for more suitable trees. In the British Columbia Interior such trees are rarely far away.

A dwarf mistletoe parasitizing Lodgepole Pine.

When they begin feeding in a tree, the beetles release pheromones, simple volatile chemicals that attract other beetles, and so another pocket of infestation begins or a small infestation becomes larger. When the tree becomes crowded with beetles, the males emit another pheromone, which deters other beetles from landing.

Serious epidemics usually begin during drought periods when trees are stressed and summer temperatures are ideal for larval growth and end a decade or so later when a cycle of higher precipitation begins. In the middle of the dry 1930s, two biologists working for the British Columbia Provincial Museum reported: "Throughout the Chilcotin we found that bark-beetles had attacked the Pine to an alarming extent. The hillsides were covered with vast patches of the dying trees." The forests recovered over the next few decades, and then a series of dry years in the 1970s triggered another major outbreak. When we drove through the forests of the western Chilcotin in 1978, the scene was very similar to that described in 1935. This epidemic spread throughout the southern province, peaking in 1984 when more than 400,000 hectares of pines were infested.

But this epidemic was dwarfed by a more recent outbreak. After a period of warm winters and hot summers starting in 1996 and 1997, the beetle populations of the Chilcotin Plateau exploded again in 1999. In two years the beetles had affected 800,000 hectares of forest, and by 2003, the epidemic seemed unstoppable, with 4 million hectares damaged. Summers continued hot and dry, and cold winter weather never came. As of 2012, the Mountain Pine Beetle had killed more than 18,300,000 hectares of Lodgepole Pines, or more than five times the area of Vancouver Island. The infestation peaked in 2005, and the rate of spread is now slowing—the latest projections indicate about 57 per cent of the pine volume in the province may be killed by 2021, significantly less than the 80 per cent projected earlier.

Large pine beetle infestations speed up the succession processes in most forests. Young firs and spruces, released from the shade of the pines, grow quickly into a climax forest. In dry forests where Lodgepole Pine is the climax species, such as forests in parts of the western Chilcotin, infected stands quickly produce more mature Lodgepole Pines for the beetles to attack, so epidemics can be more damaging and long-lasting. Outbreaks can enhance the diversity of these forests, though, by creating a mosaic of unevenly aged stands.

The forest industry, however, is unwilling to wait for the fir and spruce forests promised by widespread beetle attack. Immediate harvest has been the usual way of dealing with pine beetle infestations, resulting in the largest clearcuts in the world in parts of the Fraser Plateau. Unfortunately, these large clearcuts usually grow back into monocultures of Lodgepole Pine, gunpowder for a new beetle explosion.

New techniques using pheromones to capture or at least divert beetles searching for new trees are effective on a small and short-term scale, but as long as huge areas of the province are covered with dense stands of Lodgepole Pine, the Mountain Pine Beetle will continue to flourish. Silviculture practices that produce a high diversity of tree species and ages are the best way to reduce pine beetle epidemics. Careful thinning of uninfected pine stands, for instance, speeds the growth of spruce and fir seedlings, produces vigorous pines and increases wind flow to disperse beetle pheromone trails.

Mountain Pine Beetle

Aspens

In the autumn, the northern forests are a patchwork of dark green conifers and blazing yellow and orange Trembling Aspens. As its flickering, golden leaves seem to signify, the aspen is another tree of fire. Like its poplar relatives, aspen is a fast-growing, short-lived tree; few individuals are more than a hundred years old. Like most western deciduous trees, aspens need full sun to grow. The fluffy, buoyant seeds of aspen and other poplars are unusual in that they must germinate within a few weeks of hitting the ground. They cannot lie dormant like other plant seeds, waiting for proper moisture levels. Seedling aspens are therefore rare under normal conditions. A stormy summer produces just the germinating conditions aspens need— lightning fires open sections of the dark forest and occasional downpours water the seeds.

Like its other poplar relatives, however, the aspen usually propagates through suckers, and following disturbances such as fires it can reproduce in abundance in this way. Often extensive clones form, each originating from a single parent tree.

Aspens are valuable wildlife trees for several reasons. Moose and Elk browse their twigs and bark in winter, and aspens growing close to a pond are a favourite with Beavers. But aspens are especially favoured by woodpeckers. Most woodpeckers usually feed outside the aspen woodland—Pileated Woodpeckers in mature coniferous forests, flickers looking for ants on the ground in meadows, sapsuckers in willow and birch thickets—but they prefer to nest in aspens. Why? Most mature aspens are infected with heartrot fungus, and woodpeckers find that excavating a nest hole in an aspen is simply a lot less work than chipping away at some other tree.

Next time you are in an older aspen grove, look around and count the number of woodpecker cavities—several can usually be found in a few minutes. These homes are now available for squirrels, chipmunks, mice, small owls, swallows, bluebirds, wrens, chickadees, nuthatches, honey bees, bumble bees and the many other animals that use tree cavities for roosting and for rearing young.

Another inhabitant of aspens, the Forest Tent Caterpillar, can have a dramatic effect on these forests. In 1974 I was working in the Rocky Mountains of British Columbia. I arrived in late May as spring was in full sway, the aspens a beautiful pale green against the dark spruces and firs. But within a matter of weeks the beautiful wilderness scene quickly changed to one of apparent ecological disaster—every aspen leaf in the valley had been devoured by a swarm of millions of Forest Tent Caterpillars. The caterpillars, rather attractive on close inspection—black with blue and orange spots—were literally raining from the trees.

Local residents told me that tent caterpillars had devoured the aspen leaves the year before as well. I was amazed that the aspens had survived, but I soon found out how they did it. By July, the woods looked like early spring again—a flush of light green came over the white aspen branches as new leaves sprouted from the axils of the old leaf stems. The fat, mature caterpillars wove their small silken cocoons, many of which became food for chickadees and warblers. Those that survived soon emerged as small brown moths, equally attractive food items for warblers and vireos.

The following year, there were almost no Forest Tent Caterpillars in the Robson Valley. What had happened? Tent caterpillars, like the Douglas-fir Tussock Moth and the Spruce Budworm, have cyclic populations. Every eight to eleven years, tent caterpillar numbers increase to astronomic proportions for a couple of summers and then disappear over the next few years before mushrooming again a decade later.

Pages 224-25: In the fall, patches of genetically identical aspens can be easily picked out from the rest of the forest, since the trees within them all turn colour at the same time.

Trembling Aspen

LEAF MINERS

The Aspen Leaf Miner is a tiny white moth native to North America. Leaf mining is a popular way to make a living among some small moths and sawflies. For small caterpillars, eating a leaf from the inside out is a great way to eat as much as you want and not have to worry about getting eaten yourself. Mined leaves are filled with pale, sinuous tunnels that give infested aspen groves a silver colour rather than the normal deep green. The moths overwinter as adults and fly in great clouds on the first warm days of spring, when the leaves are in bud. Occasionally, the Aspen Leaf Miner population reaches outbreak proportions. In the far northwest, an outbreak began in Alaska in 2000 and has since spread through the Yukon and much of north-western British Columbia. Initiation of outbreaks is associated with a series of warm, dry summers. The end of the outbreak is difficult to predict; presumably, the natural control agents of the species— diseases, parasitoids—will be able to overwhelm the leaf miners at some point, perhaps with the aid of a hard frost in early fall or a cool, wet summer or two. Ongoing infestation doesn't usually kill the trees, but can result in a loss of growth and branch die-back. The Willow Blotch Miner is another small moth of the boreal regions that mines leaves, attacking most willow species. In this case, the mined leaves turn a blotchy brown, making it appear that the shrub is dying.

Aspen leaf tunnelled by a leaf miner caterpillar.

In the year of the decline, the caterpillars first appear healthy but soon become lethargic and then begin to die by the thousands. The cause of death, and perhaps the driving force of the entire cycle, is a disease agent called the nuclear polyhedrosis virus. Viral bodies on leaves are eaten by the caterpillar and replicate in the nuclei of the caterpillar's cells. Within a week or so, millions of viral bodies are produced and the caterpillar bursts, leaving a limp cadaver on the leaf and a huge number of viral bodies to spread the disease to other caterpillars. When most of the caterpillars are dead, the viral bodies have very few hosts in which to replicate, and outside their hosts, the viral bodies are slowly destroyed by ultraviolet light. A few viral bodies survive in shaded areas and after ten years or so begin to build up in the caterpillar population again as the moths start to multiply. And so the cycle continues.

WINTER IN THE SPRUCE KINGDOM

The primary story of these great forests of spruce, fir and pine is the story of winter. To fully understand them, naturalists cannot simply visit them at the height of summer when the meadows are in full bloom, tropical migrant birds sing in the trees, and insects swarm in the air. Winter is the time of reckoning here, and a midwinter trip to the spruce forests reveals many of the factors that shape them.

Animals of Winter

Winter is a quiet time in the mountain forests. Often the only sounds heard over the trees creaking in the cold wind and the trickling of ice-bound brooks are the croaks of a lonely raven and the occasional twitters of a roving band

FITTING IN

Most of the birds that escape the cold winters of North America each year for the balmy tropics don't go as far as you might think. Most stop in southern Mexico and Guatemala, and a few make it to Costa Rica—the tropical forests of South America are the major destination of only about a half-dozen of British Columbia's species. But Central America is only a fraction of the size of North America. How do most of the North American migrants fit into that small area, which is already teeming with bird life? The simple answer is that they haven't been gone long. Most of the birds that are with us in the summer—swallows, flycatchers, warblers and others—are really tropical species that dash north to breed. They take advantage of our long summer days, hordes of insects and lack of snakes to produce as many young as possible and then wing their way back home to Mazatlan and Monteverde. Their stay-at-home jungle neighbours simply don't have enough time to increase their numbers and take over the gaps vacated by the northern travellers.

Violet-green Swallow

of chickadees and kinglets. Gone are the buzzing insects and singing birds of the previous summer. The Elk have finished their autumn bugling, and the Bighorn rams have stopped bashing heads for another year. Winter is serious business here, and any animals that are active are working full-time to survive.

MON PAYS CE N'EST PAS UN PAYS, C'EST L'HIVER.
Gilles Vigneault, "Mon Pays"

Three-quarters of the birds have moved out. Half of the bird species, mostly insect eaters such as flycatchers, swallows, vireos and warblers, have gone to Mexico and beyond. Another quarter have made more modest journeys, some to California, some to the gardens of the Lower Mainland, others to the more temperate valleys of the southern Interior. The quarter that stay in the boreal forests, about twenty-eight species in all, belong to one of four loose categories: predators (hawks and owls), bark gleaners (woodpeckers, chickadees, nuthatches), scavengers (jays and ravens) and seed eaters (finches).

A male Red Crossbill searches for seeds in Ponderosa Pine cones.

Many of these winter birds will move out as well when food is scarce. Owls are forced south to find alternative prey if hare or vole populations have crashed, and if local forests are insect free, Hairy Woodpeckers will move into southern forests, searching for beetle infestations. For some species, availability of food is so unpredictable that wandering becomes a way of life; two rather bizarre species of finch, the crossbills, exemplify this nomadic lifestyle.

Crossbills are unique among the birds of British Columbia—the tips of their bills are crossed like the points of fine scissors. This feature, which looks as if it would hinder attempts to feed on anything, is an adaptation for extracting seeds from cones. In fact, crossbills rely on conifer seeds so heavily that they roam the continent in search of areas with good cone crops. One

year they might be the commonest bird species in British Columbia forests, and the next almost all of them are gone, feeding on spruce seeds in New Brunswick or pine seeds in Oregon. Where cone crops are heavy, crossbills can breed year-round; we have seen courting and nest-building pairs during our Christmas Bird Counts.

White-winged Crossbills are the smaller of the two species and specialize in spruce cones, so they are restricted to the boreal and subalpine forests of British Columbia. Red Crossbills feed on a wider variety of conifer seeds, and although their populations seem more predictable on the surface, recent research has revealed that there may be as many as six species of "Red" Crossbill in British Columbia, each specializing in a particular conifer species.

So why are their bills crossed? Craig Benkman of the University of British Columbia has shown that this unusual mechanism is needed to extract seeds from unopened, immature cones, an essential ability if crossbills are to eat conifer seeds year-round. Crossbills insert their closed bills between the scales of a cone and then pry the scales apart by moving the lower mandible sideways. When the gap is large enough, they extract the seed with the tongue.

Many of the birds of the boreal winter find enough food simply because they have personal storehouses. Chickadees wouldn't survive the long, cold winter if they didn't store insects, spiders and seeds in tree cracks all summer. Did you ever wonder what Gray Jays eat when there are no hikers or skiers around? The next time a pack of these jays (also known as whisky-jacks or camp robbers) discovers your campsite or picnic lunch, watch them—most of the time they don't eat the food right away but fly away with it to store it in a secure place.

Small birds like chickadees, nuthatches, creepers and especially the tiny Golden-crowned Kinglets, are faced with a life-threatening situation every winter night—freezing to death. Their small size forces them to use a tremendous amount of energy staying warm. Kinglets (which weigh only a fifth of an ounce) manage to keep their body temperature at 39° to 42°C all winter, even

Opposite page: A male American Three-toed Wood-pecker (identified by its yellow crown) flakes the outer bark off a spruce trunk in a never-ending search for bark beetles.

Below: This male Spruce Grouse shows the tail pattern—black with white-spotted coverts—typical of the mountain form of the species. This form is often called the Franklin's Grouse.

in –30°C weather. They feed all the short winter day long to get enough energy to survive the long winter night but would still die on a cold night if they didn't roost communally. Research has shown that kinglets reduce heat loss by 23 per cent if they roost in pairs and by 37 per cent if they sleep in a ménage à trois. So at the end of the day, a kinglet's number one priority is to find a sheltered spot and some kinglet friends to snuggle up with and conserve energy. This is why you never see a kinglet by itself on a winter day.

If you are out skiing or snowshoeing through spruce forests in the midwinter, look for woodpecker signs. Listen for quiet tapping and look for reddish trunks where American Three-toed Woodpeckers have flicked the grey scales of spruce bark away in their search for beetles just underneath. Often the red bark of infested trees stands out from a great distance, and bark scales litter the snow.

The characteristic grouse of these spruce forests is, not surprisingly, the Spruce Grouse. Blue Grouse hoot from the mountain meadows, and Ruffed Grouse drum from deciduous draws, but Spruce Grouse have the thick forests more or less to themselves. Like the Blue Grouse, the Spruce Grouse has two distinct forms in British Columbia. One is found east of the Rocky Mountains and across the northern edge of the province, and another is found on the central plateaus and mountains. How are they different? Types of grouse almost always differ in the tail, since the tail is the centrepiece of male display in most chickenlike birds, from peacocks to turkeys to Spruce Grouse. All male Spruce Grouse have a jet-black tail; in the eastern form it is tipped with a reddish-brown band. The mountain form—often considered a separate species, the Franklin's Grouse—has an entirely black tail, but the tail coverts are tipped with white, producing a spectacular spangled effect when the tail is fanned in courtship.

There are differences in the courtship itself as well. Eastern Spruce Grouse males attract females with a loud, fluttering flight up to a favourite branch. Franklin's Grouse do the same but add a distinctive touch to the descending flight. Halfway to the ground, the male throws his wings over his back and cracks them together twice, producing a loud *clap, clap* sounding just like some very short but enthusiastic applause in the quiet of a spring dawn in the mountains.

Spruce Grouse spend the winter in a quiet, retiring manner up in the trees, patiently eating the fresh needles produced in the last summer. Grouse will often pick the same tree to feed in year after year—studies in the Yukon show that these favoured trees seem to be among the most productive spruce in the vicinity, despite the continuing depredations of grouse. The needles of these trees are apparently more nutritious than the others, and the piles of grouse droppings that build up underneath them help keep them nutritious. Look for large trees with lots of needles missing near the branch tips.

Although a few mammals of the boreal forest hibernate and others live on stockpiles of food, most survive the winter just by getting by—remaining active, continually searching for food and always losing weight. For large herbivores such as Moose, times are hard because the nutritious green food they lived on all summer is gone; the plants are covered by snow or ice or have sent many of their nutrients into their root systems. Moose rely almost totally on shrubs and trees at this time, browsing the relatively nutritious twig tips from the previous season's growth. To reduce metabolic costs in winter, they lower their body temperatures somewhat, but despite this strategy their food intake is about 30 per cent less than that needed to maintain their body weight.

When you are out on your summer hikes, look for signs of browsing—willows and smaller shrubs often are obviously well pruned. Since Moose don't look under the snow for food, conifers sometimes have a skirt of snow-protected branches below an empty break; the height of the skirt tells you the depth of the winter snow, and the height of the upper branches shows how high the long-necked Moose can reach. By looking closely at the clipping points on the old branch tips, you can guess what animal did the browsing—Snowshoe Hares make neat diagonal clips, whereas Moose and other deer, lacking upper teeth, tear off the branches, leaving messy, frayed ends.

So winter is a time of weight loss for most animals—and malnutrition and frigid weather make individuals susceptible to many diseases. It is vitally important for animals such as Moose to enter winter healthy and fat. Many deer and sheep mate in the fall, however, and the males don't have time to eat much when

TRACKS IN THE SNOW

Skiing or snowshoeing across a fresh blanket of snow can be a revelation for the curious naturalist—everywhere there are signs of life in the seemingly lifeless winter surroundings. Tracks of animals that are so secretive they are rarely encountered face to face are there for all to see, and the stories of nocturnal encounters of predator and prey are spelled out on the snow. For this reason, biologists often use tracks to study the lives of animals they have difficulty studying directly. Tracks can be used to answer questions such as "What predators live in this forest? How common are grouse? How far does a wolverine travel? Where do lynx go? What do they eat?" If you wait a particular time after the last snowfall—say, two days—you can use tracks as an index of abundance of animals from time to time and from forest to forest.

Whose tracks are these? A Porcupine dragged its tail through fresh snow as it waddled by.

they are busy fighting other males and courting females. Consequently, it is the older, reproductively active males that are often most likely to die during winter.

Everyone knows that squirrels gather and store food for the lean winter ahead. In British Columbia forests, look for the middens of Red and Douglas' Squirrels—under certain conifer trees lie great heaps of cones, with tunnels leading into the core of the larder. Squirrels also gather mushrooms—look for their drying racks up in the branches of trees. Squirrels aren't the only animals that prepare for winter by storing food. Pikas, for instance, gather grasses and forbs in the height of summer and make hay piles for curing their winter food, and Beavers gather branches all summer and store them in their deep ponds for winter chewing.

In winter, most insects become inactive and spend the cold, dark months in some sort of hibernation. A few, however, are most conspicuous during cold, snowy weather, even in the high mountains or the far north of the province. In British Columbia, the two groups of snow-loving insects most commonly encountered are the wingless snow flies *Chionea* and the snow scorpionflies *Boreus*.

Snow flies are in the crane fly family but are much smaller than the garden-variety crane flies, and their wings are reduced to stubs. With slender but strong, arched legs, they look like slim spiders as they scramble over the snow (count their legs, though—there are only six!). The name *Chionea* comes from the Greek *chion*, meaning snow.

In the summer the larvae live in mammal burrows and forest litter, but little is known of their way of life. Experts speculate that unlike most of their vegetarian crane fly cousins, snow fly larvae are predators, feeding on various other small invertebrates. Adults seem to spend most of their life in mammal burrows, under rocks or logs, or in the forest litter in the narrow airspace beneath the snow. Under the snow they are well insulated from the cold, for sub-snow temperatures remain quite constant and close to freezing even when the snow cover is relatively thin. The adults usually appear on the surface of the snow only when the temperature is hovering around freezing and when the light is dim, such as at dusk or on a cloudy day. At these times, the surface temperature is relatively stable; if the temperature dropped suddenly, even these winter insects would freeze and die.

Snow scorpionflies in the genus *Boreus* are small, glossy brown or black insects that resemble minute grasshoppers with long snouts. The males have tiny, bristle-like wings with which they hold the females during mating; the wings of the females are reduced to just a pair of small scales.

Away from snow, *Boreus* are rarely seen, and are invariably associated with mosses, especially those that grow in low, compact cushions. It is curious that these snow-loving, moss-eating insects are British Columbia's only representatives of the predominantly tropical, predatory scorpionflies.

Opposite page: **The dominant trees of cold forests are spire-like to prevent them from becoming overloaded with snow, but even so the snow can load the trees heavily.**

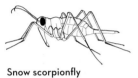

Snow scorpionfly

Caribou have broad hooves that double as snowshoes and snow shovels—in shallow snow they are invaluable in clearing snow craters to reach food.

Opposite page: **Snowshoe Hares** are familiar to most naturalists as the "rabbit" of the northern forests that turns white in winter. Basking in the April sun, this one is already showing signs of its brown summer coat.

Living with Snow

Snow can be a problem or a boon to big animals. Early in the winter, big falls of powder snow can be advantageous to animals like Moose, for their long legs can travel through it with relative ease, whereas predators such as wolves may flounder. As the snow develops a strong crust, however, the advantage swings over to the wolves, who can run along the top of the snow at speed whereas the Moose continually break through it. To combat this problem, Caribou have specially adapted hooves that spread out and essentially form small snowshoes—the ratio of their foot area to their weight (a foot-load index) is more than twice that of Moose. Caribou use their snowshoe hooves to move into forests high on mountain slopes, places that wolves shun since the snow there is deeper and stays soft much longer than in the valleys. By travelling in herds, Caribou can also share the task of moving through deep snow by taking turns leading and plowing the trail.

Mice and other small mammals live under the snow, which, like a thermal blanket, protects them against the severe cold above, though it may make food harder to find. Even in subalpine and alpine regions, temperatures in Deer Mice burrows hardly ever fall below freezing. The commonest mice of the spruce forests are the Southern and Northern Red-backed Voles, which subsist on seeds, fungi and lichens. They peak in population in years of bumper spruce cone crops, and at that time, Boreal Owls and Northern Saw-whet Owls congregate to feed on them. Hawks have a harder time finding mice hidden under snow, so most head south to the southern coast and valleys in winter. But owls stay behind and put their special talent to work—hearing. The Great Gray Owl can hear and catch mice under a half-metre of snow.

PREDATOR AND PREY: CONNECTIONS IN THE SPRUCE FORESTS

The Snowshoe Hare Story

I first ventured into the northern forests of British Columbia in the summer of 1980. Of my many memories of that summer, I most clearly remember the long days, the long roads and the abundance of animals—Snowshoe Hares almost constantly in view, bounding into the forest; dozens of lumbering Porcupines; a Lynx padding off into the aspens; families of just-fledged Great Horned Owls perched on roadside spruces in the long twilight; and, in the subalpine willows, ptarmigan literally everywhere. I returned to the same roads only three years later but found them almost empty of wildlife—I saw no Porcupine, no Lynx, one pair of owls, only one or two hares and a small flock of ptarmigan only after a strenuous hike into the mountains.

This boom and bust pattern in the populations of northern animals has long intrigued ecologists. Most of the species involved exhibit clear eight- to eleven-year cycles, and several apparently unconnected species show some synchrony in their cycles. The key to this puzzle—and one of the keystone species in the ecology of the entire boreal forest—is the Snowshoe Hare.

During the low portion of the population cycle, hares can be hard to find, with only about ten animals per square kilometre. This low phase lasts four or five years, and then the population begins to climb rapidly for two or three years, peaking at densities about fifty times that found in the low phase. Hares are literally everywhere at this point, the normally nocturnal animals feeding brazenly by roadsides during the day. Predators are everywhere as well, especially the hare specialists— Lynx, Great Horned Owls and Northern Goshawks. Other species also thrive during this period, perhaps taking advantage of the fact that most of the predators are concentrating on hares and temporarily disregarding burgeoning populations of grouse and ptarmigan. The large number of hares is usually maintained for two years, and then in the winter of the third year 95 per cent of the hares die and the population is at the low level again.

The two primary theories of the cause of the Snowshoe Hare cycle are intuitively obvious: (1) they eat themselves out of house and home, and eventually most starve to death, and (2) their predators are able to increase their own populations quickly and simply eat most of the hares. Or the cycle may be the result of a combination of the two factors. Several groups of ecologists have worked extensively on this problem, since it seems to be the key to understanding the ecological processes in the entire boreal forest. One group of scientists from the University of British Columbia and several other Canadian universities has been studying hares and other animals in the southwestern Yukon since 1977 and is beginning to shed light on this puzzle. In

AVALANCHES

Steep mountain slopes and deep snowpacks combine to create one of the most powerful forces that shape mountain forests—avalanches. The deep mountain snowpack is not a uniform mass but is built in distinct layers, each one laid down by a separate snowfall. These layers normally have different characteristics; new layers are usually soft, while old layers can have a hard, crusty surface and a loose, grainy interior. Some of these layers are bonded strongly to the layer below, but others are only loosely held.

Prolonged periods without new snow can create a layer of large hoar crystals on the snow crust, and hoar crystals provide a very poor bonding surface for a new layer of deep snow. Cold, dry weather can sublimate water out of the snowpack itself, slowly turning the firm snow into a thick layer of gravelly crystals, known as graupel, another possible source of weakness. As the snowfalls accumulate, the weight on each bonding surface increases. If the weight, or shear force, on a surface is greater than the bonding force, the slope will fail and a mountainside of snow will roar to the valley bottom.

Avalanches carry catastrophic power, and their tracks are easily visible at the height of summer—vertical, grass-green swaths through the dark conifers. Avalanche tracks are dominated by deciduous shrubs, especially alder, since these plants can regrow from sprouts if the main stem is snapped off by the avalanche. If a conifer trunk is broken off at the ground, the tree dies. Since most of the snow on avalanche tracks is swept to the valley bottom, these areas are often the first places where green grass and herbs appear in the spring. This new growth attracts hungry herbivores waking from their winter sleeps. Bears, ground squirrels and marmots are often seen on avalanche slopes in early spring.

An avalanche roars down a slope in the Rocky Mountains.

areas where hares were fed extra food and protected from predators to some extent, high numbers persisted as the population crashed all around; populations given extra food but not protected crashed as well. So it seems that predators play a key role in reducing the hare population, and this role is probably enhanced by the reduction in food supply.

The Yukon study has also provided surprising new data supporting an old but often challenged theory—that there is a connection between hare numbers and sunspots. The hare cycle can be detected for two hundred years or so in the past by examining cores from trees and counting the characteristic marks left by browsing hares in each year. Climatologists have cored even more ancient structures—the glaciers on the nearby St. Elias ice fields—and have discovered a ten-year cycle in precipitation. This cycle not only matches that of the hare cycle but lines up surprisingly well with records of sunspot activity kept for hundreds of years by European astronomers. Most intriguing of all, cycles in which sunspot activity changed only moderately fell out of

phase with the hare cycles, whereas strong sunspot cycles matched those of the hares exactly. Could sunspot activity affect rainfall patterns, which in turn could affect plant growth, which could boost the hare population to unusually high levels?

Boreal Owl

BOOM, BUST AND OWLS

Boreal Owls, like many hawks and owls, specialize in eating meadow mice, or voles. These mice have four-year population cycles, similar to those of lemmings.

Recent research has revealed that Boreal Owls have some remarkable breeding strategies. Older Boreal Owls, which have gone through one boom-and-bust cycle of mouse numbers, put a tremendous effort into raising young the first year that mouse numbers begin to climb, even though the rodents are still rather uncommon then. The following year, when mice are everywhere, the older owls relax and raise fewer young. Younger, less experienced owls raise large broods at the peak of the mouse cycle, only to have their young starve the following winter as mouse numbers crash.

Lovers of willow thickets created by wildfires and logging, Moose have prospered in the last few decades.

Connections between Caribou, Moose and Wolves

The web of life connects the inhabitants of the mountain forests in many ways, but there are few more dramatic connections than those between big predator and big prey. Moose were rare in central British Columbia at the turn of the twentieth century. Wolves hunted small herds of Caribou and what Moose they could find before the fires and logging of the past century produced vast areas of prime Moose habitat. As the Moose population soared, the wolf population climbed as well.

So who are the losers in this race? The Caribou, of course. Wolf populations are now much higher than they have been for years, and although they dine on Moose, they continue to take Caribou whenever it is convenient. The Caribou now suffer more wolf predation than ever before, and the same fires and logging that benefited Moose have shrunk the old-growth mountain forests, the critical winter habitat of Caribou. Although Caribou hunting has been curtailed, many herds around the province have greatly declined.

The problem facing wildlife managers is whether or not to try to help solve the problem using predator control. Wolf kills have galvanized protests by environmental groups, and some biologists question their effectiveness. Moose, the unknowing wild card in this hand, continue to support wolf populations.

MONTANE FORESTS

MONTANE FORESTS

O N THE LOWER PLATEAUS and mountain slopes in the lee of the Coast, Cascade and Columbia Mountains lie warm, open forests of Douglas-fir and Ponderosa Pine. These are transition forests between cold and wet and hot and dry, with thick forests and deep snowpacks above and cactus-studded grasslands below. The grassy, flowered floors of these transition forests, called the montane forests, invite exploration on foot, and we have spent much of our lives wandering the Interior hills, listening to the sharp squeals of chipmunks on hot afternoons and the rich, rambling songs of Townsend's Solitaires above the open canopy at sunset.

Like the Douglas-fir forest of the coast, the montane forest is a benign environment. Snow covers the ground in winter, but only for two or three months; summers are hot and dry but not as parched as in the lower grasslands. As in other Interior forests, the dominant force shaping both Douglas-fir and Ponderosa Pine forests is fire.

THE DOUGLAS-FIR FOREST

Descending the eastern slopes through subalpine forests, the hiker first encounters the thick, grooved bark and square tops of veteran Douglas-firs on south-facing ridges. This is a green forest, its floor swathed in bright Pinegrass and its branches glowing with the almost luminous chartreuse Wolf Lichen.

Isolated by substantial mountain ranges and adapted to more continental conditions, the Interior variety of Douglas-fir is a slightly different tree from that of the coast. Its needles have more of a bluish cast than the deep green foliage of the coastal tree, and it is much more tolerant of shade and cold. Its longer taproot also enables it to grow successfully in the dry Interior valleys.

Many Interior Douglas-firs show signs of dwarf mistletoe attack, and perhaps more than any other conifer, they react to this parasite by producing large, conspicuous witches' brooms of dense, tangled branches. These growths can reduce the vigour of the tree but rarely kill it and incidentally provide nesting platforms for large hawks, ravens and owls.

Fire and Firs

Douglas-fir has quite a different fire survival strategy from Lodgepole Pine. Rather than broadcasting millions of tiny seeds and dominating the next forest by sheer numbers of seedlings, older Douglas-firs protect themselves with a thick armour of bark. This armour, a corky layer up to 15 centimetres thick, allows the large trees to survive most ground fires and dominate the succeeding forest as scattered veterans.

In the drier parts of the zone, Douglas-fir cannot easily propagate in open, sunny conditions. So in most montane forests south of the Cariboo Plateau, Ponderosa Pine is the fire pioneer species. In the relatively moist conditions of this zone, Ponderosas grow to great sizes in open woodlands, their thick, red trunks dwarfing those of their relatives on the arid slopes below. But pine seedlings are not well adapted to the cool shade that their parents have created and are less efficient photosynthesizers than Douglas-firs that are given adequate moisture. So if fire does not intervene, Douglas-fir seedlings eventually spring up in dense, green thickets beneath the canopy of veteran Ponderosas. These woodlands of huge Ponderosa Pines and Douglas-firs are to me just as spiritually uplifting as the majestic old-growth forests of the West Coast. The sense of warmth, openness, light and space among the big trees invites you to wander among them and rejoice in life.

Below the true Douglas-fir Zone in the realm of the Ponderosa Pine and the Bluebunch Wheatgrass, Douglas-fir can still be found in certain places, growing large and vigorously. But these places are usually shady canyons, or where the Douglas-firs are on hot, sunny slopes, they are filled with boulders

Pages 242–43: Arrow-leaved Balsamroot flowers carpet the open, grassy floor of a Ponderosa Pine forest near Princeton.

Douglas-fir

FIRESTORMS

Humans have been inextricably linked with fire since the dawn of humanity. We may not often ponder our relationship with fire, but recent summers of devastating wildfires in the southern Interior of British Columbia have brought that ancient connection to prime-time news and banner headlines.

Fire ecologists divide forest fires into two main types—low-intensity, or stand-maintaining fires, and high-intensity, or stand-destroying fires. Low-intensity fires generally occur in fall and spring, burning low on the forest floor, killing small trees, shrubs and dry grass but leaving large, live trees to create an open, parklike forest of Douglas-firs or Ponderosa Pines.

High-intensity fires happen at the height of summer, when the forest is tinder dry and the humidity is low. Ignited by lightning or a careless human, they quickly leap off the grass and brush and into the tree crowns. Afternoon winds, common on hot summer days, send them roaring through the forest, killing almost everything in their path, leaving a moonscape of black snags and white ash.

Evidence from tree rings and historical sources suggests that low-intensity fires were once common events in the dry forests of British Columbia, burning any given patch of woodland every five to thirty years until the late 1800s. After that date, low-intensity fires essentially vanished from the

Catastrophic fires at the interface between cities and forests may become more common as drought periods lengthen and fuel loads build up from years of fire suppression. This fire burned open forest and grasslands on the edge of Penticton in 1985.

forests of western North America. Why? Fire suppression in the style of Smoky the Bear did not become effective until about 1940. Overgrazing by cattle, which were brought into British Columbia valleys by the thousands in the 1860s and 1870s, may be part of the reason, as the cows ate most of the grass that helped fuel these ground fires. But more and more evidence links historical low-intensity fires to the environmental management practices of aboriginal people.

The indigenous peoples of the British Columbia Interior regularly used fire as a tool to create habitat for berry-producing shrubs in high-elevation forests and to enhance habitat for other food plants, such as Arrowleaf Balsamroot and Spring Beauty. Indigenous peoples used fire to create game animal forage and also to protect their own villages from high-intensity wildfires. Some bands had families who were the firekeepers for the village, directing the time and place of annual burns. Large fires, to clear off a mountainside or valley, were set in the late fall when the lowland grass was still dry but the first snows would keep the fire from spreading into thick forests at higher elevations. Smaller fires were set in spring for more specific situations. Areas were burned every three to fifteen years, depending on the fuel load in the forests and the desired result—berry patches, for instance, were usually burned more often than open forests. In the latter half of the nineteenth century, indigenous peoples were confined to reservations and their traditional practices severely disrupted.

High-intensity fires, on the other hand, continued unabated until fire suppression efforts significantly dampened their frequency in the middle of the twentieth century. Early logging quickly removed most of the large, fireproof trees from the landscape, and the forest filled in with thick stands of young trees and a shrubby understorey. In these dry forests, organic material does not decay very quickly, and the production of leaves and branches vastly exceeds the decomposition rate. Fuel loads, in the form of dead branches, shrubs and grass, quickly build up. Without periodic ground fires to clear away this fuel, the forest is soon ready for a major firestorm.

So what can we do? Prescribed burns are being set more frequently by forest managers to alleviate the problem, but in many areas there is simply too much fuel in the forests to safely do this. Careful removal of lower branches, small trees and shrubs must be done mechanically before fire can be used to complete the job. These projects can be expensive, but generally cost only a fraction of the amount spent fighting a major forest fire, to say nothing of the economic loss caused by such a fire. Public concerns about air quality during prescribed burns and fears about runaway fires must also be addressed, but the greater fear of seeing whole communities razed by fire may allow land managers to reintroduce fire as the important ecological tool it was to indigenous firekeepers for centuries.

Whatever we do, these firestorms will likely increase in frequency and intensity over the next few decades as climate change brings longer, hotter summers. The fires will be the agents of long-term change in these dry forests, turning Ponderosa Pine forests into grasslands and Douglas-fir forests into Ponderosa Pine woodlands. For the hot summers not only bring fires, but also make it difficult or impossible for young trees to germinate from the ashes. The area of British Columbia climatically amenable to these forest types is predicted to double by 2050, but how quickly the forests themselves will change is difficult to assess.

and talus. In these places, the rocks act as umbrellas, sending the meagre rainfall to the cracks between them, where the shallow roots of the Douglas-firs have an easy time imbibing the runoff.

Larch Forests

In the wetter parts of the Interior Douglas-fir forest—the Kootenays, the southeastern Shuswap and the eastern Okanagan Highlands—another tree dominates the forests after fire. Western Larch is a seral species, one that germinates much more successfully on ground that has been cleared by fire or mechanical means than on uncleared ground. Young stands are often almost pure, but older larches are always growing with other tree species. Western Larches grow faster than any other local conifer in their first century of life, resulting in forests dominated by mature larches. Their inability to germinate well in shady, undisturbed ground means, however, that larch forests that escape fire or other disturbances for several centuries gradually become dominated by Douglas-fir, Engelmann Spruce or Subalpine Fir.

The Western Larch is one of the most beautiful trees in the province. Mature larch forests are open and parklike, carpeted with lush Pinegrass sprinkled with clumps of pink Fairyslippers and nodding Tiger Lilies. The huge pale reddish larch trunks, similar to those of Ponderosa Pines, contrast perfectly with their light green needles. Like all larch forests, these woodlands are most spectacular in fall, when the needles turn yellow against the blue October sky and then carpet the forest floor in gold.

Birds

As in other forests, many birds of the montane forest carry out their lives largely unseen from the ground below. One of the most colourful songbirds in the province, the Western Tanager, is commonest in this habitat, but the male's scarlet, black and gold plumage is hidden in the green treetops most of the summer. Cassin's Vireos and Hammond's Flycatchers are also common, but their presence is usually noticed only by people familiar with their songs.

The open trunks of the Western Larch make them a favourite with woodpeckers and other hole nesters—about one-quarter of the birds in larch forests fall into this category. It is common to find a big larch acting as a true bird apartment building—Mountain Chickadees near ground level, sapsuckers on the second floor, flickers higher up and the big, oval holes of the Pileated Woodpecker near the top. One of Canada's rarest woodpeckers, the Williamson's Sapsucker, is found most often in these forests in British Columbia. The handsome males are largely black with a red throat and bright yellow belly; the females are brown with a black chest patch. In fact, the sexes look so different that early biologists thought they were two species. It was

Western Larch

Opposite page: Fairyslippers deceive pollinating bees with their beauty—the exquisite flowers contain no nectar reward and are pollinated only by naive young bees.

only after several instances of "hybridization" were reported that someone realized the truth.

The old larches are also favourite nesting sites for Barred Owls and occasionally their big cousin, the Great Gray Owl. The abundance of woodpecker holes also makes larch forests a good breeding habitat for the tiny Northern Pygmy-Owl. This diminutive predator—little bigger than a sparrow—hunts during the day, looking for small forest birds as well as shrews, voles and large insects. Because it is diurnal, it lacks the two main owl adaptations for night hunting: a big, round face for sound reception, and soft, silent wings.

Mammals

South-facing slopes where old-growth Douglas-firs are interspersed with grassland and snow depths are low are important winter ranges for Elk, Mule Deer, White-tailed Deer and Bighorn Sheep. Deer particularly prefer to browse the new growth of Snowbrush, a common understorey shrub in these dry forests. Elk and Bighorn Sheep are grazers. Elk live where fires have created a mosaic of grassland and open forests; Bighorns are locally common where grassy benches are interspersed with steep escape terrain, usually rock cliffs.

The Yellow-pine Chipmunk is a ubiquitous mammal of the montane forest. Whereas most small mammals are cryptically coloured and strictly nocturnal, chipmunks' striped backs and faces, jaunty tails and hyperactive personalities make them conspicuous members of forest communities. Four species of chipmunks live in the province, all very similar in appearance. Besides the Yellow-pine, there is the Least Chipmunk, which is found in open habitats in the far north, along the spine of the Rockies and locally in the Selkirk Mountains. The Red-tailed Chipmunk is a rare denizen of the southern Kootenays, and Townsend's Chipmunk is a big, dull-coloured species of the coastal rain forests.

MOB PSYCHOLOGY

When a small bird discovers a pygmy-owl, it doesn't immediately dive for the nearest cover but almost always begins calling loudly and flying back and forth very close to the owl. This behaviour attracts other small birds, and soon a clamorous mob is pestering the little predator. Mobbing is a somewhat paradoxical behaviour, since it puts the birds doing it at risk and is often directed at rather inappropriate victims—for example, hummingbirds may mob a large owl that normally eats hares. There seem to be two main benefits to mobbing. One is the most obvious—if the chickadees and nuthatches harass the pygmy-owl long enough, it will eventually leave its neighbourhood. The second advantage is that if smaller birds can keep a predator in sight, it can't hit them from behind, as most predators like to do.

Mobbing is a learned behaviour—young birds won't attack another animal unless they have seen other birds doing it. This learning is often generalized by the young birds. After a few lessons with small owls that actually eat small birds, a hummingbird could become riled up by seeing the round face of a much bigger owl. Even the call of the predator is enough to trigger the response. Birders have learned this lesson as well, and imitating the call of a pygmy-owl is a great way to see close at hand small birds that are foraging quietly, hidden in the forest. A series of whistled *kook* notes given at a rate of one every two seconds will attract any small birds that know about pygmy-owls, and often the owl itself. Be careful with this power though—I still feel a little guilty about the time I called in a flock of Pine Siskins with a pygmy-owl call, only to have a pygmy-owl swoop down and pick off one of the siskins as it mobbed me.

Northern Pygmy-Owls are daytime predators of small birds and mammals.

Chipmunks live in underground burrows, usually dug at the base of a tree, where they bear their young and add to their storehouse of winter food. Some have separate summer homes, usually in an old woodpecker nest or other tree cavity. Chipmunks sleep most of the winter but not as deeply as their ground squirrel and marmot cousins. Since this light sleep uses up their fat reserves more quickly, chipmunks must wake up regularly in winter to refuel from their food pile.

Reptiles

Although they are not as attractive to reptiles as the hot grasslands of the southern valleys, Douglas-fir forests are home to several interesting species. Northern Alligator Lizards are common where talus slopes and woodpiles provide some shelter. Like many northern reptiles, female alligator lizards give birth to live young. The Rubber Boa, the only Canadian representative of

A Yellow-pine Chipmunk (right) meets its larger, look-alike cousin, a Cascade Ground-squirrel.

the boa family, is less often seen because it is strictly nocturnal. This small snake has a characteristically blunt tail that it waves over its coiled body when threatened. It uses this trick most often when consuming young mice; the frantic mother mouse repeatedly attacks the headlike tail while the real head is catching her young.

Garter snakes are the commonest reptiles in these forests. Predators of mice, birds, insects, amphibians and small fish, both the Common Garter and the Western Terrestrial Garter Snakes are often encountered in sunlit forest meadows. Garter snakes spend the winter underground in groups. The number of snakes in each group is usually quite small, but occasionally hundreds or even thousands of garter snakes will mass together in a hibernacula. In spring, the males emerge from the hibernacula first and wait near the entrance for a week or two for the females to come out. As each female emerges, it is entwined in a writhing mass of males competing for mating rights. Young are born live in midsummer.

PONDEROSA PINE WOODLANDS

For middle-aged coastal dwellers, the word *ponderosa* may bring forth images of *Bonanza* more readily than it does of the deep valleys of the southern Interior of British Columbia. The sunny, dry woodlands of aromatic pines are a different world from the cool, moist and dark forests of the coast.

Ponderosas are easy to identify—their orange, jigsaw-puzzle bark, long needles and large, egg-shaped cones are unlike those of any other British Columbian tree. Like many forest zones in the province, this one can be identified by smell too. On warm, calm days, Ponderosa forests fill with the sweet aroma of vanilla. For a stronger whiff, smell the bark itself—it contains pure vanillin, the same chemical as the popular flavouring.

Ponderosa Pine

LINING THE RIDGES OF THE SOUTHERN INTERIOR VALLEYS
IS A STRING OF TREES MUCH TOO WIDELY SPACED TO
BE CALLED A FOREST . . . THE TREE SPECIES THAT DOMINATES
THIS DRY, HOT LAND IS PONDEROSA PINE . . .
IT IS THE UNDISPUTED KING OF ITS ENVIRONMENT.
Cameron Young, *The Forests of British Columbia*

Ponderosa Pines form pure stands along the lower timberline of southern Interior valleys, just above the grasslands nestled in the rain shadow of the Coast Mountains and Cascade Range. There, the summer drought is intensified by high daytime temperatures, which hasten the evaporation of what little moisture is in the soil. Below a critical lower elevation, soils are too hot and dry in summer for tree germination, and the hillsides are covered with grasses and shrubs such as Big Sagebrush and Antelope-brush.

Just above this lower timberline, Ponderosa Pines are able to grow in conditions unfit for almost any other tree. Unlike most local conifers, Ponderosa Pines have a substantial taproot. A seedling may be only 7 centimetres high after its first year, but its taproot is over 50 centimetres long! The lateral roots of older trees can extend up to 46 metres from the trunk, and so open parklands with scattered Ponderosa Pines are underlain with an almost complete mat of pine roots. The seedlings can withstand ground temperatures of up to a sizzling 72°c, although substantial injury often occurs above 55°c. Shade or a series of relatively wet summers greatly increases the survival of seedlings at lower treeline.

Fire Forest

Young trees are susceptible to the grass fires frequent in this habitat, but after a tree has grown beyond the sapling stage it develops a thick bark that can withstand all but the most violent conflagrations. Indeed, large Ponderosa Pines seem to encourage ground fires by producing quantities of highly flammable fuel—old pine needles. Like all conifers, Ponderosa Pines shed their needles periodically. In the dry Interior climate the needles, filled with natural preservatives, decay very slowly, and a deep layer builds up under older trees. This layer can be so deep that as children we often used to build forts under old pines by piling needles into walls almost a metre high. In summer, this layer is tinder dry and the volatile chemicals in them are so flammable that any spark will start a ground fire.

The fire, fuelled as well by the dry grasses among the pines, clears the open forest of any small trees and shrubs that might be competing with the large pines for the precious water supply. The larger trees usually escape such fires with some blackened bark and can even survive more serious blazes that burn right through the bark on one side of the trunk and destroy up to half of the crown.

This regular cycle of fires creates a parklike landscape of large pines with an understorey of bunchgrass and flowers. Most of the plants in the understorey also grow in the grasslands found just below the pine forests. The creamy blossoms of Squaw Currants lure Calliope Hummingbirds north in April, just as the Red-flowering Currant blooms do for Rufous Hummingbirds on the coast. Saskatoon bushes bloom in April and bear sweet berries in early July. Some hillsides turn butter-yellow in early May when the sunflower-like Arrow-leaved Balsamroot blooms and Mock-orange blossoms fill the warm June evenings with the sweetest scent in the forests.

Ground fires in British Columbia Ponderosa Pine forests still occur regularly but are much rarer now than they were a century ago. Overgrazing by cattle has reduced the amount of dry grass fuel, and this reduction, along with modern fire suppression policies, has greatly limited the extent of fires in this zone. In the absence of fires, large, dense stands of young pines with little grass and shrub understorey are now common. These pines grow more slowly than those in open stands and are much more susceptible to pine beetle infestations. Some of these stands are now being thinned, increasing the vigour of the trees and making the woodland more attractive to wildlife of all kinds.

Ponderosa Birds

A number of animals, especially birds, are found only in and around Ponderosa Pines, probably attracted by the unique, open structure of both the trees and the forest. Perhaps the most characteristic bird species here is the Pygmy Nuthatch. Nuthatches use their sharp beaks to probe in the bark for insects, reach into ripe cones for seeds and dig nest holes in soft wood. Small bands of Pygmy Nuthatches, keeping track of each other with shrill, peeping calls, can be found wherever Ponderosa Pines grow in abundance and are almost never out of sight of their favourite tree.

Pygmy Nuthatches spend more time foraging out towards the end of branches than do their relatives, the White-breasted and Red-breasted Nuthatches, which forage primarily on tree trunks. Pygmy Nuthatches spend the summer searching for insects, storing excess food in the ample bark

Opposite page: A Rocky Mountain Wood Tick "questing" from a sagebrush. Although popular lore has ticks jumping from trees onto the heads of mammals, they actually get there by grabbing passing legs and climbing up. Check yourself thoroughly for ticks after a spring hike in the southern Interior; ticks should be removed promptly to prevent tick paralysis, a potentially fatal syndrome caused by a neurotoxin in the tick's saliva.

cracks of the pines. In winter, they are usually found in flocks of 20 to 50 birds and roost communally in tree cavities. Sometimes as many as 120 birds share one cavity. The ones on the bottom are so squashed by the late arrivals that they are forced to spend the night in torpor—an essentially breathless sleep akin to hibernation.

White-breasted Nuthatches are much bigger, the size of small sparrows, and have an all-white face and characteristic *eh-eh-eh-eh* call, somewhat like a short, soft chuckle. They too are largely restricted to Ponderosa Pine forests in British Columbia but are not quite as tightly bound to them as are Pygmy Nuthatches. The Red-breasted Nuthatch has a much more catholic taste in forests, and its *yank-yank-yank* call can be heard throughout the province.

Another bird partial to Ponderosa Pine branches is the White-headed Woodpecker. Unlike most woodpeckers, which drill holes in tree trunks to get at insects, the White-headed Woodpecker spends most of its time out on

POLYGAMY IN THE NIGHT

The commonest owl in Ponderosa Pine forests is the Northern Saw-whet Owl. These small owls, the size of a beer can and the colour of brown autumn leaves, spend the nights perched on low branches or shrubs, listening for the rustle of mouse feet in the dry grass. The meal they most often encounter is the Deer Mouse, an abundant nocturnal mouse with big ears, big eyes and a diet that encompasses anything edible.

In late winter, a male saw-whet finds a suitable nest site—a roomy woodpecker hole in a snag—and begins calling with a monotonous series of whistled toots to attract a female. By early March, he has usually succeeded, and the female settles in the nest to lay the eggs. Like the males of all owl species, the male saw-whet does all the hunting for the pair while the female incubates the eggs and broods the small young. If mice are easy to come by, the male can satisfy the female's hunger quite quickly and then spends the rest of the night whistling at the other end of his territory, hoping to attract a second mate. If he is successful, his real test of mouse-hunting ability comes a month or so later when he has two families of ravenous young to feed. One male in the south Okanagan Valley kept twelve young fed—six each in two nests only 200 metres apart!

A female Northern Saw-whet Owl peers from her nest, a hole excavated by a Northern Flicker in a Black Cottonwood.

the branches, gleaning insects from the needles and whacking open the big cones to eat the hefty seeds. This reliance on Ponderosa Pine seeds to make it through the winter may be the reason for the bird's rarity in Canada—the pines produce good seed crops only once every three to five years.

The Lewis's Woodpecker acts even less like a woodpecker than the White-headed. It looks like a small, glossy crow with a bright pink belly and is found in stands of large Ponderosa Pines, Douglas-firs or cottonwoods near grasslands.

Lewis's Woodpeckers peck wood only to dig nest holes or to store food; they spend most of the summer flying around catching insects like overgrown swallows or flycatchers. When cherries ripen in Interior orchards, Lewis's Woodpeckers often take a break from fly-catching to feast on fruit. In late summer they again break normal woodpecker protocol by gathering in small flocks and winging their way south to winter in the almond orchards of California.

After Dark

As the western sky fades from yellow to green to indigo, the Ponderosa Pine forest awakens to one of the liveliest natural nightlives in Canada. Animals unseen by day announce their presence as dusk falls. A fledgling Great Horned Owl lets out a startling *khheee-ik!* and is reassured by its father's *Hoo-hoo-hoo-HOOO!* which sets off a small pack of Coyotes yapping up the hill. A soft chittering followed by a scratchy thud on a nearby pine trunk signals the arrival of a Northern Flying Squirrel, beginning its nightly search for mushrooms, truffles and other tasty items on the forest floor.

Common Poorwills call their name—a rich, whistled *poor-will, poor-will*—from rocky hillsides, while the soft, ventriloqual *boo-boot* of a tiny Flammulated Owl emerges from the big pines and firs upslope. The poorwills fall silent quickly as dusk turns to black night, but the Flammulated Owl will hoot all night if it is searching for a mate. Both of these birds are insect specialists, the poorwills fluttering up from the ground to snap up large insects in their

BAT MATERNITY WARDS

The squeaking masses of bats that occasionally take up summer residence in attics are a special section of the bat community: they are all mothers and their children. The males lead solitary lives all summer, but females gather in maternity colonies to give birth in May and June. The large young—up to a third of their mother's weight at birth—usually stay at home, hanging from the rafters while their mother goes on feeding flights. By late summer they are strong enough to fly on their own, and in September the maternity colonies disperse, the bats returning to hibernation caves, sometimes several hundred kilometres away. There the females find males calling for them in the dark, and mating takes place with a minimum of courtship and absolutely no pair bonding. Since the young must be born in spring to survive, female bats use a rare technique to delay fertilization; they store live sperm all winter, feeding them at special cells in their uteruses.

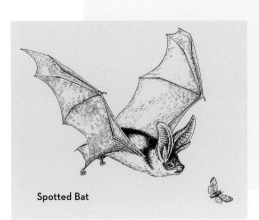

Spotted Bat

huge mouths and the owls snatching moths, beetles and crickets flying through the canopy of the big pines.

Overhead, a remarkable array of bats—more than ten species—forages for insects, their echolocation clicks unheard by human ears except for the descending buzz as they home in on and catch an unlucky moth. One species, the spectacular Spotted Bat, does produce clicks in our hearing range and can be heard most summer nights in the Ponderosa Pine forest—listen for a high-pitched *tsip-tsip-tsip-tsip* coursing overhead. Spotted Bats hunt in regular routes at treetop level around forest openings, and their huge ears and the low frequency of their echolocation call allow them to detect moths at great distances.

The loud buzzing of cicadas is replaced at night by the trills of ground crickets and the measured peeps of the tree crickets. Crickets sing by rubbing a file on one front wing over a scraper on the other. Each of the six tree cricket species that live in the southern Interior has a different song. Two call in measured chirps, whereas the other four give melodious trills, and each differs from the others in the pitch or frequency of the chirps.

Snowy Tree Cricket

Male Snowy Tree Crickets produce a loud chorus by synchronizing their chirps. This species is sometimes called the thermometer cricket because observers in eastern North America have calculated that the frequency of its chirps is directly related to temperature—you can get a good estimate of temperature in Celsius degrees by counting the number of chirps in seven seconds and adding five! Since there are a number of tree cricket species in British Columbia—and each has its own pattern of chirping—it's probably best to construct your own cricket thermometer by counting the chirp rates you hear over a range of temperatures. The crickets in my yard in Penticton (probably Riley's Tree Crickets) have a slower chirp rate than Snowy Tree Crickets, so to get the actual temperature in Celsius degrees, I count the chirps in ten seconds and add five.

GRASSLANDS

GRASSLANDS

MOST PEOPLE MAY not associate grasslands with British Columbia, which is known for its vast forests and towering mountains. But grasslands are born of mountains, forming in the rain shadow of high ranges. Behind the glaciers of the Coast Mountains and Cascade Range, fingers of the Columbia Basin work their way north into southern British Columbia, benchlands of bunchgrass and sagebrush amid the dark green conifers. To the history buff, this is the land of stagecoaches and cattle drives; to the naturalist, it means meadowlarks, mariposa lilies and rattlesnakes. Having grown up on a dry, grassy bench in the south Okanagan, to this day we are more at home with curlews and cactus than we are with slugs and redcedar.

From certain vantage points, these grasslands appear to stretch forever, but they are in fact quite restricted in British Columbia. Hugging the lowlands on the east side of the Island, Coast, Cascade and Purcell Ranges, they are sinuous golden islands in a sea of green forests; smaller outlying archipelagos dot the adjacent dry plateaus. In the far northeast, the grain fields of the Peace River parklands grow where the prairie grasslands once mingled with the edge of the boreal forest in the rain shadow of the Rocky Mountains.

Although they are not extensive, grasslands in British Columbia are surprisingly diverse. The most extensive are the bunchgrass steppes of the southern Interior, but there are also the Garry Oak meadows of southern Vancouver Island, the parklands of the Peace River country and the cold, mountain grasslands of the northern Rockies. All of these are quite different ecosystems. And within these broad divisions, there are many different grass communities—in wet and dry areas, in sandy and silty soils, and in grazed and ungrazed conditions. The diversity of grassland plant communities is paralleled by a diversity of animals, both vertebrate and invertebrate. The open nature of grassy meadows and their abundant and diverse forbs offer homes to many species of butterflies, wasps, bees and other sun-loving insects.

BUNCHGRASS STEPPES

The common feature over the dry intermountain valleys, or steppes, is bunchgrass. Bluebunch Wheatgrass and the other bunchgrasses it associates with are of northern origin; as the mountains rose in the north, they created the rain shadowed dry country in which these grasses evolved.

What is a steppe? A steppe is a cool, continental environment that is too dry for trees to thrive in. Grasses succeed in these harsh places because they have small, simple, ephemeral structures above the ground and huge, fibrous root systems below. Bunchgrasses also tolerate drought well because their leaves contain a great deal of dry support tissue—rather than wilting as orchard grass would, they just become dormant. The leaf bunches act as big funnels, gathering the rainwater from above and guiding it to their roots below.

The bunchgrasses of southern British Columbia are not affected by summer drought because they actively grow only in the late autumn and again as soon as the snow melts in late winter and spring. Growth is essentially over by mid-July. This absence of green summer forage in the dry intermountain valleys may explain the absence of Bison west of the Rockies. On the central Great Plains, the early summer is as moist as the spring, and the sod grasses the Bison fed on grow well into the summer.

The Lower Timberline

The fingers of grassland in the valleys of the Fraser and Columbia watersheds generally lie in the valleys and basins beneath the dry montane forests. The dividing line between the bunchgrass and the montane forest is the lower timberline, in many ways analogous to the alpine timberline. Lower timberline is determined by a combination of aridity, soil texture and the history of fires in the area.

Aridity is the consequence of a number of factors, including low precipitation and high evapotranspiration (the combination of water loss from direct evaporation and from transpiration through plants). In mountainous terrain, precipitation decreases and evapotranspiration increases as one moves down the mountain slopes. At the boundary between the lower stands of Ponderosa Pine and grassland, the hot summer sun pulls much more water out of the soil than rain puts in. These dry benchlands receive less than 30 centimetres of precipitation annually, and less than half of this precipitation falls during the growing season.

The bunchgrass steppes also experience extended periods of drought; that is, the rain in summer can come in showers separated by two or more weeks of hot, sunny days. Despite what some prairie farmers may tell you, the dry Interior of British Columbia has an even greater tendency towards drought than southern Saskatchewan. These long summer droughts can effectively eliminate tree seedlings from establishing new forest outposts in the grasslands. The hot summer sun of the open grassland can also kill tree seedlings directly by heating the soil surface beyond a critical temperature, about 55° to 70°C for Ponderosa Pines.

But if a few trees can become established out in the grasslands during a series of cool, wet summers, their shade can help new seedlings to survive by decreasing the rate of evapotranspiration. The soil around them will thus be cooler and less arid than in the surrounding grasslands. Single pioneer trees soon harbour clumps of small trees, the forest grows larger, and the lower timberline advances downwards into the grass.

THIS KIND OF ENVIRONMENT WAS OUR CRADLE,
THE MEETING OF FOREST AND GRASSLAND, THE DYNAMIC
EDGE, THE OPEN/CLOSED LANDSCAPE, THE ONE
OF TENSION, THE FIRE-MAINTAINED MOSAIC.
Don Gayton, *The Wheatgrass Mechanism*

Soil texture also plays an important part in determining the lower treeline. Fine soils like those on the silt benches of the Thompson, Okanagan and Columbia Valleys retain rainwater near the surface, but, paradoxically, this water retention does not help trees survive. Water held near the soil surface either evaporates or is absorbed by the fibrous grass roots before it can soak down to the level of the pine roots. Conversely, in gravelly or rocky soils, the water quickly drains below the grass roots to the level of the tree roots, where it will not evaporate.

Natural fires can, of course, eliminate the pine or fir forest, and succession from the resulting grassland back to forest can be exceedingly slow. Before fire suppression, fires occurred every seven to ten years on average in the grasslands of the Rocky Mountain Trench. Ponderosa Pine and Douglas-fir parkland has a grassland understorey that is essentially identical to the adjacent grassland; there the grassland is maintained by periodic cool fires that eliminate the small trees and shrubs that spring up in the shade of the veteran trees.

Ponderosa Pines or Douglas-firs could extend farther into these lower grasslands if a series of moist summers allowed the seedlings to get a good start and if fires occurred infrequently, allowing the seedlings to grow large enough to escape a quick, cool fire. In fact, this is just what is happening in the Rocky Mountain Trench, where, as a result of fire suppression, the forest has taken over about 30 per cent of the grasslands since 1960.

Sunny Slopes

In temperate mountainous regions, the direction a slope faces affects the vegetation that grows there. At British Columbia's latitudes, south-facing slopes receive sunlight much more directly than north-facing slopes and consequently are warmer and, because of greater evaporation, drier. Generally speaking, the steeper the slope, the greater the effect. On steep

South-facing slopes are sunnier, warmer and drier than north-facing slopes, as shown in this aerial view of Testalinden Creek near Osoyoos. If you get lost in the dry Interior of British Columbia, you don't have to see which side of the tree is covered in moss to find north—just look for the side of the mountain with trees on it!

south-facing slopes, grasslands can reach all the way to mountaintop tundra, whereas on steep north-facing slopes, mossy-floored forests can reach the valley bottom.

The Spring Bloom Wave

In spring, when the soil is moist from melting snow and spring showers, these grasslands are verdant with new growth and blossoming with wild-flowers. Like that of the subalpine meadows, the first bloom wave of the low grasslands features members of the buttercup and lily families. Sagebrush Buttercups brighten the brown, matted grass in March; they are followed by the Yellow Bells and shootingstars of April.

The real show begins in late April and early May when Arrow-leaved Balsamroots spread their brilliant yellow sunflowers across the green slopes. Flashy pink Bitterroot flowers appear as if by magic out of the ground, joined by swatches of another pink flower, the Long-leaved Phlox. In moister swales, the cream-coloured plumes of Meadow Death-camas carpet the grassland.

In June, the hills are splashed with the blue, yellow and red of Silky Lupines, Brown-eyed Susans and Scarlet Gilias. The Sagebrush Mariposa Lily, with its water-retaining bulb, is one of the few flowers that bloom into the hot, dry days of early July.

The main strategy of these perennial plants is to bloom and grow while there is enough moisture in the soil and then to withdraw the nutrients into the root system and wither away before the dry summer kills them. It is surprising how quickly a big, leafy plant like Arrow-leaved Balsamroot can shrivel to a few thin, dry stalks sticking out of grey leaf litter on the ground. Bitterroot takes this strategy even further. Its rosettes of fleshy, cylindrical leaves appear immediately after the snow melts and pump food into the thick, starchy root. By early May the leaves have completely disappeared and the flowers sprout out of the ground without any sign of green, as if the plant was some leafless saprophyte.

Most of these plants are found over a range of altitudes, and the bloom waves are delayed on the higher or north-facing slopes. One of the main advantages of being a naturalist in mountainous country like British Columbia is that if you miss a certain part of the bloom wave in the valley, you merely have to find a hillside where the flowers are still in perfect condition. On top of Mount Kobau near Osoyoos, Bitterroot is in full bloom in late July.

Small annual wildflowers like whitlow-grasses and Small-flowered Blue-eyed Mary also grow quickly, bloom and then wither, leaving only seeds to carry their genes through the dry months ahead. These seeds are programmed not to germinate unless the soil is soaked—usually after the snow melts in spring—but these plants are occasionally fooled by heavy autumn rains. In dry country like this, "annuals" may not appear annually— many wait patiently as seeds in the soil for a number of years for that one exceptionally moist spring.

One of the common strategies of the plants that keep their leaves through the summer is to cover them in hairs to reduce evaporation. Masses of small hairs give the leaves of Big Sagebrush, Common Rabbit-brush, Low Pussytoes and Silky Lupine a distinctly grey, silvery look.

The Grassland Communities

In the bunchgrass steppes of southern British Columbia, three distinct grassland communities are discernible to the naturalist who takes out a grass guidebook. These were formerly known as the Lower, Middle and Upper Grasslands, and although they have now been classified as a number of associations within the Bunchgrass, Ponderosa Pine and Interior Douglas-fir Biogeoclimatic Zones, it is probably simplest for us to leave them with their former names.

The Lower Grasslands are characterized by a hot and arid community of Big Sagebrush and Bluebunch Wheatgrass. This community, commonly called a shrub-steppe by ecologists, occupies the bottom of the Thompson and Okanagan Valleys, usually below 500 metres elevation. It is the home of such Great Basin specialties as Brewer's Sparrows, Sage Thrashers, White-tailed Jackrabbits and Nuttall's Cottontails. It is also characterized by the pungent scent of sage after a warm rain and the clear song of Western Meadowlarks. Compared with the Upper Grasslands, the shrub-steppe is poor in wildflower species.

In the Middle Grasslands, the vegetation is dominated by Bluebunch Wheatgrass and Sandberg Bluegrass—Big Sagebrush is essentially absent, but Common Rabbit-brush, Prairie Sagewort and Junegrass are important secondary species. Look for these grasslands in places like the Nicola Valley or on north-facing slopes down in the main valleys.

The Upper Grasslands lie above about 800 or 1000 metres elevation, on mountainsides and plateaus in southern British Columbia. Bluebunch Wheatgrass is still an important component, but various species of fescues usually dominate the cover. Like wheatgrass, the fescues grow in bunches, but the clumps are more compact and closer together. These grasslands are moister than the Lower and Middle Grasslands and are usually much richer in wildflowers. Nuttall's Larkspur, a beautiful but poisonous wildflower, is widespread, as are Silky Lupine, Scarlet Gilia, Narrow-leaved Phacelia and Parsnip-flowered Buckwheat. In the Cariboo and Chilcotin Plateaus, Bluebunch Wheatgrass and needlegrasses dominate the upper grasslands and fescues are absent.

Bluebunch Wheatgrass

Sandberg Bluegrass

Junegrass

Needle-and-thread Grass

Cheatgrass

Rough Fescue

The "Pocket Desert"

The sandy, dry benchlands of the south Okanagan Valley have often been referred to as Canada's Pocket Desert. This area certainly looks like a desert—the sandy hills are dominated by the dark, angular shapes of Antelope-brush, abundant patches of Brittle Prickly-pear Cactus and sparse clumps of Red Threeawn and Bluebunch Wheatgrass. Antelope-brush is found south to northern Mexico, linking the Okanagan with the high plateaus of Arizona and Sonora.

Although the desert appellation may be good for attracting tourists, technically this area is not a desert. First, it is simply not dry enough, with annual precipitation averaging over 300 millimetres—deserts are generally defined as receiving less than 250 millimetres. Second, it is too cold—the mean annual temperature of 10°C is lower than the minimum 12°C for true deserts. Climatologists instead refer to this region as a mid-latitude steppe. Narrow valleys closer to the Coast Mountains, such as the Similkameen and lower Nicola, are actually much drier than the Okanagan, with only 200 millimetres of precipitation per year, but are even colder in winter.

Desert or not, the south end of the Okanagan and Similkameen Valleys is a special place. About a third of British Columbia's rare or endangered plants and animals make their home there. Birders come from all over the continent to see the special birds of the grasslands and the dry pine forests. And the invertebrates are unusual too—a recent collection of wasps on the sand benches north of Osoyoos netted thirty-five species, thirteen of which were previously unknown to Canada.

Pages 268–69: Although the waxy flowers of the Brittle Prickly-pear Cactus don't produce a show on a grand scale, they are individually spectacular—look closely in June on sunny, sandy hillsides for mature cactus clumps and you will be rewarded with gorgeous yellow flowers, produced one per day.

Opposite page: Desert Nightsnakes are rare, nocturnal denizens of the dry rocky hillsides of the south Okanagan and Similkameen Valleys where they specialize in hunting small reptiles and amphibians.

THE SPACE BETWEEN: THE CRYPTOGAMIC CRUST

True to their name, bunchgrasses grow in discrete bunches, and the ground between them appears relatively free of life—until you look closely. Connecting the grass clumps and mantling the soil of undisturbed grasslands is a fragile organic layer of lichens, mosses, liverworts and cyanobacteria—collectively called cryptogams. Despite its relative obscurity, this cryptogamic crust is a critical part of bunchgrass ecosystems. It stabilizes the soil, restricts establishment of weedy species and helps to retain soil moisture; in addition, the cyanobacteria fertilize the soil by converting atmospheric nitrogen into nitrates.

The cryptogamic crust is also a colourful and beautiful little ecosystem to watch close up. Unfortunately, it can be difficult to find nowadays. Except in a few, relatively undisturbed grasslands, it has been trampled and shattered by horses and cattle. The crust is especially fragile on dry, sandy soils, where it takes a long time to recover its former structure and function. The opening of the soil surface and the subsequent invasion of alien weedy plants may have just as great an effect on grassland communities as the actual grass grazing does.

SHRUBS OF THE STEPPES

Because they are both grey, Big Sage-brush and Common Rabbit-brush are often confused by would-be botanists—but they are easily distinguished. Big Sagebrush has leaves that end in three teeth, has plumes of inconspicuous, brownish-yellow flowers that bloom in late September and early October, and exudes a strong, luscious scent when crushed. Common Rabbit-brush, in contrast, has soft, needle-shaped leaves and is crowned by brilliant golden flower heads in late summer. Despite the plant's specific name, *nauseosus*, the foliage does not give off a strong odour when crushed. The third shrub of the steppes, Antelope-brush, is a large, gangly shrub with dark, dull green leaves that, like sagebrush leaves, have three teeth. Masses of small yellow flowers appear along its branches in May.

Big Sagebrush

Common Rabbit-brush

Antelope-brush

MILKWEED AND MONARCHS

Thriving in moist meadows and ditches in the hottest part of the Interior of British Columbia, the Showy Milkweed initially grabs your attention with its large clusters of pink flowers. On closer inspection, these flowers are not only beautiful but are also marvellously odd and complex—for example, what appear to be petals are actually parts of the stamens, designed to ensure cross-pollination. But the most fascinating story about milkweeds begins with their chemistry. The entire plant contains cardiac glycosides, chemicals related to digitoxin that stimulate the heart in small dosages.

Glycosides not only taste terrible but also stimulate vomiting and can be downright poisonous in higher concentrations.

Because of these bitter chemicals, the milkweed is shunned by cattle and most insect herbivores. Some insects not only are able to eat milkweed, however, but manage to store the glycosides in their own bodies and make themselves noxious to predators. Perhaps the best example of a milkweed insect is the Monarch, a large orange-and-black butterfly that migrates to the Okanagan and Thompson Valleys every summer from Monterey, California. The Monarch lays its eggs on milkweed leaves, and the hatchling caterpillars chew their way to maturity, gathering glycosides along the way. When they pupate and then emerge as adult butterflies, they keep the bitter poisons with them and store them throughout their body, even in their wings. Extensive research has shown that birds and other predators learn very quickly that Monarchs are not good for them and subsequently leave them alone.

The bright red-orange and black pattern on Monarch wings is a classic example of warning coloration—the same colours are used throughout the animal world to warn predators away from poisonous or stinging prey. We instinctively use the same colours to warn motorists of dangers on the road. In fact, the other two insects that commonly feed on milkweeds in British Columbia—the Small Milkweed Bug and the Milkweed Beetle—use the same colours. Both these insects are colourful exceptions in families where the predominant colours are more conservative browns and greys.

THE OTHER GRASSLANDS

Northern and Mountain Grasslands

Grasslands are scattered throughout northern British Columbia, especially on south-facing slopes. The common northern grassland is a steppe related to the bunchgrass steppes of the south. In the north, Big Sagebrush is replaced by its diminutive boreal relative, Prairie Sagewort, and Bluebunch Wheatgrass is replaced by the closely related Slender Wheatgrass.

On the steep, south-facing slopes along the Peace River, Slender Wheatgrass and Western Wheatgrass share the sun with needlegrass, sedges and Prairie Sagewort. These special grasslands, also known as breaks, are related to the mixed grasslands of the Great Plains and, like them, are a threatened ecosystem. Most of the level grasslands in the Peace River area have been plowed, and those on steep riverside slopes have either been flooded by dams or are threatened by proposed ones. These grasslands are home to many animals and plants that are unusual in a British Columbia context.

Coastal Prairies

Probably the most threatened grasslands in British Columbia are the meadows associated with open Garry Oak woodlands on the dry, southeastern side of Vancouver Island and on the Gulf Islands. These meadows are filled with plants and animals found nowhere else on the coast, and one of the small flowers blooming in these meadows, Macoun's Meadow-foam, is found nowhere else in the world. When warm spring days and moisture from winter rains mix to provide perfect growing conditions for flowers, Common Camas, Sea Blush, Yellow Monkey-flower and many other blooms carpet the meadows with colour. On particularly dry sites you can even find Brittle Prickly-pear Cactus.

> I THINK THIS IS THE MOST BEAUTIFUL PLACE I WAS EVER IN, THE PRAIRIE THOUGH SMALL IN COMPARISON TO THE ONES ON THE OTHER SIDE OF THE MOUNTAINS, IS MOST LOVELY, COVERED WITH FLOWERS— STRAWBERRIES—EVEN IN THIS EARLY PERIOD OF THE YEAR THE GRASS IS NEARLY UP TO THE WAIST.
>
> Diary entry of Charles Wilson, at Chilukweyuk [Chilliwack] Prairie, June 16, 1859

Substantial grasslands were once associated with the so-called raised delta lands along the Fraser River. Built on fine, rich soil, the lush meadows of Langley Prairie and Matsqui Prairie bloomed with paintbrush, alumroot and many other wildflowers. We know very little about these grasslands, since

they disappeared before they could be adequately studied. Gone with them are animals such as the coastal Gopher Snake. The Streaked Horned Lark, a subspecies found only in coastal grasslands of the Pacific Northwest, may also have disappeared from British Columbia——it last nested on the grounds of the Vancouver International Airport. Similarly, the coastal subspecies of the Vesper Sparrow is now restricted to the Nanaimo airport, where in some years only a single male sings on territory. The flora and fauna of these grasslands may have been similar to those of the grasslands of the southern Puget Sound area, fragments of which still exist on military reserves.

Old field meadows can still be found in parts of the Fraser Delta, especially in the Boundary Bay area. These are not native meadows, but they mimic them well for the animals that depend on them; the tall, rank grass is still home to Townsend's Voles and other creatures. The abundant voles make these meadows one of the best wintering habitats in Canada for a number of hawks and owls, including Rough-legged and Red-tailed Hawks, Northern Harriers, and Short-eared and Barn Owls.

Opposite page: **The spectacular Golden Paintbrush survives only on five grassland sites in southern Vancouver Island and the Gulf Islands and a few other sites on the American San Juan Islands.**

GRASSLAND ANIMALS

Like the plants, the animals of the southern grasslands are intimately tied to the steppes' cycles of water and warmth. In the short days of winter, the grasslands are virtually inanimate. Mice are busy under the thin layer of snow and are hunted by a few migrant shrikes and hungry Coyotes, but almost all other vertebrates have left or are hibernating. Even resident birds like Sharp-tailed Grouse spend much of their time in the cover of creekside woodlands. But when the warm winds blow in from the south and the melting snow moistens the ground, the action begins.

In February and March, early migrants like Say's Phoebes, Horned Larks, Mountain Bluebirds and Western Meadowlarks return, brightening the scene with their colours and songs. The warm rains of April and early May further revive the grasslands, awakening slumbering spadefoot toads. The peak of plant growth and insect activity in May and June coincides with the breeding season of the birds and many other grassland animals.

In the hot days of July, the frenzied activity quickly declines and some of the breeding birds begin to vacate the parched steppes, long before there is a hint of autumn. Long-billed Curlews leave in mid-July, just after the young learn to fly, and Western Kingbirds leave in early August.

The term *grassland amphibian* may seem to be an oxymoron, but Great Basin Spadefoots are the perfect symbol of the survival of water-loving life in a water-starved environment. In May, these toad-like amphibians emerge at night to gather at an ephemeral pond or a shallow lake. The males' hoarse, rising croaks are as much a part of the nocturnal spring chorus as the clear song of the poorwills.

Larval development is rapid; the eggs hatch in about four days, and the tadpoles metamorphose in less than a month. It is a race against drought as the pool quickly shrinks in the hot June sun. Some spadefoot larvae speed the process even further through a remarkable adaptation. Instead of scavenging food from the bottom of the pond as other spadefoot larvae do, they become predacious cannibals, growing fast on a high-protein diet of their own kind.

On wet summer nights the young adult spadefoots leave the water and hop across the sagebrush steppe. They continue to forage at night throughout the summer, spending the day underground to avoid the hot, desiccating sun. Their name refers to a cornified flange on their hind feet that allows them to burrow rapidly into loose soil. When they go into hibernation in October, they secrete a gelatinous coat in their burrow that mixes with the surrounding soil to form a hardened case.

Birds

To most naturalists, the most obvious animal inhabitants of the grasslands are the birds. The avian community of southern Interior grasslands is small but distinctive. Its two commonest inhabitants are the Western Meadowlark and the Vesper Sparrow, whose songs can be heard on spring mornings from

Cranbrook to Quesnel. Much rarer are two species of the sagebrush steppe that barely make it into Canada—the Sage Thrasher and the sagebrush sub-species of the Brewer's Sparrow, both found regularly only in the southern Okanagan and Similkameen Valleys. Another rare species sought after by local birders is the Grasshopper Sparrow, which lives in lowland Okanagan grasslands but shuns sagebrush.

Mammals

Although the most obvious mammals of the grasslands are the big ones—Elk, Mule Deer, Bighorn Sheep and Coyote—the most intriguing in many ways are the small ones. The hot, dry Interior is home to more bats than any other area in Canada—about fourteen in all (see Chapter 8 for more details about them). Several of these bat species were thought to be restricted to the Okanagan and Similkameen Valleys in Canada, but recent searches by biologists and natural-ists have revealed that Spotted Bats, Western Small-footed Myotis, Fringed Myotis and probably even Pallid Bats are found all the way up the dry canyon of the Fraser River to Williams Lake.

The bat that is tied most to the sagebrush grasslands is the Pallid Bat. This rarely observed bat is unique among local bats in that it does not use sonar to hunt. Instead it hunts as an owl would, relying on its huge, sensitive ears to locate the faint rustles of its ground-dwelling insect prey. This hunting strat-egy is most effective over open ground, where beetles, crickets and scorpions can easily be tracked down.

If on your walks through the sagebrush or Antelope-brush steppe you see mounds of earth under the bushes punctuated with small holes, you have found the living quarters of Great Basin Pocket Mice. These diminutive rela-tives of kangaroo rats are nocturnal, emerging from their tunnels at night to feed on leaves, buds, seeds and insects. Their name refers to an external fur-lined pocket in each cheek, which is used to store food. Like their kanga-roo mouse cousins, they are capable of existing without access to water.

Another little-known mouse that is restricted to the southern grasslands is the Western Harvest Mouse. This, the smallest mouse in British Columbia, is so far known only from the Okanagan and south Similkameen Valleys, where it lives in dense grasses, rose thickets and wooded ravines in the moister areas of the grassland.

"Cold-Blooded" Animals in the Hot Grasslands

The sunny and warm nature of grasslands makes them ideal places for "cold-blooded" animals like lizards, snakes, insects and spiders. Look at your feet the next time you walk through dry grassland, and besides seeing the cactus you might have stepped in, you will be amazed at the variety of insects. Female velvet ants—furry, wingless wasps—scurry along the ground searching for

Opposite page: Without a doubt, one of the most beautiful of grassland birds is the Mountain Bluebird. Unlike its woodland counterpart, the Western Bluebird, it hovers a lot in its search for insects, a necessity in a habitat where perches are almost nonexistent.

the nesting burrows of solitary bees to parasitize, big robber flies buzz through the air, brilliant green tiger beetles with bulging eyes and massive jaws watch intently, and fuzzy yellow beeflies with intricately patterned wings hover over the dry grass. Watching them is so easy in open country.

Many people are surprised that there are scorpions in British Columbia, but the Northern Scorpion is actually fairly common in the Okanagan. It is a small scorpion with a sting that is painful but nowhere near fatal. During the day it stays out of the hot, drying sun in crevices under flat rocks; at night it emerges to hunt for small invertebrates. Even more curious are the five or so species of sun scorpion that inhabit the Okanagan and Similkameen. These are not true scorpions but are closely related to them, just as spiders are. They lack the stinging tail and grasping claws of scorpions, instead relying on massive jaws to subdue their prey.

The south Okanagan is also home to Canada's only native praying mantis. The Ground Mantis is a small member of its family and, perhaps because of its remarkable resemblance to a sage twig, is rarely seen. The females are wingless, but the adult males are fully capable of flight and occasionally come to porch lights in the Oliver area.

Perhaps the most infamous reptile of the grasslands is the Western Rattlesnake. The sudden *chchchch!* of a rattlesnake's warning buzz is a sound that stops you in your tracks. Chances are that the snake is already sliding away quietly through the sagebrush, but you stand still, scanning the immediate surroundings for a rattlesnake poised to strike. The bite of a Western Rattlesnake is dangerous, but bites are rare and fatalities even rarer in British Columbia. The Western Rattlesnake is generally a shy, retiring animal, preferring camouflage, warning and retreat as a defence rather

HOT-BLOODED LIZARDS

We are taught early in school that mammals and birds are "warm-blooded," whereas the rest of the animal kingdom is "cold-blooded." This unfortunate choice of terms gives us the idea that lizards and insects are cold, sluggish beings, when the opposite is often true. The real situation is that "cold-blooded" animals get their warmth from the environment, not from biochemically generated heat, as mammals and birds do. In the winter, lizards and insects are extremely sluggish, if not totally inactive—just like mammals that lower their body temperature to hibernate. In the summer, however, they actively regulate their body temperature by choosing their microclimate carefully. In the morning, they may bask in the sun before going out foraging; in the afternoon, they may cool down by lying in the shade—just as we do. While they are active, however, they are just as "warm-blooded" as we mammals and at least as quick moving. Because of this confusion, scientists prefer to use the terms *ectothermic* (meaning heat from outside) in the place of *cold-blooded* and *endothermic* (heat from inside) in the place of *warm-blooded*.

than outright attack. Its venomous nature, however, has resulted in extensive and often unwarranted persecution, both organized and opportunistic. This persecution, as well as an accelerating rate of habitat loss, has put the Western Rattlesnake on British Columbia's Blue List of vulnerable species. Biologists believe that in the absence of conservation action, it may become an endangered species in this area.

The Ground Mantis is Canada's only native praying mantis.

In British Columbia, Western Rattlesnakes are restricted to the hot, dry grasslands and woodlands of the south-central Interior, ranging as far north as Lillooet and Kamloops and as far east as Christina Lake. Unlike many other species of small animals in the province, we actually know a little bit about the biology of rattlesnakes in British Columbia, especially how rattlesnakes survive at the northern limit of their range.

Rattlesnakes overwinter in communal hibernacula in deep crevices or talus on sunny, warm slopes. Deep in the rocks the temperature never falls below freezing, and the snakes stay a few degrees warmer than the air temperature by snuggling up together. The rattlesnakes emerge from hibernation in late March or April and spend some time basking on the rocks. But they soon move to nearby foraging areas, where they spend the summer. Although they don't return to the winter den during the summer, they don't venture too far away either, usually staying within 1.5 kilometres of it the entire active season.

Rattlesnakes farther south in the United States feed a great deal on small lizards and amphibians, but Okanagan snakes seldom eat lizards, if at all—their diet is 91 per cent small rodents, 5 per cent shrews and 4 per cent small birds. This dependence on mammals may be a significant hindrance to growth and survival, especially for small newborn snakes.

The reproductive cycle of rattlesnakes at this northern latitude is a fascinating story of adaptation and the struggle for existence in a short active season. Mating takes place in late summer on the foraging range, but females store the sperm and the eggs are not fertilized until after they emerge the following spring. This delay allows the embryos to grow throughout the summer, when the females can bask in the warm sun to encourage their babies' development. Unlike the rest of the rattlesnakes, pregnant mothers remain around the den site all summer. Each mother gives birth to about five young in the fall. The mothers immediately go into hibernation, while the young remain at the surface for about two weeks, until they shed their skin for the first time.

The most remarkable part of this story is that the mothers do not eat during this entire period—they fast for about one and a half years, from the time they enter hibernation after mating, through the summer of their pregnancy and through another entire winter! This pattern of late summer mating and autumn births means that females can only give birth every second year at best, and in British Columbia it appears that every third year is more usual. Female snakes are very emaciated after giving birth and must double their weight before mating again. In the short snake season of the Okanagan Valley, most cannot do this in a single summer.

Females must also be at least 65 to 75 centimetres long from snout to vent before they become sexually mature, and in British Columbia this require-

Opposite page: **Western Rattle-snakes are pit vipers, so named after a pair of pits between their eyes and nostrils which contain masses of cells that are extremely sensitive to infrared radiation, or heat. These infrared "eyes" allow rattlesnakes to hunt mice and other endothermic prey by following the heat trails that they leave behind. They hunt mostly at night, when these trails are most conspicuous.**

ment means that they are five to eight years old before they mate. In addition, like many other male animals, male rattlesnakes fight each other during the breeding season. Presumably larger snakes have an advantage in attracting females; in British Columbia, researchers have never seen males less than 72 centimetres long (snout to vent) aggregating with females.

All these factors taken together mean that the reproductive rate of rattle-snakes in British Columbia is extremely low for animals of their size. They are therefore very vulnerable to environmental disturbances, and small populations are particularly susceptible to extirpation. So take care when walking in rattlesnake country, and don't harm them unless you are in real danger. Be especially careful around possible den sites—not only for your own safety but for the well-being of the rattlesnakes.

ROCK AND ROLL: CLIFFS AND TALUS SLOPES

Cliffs are special places. Rising out of the grasslands and extending into the dry forests above, the cliffs of the dry southern Interior of British Columbia are home to flora and fauna found nowhere else in Canada. What makes them

In Canada, the Canyon Wren is found only on the rock cliffs of the south Okanagan and adjacent valleys.

so special? First, the narrow ledges and crevices of the rock walls provide the ultimate in security for most of their inhabitants. Talus slopes, the steep fans of jumbled boulders that lie at the base of cliffs, also provide safe, secure homes to many creatures. But cliff walls are also great heat storage units—they soak up the sun's rays all day and cool only slowly through the night, thus providing a warm microclimate for many animals, especially the ectothermic snakes, insects, spiders and scorpions.

Deep talus slopes also provide a wide range of temperatures for such animals as reptiles and insects, whose body temperatures are determined by their environment. Rattlesnakes and skunks hibernate in the cool, cavelike interiors of such slopes and bask on the warm rocks in the spring sunshine.

Some animals, like Bighorn Sheep and Spotted Bats, make use of the security of the cliffs but spend much of their time foraging elsewhere; others, like Canyon Wrens, spend their entire lives on the face of cliffs or among the big rocks at their base.

Cliffs and rocks also act as umbrellas, shedding water in sheets during summer rains or spring thaws. Consequently, plants that grow at the base of cliffs or between rocks at the base of talus slopes receive significantly more water than those a few metres away on the dry grassland. Mock-orange, Saskatoon, Tall Oregon-grape, Poison-ivy and Smooth Sumac all thrive in this narrow band of moisture.

THE RISE AND FALL OF GRASSLANDS

Imagine standing amid the tall sage and golden grass in the hills outside Kamloops. It is an evening in late summer, and the heat of the sun has been tempered by the lengthening shadows and a cool afternoon thundershower. If you squint your eyes and smell the moist sage, you can almost experience the grasslands of two hundred years ago, before the Coquihalla Highway, before the sprawling suburbs, before the railway and before the cow.

People have not been kind to grass in this country. Growing up in the grasslands of the Okanagan, we have watched as knapweed and Cheatgrass have invaded the overgrazed steppe, watched as dirt bikes have scarred the grasslands' delicate skin, watched as plows and harrows cut huge swaths through the native soil and replaced the bunchgrass with foreign Crested Wheatgrass in their wake, watched as grasslands became alfalfa fields, vine-yards, golf courses, houses, roads, gravel pits and landfills.

Grasslands Then

Two hundred years ago there were impressive grasslands in the southern Interior. They filled the valleys below the Douglas-fir and Ponderosa Pine woodlands and were home to badgers, Burrowing Owls, White-tailed Jackrabbits and Sharp-tailed Grouse. Because there were few large herbi-vores, the grasslands were untrampled and the grass grew tall. The spaces between the grass bunches were covered in a diverse and healthy crust of lichens, fungi, mosses, liverworts and algae.

It was originally thought that Big Sagebrush was uncommon in these grasslands and that overgrazing led to a large increase in sagebrush. Indeed, the pollen record of the late 1800s tells us that only a small amount of sage-brush existed then. But the scarcity of sagebrush in the last century is now attributed to widespread burning at that time—sagebrush populations today are probably not much more extensive than they were in pre-settlement times.

Grasslands Now

It is remarkably difficult to find a grassland resembling the one described above today. Grazing practices have improved over the past fifty years, but even where cattle grazing is now light, the crust is broken and dozens of species of introduced grasses and weeds have taken its place. All types of grassland have disappeared under the bulldozer or plow, becoming alfalfa fields, vineyards, golf courses, housing developments and theme parks.

How are the grassland animals doing? Badgers, the subjects of widespread persecution earlier in the century, are still very scarce in the Okanagan grasslands, although they may be making a comeback in the Kootenays. Burrowing Owls have disappeared, in part because of the decline of Badgers. Great efforts are being made to reintroduce these birds, but success is by no means assured. Long-billed Curlews are hanging on but have declined considerably—they at least prefer the short grass left after grazing. White-tailed Jackrabbits and Sage Grouse, both lovers of big expanses of grass and sagebrush, are gone. Sharp-tailed Grouse, once so abundant, have disappeared from the Okanagan and East Kootenay grasslands and have declined in the Thompson country. And the list goes on.

Grazing

Grazing by cattle changes grasslands, especially if too many are put out onto the range or if they are allowed to graze for too long in a particular area. The impact of grazing is most obvious around ponds and along creeks, where cattle congregate to find water and shade.

Bluebunch Wheatgrass and fescues are preferred foods of cattle and so generally decline with grazing; other, less palatable or weedy species increase or invade at their expense. In the hot, dry Lower Grasslands, Big Sagebrush, Brittle Prickly-pear Cactus, Low Pussytoes, Needle-and-thread Grass and Cheatgrass become dominant after too much grazing has taken place. In the Middle Grasslands, Sandberg Bluegrass and Needle-and-thread Grass increase, and if disturbance is more extreme, Cheatgrass and knapweed take over. In the Upper Grasslands, Prairie Sagewort, Junegrass, Woolly Cinquefoil, Kentucky Bluegrass, Silky Lupine, Timber Milk-vetch and Yarrow increase, and Yellow and Meadow Salsify, Cheatgrass and Cut-leaved Daisy invade.

Animals that inhabit the grasslands also increase or decrease with grazing. Upland Sandpipers and Sharp-tailed Grouse prefer the cover of ungrazed grasslands, but Long-billed Curlews and Horned Larks prefer the more open nature of grazed areas. Grazed grasslands have less diversity of insects than ungrazed ones, but interestingly enough, at least some species of grasshoppers are most common in heavily grazed areas.

Not only do cattle eat vegetation, they trample it. The cryptogamic crust is most sensitive to trampling, and the destruction of this crust can have serious consequences for grassland communities (see the box entitled "The Space Between: The Cryptogamic Crust," page 270).

How long does it take grassland to recover from heavy grazing? To answer this question, cattle were excluded from a series of fenced plots in British Columbia grasslands beginning in the 1930s. The badly overgrazed sites changed little in the first ten years, but after that the natural community slowly began to re-establish itself. After twenty-five years average herbage production inside fenced Ponderosa Pine/Bluebunch Wheatgrass sites was 124 per cent greater than production on the rangeland outside. In general, it took twenty to forty years for the sites to return to excellent range condition.

Frustrated by this slow recovery time, some range managers have taken the drastic measure of plowing and reseeding to Crested Wheatgrass. Although this practice provides a quick crop of grass, it utterly destroys the natural grassland community by replacing it with an alien monoculture. The effects of this practice on grassland biological diversity are detrimental and long-lasting.

After all the plowing, bulldozing and overgrazing, the dry grasslands of British Columbia have been devastated by another agent: knapweed. A close relative of the artichoke, knapweed produces masses of prickly seed heads, making the plant unpalatable to cattle. Two species of knapweed were accidentally introduced from eastern Europe or western Asia around the turn of the century and have invaded most of the Interior grasslands. As well as being unpalatable to cattle, they are also drought resistant and produce allelopathic substances—chemicals that prevent other plants from growing near them. Attempts at biological control have centred on two species of fly whose larvae eat only knapweed seeds and a beetle whose larvae devour the long taproots.

Fire

Fire has always played an important role in shaping the grasslands of British Columbia. For millennia, indigenous peoples have used fire to maintain grassland habitats. Since this practice was stopped in the late 1800s, grasslands have gradually changed in British Columbia. Ponderosa Pines and Douglas-firs have spread onto grasslands, shading out the sun-loving plants characteristic of this open habitat.

While habitat managers have been trying to counteract this forest ingrowth by setting prescribed burns in small areas, climate change may be stepping in to play a major role in the future growth of grasslands in British Columbia. With predictions of longer, hotter summers throughout the province, wildfires may become more common and more intense. Dry, low-elevation forests consumed by fire may not grow back to forests in this new climate regime, since hot summer droughts limit the germination of new trees. In 1970, we watched a large fire consume about 5000 hectares of Ponderosa Pine forest in the south Okanagan Valley; today, more than forty years later, most of that land remains shrubby grassland with essentially no regrowth of pines.

CHAPTER TEN

THE WORLD OF FRESH WATER

THE WORLD OF FRESH WATER

RIVERS AND LAKES are not only the circulatory system of terrestrial life—transporting, filtering and storing water and nutrients—but also worlds of life unto themselves. Creeks, rivers, lakes, ponds, marshes and bogs add a physical and natural diversity to the landscape cherished by naturalists everywhere.

MOVING WATER

British Columbia's mountainous terrain keeps water moving downhill, and most of its creeks and rivers tumble and turn quickly towards the sea. Still, there is a great variety of moving water in British Columbia—from cold mountain rivulets to powerful, rushing rivers, and from warm, slow, peat-stained beaver-dammed creeks to the great silt-bottomed, meandering main-stem rivers.

Cold Mountain Creeks

Mountain water begins its journey to the sea in small rivulets flowing from the edges of summer snow fields or the toes of glaciers. Clear and cold, these creeks support little plant life except a slippery film of diatoms on the rocks and a few clumps of filamentous green algae clinging with special holdfast cells to the stones. This is no place for plankton; any unattached animal or plant is swept unceremoniously downstream, and unless it can swim against the current it will never return home.

It is not easy for tiny creatures to stay put and live in the rushing waters of a cold mountain stream, but these organisms have to come to grips with the problem.

The simplest remedy is to avoid the current altogether. Some mayfly and stonefly larvae with long, narrow bodies squeeze among stones and gravel. Flat *Stenonema* mayflies live in sheltered spots under stones, and the flattened larvae of clubtail dragonflies burrow in the sand and wait for unwary prey to walk, swim or drift by. Bodies flattened top to bottom and widely splayed legs are also typical of larvae such as those of the mayflies *Epeorus* and *Arthropleona* that live on exposed rocks. Actually, because of friction, there is a rather still boundary layer in the water 2 to 3 millimetres above the bottom, and small, flattened bodies can exploit this lack of current.

Baetid mayfly larvae, among the most abundant animals in stony, fast-flowing streams, display streamlining to perfection. Rather than avoiding the current, they revel in it, standing high on legs with abdomens free in the water. Their three long tail-like cerci swing from side to side, acting as vanes to keep the head turned into the current and making the insect's stance very stable. Many mayfly and stonefly larvae sport these long, stabilizing tails. Caddisfly cases are often long and tapering for the same reason.

Net-winged midges live along tumbling mountain streams where the larvae are firmly attached to smooth rocks by suction cups. The pupae resemble miniature limpets, complete with abdominal adhesive pads. In mayflies, a friction pad made of felty backward-projecting hairs covers the belly of *Drunella* and sticks it to stones; in *Rithrogena* the front pair of abdominal gills is enlarged and turned under its body, greatly increasing the area of close contact with the rock.

> A RIVER IS NEVER QUITE SILENT; IT CAN NEVER,
> OF ITS VERY NATURE, BE QUITE STILL; IT IS NEVER QUITE
> THE SAME FROM ONE DAY TO THE NEXT. IT HAS ITS
> OWN LIFE AND ITS OWN BEAUTY, AND THE CREATURES IT
> NOURISHES ARE ALIVE AND BEAUTIFUL ALSO. PERHAPS
> FISHING IS, FOR ME, ONLY AN EXCUSE TO BE NEAR
> RIVERS. IF SO, I'M GLAD I THOUGHT OF IT.
> Roderick Haig-Brown, *A River Never Sleeps*

Hooks and grapples are liberally used. Prominent hinged claws firmly anchor free-living *Rhyacophila* caddisfly larvae, and the seven pairs of lobes on the abdomen of mountain midges bear row after row of toothed hooks that grip any irregularity.

Silk and sticky secretions help to overcome the dangers of current. Many animals, from snails to stoneflies, lay adhesive eggs, preventing these vital

Pages 286–87: The waters of the meandering Mitchell River give life to the rich wetlands above Quesnel Lake.

Stonefly larva

Mayfly larva

Caddisfly larva

Streamside Moss

Longnose Dace

Tailed frog

objects from being washed away from their proper homes. Most stream-dwelling caddisfly larvae build their cases from stones or sand glued with silk. Obviously, this is readily available material, but its weight also prevents the insects from being swept away. In some groups, the faster the current, the larger the stones incorporated into the case. Velcro was invented by black flies—larval salivary glands make sticky silk that is smeared on rocks, and masses of tiny hooks on the larva's rear end grasp the tangled silken mat. The larva also anchors a silk strand to the rock so that if dislodged, it is carried away on a lifeline.

As the streams flow downward into the forests, they gather more plant debris and gain size with every creek that joins them. Aquatic mosses such as Streamside Moss grow on rocks in the splash zone, providing food and refuge for small invertebrates.

And of course there are fish. When most of us think of creek fish, we think of trout and char—in British Columbia this means Rainbow Trout, Cutthroat Trout, Bull Trout and Dolly Varden. These sleek predators hide in the shadowy eddies below boulders, snapping up any insect that loses its grip on its rock and leaping for the slow-flying adult mayflies dancing over the green pools. But there can be many more fish in a creek than these—Mountain Suckers, Bridgelip Suckers, Longnose Dace, Torrent Sculpins, Prickly Sculpins, Slimy Sculpins, Mottled Sculpins and many others all find a place.

The Longnose Dace is a minnow that, as its scientific name, *Rhinichthys cataractae,* suggests, is well suited to rushing mountain streams. The species name, *cataractae,* refers to waterfalls—the type specimen was, in fact, collected at Niagara Falls. *Rhinichthys* means "snout fish" and refers to the fish's prominent nose. Its profile does come in handy, because in fast water the current hits its long, angular head and forces the fish down towards the bottom of the stream, keeping it from being washed away. Adult Longnose Dace have smaller swim bladders than other fish—a large, buoyant swim bladder would bob them back up to the surface, where they might again be in danger of being swept downstream.

Along the mainland coast and in the Flathead River valley of British Columbia's southeast corner live two of the strangest denizens of mountain creeks, the Coastal Tailed Frog and the Rocky Mountain Tailed Frog.

Tailed frogs are peculiarly adapted to life in rushing water. The "tail" is found only on males and is essentially a penis used for internal fertilization. The external fertilization common to other amphibian species is inefficient in the tailed frog's tumbling streams, since most of the sperm would be swept off to the Pacific before they even came close to the eggs. The tadpoles, like many other stream algae eaters, have a big suction cup on their bellies so that they can stick to the boulders.

Another amphibian of cold mountain streams is the Pacific Giant Salamander. In British Columbia, this large—up to 33 centimetres long—salamander is found only in the Chilliwack area. For an amphibian it is a ferocious predator, eating insects, slugs, amphibians, shrews and even small snakes and mice. Giant salamanders have a powerful bite and can even bark when agitated.

Pacific Giant Salamanders live in the pools of clear, fast-flowing streams.

> THE OUZEL (DIPPER) NEVER SINGS IN
> CHORUS WITH OTHER BIRDS, NOR WITH HIS KIND,
> BUT ONLY WITH THE STREAM.
> John Muir, *Mountains of California*

If you look closely along almost any creek in British Columbia you can see an American Dipper, a grey tennis ball of a bird nervously doing knee bends on the polished rocks. Named for their frequent plunges into the cold water, dippers use their short wings to manoeuvre underwater along the stony bottom, looking under small rocks for insect larvae and fish eggs. Facing upstream, they angle their wings under water so that the current keeps them on the bottom. Their constant knee bending is a habit peculiar to birds living near running water. Spotted Sandpipers, waterthrushes, wagtails and pipits

Above: **American Dippers are very territorial about their waterfront property, proclaiming ownership year-round with a beautiful, warbling song, which is often barely heard over the roar of the rushing water.**

Below: **Harlequin Ducks court and nest along fast-moving mountain streams.**

all bob up and down or wag their tails, perhaps imitating the movement of branches caught in the current.

The rather spherical shape of a dipper—very short tailed and almost neckless—is an adaptation to reduce the surface area available for heat loss in frigid water. A dipper will often stay on a productive stretch of creek all winter as long as there are one or two holes in the ice to provide access to the food below.

Whereas ponds and lakes are often host to large, diverse flocks of waterfowl, cold mountain creeks have few such visitors. The most characteristic duck of these streams is the Harlequin Duck, the handsome male decked out in elegant slate grey boldly patterned in white and chestnut, the female almost invisible in dark brown spotted with white. Harlequins spend most of the year in that other wave-washed environment, the rocky coast of British Columbia. Pairs fly in to the Interior in late April and May, taking up summer residence on a wide variety of rushing rivers and streams. The females lay their eggs in down-lined nests hidden among the overhanging roots of the river banks or in hollow trees; shortly thereafter the males wing their way back to the coast to moult amid the Bull Kelp forests along the shore. The female Harlequin Duck raises the young on her own but then abandons them in mid-August to return to the coast herself. The young are left to find their own way to the sea—the few that survive usually appear there in early September.

WATER SHREWS

Shrews are hard to see, since they are mostly nocturnal and live in hidden places. The Water Shrew is no exception. But fetching water some early morning from a tumbling creek by your mountain campsite, you may cross paths with one, hunting on the bank. And you may be astonished at its un-shrewlike behaviour as it skitters across the water and plunges under the foam. It rarely stays below the surface for more than half a minute; longer immersion may wet the fur, resulting in irrecoverable heat loss. Shrews, with their tiny bodies, have a very large surface area relative to their mass, and the heat generated by their hyperactive metabolism is quickly lost. The silvery film of air bubbles trapped in the coat reduces this heat loss under water, but makes their light bodies even more buoyant. They must paddle hard with their big feet to stay under. Rows of stiff hairs line the toes and margins of the hind feet; these make the paddling surface even larger and trap air bubbles that further increase buoyancy, allowing the tiny mammal to walk on water for short periods. Like many aquatic animals, Water Shrews are distinctively coloured dark above and pale below, making them harder to see from either angle when in the water.

To maintain their body heat, shrews eat voraciously. Water Shrews devour anything they can subdue in their travels, including insects, snails, small fish and amphibians. To help preserve body heat, anything captured underwater is brought to land to eat. Many shrews have a surprising repertoire of vocal signals to communicate with each other and, like bats, apparently use sounds for echo-location. Water Shrews emit staccato, high-pitched squeaks. These may be effective in pinpointing prey and obstacles underwater, where an acute sense of smell is of little use.

Although Water Shrews are rare, they live throughout British Columbia except at lower elevations in the Fraser Valley, where they are replaced by the similar Pacific Water Shrew. They are absent from coastal islands except for Vancouver Island, which supports the only island population along the Pacific coast of the continent.

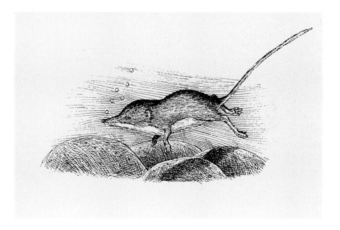

Warm Streams

Mountain creeks have little chance to become warmed by the summer sun. Much of the time they are shaded by dense coniferous forests, and any surface water warmed by a sunlit stretch is soon sent to the cold rocks below. Even in midsummer, the temperature of these creeks may be as low as 10°C. Water reaching a lake, however, is calm enough to develop a warm surface layer in summer, which is skimmed off and sent down the creek or river emptying the lake. These warm outflow streams can have maximum temperatures as high as 25°C and have a different flora and fauna from the chilly waters that flowed in.

In British Columbia, the black and yellow Grappletail dragonfly is found only in warm creeks flowing off the mountain slopes surrounding the Lower Mainland.

The invertebrate diversity of these streams is much higher than that of mountain creeks. Alderflies, dobsonflies and some dragonfly groups—such as the spiketails and clubtails—are specialized river predators. Their larvae skulk in the bottom debris, waiting to snatch other insect larvae.

Rivers

British Columbia's rivers can be divided roughly into three types based on where they get their water and when their flows peak. Small coastal rivers receive most of their water from rainfall, so their maximum flow occurs in winter. This flow can fluctuate dramatically, since runoff from rainfall is rapid. Most Interior rivers peak in late spring or early summer, coinciding with maximum snowmelt in the mountains. Rivers that predominantly drain large glaciers—like the Alsek and the Taku in the far northwest—are highest in midsummer, when the glacial ice wastes away under the hot July sun.

The Pacific Salmon

The five species of Pacific salmon that live in British Columbia waters have fed and fascinated humans for thousands of years and have been keystones in the ecology of both coastal waters and hundreds of streams throughout much of the province. Their lives are part of a great cycle—the migration of fry or smolts from freshwater streams to the ocean; the grand travels of silvery adults through the North Pacific; the arduous migration upstream to their natal stream reach; the battles and lovemaking of gaudily coloured, distorted bodies on the spawning grounds; and the inevitable swift decay and death of the battered fish among the eggs of the generation to follow. All aspects of this cycle have stirred the human imagination.

Although Pacific salmon all share the same basic cycle, different species spend different lengths of time in fresh water as juveniles and in the ocean as adult fish, they spawn in different kinds of streams and at different times of the year, they travel to different parts of the ocean, and so on.

EULACHON: GIFTS OF GREASE

In the promising days of spring, beginning in mid-March, millions of small, silvery fish leave the protected marine inlets and enter coastal rivers. The Eulachon swim upstream—up the Nass, the Skeena, the Kitlope, the Klinaklini, the Fraser and a host of other streams—but they don't swim far. They swim just far enough to find good spawning gravel for their eggs. In the Nass, they don't go more than 35 kilometres upstream; in the Fraser, most spawning takes place between Chilliwack and Mission.

The First Nations peoples welcomed the return of the Eulachon because they came at the end of the cold, wet winter and they came bearing rich gifts—bodies laden with energy- and vitamin-rich oil. In an industry full of tradition and ceremony that is still very much alive, the Native people netted the fish in tremendous quantities and extracted the oil.

The name Eulachon is from the Chinook trading language—and the Eulachon was indeed a major commodity of trade, for both oil and fish were carried through the Coast Mountains on well-trodden kleena or "grease" trails. Both the Klinaklini River and the settlement of Kleena Kleene on the Chilcotin Plateau derive their names from this trading network. Indeed, the Eulachon trade was so important that the eastern Cree pronunciation of the word—*oorigan*—gave rise to the name of the near-mythical "River Oregon," for which Lewis and Clark searched in vain, but which is now suspected to be the Fraser River.

But the migration of the Eulachon was not just a boon for the humans along the coast—it was and is the centre of one of the great natural spectacles of spring in British Columbia. Killer Whales, Harbor Seals, salmon, Spiny Dogfish and Pacific Halibut gorge on the Eulachon as they mass for their spawning run. Hundreds of California Sea Lions—and a few Northern Sea Lions as well—gather at the mouth of the Fraser River to intercept them, and some even follow them all the way up to the spawning grounds. In the depths of the Fraser, huge White Sturgeon stock up on the tiny fish just before their own spawning season begins.

Loons, mergansers and other fish-eating birds also home in on the action, and the course of the migration is marked overhead by circling swarms of gulls, interspersed with huge black forms of soaring Bald Eagles. When the Eulachon run on the Nass, thousands of gulls from the entire north coast converge on the river mouth. One early account compared the cloud of gulls over the Eulachon to a heavy fall of snow.

Eulachon spawning populations in the Fraser River and along the central coast crashed in the 1990s, declining by 90 per cent to 98 per cent, and are now listed as Endangered. The cause for this decline is unknown but seems to be related to conditions at sea, and may well be connected to water-temperature fluctuations and other effects of climate change. The northern populations spawning in the Nass and Skeena Rivers seem to be still healthy.

Scientists still are not sure exactly how salmon find their birthplace, but they certainly use their noses—fish with plugged noses cannot find their way back. Unique stream odours probably become imprinted on juvenile salmon as they travel downstream, and they follow these as they travel back up the stream several years later as adults. If this sounds amazing, just recall how specific smells from your childhood can take you instantly back (in your mind, at least) to your schoolyard or family kitchen.

In addition, salmon may be helped by the fact that they travel upstream in the company of their brothers, sisters and other fellow spawners. They may be able to recognize members of their own stock by specific smells released by the fish. And when many fish are trying to find the same place, it is far less likely that any will go astray than if they tried on their own.

Although most salmon find their way back home, a small per centage do stray into unfamiliar streams, either on their own or in the company of salmon that belong in those streams. Straying may or may not be advantageous to individuals, but a small amount of it certainly aids in the survival of the species. Strays introduce genetic variation into breeding stocks and, without them, rivers would not be recolonized following glaciation or natural disasters such as volcanic eruptions and landslides.

LONG BEFORE THE ENVIRONMENTAL STRESS ON A RIVER BECOMES OBVIOUS TO MOST OF US, IT SHOWS UP IN THE FISH. THEY ARE CANARIES IN A MINE—BUT CANARIES THAT CANNOT SING. WE MUST PAY ATTENTION TO WHAT THE FISH ARE TELLING US, AND TO THE WHISPERING VOICES OF OUR RIVERS, FOR THEY ARE SPEAKING ABOUT OUR FUTURE.

Mark Hume, *The Run of the River*

The cycle of the salmon is one of the great connecting agents in the ecology of British Columbia, for in their spawning migrations they bring riches from the sea to distant valleys of the Interior. The First Nations peoples living along salmon-bearing streams depended on these fish for sustenance, and they became an integral part of Native culture. But beyond humans, both the aquatic and terrestrial ecosystems of salmon watersheds revolve around the return of the seagoing fish. Black and Grizzly Bears greet them with swats of their great paws; sleek River Otters pursue them underwater; American Dippers, goldeneyes, Common Mergansers and fish such as Dolly Vardens gorge on the eggs; and scavengers large and small—from Bald Eagles to stoneflies—gather to feast on the carcasses that pile up in quiet waters downstream. Any nutrients that remain in the river fertilize algae and other aquatic life, giving an enormous, vital boost to the river's food chain.

University of Victoria biologist Tom Reimchen's studies of Black Bears at a Chum Salmon run on the Haida Gwaii have detailed some of the remarkable contributions of salmon to the forest ecosystem. There, the bears hunt the salmon primarily at night when the fish cannot see them well and so are easier to catch. Amazingly, they consumed 4000 of 5000 salmon in the run, although three-quarters of these had already spawned. They dragged the fish into the adjacent forest to eat them in peace, and in doing so brought

4000 kilograms of fish to every hectare of forest. The bears only ate half of each carcass, so there was plenty left for scavengers such as crows, gulls and marten. After the big animals had had their turn, insects consumed the remaining flesh.

One of the great wildlife spectacles in British Columbia is the gathering of Bald Eagles along rivers with winter salmon runs. Eagles from all over western North America fly in to take part in the feast. In mid-January, more than 2500 well-fed eagles perch in the cottonwoods and firs lining the Cheakamus and Squamish Rivers, and a similar number can be found at the junction of the Chehalis and Harrison Rivers and along nearby channels of the Fraser. Eagles fly back and forth between these rich areas; sometimes a string of them can be seen flying over the North Shore suburbs, commuting from Squamish to Harrison! On northern Vancouver Island, over 800 gather at the mouth of the Nimpkish River.

Chinook Salmon
The Chinook, also known as King Salmon, Tyee and Smiley, is the biggest of the Pacific salmon, usually growing to 13 kilograms and occasionally to 30 or even over 50 kilograms. It is also a biologically and ecologically plastic species. Some of the Chinook's varied ecological strategies can be explained by the existence of two separate races, but even within a race, Chinooks exhibit a flexibility of lifestyles that enables at least some of them to survive the unpredictable disasters that can befall salmon stocks.

The two races—an "ocean" type and a "stream" type—are thought to have diverged during the Pleistocene glaciations, when the stream Chinooks spawned and were reared in Beringia and Asia and the ocean Chinooks lived south of the ice sheets in California, Oregon and Washington. For the most part, they remain separated today. Stream Chinooks are found in northeastern Asia and North America south to the Stikine River; in rivers south of the Stikine, they are restricted to the headwater reaches, leaving the lower reaches to ocean Chinooks. In the Fraser River, stream Chinooks make up 34 per cent of the spawning population, and in the Cowichan, 10 per cent.

Stream Chinooks enter rivers in early summer (hence the alternative name Spring Salmon) and spend several months in the river before spawning. After they emerge the following spring, the fry spend one or more years in fresh water before migrating to the ocean. Once in the ocean, they tend to make long journeys offshore. Ocean Chinooks, in contrast, arrive at the spawning rivers later in the summer or fall and spend only a short time in the river before spawning. Similarly, the juveniles remain only a few weeks in their natal stream before reaching the ocean; when they reach the ocean they tend to remain in coastal waters.

The Pacific Salmon of North America:

♂

♀

Chinook

♂

♀

Coho

♂

♀

Sockeye

♂

♀

Pink

♂

♀

Chum

Coho Salmon

Coho, or Silver Salmon, are small cousins of Chinook Salmon, growing to 2.5 to 4 kilograms on average. They are aggressive and opportunistic fish—aggressive and tenacious in their determination to reach small headwater streams that other salmon cannot navigate (they can make leaps of 2 metres), and opportunistic in their use of a variety of habitats when they are juveniles. Coho usually spend a full year in their spawning stream or a nearby lake as territorial fry before migrating to the sea. The small headwater spawning streams they inhabit are ideal for rearing, being cool, stable and rich in aquatic invertebrates. Although the small rearing area provided by these streams limits the number of surviving fry, those that reach the sea are healthy, large smolts and their survival is high compared with that of other salmon.

> FROM PORT HARDY ONE MORNING I CAST OFF MY LINES
> THE SEA IT WAS SMOOTH AND THE WEATHER JUST FINE
> AND TO CASTLE ROCK I WAS HEADED AWAY
> WHERE THE COHO FLASH SILVER ALL OVER THE BAY . . .
> Lloyd Arntzen, "Where the Coho Flash Silver"

After spending one and a half years in the ocean, adult Coho usually return to their natal streams as three-year-olds. In British Columbia, the first returnees arrive at the stream mouth in September or October, but are not ready to spawn until November to January. The red-sided Coho are stimulated to enter shallow coastal streams by an increase in flow following the onset of autumn rains. In large rivers, Coho usually migrate farther than Pink or Chum Salmon but not as far as Sockeye or Chinook. Most do not travel more than 250 kilometres, but some swim 680 kilometres to the tributaries of the middle Fraser.

Sockeye Salmon

Sockeye, originally transcribed as *sukkai*, is the name given to this salmon by the Coast Salish people—the literal translation is "fish of fishes." With its rich, red flesh and its scarlet and green mating colours, this fish stands out among all others. Unlike other salmon, it has inserted a lake phase into its life cycle— fry usually spend one or two years feeding and growing in a lake near the spawning stream. Sockeyes spend two or three years in the ocean, returning to their natal streams at age four or five.

In the lakes, the fry are plankton feeders in open waters. Because there is nowhere to hide in the waters they feed in, juvenile Sockeyes usually spend the daylight hours deep in the dark waters below the lake's thermocline, coming up to feed in warmer, plankton-rich waters at dusk and dawn. One of the greatest lakes for Sockeyes is Shuswap Lake, which is the rearing ground for fry from

the runs on the Adams River and other tributaries. In good years, 93 million young Sockeyes may be in the lake—a remarkable 3000 per hectare. Because lakes have a larger rearing area than streams, Sockeyes are more abundant than stream-developing species such as Coho and Chinook Salmon. The lake-rearing habit of Sockeye Salmon has independently given rise to a number of populations that remain in the lake and never make the dangerous trip to the ocean and back. These fish are called Kokanee or, occasionally, Kickininee.

In order to find their nursery lake, emerging young Sockeyes have innate swimming responses in terms of direction and current. For example, some are "hard-wired" to swim north and upstream, others east and downstream. Because of this genetically determined behaviour, it has proven extremely difficult to re-establish Sockeye runs that have been eliminated by overfishing or some other disaster.

Pink Salmon
Pink Salmon are the most marine—or perhaps it is better to say least freshwater—of the Pacific salmon. The adults usually travel only a short distance up streams to spawn, and when the fry emerge from the spawning gravels,

GIANT IN PERIL: THE WHITE STURGEON

The biggest fish in Canada lies resting somewhere in the bottom of a deep pool in one of the big rivers of British Columbia. It is a White Sturgeon—one of the most intriguing yet little-known fish of our waters. Ironically, we are only just beginning to understand the sturgeon's life, just as we are threatening to end its chapter in British Columbia's natural history.

Before the turn of the century, White Sturgeon were abundant in the Fraser, Columbia and Kootenay Rivers. Abundant and huge. One taken opposite New Westminster on 14 August 1897 weighed in at 630 kilograms, and another, unsubstantiated catch from the Fraser near Mission was claimed to weigh over 800 kilograms! These monster fish were probably on the order of 6 metres long. How do they get so big? They grow slowly but surely—and live well over a hundred years.

But like the veteran Douglas-firs and Sitka Spruce along the Fraser, the big sturgeon of that mighty river wouldn't last long. The fishery began in earnest only after 1880; by 1894 there was an export market, and 517,135 kilograms of sturgeon were caught in 1897. But this peak catch was followed by a 93 per cent decline over the next decade to almost commercial extinction.

The sturgeon of the other rivers in British Columbia weren't threatened much by humans until the 1950s and 1960s, when the Nechako, Kootenay and Columbia Rivers were dammed. The upper Kootenay River was the last to have its spring freshet harnessed, when a large dam was built near Libby, Montana, in 1972. These dams not only flooded some of the traditional spawning and rearing grounds of sturgeon and cut off their migration routes but reversed the flow cycles of their rivers.

Biologists believe that White Sturgeon spawn in the powerful currents of the spring runoff. Hydroelectric dams take that water away from them by holding they migrate quickly to the ocean. In short coastal streams, the fry migrate at night to protect themselves from predators, but in big silty rivers such as the Fraser, they move during the day, safely hidden in the murky waters.

Pinks are unique among Pacific salmon in having a fixed, two-year life span. After only one and a half years at sea, they return to the streams of their birth to spawn and die. Because of their short lives, they are the smallest of Pacific salmon, averaging only 1 to 2.5 kilograms as adults. Their two-year life span also results in genetically isolated runs in even and odd years. In many streams, the odd- or even-year run may completely dominate the other—Fraser River and Puget Sound Pink Salmon, for example, spawn almost exclusively in odd years. And up and down the coast, Pink Salmon spawning in odd years

back the spring freshet and releasing its waters the following fall and winter, when electrical demands are greatest. What has happened to the sturgeon? Recent studies have shown that all populations below dams in British Columbia are now dominated by older fish—there is a disturbing shortage of sturgeon younger than the dam above them.

Because they live a long life, sturgeon have the unenviable opportunity to absorb and concentrate a variety of toxins that now exist in our rivers. The effect of these toxins on sturgeon is not known. None have been proven to die from them, but recent, mysterious deaths of a number of large sturgeon in the lower Fraser have caused biologists to wonder about what these venerable giants are telling us. Sturgeon are a symbol of what our great rivers once were—and could be once again, if we learn to respect flowing waters and the life within them.

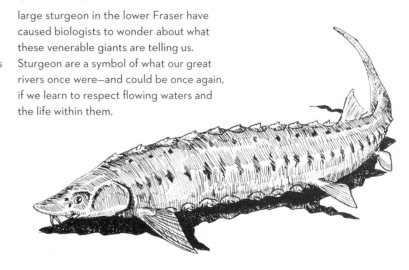

are genetically more closely related to each other than to Pinks spawning in even years in the same streams.

Despite their name, the spawning dress of Pink Salmon is rather dull. The males, however, develop a striking hump on their backs, which gives them an alternative name, Humpback Salmon.

Chum Salmon

Chums are the most widely distributed of the Pacific salmon species, spawning in more than eight hundred streams in British Columbia, with few large runs. Like Pink Salmon, the fry migrate directly to the sea after they emerge. On the south coast of British Columbia, the young salmon spend up to three weeks maturing in the river's estuary before heading out to sea. They spend a number of years at sea, returning to spawn at age two to five, and occasionally up to seven years of age. When they are mature, they are the second-largest Pacific salmon, weighing in at 4.5 to 6.5 kilograms, and sometimes more than 10 kilograms.

Chums are the least fatty, and thus the least tasty, of the Pacific salmon and in past years were consequently considered the least desirable catch. The First Nations peoples fed them to their dogs, resulting in the name Dog Salmon.

On the north coast, spawning generally takes place in the summer, from July to September, but on the south coast it is considerably later—October to January. Spawning fish enter the river ready to mate and in full calico coloration. Like Coho, Chum Salmon are stimulated to enter the river by an increase in stream runoff following autumn rains.

LAKES AND PONDS

Unlike some other parts of Canada, British Columbia is not dominated by lakes. It has few broad plains covered with small lakes and ponds, and its largest natural lake, Atlin, doesn't even make it into the top fifty in Canada. Less than 2 per cent of its surface is covered in fresh water, and that water is trapped in narrow valleys and always seems to be rushing to the sea. Nevertheless, there are over sixteen thousand lakes in the province. Ranging in size from mountain tarns to great bodies of water more than 500 square kilometres in area, these lakes are home to flourishing aquatic communities— communities largely unknown to most humans. Anyone who has fished in lakes knows they are full of living things, but most of us don't often wonder what goes on under the waves. What is life like down there?

Rich Lakes, Poor Lakes

There are different kinds of lakes, and one of the ways to classify them is based on how rich in nutrients they are. Lakes and ponds rich in nutrients such as nitrates and phosphates are crammed with life—think of Cariboo duck ponds or the shallow, marshy lakes of the north—and are called eutrophic (rich in nutrients). The water feeding them flows over and through glacial till, limestone, shale and other easily dissolved nutrient sources. Another contributing factor is the low rainfall and high evaporation rates in some Interior regions—minerals can become concentrated in lake basins where summers are hot and dry. Because there is abundant, respiring life in them, eutrophic lakes tend to be relatively low in oxygen in their deep, near-bottom waters.

At the other end of the scale, lakes that are virtually free of dissolved nutrients are said to be oligotrophic (poor in nutrients). Lakes that receive pure, clean water flowing over the resistant granitic bedrock of the Coast Mountains are good examples of this type of lake. The high rainfall along the coast also contributes to the low concentrations of minerals in solution. Oligotrophic lakes are clear and relatively rich in oxygen but sparse in life. Lake size and shape also influence the amount of nutrients. The big, deep

Productive lakes such as Lac du Bois near Kamloops are host to a diverse but largely unseen community of plants and animals.

fiordlike lakes of the Interior tend to be nutrient poor because their water volume is so great compared with the shallow, productive region along their edges.

Warm Water, Cold Water

It is obvious to anyone who has swum in the warm waters of a lake in July and skated over its clear, hard ice in January that lakes change through the seasons. But some of the most important changes aren't so obvious to beings like us who look at a lake from the dry side.

After the ice has melted in the spring thaw, the water in a lake is usually one temperature from top to bottom—about 4°C. And since all the water is at the same temperature and density, it intermixes freely. Spring breezes create circulating currents that move water from the bottom of the lake to the surface and back down again. But as spring becomes summer, the upper layer of water in the lake warms up and becomes less dense than the

FIGURE 10.1
An Interior lake through the seasons.

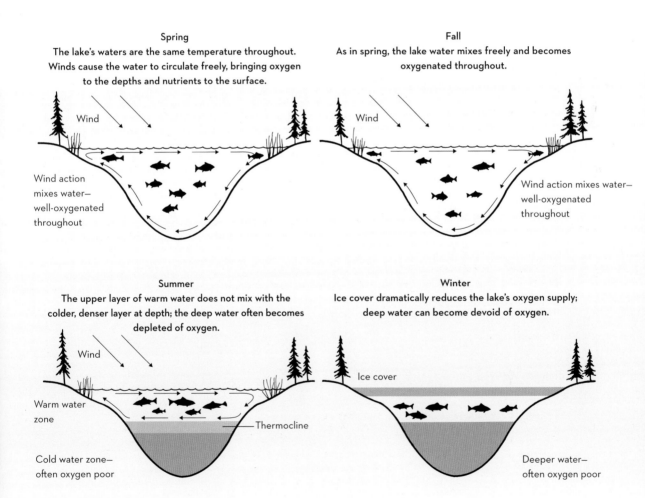

Spring
The lake's waters are the same temperature throughout. Winds cause the water to circulate freely, bringing oxygen to the depths and nutrients to the surface.

Wind

Wind action mixes water—well-oxygenated throughout

Fall
As in spring, the lake water mixes freely and becomes oxygenated throughout.

Wind

Wind action mixes water—well-oxygenated throughout

Summer
The upper layer of warm water does not mix with the colder, denser layer at depth; the deep water often becomes depleted of oxygen.

Wind

Warm water zone

Thermocline

Cold water zone—often oxygen poor

Winter
Ice cover dramatically reduces the lake's oxygen supply; deep water can become devoid of oxygen.

Ice cover

Deeper water—often oxygen poor

water below. As the temperature and density differences increase, it becomes harder and harder for the two layers to mix. As long as the summer sun warms the lake, the warm, upper water does not mix with the cold, bottom water. In between them is an invisible barrier—the thermocline. In most lakes, this barrier lies somewhere between 5 and 15 metres deep (Figure 10.1).

This division of summer lakes into warm surface and cold bottom layers has a great effect on life within them. The surface waters are warm and usually rich in oxygen. Consequently, they are usually rich in life also. This is where the summer action is—where the algae bloom, where the zooplankton graze and where the fish feed.

But the story is reversed below. Not only is the bottom layer cold, but especially in more productive lakes, it soon becomes depleted of oxygen. Any life that is respiring down there, including all the bacteria consuming the detritus raining down from the action above, gradually consumes the oxygen dissolved in the water. And because the water in the bottom layer does not mix with the water that is getting oxygen from the air, the water in the bottom layer cannot easily replenish its oxygen.

With the return of the long, cold nights of autumn, however, the surface of the lake gradually cools. When it reaches 4°C again, it becomes the same density as the lower layer and the entire lake is able to mix freely once more. All it takes is a good autumn wind to move the surface water over a bit and the bottom water rises from below, creating a circular current in the water column. The lake "turns over," and its water becomes recharged with oxygen from top to bottom. This is a critical event, because winter ice cuts off the lake's water from the oxygen-giving air and reduces oxygen-producing photosynthesis by aquatic plants. All the animals spending winter beneath the ice have to survive until the next spring on the oxygen within the water. By early spring in many lakes, only a thin band of oxygenated water lies immediately beneath the ice. Large lakes with massive, well-oxygenated deep-water zones, however, have more than enough oxygen to last the winter. And most lakes at low elevations on the south coast of British Columbia rarely freeze, so they circulate throughout the winter.

Lake Life

Let's get into a canoe and paddle around a lake—imagine one of the popular fishing lakes on the central plateau—and have a look at the life within it. We'll look at its three different regions: the littoral, limnetic and profundal zones. The first one we'll explore is the littoral zone, the shallow water over the lake's sloping shoreline. Life is rich here because the water is warm, light is abundant, and the lake bottom supports a variety of plant and animal life.

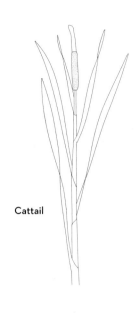

Cattail

Hard-
stemmed
Bulrush

The rich shore

We set out in a protected bay that is rimmed with dense marsh vegetation. Two of the common emergent plants along the lake's shoreline here are Cattails and Hard-stemmed Bulrushes. Cattails have long, flat leaves and round stems with flowering heads that look like fuzzy weiners on the end of them—the cat tails. Bulrushes, in contrast, have round, pith-filled leaves and droopy heads of brownish flowers. The dense growth of bulrushes and Cattails, both underwater and above water, provide cover for a great variety of animals.

A few American Coots and Ruddy Ducks paddle into the green wall in front of us; these and other waterfowl nest within the safety of the green wall as well. Columbia Spotted Frogs, the common aquatic frogs of the Interior, swim unobtrusively away; we'll rarely hear them, for unlike the Pacific Tree Frogs and their loud *ribits* on spring nights, the croaks of spotted frogs are barely audible. Along an open stretch of gently sloping shoreline are what seem to be millions of tiny frogs—but these are actually transforming Western Toads. As tadpoles, these toads school up in black masses in the warm shallows of Interior lakes and, when transforming, march out of the lake like tiny amphibian armies.

North of here, or up in the mountains, the common shoreline plants are sedges. These look like big, coarse grasses, but if you try to roll the base of a sedge stem, you will find that it is solid and triangular, not round and hollow like a grass stem.

Back to the canoe now, where insects of all shapes and sizes are buzzing around our heads. It is too hot and sunny out for the mosquitoes—they'll be out in the evening when the humidity rises—but female horse flies are out searching for blood meals. Beneath our paddles, hundreds of bugs (members of the order Hemiptera), beetles and other insects are paddling, too.

BEAVER PONDS

Although Beavers are often considered destructive by anyone who happens to own property that these animals decide to log or flood, they perform a multitude of ecological services in a land of running water. In British Columbia's narrow, steep valleys, numerous small lakes and their inhabitants owe their existence to the stick and mud dams built by Beavers. In dry country, the pond behind the dam is an oasis, holding back the spring freshet and doling it out gradually through the summer. The Beavers' logging and flooding create sunny borders of sedge marsh and willow swamp, where Willow or Alder Flycatchers sally out after caddisflies; Common Yellowthroats, Northern Waterthrushes and Lincoln's Sparrows sing from the bushes; and Moose munch in the shallows. The flooded, dying trees that remain standing along the pond's edge become homes for woodpeckers, goldeneyes and Tree Swallows.

Swimming in short bursts along the bottom with the bugs and beetles are a host of what most of us would call freshwater shrimp. Although these are crustaceans, they are not true shrimp—they are the amphipods *Gammarus* and *Hyalella*. They breed prolifically in productive lakes like this one that are rich in calcium. The *Gammarus* that have orange brood pouches on their undersides are pregnant females, which are especially favoured by trout.

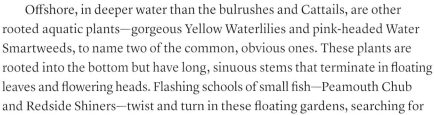

Western Toad

Offshore, in deeper water than the bulrushes and Cattails, are other rooted aquatic plants—gorgeous Yellow Waterlilies and pink-headed Water Smartweeds, to name two of the common, obvious ones. These plants are rooted into the bottom but have long, sinuous stems that terminate in floating leaves and flowering heads. Flashing schools of small fish—Peamouth Chub and Redside Shiners—twist and turn in these floating gardens, searching for the insects that thrive among them. Along the bottom are masses of shrubby-looking water plants— but on close examination we find that they are a type of green algae called *Chara*. This alga is brittle and crunchy, with a skeleton of calcium carbonate, and its presence tells us that the lake is rich in calcium.

The Redside Shiner is a common minnow of British Columbia lakes, ponds and slow rivers.

All the marsh life we've seen along the lakeshore brings up the question "What makes a marsh different from a lake, anyway?" In simple terms a marsh is simply a shallow lake—a lake where the emergent vegetation of the littoral zone covers the entire water body. The animals and plants that live in a shallow, protected bay of a lake will be just the same as those in a nearby marsh.

Open water

Paddling out beyond the littoral zone, past the dropoff, we come to the open waters of the lake—the limnetic zone. Here the water is more than 8 metres deep, too deep for rooted plants. Still, it is productive water, filled with microscopic algae that are busy growing and making food for tiny zooplankton such as the little crustaceans *Daphnia* and *Bosmina*.

Sometimes, in especially rich waters, the algae can "bloom" in midsummer and produce dense mats of filamentous algae or something resembling thin green soup. The cyanobacterium *Aphanizomenon* can form a bloom that looks like masses of small grass clippings but doesn't smell at all like a freshly mown lawn.

Out in the middle of the lake a pair of Common Loons is swimming and occasionally diving, disappearing for minutes at a time. The birds are fishing, but at midday the trout are far below, in the lake's dark depths.

The dark depths

Peering down into the depths of the lake, below 8 metres or so, we can imagine we see the profundal zone. Little light penetrates this deep, so few plants can photosynthesize and produce food and oxygen. Below the thermocline, the water is cold as well. It is not at all like the sunny shoreline paradise we were looking at a short time ago. The animals that live down there are scavengers or predators on scavengers, all dependent on the rain of food from the productive limnetic and littoral zones.

On the mud bottom of the lake live freshwater clams and millions of tiny worms: tubifex worms (distantly related to our garden earthworms) and bloodworms, which are actually larval midges. The midge larvae come in several dull colours besides red, but it is the big red ones that attract attention. The name bloodworm is a good one, since the red pigment is haemoglobin, which is used by the insect to snatch up the sometimes scarce oxygen down on the mud surface. When the midge larvae pupate and then emerge on the water surface as adults, they form the whining swarms of tiny flies that can form towering clouds over shrubs, trees and people along the lakeshore. Don't panic—they won't bite! They are simply mating swarms of males that are dancing en masse, hoping to attract a female to their party.

A distinctive community of fish preys on the invertebrates that live at the bottom of the lake, including Lake Chub, Lake Whitefish and Longnose Sucker.

Water insects

Although the label "true bug" doesn't inspire fear in most people, the aquatic members of the insect order Hemiptera are, milligram for milligram, among the fiercest predators in local ponds. Whereas their terrestrial cousins are often mild-mannered, plant-sucking citizens, aquatic bugs are invariably predacious. And they are predacious in diverse and remarkable ways. They do share a common, final modus operandi, however—all of them kill and consume their prey by stabbing them with a short beak, injecting them with digestive enzymes and sucking out the resulting nutritious broth. This last feature, among others, distinguishes the true bugs from beetles, which they superficially resemble.

Probably the most familiar bugs to all pond watchers are the water striders, or pond skaters. These graceful insects spread their weight out on long, thin legs that have pads of waxed hairs on the feet so that they can skate freely over the surface of the water. The water's surface tension not only gives them their skating rink but provides them with food as well—these predators specialize in prey that has become inadvertently trapped in the surface film.

Backswimmers are mirror image cousins of water striders, not in the sense that they look similar—they don't—but in the sense that they are upside-down hunters of the surface film. Instead of racing around on top of the pond, they swim gracefully on their backs just below the surface, powerfully propelled by large, oarlike hind legs.

Backswimmers are often mistakenly called water boatmen because of their big, rowing legs. But real water boatmen belong to a related family of bugs that swim right side up—look for their dark, folded wings on top. They are primarily plankton feeders, capturing small crustaceans and the like with their spiny, scooplike front legs. Water boatmen are especially abundant in the warm shallows of saline lakes of the Interior, where they form the bulk of the insect biomass.

The largest aquatic insect in British Columbia is the Giant Water Bug, a flattened, winged ovoid the size of a small frog with front legs that end in a sharp hook for capturing hapless insect larvae, tadpoles and small fish. It is often called toe-biter, for obvious reasons. In the warm evenings of late summer, these bugs—and the other bugs of the pond, too—take to the air, flying on strong wings to find new ponds.

A slender giant is the Water Scorpion, a bug that looks for all the world not like a scorpion but an aquatic praying mantis. The scorpion appellation comes from its straight, strawlike tail, which is just that—a straw through which it breathes air from the surface.

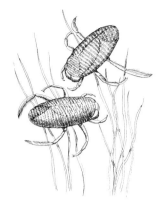

Water boatmen

Giant Water Bug

A backswimmer rests below the pond's surface film, waiting for prey.

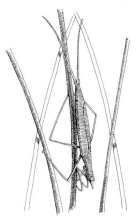

Water Scorpion

The water beetles most familiar to small children and curious adults are the predacious diving beetles. In British Columbia, these range in size from tiny to disturbingly large beetles, but all are smooth, streamlined, well-waxed insects superbly adapted to underwater life. Like water boatmen, they have long, hairy hind legs that row simultaneously for efficient swimming, and they carry air down from the surface under their wings. The larvae of predacious diving beetles are flattened, streamlined, quick and armed with hollow, sickle-shaped mandibles with which they capture, inject enzymes into and consume their prey. They well deserve their special name, water tigers.

The exquisite aerial forms of dragonflies are known even to people whose only experience of wetlands is the lily pond in a city park or golf course. The underwater lives of dragonflies are probably less well known to the general public. Dragonflies are, as their name suggests, active predators, both as larvae within the pond and as adults winging through the air. There are two primary groups of dragonflies—the robust, "true" dragonflies and the more delicate but equally predacious damselflies. The larvae of damselflies can be

SALAMANDERS VERSUS TROUT

I can remember walking through shallow, alkaline ponds as a boy, seeing great schools of fish scatter before me, rippling the surface of the warm waters. But then I discovered that these were not fish but salamanders—Tiger Salamanders, top dogs of the pond world.

Tiger Salamanders reach the northern edge of their range in the south Okanagan Valley and the Boundary country around Grand Forks. There they can be extremely abundant in ponds and lakes that meet their needs. Such ponds are rich in invertebrate life but lacking in fish. Where fish are absent, as they are in many small bodies of water that lack inlet or outlet streams, salamander larvae and frogs can become the top predators of the ecosystem. In permanent ponds that are fish-free, some Tiger Salamander larvae don't transform into the terrestrial adult form but instead grow and reproduce as gilled larvae, or neotenes. Neotenic larvae can reach the same impressive sizes as terrestrial adults—some grow to more than 30 centimetres in length!

A few years ago, lakes like Yellow Lake near Keremeos and Burnell Lake east of Oliver were salamander kingdoms. Attempts had been made to introduce trout into Yellow Lake, but the fish that weren't caught in the summer perished in the winter, suffocating in the oxygen-poor water beneath the ice, where salamaders are able to survive. But there is no sport in "fishing" for salamanders, so the provincial government decided to help the introduced trout by pumping air into the bottom of Yellow Lake to create an upwelling and bring the oxygen-starved water to the surface. This was a great success, and the present popularity of Yellow Lake as an all-season fishing destination attests to this.

But where fish flourish, salamanders get eaten—and few, if any, Tiger Salamander neotenes can be found in Yellow Lake today. The salamander kingdom is gone, unappreciated and unknown. What invertebrates lived with them? How did this ecosystem work? We don't have a distinguished by their slender bodies waving a triad of mottled, leaflike tails— true dragonflies are chubbier and lack the leafy tails. But the predacious lifestyle of both groups can be confirmed by one of the features they do hold in common—an incredible, hinged lower "lip" that flicks out and grasps unsuspecting prey in a flash.

Adult caddisfly

The other abundant group of insects commonly inhabiting British Columbia lakes is the caddisflies or, as fly-fishers call them, sedges. They're called sedges because at times the band of sedges along a lakeshore can be seething with them—brownish insects that look like small, elongate moths. They are related to moths, but instead of scales on their wings, they have thousands of short hairs. They can be hard to spot in the sedges, but when they skitter across the water's surface after emergence or when laying eggs, they look like tiny hydroplanes. The trout go crazy trying to catch them.

Larval caddisflies, which look like caterpillars, build "houses" of vegetation fragments, grains of sand or even strands of filamentous algae. They roam the lake floor, dragging their abode along with them as they scavenge for food.

clue. All we know is that it is completely different now. But the real tragedy is that these events are not unique to Yellow Lake—they have occurred at other lakes as well. And it goes beyond the range of Tiger Salamanders— similar scenarios have been repeated in lake after lake around the province. Lakes have been stocked and restocked with introduced Rainbow Trout or poisoned and then stocked or aerated and stocked. Today so many plateau lakes have been changed by foreign fish that it is difficult to find a natural ecosystem.

Tiger Salamanders are often the top predator in fish-free ponds in the south Okanagan and Boundary country.

Saline Lakes

Scattered through the grasslands of British Columbia are ponds and lakes that are encircled by shining white crystalline shores of salt. These strange-looking bodies of water occur where evaporation is greater than rainfall. Dissolved minerals are drawn into lake basins and, if no outlet stream exists, become concentrated as the water evaporates during the summer. Many such blind basins exist in the kettled terrain of glacial till, and where the surrounding till contains soluble minerals, lakes that contain high concentrations of various salts can develop. The distribution of minerals in the till and the movement of groundwater can interact in mysterious ways—a fascinating feature of a series of lakes in kettle terrain is that a very salty lake may lie within 100 metres of a very fresh one.

These lakes are not salty with table salt (sodium chloride) but instead contain baking soda (sodium bicarbonate), epsom salts (magnesium sulfate) or a variety of other salts made up of sodium, magnesium, carbonate, bicarbonate and sulfate. In a few lakes the salt concentration approaches that of seawater. As the water level falls in the late summer, bright white borders of

WHY DO WHIRLIGIGS WHIRL?

Unlike other aquatic insects, whirligig beetles make no attempt to hide from potential predators. Although they can be lone hunters at night, during the day they aggregate, sometimes in groups of hundreds or thousands—a fish could swallow many in a single bite. But whirligigs contain a number of nasty-tasting chemicals that are released when the insects are disturbed. These include at least five steroids such as cortisone and testosterone and a group of aldehydes collectively called gyrinidal, named after the whirligigs' family name, Gyrinidae. As ecologist Bernd Heinrich puts it, "There is only one thing more noxious than one gyrinid, and that is many." If the beetles stick together, they can be reasonably sure that fish or other predators in the area have tried to eat one or two and have learned their lesson.

Whirligigs aggregate by trying to follow each other. As they leave the group on their nocturnal hunting forays, they swim in a purposeful, straight line, but on their return they try to follow any fellow whirligig they encounter. More and more beetles join the weaving line, and then different groups lock onto one another. The swimming gets more and more confused and soon the big aggregation becomes stationary.

DRAGONFLY WATCHING

Dragonfly watchers and bird-watchers have a lot in common, and the reason is simple. Dragonflies act a lot like birds—they are large, colourful, active fliers that live in a sunlit, visual world. Their breeding behaviour has parallels as well; for instance, many male dragonflies defend territories at ponds or along streams where females will predictably show up to lay eggs. One feature that makes dragonfly watching even more exciting than bird-watching is that everything happens in a compressed time frame. Territories are established, defended and lost in an afternoon. Another advantage of studying dragonflies over birds is that dragonflies are active only when it is sunny and warm, so the dragonfly watcher doesn't need to get up before dawn or go out in the rain.

Most of the dragonflies that you see at ponds are males—they are waiting and watching for females, which usually only visit the pond for a short time to mate and lay eggs. If you watch these male dragonflies for a while, you will notice that not all of them are holding territories. In fact, you can divide male dragonflies into two groups according to this feature. Some, like the bright red meadowflies, hold territories by sitting on a favourite perch and flying out to challenge intruders; for this reason they are often referred to as perching dragonflies.

In some species, however, the females are less predictable or less visible, and it pays the males to range around the entire pond looking for them. This is what the blue darners do—they are often called patrolling dragonflies. Watch them as they course around the pond's edge, poking their heads into reed clumps and looking around logs. If they meet another male, they tussle for a second or two, separate and go in opposite directions; in this way, they space themselves out as much as possible.

When a blue darner male finds a female, he literally carries her off by grasping her head with claspers at the end of his abdomen—dragonfly biologists call this the tandem position. If she doesn't want to have anything to do with him—often the male has made a mistake and picked up the wrong species—she rejects his advances, and after a brief struggle they part company. If his actions are appropriate, however, she swings her abdomen up and latches onto the base of his abdomen, where he has previously stored his sperm. Thus engaged in the "wheel position," they fly into the protection of the forest, where they spend an undisturbed hour together.

A pair of White-faced Meadowflies mates in the wheel position.

crystalline salts appear around the shores of the lake. Embedded within the white ring and surrounding it are rings of other colours—a bright red ring of European Glasswort, a yellow ring of Alkali Saltgrass and so on, each ring representing a species of plant with a certain tolerance for salt and moisture. Unlike the fresher pothole ponds, saline lakes have little or no submerged vegetation and few clumps of typical emergent marsh plants such as Hard-stemmed Bulrushes.

Although few species can tolerate saline lakes, these waters can be crammed with life, for the water is warm and rich in nutrients. Alkali Bluet damselflies flit about the shoreline, capturing fragile adult midges, whose larvae mass in the mud at the bottom of the pond. Schools of water boatmen swarm in the shallows, joined by small predacious diving beetles. In a few extremely saline ponds in the Thompson and Okanagan Valleys, Brine Shrimp teem in the warm water.

FROZEN TURTLES

Painted Turtles are a symbol of summer in the ponds of the southern Interior, basking on logs in the hot sun. In late June and July, the female turtles lay their eggs in nests dug about 5 centimetres deep into south-facing banks of gravel and sand. The young hatch in early fall and immediately do a very unexpected thing—nothing. Instead of wriggling to the surface and joining their parents in the pond, they stay underground all winter. In early winter, the ground begins to freeze, and the tiny turtles freeze with it. Their body fluids stay liquid down to -3°C, but below that they are frozen solid.

Freezing normally kills all organisms, since the ice crystals rupture every cell membrane in the body as they grow. Painted Turtles have two lines of defence against this phenomenon. First, they move a lot of water out of their cells into blood vessels and other body cavities and then distribute special proteins throughout these spaces. These proteins promote the crystallization of ice but in a very regulated manner so that the crystals don't get big enough to do damage. Second, they fill their cells with antifreeze chemicals such as the sugar glucose. So their body fluids—blood, lymph and so on—freeze quickly, but the fluids inside cells do not, at least not down to temperatures of -10°C or so.

A few other pond dwellers, notably northern frogs such as the Wood Frog and the Striped Chorus Frog, share this strategy with young Painted Turtles. One of the strangest things about the ability to freeze solid is that it is totally lacking in adult turtles. They apparently cannot make the special ice crystallization proteins and so are forced to hibernate in the manner of most pond denizens—by burying themselves in the muddy bottoms below the frost line.

A Painted Turtle basks on a log in Langford Lake near Victoria.

BOGS AND FENS

Bogs and fens are peatlands, or wetlands where the substrate is made up primarily of organic matter—for example, undecayed or decaying mats of moss or sedges. The peat can form as a mat over open water along old lakeshores, resulting in "quaking bogs," which can result in unpleasant soakings for the unwary bog treader.

Bogs are dominated by peat mosses, which hold water like a sponge and over the years raise the wetland above the surrounding water table. Bogs often develop in nutrient-poor, acidic areas, but because peat mosses actively secrete acid, bogs become even more acidic than their surroundings (the pH is generally less than 4.0).

Because the vegetation within them doesn't decay easily, and because they are blocked from nutrient-bearing groundwater by peat—the only water they receive comes directly from rain or snowfall—bogs are also poor in nutrients.

In contrast, fens are dominated by sedges, grasses and mosses other than peat mosses—such as Golden Fuzzy Fen Moss, Sickle Moss and Giant Water Moss. Fens can be slightly acidic, but the pH is greater than 5.0. And unlike bogs, they receive nutrient-bearing groundwater. In other words, fens are peatlands that are friendlier and richer places to live for wetland plants and

Some shallow lakes with high concentrations of magnesium sulfate (epsom salts)—such as Spotted Lake, west of Osoyoos—produce giant circular patterns as the water evaporates and the salts crystallize.

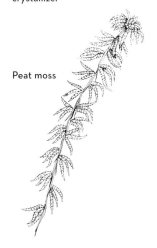

Peat moss

A small, relict population of Sandhill Cranes lives in Burns Bog. These are magnificent birds that have largely disappeared from the populated valleys of southern British Columbia.

BURNS BOG

Embedded firmly within the southern tier of Vancouver's suburbs is a huge wetland called Burns Bog. Four thousand hectares in extent, it is the largest domed bog on the Pacific coast of North America and the largest undeveloped tract of land in urbanized Canada. Seen from the air, it is a dark-green island in the midst of a grey and brown mosaic of industry, landfill, residential developments and intensive agriculture. Seen from the ground, it is a lowland northern wilderness with southern skyscrapers on the horizon. Bog Coppers and Muskeg Darners flutter and fly over the mossy carpet, as many as a dozen Black Bears feast on blueberries and cranberries, and even a handful of Sandhill Cranes make the bog their home.

Five thousand years ago, Burns Bog was a wetland right at the mouth of the Fraser River. As the delta passed it by, its stagnant waters—probably choked with slowly rotting logs—were gradually overtaken by peat mosses. The moss layer became thicker and thicker, the water rose with it, and the bog grew higher and higher. The centre of the dome is now almost six metres above the river!

animals. Features of bogs and fens can intermix in the same wetland—acidic peat moss mats, for example, can be dissected by sinuous groundwater creeklets that are surrounded by fen formations on either side.

Peatlands are most common in areas of high precipitation, since high precipitation usually results in nutrient-poor wetlands and forests. Peatlands are abundant along the rain-lashed outer west coast but are sparse across the southern Interior plateaus until you reach the Interior wet belt in the Cariboo, Monashee and Selkirk Mountains. In the far northeast, they reach their zenith in areas like the Fort Nelson Lowlands that are underlain by frozen soil much of the year.

But just because bogs are acidic and nutrient poor—and consequently stressful places to live—doesn't mean that they are devoid of life. A few plants and animals that can tolerate these conditions create a unique ecosystem. On the high moss hummocks grow a few shrubs, almost invariably including Labrador Tea. This plant's spicy scent is one of the singular smells of northern Canada, and its distinctive, rolled leaves with rusty undersides make it easy to identify. Bog-rosemary and Western Bog-laurel often brighten the scene with their fair pink flowers, and the snow-white tufts of cottongrasses nod in the breeze. On slightly higher ground grow Scrub, Low or Paper Birches and stunted Lodgepole Pines.

But the plants that trail along the moss are the most interesting, both biologically and gastronomically. Because nutrients are in short supply, a number of plants have become carnivores. In almost every bog in British Columbia live sundews, beautiful little plants that capture flying insects with delicate but effective leaf hairs tipped with a sticky fluid. Butterworts have

Sickle Moss

Giant Water Moss

Labrador Tea

Bog-rosemary

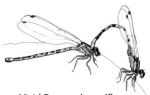

Western Bog-laurel

attractive, nectar-filled purple flowers, but small insects are attracted as well to the yellowish leaves, which trap them in a surface slime. Most naturalists have heard of pitcher-plants and their unique way of capturing prey; in British Columbia these plants are restricted to the muskegs of the far northeast. In late summer, however, the bog plants that attract humans the most are the Bog Blueberries, Bog Cranberries and Cloudberries.

HOT SPRINGS

Hot springs are scattered throughout the mountainous regions of British Columbia. They occur where water can percolate down through porous rocks to depths where the temperature rises over the boiling point. If the superheated, mineral-rich water finds fractures that can take it rapidly to the surface, it follows them upward and emerges as a hot spring.

Hot springs are full of specialized life. For example, the Vivid Dancer is a beautiful damselfly of particularly intense blue coloration that lives in cool, spring-fed streams south of the 49th parallel, but in the snowy mountains of southern British Columbia it is restricted to a handful of hot or warm springs. There it is probably a relict of the warm age that followed the retreat of the glaciers. That is, it was probably more widespread seven thousand years ago or so but has since survived only in the warm waters flowing from hot pools.

Other relicts of that warm age include several intriguing organisms living in the Liard River Hot Springs, near Liard Crossing on the Alaska Highway. A small snail, the Hotwater Physa, lives here and nowhere else. Another damselfly, the tiny Plains Forktail, lives here and nowhere else in British Columbia—its nearest relatives live in streams on the Great Plains, as far north as southern Saskatchewan. A race of Lake Chub with a unique hot springs lifestyle also makes the warm streams and marshes of Liard home.

The human attraction to naturally hot water has spelled disaster for the specialized, dependent inhabitants of most hot springs, for if the springs are of any size and consequence, they are soon dammed or piped away to concrete pools in commercial resorts. If they are lucky, the former inhabitants find refuge in the trickles that escape the pipes—at Fairmont Hot Springs in the East Kootenay, for example, the four remaining sterile clumps of Southern Maidenhair Fern in Canada cling to a single ledge.

RIVERSIDE FORESTS AND MEADOWS

Stretching like long green ribbons along the rivers and creeks of the province are moist forests quite unlike those on the surrounding hills. They are usually dominated by fragrant Black Cottonwood, but Western Redcedar also prefers the rich, well-watered soil of floodplains. In time, if the river doesn't reclaim

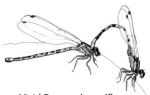

Vivid Dancer damselfly

the land first, spruces, pines or firs also colonize the levees and grow to immense sizes. Giants such as the Sitka Spruces of Carmanah Creek and the Douglas-firs of Cathedral Grove and Nimpkish Island all grow in well-watered and well-fed streamside forests.

The short trunks and rounded, clumped tops of these bog-dwelling Lodgepole Pines in Naikoon Park are a result of phosphorous deficiency.

Called riparian forests by ecologists, these woodlands are home to a diverse community of animals and plants, but too often they are the first ecosystems to feel the effect of development. The cottonwoods grow large quickly but begin to die relatively young. In a mature stand, many trees are hollow and have broken tops or have lost large branches, which provide inviting shelter for birds such as Western Screech-Owls, Northern Saw-whet Owls, Barred Owls, Vaux's Swifts and Lewis's Woodpeckers as well as a variety of bats. Large entrances often lead to the abodes of Raccoons or the winter homes of Black Bears. Mature cottonwoods have sturdy, horizontal branches that provide excellent platforms for nesting Red-tailed Hawks, Northern Goshawks, Bald Eagles and Great Blue Herons.

The understorey of riparian forests is a complex assortment of plant communities, from a tangle of tall shrubs dominated by species such as Red-osier

Dogwood to meadows of orchids, lilies, violets and other wildflowers. These rich habitats are also home to special bird communities—in the southern Interior valleys, for example, Veeries, Gray Catbirds, Black-headed Grosbeaks and Yellow-breasted Chats all sing from shrubby forests along watercourses. The lush, grassy meadows are home to thriving populations of voles, which provide abundant food for nesting hawks and owls. In southern British Columbia, these swards are graced with the jumbled song of the Bobolink and the insectlike buzz of the Savannah Sparrow.

Pages 320–21: The warm marshes below Liard Hot Springs are home to a special snail, damselfly and fish.

Right: The Interior subspecies of the Western Screech-Owl is restricted in Canada to a few remaining cottonwood and aspen riparian forests in the Okanagan and adjacent valleys.

Riparian forests and meadows are the link between water and land. Not only does fresh water support an abundance of life in these habitats, but riparian ecosystems are vital for aquatic life as well. The trees provide shade, their root networks stabilize the shore, fallen leaves fertilize the river, and fallen insects feed aquatic invertebrates and fish. When old trees are uprooted by spring floods, their fallen trunks stabilize the stream flow and create pools that are critical to animals such as fish, salamanders and dragonflies.

CLIMATE CHANGE IN THE WORLD OF FRESH WATER

Freshwater habitats will be drastically affected by climate change over the next century. For rivers and streams, the flow patterns described earlier in this chapter will shift along with temperature and precipitation patterns. As winters become warmer and wetter, more precipitation will fall as rain and less as snow. This variation will increase winter stream flows in low-elevation coastal rivers that are fed predominantly by rainfall, resulting in more flood risk in valley bottoms. For river flows dominated by snow melt, the decrease in winter snowfall combined with earlier, warmer springs will shift peak flows to earlier in the spring, and those peaks will be smaller. Longer, hotter summers will result in very low flows from July through October in most streams across the province. Hotter summers are already melting glaciers in British Columbia mountains at a tremendous rate. Rivers fed predominantly by summer glacier melt will therefore experience higher summer flows for a number of decades as the glaciers shrink, then revert to a pattern of spring peak flows as the water produced by summer glacial melt drops to insignificant levels compared to spring snowmelt freshets.

Any of these changes in stream flow pattern will have impacts on stream ecology. Runs of spawning salmon are delayed when river flows are low and water temperatures high, reducing the number of fish that manage to reach the spawning grounds. Populations of salmon and other river-dwelling fish will also be impacted if winter flood events scour spawning beds more frequently.

Small water bodies throughout the province, but especially in the southern Interior where summers are typically dry and warm, are already shrinking in the face of longer, hotter summers. These wetlands provide critical habitat to many species of plants and animals, so any substantial change in their size and distribution could have important impacts on the ecosystems around them.

THE FUTURE

THE FUTURE

THIS BOOK HAS focussed on the "natural" world of British Columbia, a world that seems somehow separate from human civilization. But humans are an integral part of nature, especially now that our ecological footprints are so huge and heavy. It is a cruel paradox that even as our daily lives become more isolated from nature, our increasing hunger for resources means that we have a greater effect on the "natural" ecosystems of this province.

The face of the world has been radically changed over the last century. The human population is increasing by a quarter of a million people every day. Many of the world's forests have been felled, and everywhere they are falling faster and faster. The ocean has been efficiently scoured; fishery after fishery has boomed and then collapsed. As prosperity in the developed world increases, people consume more resources and use more energy. And as consumption of fossil fuels increases, so does the production of carbon dioxide and other greenhouse gases. Chlorofluorocarbons and other ozone-eating chemicals slowly filter towards the upper atmosphere, cutting holes in the earth's ultraviolet light barrier.

This litany of environmental changes could go on and on, for we are living in a period of incredible change, a period in which much of the world's natural diversity is being replaced by a human monoculture. But British Columbia is a fortunate part of the world—or is it?

Not long ago it was a wilderness with only a few aboriginal communities living off the land in relative harmony with the natural ecosystem. For many years its rugged mountains resisted colonization and exploitation. Even today, most of the land in British Columbia sees few people.

But British Columbia is no longer a vast, untamed land of limitless resources. Highways and logging and mining roads have penetrated formerly impenetrable mountain ranges, and the deep, rich valleys have been plowed, paved and flooded.

What is the state of British Columbia's natural ecosystems today? What can we learn from the past? And what does the future hold?

THREATENED ECOSYSTEMS

Shangri-La: The Lost Valleys

British Columbia is a land of mountains and high plateaus—about three-quarters of its land lies above 1000 metres in elevation and more than 18 per cent is rock, ice or tundra. It is, by and large, dominated by steep terrain with long winters at high elevations. Only a very few people live above 1000 metres, even on the flat plateaus. More than 80 per cent of the province's human population crowds into the coastal plains and deep valleys of the southern sixth of the province, where the land is flat, the soil fertile and the winters short.

The population is also growing fastest in the lowlands. From 1986 to 1991, the Fraser Valley's population grew by 17 per cent and the Okanagan Valley's by 15 per cent. By 2016, the total population of British Columbia is projected to reach 4.9 million, up 40 per cent from 1995.

Major environmental change began soon after European and Asian settlement in the lowlands; the settlers cleared lowland forests and plowed the rich bottomland and benchland soils. The Fraser River Delta and smaller estuaries on the east side of Vancouver Island were diked and drained. In 1948 there were already 1.8 million hectares of farmland in the province; by 1971 there were 2.4 million hectares.

And the changes continue. In the Lower Mainland, on the east side of Vancouver Island, and in the Okanagan Valley, urban and suburban sprawl is consuming both agricultural areas and the remnant natural ecosystems. In British Columbia as a whole, almost 600,000 hectares have been developed for urban and rural settlement and transportation. The remaining farmland is also being more intensively worked—edge habitats are being converted to agricultural land with little or no regard for their value as wildlife habitat, and fertilizers and pesticides are being used to increase production.

Pages 324-325: The massive roadwork of the Sea to Sky Highway arcs through a coastal forest north of Vancouver.

The Columbia River valley, cleared in preparation for flooding behind the Revelstoke Dam in 1981. In the cause of electrical power and flood control, a number of rivers and their valley bottoms have been sacrificed under the floodwaters of dams, small and large: 102,000 hectares in the Columbia system, 175,000 hectares in the Peace and 91,000 hectares in the Nechako.

Most of the plant and animal species we share the province with also prefer or even require the disappearing natural ecosystems of British Columbia's valleys, which are benign, rich places. Fully half of the animal species on the provincial Red List—those that may be threatened or endangered—are confined to low elevations.

Grasslands and Savannas

Globally, grasslands are one of the most threatened ecosystems. In North America, no other terrestrial ecosystem has lost so much of its land base to human development. Between 76 and 99 per cent of the native grasslands of Canada's prairies have been eliminated by cultivation and other development. Despite this incredible decline in grassland area, the problem has received little media attention. The lack of attention might be better ascribed not to the media but to the fixation of many conservation groups on wetlands and the giant trees of coastal forests.

The grasslands on British Columbia's plateaus are not as imperilled by development as their lower-elevation and prairie cousins, but they are still grazed extensively. Although overstocking with cattle is not the problem it once was, studies in British Columbia have shown that twenty to forty years of full rest are required for range sites to recover from poor to excellent condition.

Besides grazing, one of the main effects that humans have had on grasslands is fire suppression. Grasslands are ecosystems that live by fire, and when humans control fires, the conifer forests surrounding the islands of grass begin to invade. In British Columbia, this invasion is especially evident in the cooler, moister grasslands of the central plateaus and eastern valleys. In these areas, about 30 per cent of the grasslands have returned to forest and woodland since 1960.

Our system of parks and reserves, built over the last century largely with recreation in mind, has protected many mountains and high, forested valleys, but less than 1 per cent of British Columbia's grasslands have been set aside for their natural flora and fauna to flourish without interference from humans and their livestock. In a report on the grasslands of the Cariboo and Chilcotin Plateaus, Tracy Hooper and Michael Pitt of the University of British Columbia recommend that large, contiguous, representative areas of grassland be conserved.

But if these endangered ecosystems are to survive, cooperative steward-ship agreements with private landowners must be made. In most cases, grassland communities can coexist with sensible grazing practices.

Old-Growth Forests

The pace of logging in British Columbia has increased dramatically in the last twenty-five years. On the coast, over half of all trees cut have been felled since 1967, and in the Interior, over half of all trees cut have been felled since 1977. The Forest Service has calculated the long-run sustainable yield for the province to be about 59 million cubic metres of wood per year. In 1975, about 60 million cubic metres were cut, and this number increased throughout the 1980s; in 1991, almost 75 million cubic metres were cut. Although the amount of old-growth forest remaining is a matter of controversy, it is clear that at present rates of cut, little will be left in a few decades.

Regardless of how they are defined, old-growth forests are home to dif-ferent animal, plant and fungus communities from those of younger forests. And although we have learned a great deal about how to cut and grow trees fast and efficiently in the past few decades, we are only just beginning to learn how the forest works as a community. But, as we should have expected, the interrelationships among its inhabitants are strong in an old-growth forest. Spotted Owls and Northern Flying Squirrels both need large trees for nesting sites; the owls depend on flying squirrels for food, and the squirrels, in turn, depend on truffles. The truffles depend on the flying squirrels to disperse them and the big trees, in turn, depend on the truffles' fungal threads for sustenance.

Scientists still know appallingly little about the invertebrate and fungal communities in old-growth forests, but initial research is showing that these communities are diverse and critical to the long-term survival of the forest's trees. In some cases, they are unique—living among the nesting Marbled Murrelets in the moss carpets of the upper branches of giant Sitka Spruces is

a community of unusual springtails and other insects that are found nowhere else in the world. But the real diversity in old-growth forests is probably found in the slowly decaying humus on the forest floor—and scientists know virtually nothing of this complex community of invertebrates and fungi.

Today's system of logging is only beginning to take this information into account. Even if the forest was harvested in a sustainable manner, only isolated remnants of old growth would remain after the first cycle of cutting. And since the second cut would go through after eighty or a hundred years, no harvested blocks would ever regrow to become old forests again. Clearcutting, the main method of logging in most British Columbia forests, leaves no large, living trees or dead snags to carry over some of the critical features of old growth to the new stand and, once the big logs and stumps of the first cut have rotted away, there will be none left for the termites, salamanders, voles and martens to live in.

"Who speaks for the forest in British Columbia? The silent constituent in all of our conflict and uncertainty over forest use is the forest itself." —Herb Hammond, *Seeing the Forest among the Trees*

Wetlands

Below our childhood home near Penticton was a large marsh on the floodplain of the Okanagan River at its outlet from Okanagan Lake. In the early 1950s the channellization of the Okanagan River cut off its direct water supply and Highway 97 divided it in two—but the marsh persisted. The strange, pumping calls of bitterns and squeals of rails still emanated from the cattails on summer nights, and waterfowl lingered on their southward journey in the autumn. But perhaps the most welcome denizens of the reeds were the Red-winged Blackbirds that returned early every spring and made the dry, brown cattails come alive with their loud *onk-er-ee!* cries and flashing red shoulders.

But over a period of more than a decade the marsh died a slow death. Clean Fill Wanted signs ringed the edges, and the cattails were slowly and inexorably smothered in earth and concrete rubble. Eventually, the only water that remained was in the narrow ditch between the fill and the highway—and there a few remaining blackbirds made their home in the last of the cattails. And with the cruel irony that seems to accompany so many developments, the new walled community that rose from the marsh was named Redwing Estates.

This scene has been repeated innumerable times throughout British Columbia. Flying over verdant river valleys, one sees only the green ghosts of oxbow ponds in the hay meadows along diked rivers. In other, less fortunate valleys, whole wetland systems have been drowned under reservoirs.

SPOTTED OWLS

Spotted Owls are symbols of what the coastal slope of the Pacific Northwest used to be—a virtually unbroken forest of towering conifers blanketing the valleys and mountains from the coast to the dry forests in the rain shadow of the Coast Mountains and Cascade Range.

Dependent on large expanses of old-growth forest for both foraging habitat and nesting sites, Spotted Owls have declined drastically in the face of large-scale logging in the core of their range in Washington and Oregon.

At night, in the open forest halls beneath the high green canopy, they hunt flying squirrels and woodrats. A single Spotted Owl consumes an average of two hundred flying squirrels in a year, providing a possible explanation for why they require such large tracts of old-growth forest—about 3200 hectares per nesting pair.

In British Columbia, Spotted Owls have been found at only thirty-nine sites. Undoubtedly fewer than ten pairs remain, restricted to the scattered, unlogged headwater valleys of creeks and rivers from Vancouver's North Shore east to Manning Park and north to the Birkenhead Lake area. The Committee on the Status of Endangered Wildlife in Canada has declared the Spotted Owl an endangered species in this country.

The primary threat to the persistence of Spotted Owls is fragmentation of the remaining old forest. Not only do adult Spotted Owls not hunt over open clearcuts or in regenerating forest, but juvenile owls are apparently easily killed by larger predators such as Great Horned Owls as they move across open country in their search for a new home.

How we go about sharing the remaining old-growth forest in southwestern British Columbia with Spotted Owls will say a lot about how much we are willing to sacrifice to ensure that not only these owls but this entire magnificent forest ecosystem will not perish.

Wetlands are seen as wastelands. Some of the finest, such as Burns Bog in Delta and Alki Lake near Kelowna, have suffered the worst fate and become huge garbage dumps.

Like most aspects of the environment, the statistics on wetlands are depressing, especially in the southern valleys. The once meandering Okanagan River has been channellized and 85 per cent of Okanagan wetlands are gone. At the mouth of the Fraser River, 70 per cent of the delta has been diked and drained, and habitats such as seasonal wet meadows and bogs have virtually disappeared. The vast wetlands of Sumas Lake are gone forever. The Kootenay River at Creston has been diked and much of the floodplain converted to agriculture. The remaining marshes within the Creston Valley Wildlife Management Area only persist because of intensive manipulation by the Management Authority, since the life-giving floods of the Kootenay River have been eliminated by the Libby Dam upstream—and the same dam has drowned the floodplain of the upper Kootenay River south of Cranbrook.

Filling or draining has eliminated 85 per cent of the Okanagan Valley's wetlands.

FOR THE THIRD GENERATION . . . ON THE OLD FARM . . . THE DAYS OF THE HUNTER'S PARADISE WERE AT THEIR BEST. TO THE WEST, SUMAS LAKE, 10,000 ACRES OF WATER AND 20,000 ACRES OF MARGINAL LANDS AND SLOUGHS, WAS THE RESTING PLACE AND FEEDING GROUND OF MILLIONS OF DUCKS AND GEESE. TO THE EAST WAS THE BIG INDIAN PRAIRIE, THOUSANDS OF ACRES OF SWAMPY MARSHY LAND, FEEDING GROUNDS FOR COUNTLESS SWARMS OF MIGRATING WATERFOWL . . . FOR HOURS AT A TIME GREAT FLOCKS FILLED THE SKY AS THEY WINGED BACK AND FORTH FROM ONE FEEDING GROUND TO ANOTHER. FOR WEEKS THE VALLEY WAS FULL OF MIGRATING WATERFOWL.

Oliver Wells, in *Waterfowl on a Pacific Estuary* by B. Leach

Riparian forests stretch like long thin green ribbons along the rivers and creeks of the province. These moist forests are usually dominated by Black Cottonwood, but Western Redcedar also prefers the rich, well-watered soil of floodplains. In time, if the river doesn't reclaim the land first, spruces, pines or firs colonize the levees and grow to immense sizes. The problems of riparian forests can be explained by simple geography. In a mountainous area, floodplains, however small, are often the only flat land in a valley. Consequently, they are traversed by road and rail corridors and power line rights-of-way and are cleared for housing and commercial development. Their rich soils make them especially attractive as future pastures and croplands. Although they once threaded their way throughout the province's major valleys, they are now uncommon, fragmented or degraded in most areas.

The Sea

When we look into the sea, we tend to see a reflection of the sky more than the real picture of the ecosystems beneath the waves. Because we are land-based creatures, we are ignorant of the sea. And we ignore that of which we are ignorant.

British Columbia's deep, cold waters with strong tidal currents along a rugged coastline have partially protected the sea from fouling and pollution, but they haven't protected it from exploitation. The overharvesting of otters, whales and fish has significantly changed the ecological dynamics of the coastal waters of British Columbia.

An efficient whaling industry eliminated Humpback Whales from the Strait of Georgia by the early 1900s and virtually wiped out Humpbacks and Blue Whales on the west coast of Vancouver Island in the middle of the century. From 1913 to 1968, organized government slaughters of Northern Sea Lions killed over 55,000 individuals and eradicated some of the breeding rookeries north of Vancouver Island. The rookeries have not recovered their former numbers, although sea lions have begun a new, large rookery in southeastern Alaska. A more alarming trend has begun in their strongholds in the Aleutian Islands of Alaska, where about 60 per cent of the world's population of Northern Sea Lions has disappeared in recent years, probably because the fish community they depended on has been overharvested.

> THERE IS NO REASON TO DOUBT—INDEED, THE FACT IS BEYOND QUESTION—THAT THE NUMBER OF SALMON NOW REACHING THE HEAD WATERS OF STREAMS IN THE COLUMBIA RIVER BASIN IS INSIGNIFICANT IN COMPARISON WITH THE NUMBER WHICH SOME YEARS AGO ANNUALLY VISITED AND SPAWNED IN THESE WATERS.
>
> Marshall McDonald, United States Commissioner of Fisheries, 1894

One of the most telling tales of our treatment of aquatic ecosystems is the story of declining Pacific salmon. These are fish that we know and love, that are part of our culture and that give us economic benefit. Yet they are vanishing and will continue to vanish unless we make strong commitments to reverse the trend. In British Columbia, as of 1996, 124 stocks of anadromous (fish breeding in fresh water and maturing in the ocean) salmonids were known to be extinct and 624 were at high risk of extinction.

The Department of Fisheries and Oceans estimates that loss and degradation of spawning habitat accounts for 20 to 30 per cent of the disappearance of small salmon populations. This loss is especially acute for Coho Salmon, which have suffered a 90 per cent decline in the Strait of Georgia. Even after the Coho spawn, vast numbers simply disappear when they get to the ocean.

Is the culprit starvation due to a decline in herring stocks, increasing incidence of toxic algal blooms, competition with hatchery fish, or predation by mackerel spreading north in the warm waters of El Niño? Or is it that global warming has changed the timing of the spring freshet and thus the timing of the spring plankton bloom that feeds young salmon? Most fish biologists agree that, although other factors compound the problem, human greed is firmly behind the collapse of our coastal symbol. We have been catching too many salmon.

Dams have had an enormous impact on anadromous fish; the many dams on the Columbia River have eliminated seventeen British Columbia salmon stocks, and dams have also wiped out stocks in the Coquitlam and Alouette Rivers.

In our preoccupation with salmon we have often ignored the health of other species. The overall Strait of Georgia fishery has declined almost 50 per cent in the past ten years alone. This includes numerous fish: Pacific Herring, Lingcod, Pacific Halibut, sole and many species of rockfish. The halibut fishery was regulated in 1932, but not before inshore bank populations had been fished out. Rockfish take twenty years to mature, can live longer lives than humans, and stay in one place throughout their lives, all characteristics that make them unsuitable to sustain a fishery. They have suffered drastic declines. The commercial Lingcod fishery has been closed in the Strait of Georgia now that the population has been reduced by a staggering 97 per cent.

The fishery for Pacific Herring, one of the key species of the coastal ecosystem, collapsed in 1950 because of overfishing for fish meal. It was reopened in 1970 for roe, but has since collapsed again. A serious flaw in the management of herring has been the assumption that overfished stocks in one area will be replenished by successful spawning elsewhere. However, recent research by Jeff Marliave of the Vancouver Aquarium has shown that herring larvae spend less time dispersing as plankton and cover less distance than previously thought. As a result, overfished populations have simply been wiped out. Where herring have failed, so too have groundfish, Lingcod and rockfish. Knowing the reliance of Bald Eagles, ducks and other seabirds on herring, one must ask how these species will be affected as well.

Invertebrates have not escaped the plunder. Long-lived species such as Abalone and Geoduck are both susceptible to overexploitation. There is now a moratorium on the Abalone fishery, and the harvesting of Geoduck clams has been described by University of British Columbia marine biologist Mike Hawkes as "the underwater equivalent of strip mining." Recent experimental fisheries using sea cucumbers and sea urchins indicate that although seemingly plentiful, marine invertebrates are not good candidates for sustainable fisheries. Marine invertebrates tend to be long-lived and, although they may successfully spawn each year, development and settlement of the larvae and juveniles may occur only once in ten years.

Pacific Herring

Our knowledge of marine invertebrate biology needs to be expanded not only for the sake of individual species of invertebrates but also to understand the importance of complex invertebrate communities in the overall picture of ocean ecology. The destruction of benthic marine invertebrate communities through deep-water trawling is now known to be related to the collapse of many groundfish stocks. Slow-growing ancient communities of sponges, bryozoans and other animals that grow like tangled vines and bushes on the ocean bottom likely act as nurseries for juvenile fish. Trawling equipment used to harvest deep-sea, bottom-dwelling fish has had a devastating effect on the entire seafloor habitat; each pass of a trawl removes up to 20 per cent of seafloor animals, so a series of ten trawls results in total depletion.

Geoduck

THE OCEAN IS GOING WRONG, BIG TIME. IT'S PROGRESSING.
IT'S GETTING WORSE. AND IT'S STILL A MYSTERY.
Dr. Carl Walters, in "The Fate of the Strait," by Mark Hume,
Vancouver Sun, June 5, 1998

All over the world, we are fishing down the food web. When salmon, Lingcod, rockfish and halibut stocks decline, pressure intensifies on herring, prawns and krill. If those stocks fail, the entire ecosystem collapses. As fisheries expert Daniel Pauly says, we have all but eliminated the fish at the top of the food web. "We are now eating bait . . . and we're headed for jellyfish."

British Columbia's marine aquaculture industry is based almost entirely on salmon farming. This production of Atlantic and Pacific (Chinook and Coho) salmon now exceeds the value of the total commercial catch. About 130 farms now produce more than 25,000 tonnes of fish each year, and that number could rise now that a moratorium on new salmon farms has been lifted. The bounty produced in these farms does not come without an environmental price, though the exact nature of that price is controversial.

More than five hundred Harbor Seals are reported shot by salmon-farm employees each year, and the unreported toll is likely much higher. Attempts to scare off seals and sea lions using recordings of predatory Killer Whales have been shown to alter the behaviour of all marine mammals—including whales and porpoises—within miles of the speakers and are ultimately ineffective, as local seals habituate to the sounds.

Another serious problem with open-net fish farms is accidental escapement. Each year, more than sixty thousand salmon escape into the open ocean, almost all of them Atlantic Salmon. Some of these have spawned successfully in the wild, as a few newly hatched Atlantic Salmon were found in the Tsitika River in 1998. Disease is another concern. In 2001, juvenile Pink Salmon in the Broughton Archipelago off the northeast coast of Vancouver Island suffered high mortality at sea, almost certainly because of an infestation of sea lice (mostly *Lepeophtheirus salmonis*) that was clearly linked to nearby salmon farms. The high juvenile mortality that year resulted in a dramatic drop in the numbers of adults returning to spawn in 2002.

Most early salmon farms in British Columbia were located in protected bays, but these proved to be unsuitable locations. Problems arose with the frequency of toxic algal blooms, accumulation of feces and high nutrient levels in the water. The combination of more knowledgeable site selection, more efficient diets and feeding strategies, improved pen design and solid bag technology may not only reduce the escapement of fish but also reduce overall pressures on the environment.

INTRODUCED SPECIES

Most people would be surprised, if not shocked, if they knew how many of British Columbia's wild species of plants and animals have arrived with humans from Europe and Asia. Surveying a meadow of golden grass and bright yellow broom on the Gulf Islands, you might find it hard to believe that the broom and most, if not all, of the grasses you are looking at are foreign species that have displaced the native grasses and wildflowers.

In fact, over four thousand species—more than five hundred of them plants—have been introduced by humans either accidentally or purposely to British Columbia. For plants, that means about one in five of the total flora. Most of these species are first established in areas where the native plants have been removed or disturbed—areas that have been plowed, bulldozed or overgrazed, for example—and most of them stay there. But some, like broom and the Purple Loosestrife that is taking over the wetlands in the southern valleys, are successful invaders that can completely choke out the plant community that existed before their arrival.

Although many fewer animal species than plant species have been brought into North America, their effects on the native ecosystems have been no less significant. The European Starling, first released in New York in 1896, reached British Columbia in the mid-1940s and was common throughout the southern part of the province by the 1950s. House Sparrows arrived even earlier, probably around the turn of the century. Both these species had long-standing ties to cities and agricultural areas in Europe, and both were immediately successful in similar habitats here. In fact, they perform valuable ecological services in such habitats, where few native species have prospered. They probably wouldn't be considered pests in British Columbia were they not hole-nesting birds, and aggressive ones at that. The arrival of the European Starling is closely tied to the decline of native species, such as Lewis's Woodpeckers, Western and Mountain Bluebirds, and Purple Martins, that it vigorously competes with for the limited number of nesting cavities.

Terrestrial Invertebrates

Most of the thousands of foreign species in British Columbia are invertebrates, but because these are usually small, unfamiliar or otherwise hidden to us, we frequently don't see the often massive changes they bring to their ecosystems. The following cases are a small sample of literally hundreds of stories that could be told.

Perhaps the best example of this is the earthworms. There are at least twenty-four species of earthworms in British Columbia, and twenty of them are exotic species from Europe. The four native species are restricted to limited areas of coniferous forest soils on the West Coast. Most of us have been taught that earthworms are beneficial miners that create rich, aerated soil. This is true in some ecosystems, but in previously earthworm-free forests, they can be devastatingly efficient ecosystem engineers. Simply put, they consume the complex litter layers of the forest and turn them into more homogeneous soil. Each earthworm species affects the soil in a slightly different way, so the greater the diversity of earthworms, the more extreme the changes wrought by them. Critical nutrients that formerly trickled into the soil are released quickly and may soon be leached away. The herbaceous plants that were beautifully adapted to exploiting the forest litter often simply vanish. Trees suffer when their fine roots are damaged or destroyed and critical mycorrhizal associations are disrupted.

You may think that an earthworm invasion would happen in extreme slow motion, and indeed they only move about 10 metres per year on their own—but humans are moving them around much more quickly, both as fishing bait and in soil picked up by earth-moving equipment. This invasion is happening across a broad swath of eastern North American forests; in British Columbia, few details are known, but exotic earthworms are widespread and they are changing our native forests, both coniferous and deciduous.

We all know lady beetles (ladybugs), the cute predators of our gardens and woodland meadows. Most of us, however, would not be able to tell the difference between an exotic Multicolored Asian Lady Beetle and one of British Columbia's native species. This species was introduced from eastern Asia into North America numerous times throughout the last century in attempts to control aphids, but for some reason it didn't become established in North America until the 1990s. But then it made up for lost time—it is now by far the commonest lady beetle in southern British Columbia. Native species such as the Transverse Lady Beetle have declined significantly in southern British Columbia since its arrival, and this is probably no coincidence. And not only does the Multicolored Asian Lady Beetle outcompete and even eat native lady beetles, but it loves to overwinter inside houses and exudes an extremely unpleasant odour and stain when frightened.

A European Paper Wasp queen begins a new paper nest.

When we were growing up in the Okanagan, native Northern Paper Wasps were constant summer companions around our house, and their small paper nests adorned the undersides of our eaves. The wasps patrolled our garden, hunting for caterpillars that they fed to their young. However, within the last decade, they seem to have become scarcer, which coincides with the arrival of their sibling, the European Paper Wasp. These handsome wasps have quickly become the commonest paper wasps in southern British Columbia. But how do they push their native relatives out? First, they feed on a much wider variety of insects, not just caterpillars; and they are also more productive than Northern Paper Wasps, foraging earlier in the day and producing workers about a week earlier than the native species.

The Common Eastern Bumble Bee is, as its name suggests, familiar to many gardeners in eastern Canada. It has a tongue of medium length, which means that it can forage from a wide variety of plants, including many crop species. It is an especially good pollinator of tomatoes and sweet peppers, both of which require buzz pollination—a bumble bee specialty in which pollen needs to be vigorously shaken out of the anthers. For this and other reasons the Common Eastern Bumble Bee has become the bee of choice for managed pollination in greenhouses. It is this work that has brought the Common Eastern Bumble Bee to British Columbia but, as might be expected, it hasn't stayed confined to greenhouses. In fact, in 2013, it was found in the wilds of the Okanagan. Will it push its western cousins aside? Its success in its native range may foreshadow a serious threat to the diverse native bumble bee fauna of the west.

SEX AND THE DECLINE OF BEES

The decline of bees has been in the news a great deal in the last few years—and there is good reason for us to pay attention. The pollination services of bees are, after all, vital to the health of the natural and agricultural ecosystems we live among and depend on. Although honey bees (which are not native to North America) are vital to the production of many crops, the hundreds of species of native bees in British Columbia are crucial pollinators as well. And although the decline has been best documented within the honey bee industry, some native bees are declining as well. For example, the Western Bumble Bee has largely disappeared from the populated and intensively farmed lowlands, and its nest parasite, the Gypsy Cuckoo Bumble Bee, hasn't been seen in the province for a quarter century.

What is causing this decline? The short answer is that no one really knows. Pesticides, including the new neonicotinoids, seem to be killing bees even at what ought to be safe levels. Parasites such as the microsporidian *Nosema* are often abundant within the guts of bees—but sometimes, too, these are abundant in populations that are thriving. Viruses such as the Israeli acute paralysis virus have been implicated in colony collapse of honey bees. For some native bumble bees, the introduction of foreign species for pollination work in greenhouses can cause unforeseen competition and spillover of diseases. Large agricultural monocultures deprive bumble bees of their need for a diverse community of flowers through three seasons. And the fragmentation of natural habitats simply reduces the size of bee populations. Perhaps in the end we'll discover that the decline is the result of the cumulative effects of all of these threats and more.

But there is one thing about bees that make them especially vulnerable to spiralling declines when their numbers are depressed, and that is how sex is determined. In humans, sex is determined by the number and type of sex chromosomes: if you have two X chromosomes, you are female; if you have one X and one Y, you are male—simple, and apparently logical. So it might surprise you to find out that bees do things quite differently. Bee females develop from fertilized eggs (which contain two copies of each chromosome: they are "diploid"), and males develop from unfertilized eggs (which contain only one copy of each chromosome: they are "haploid"). This system automatically reduces the genetic diversity of the population, since males have only half the genome and thus half the diversity of the females—and we know that genetic diversity is one of the main bulwarks against the threat of changing environments. So why would this apparently crazy system evolve? Well, probably because it does a wonderful job of weeding out undesirable genetic mutations because haploid males are stuck with what they've got, and those with nasty mutations will die before mating.

But the bee sex-determination system has a dark side. It turns out that what you learned in the paragraph above is somewhat oversimplified; bee sex is determined by a single gene, not an entire chromosome. If a bee possesses two *different* copies of that gene, it is a female. If it possesses only one copy of that gene, it is a male. So far, the story of diploid females and haploid males explains this. *But if a bee possesses two identical copies of that gene, it becomes a sterile male.* In other words, some of the progeny that we would have expected to be productive females are actually genetic deadwood. This is not a problem for large, healthy populations of bees, since there are usually twenty or so different versions of the gene in the population, and thus sterile males make up only a tiny portion of the bee world. But as populations get smaller the diversity of the sex gene gets smaller, which causes the proportion of sterile males to increase, which in turn reduces the size of the population—and the species enters an extinction vortex.

There are, however, more benign aliens, and this seems to be the description we could give to the European Ground Beetle. Even though this predaceous species arrived in North America before 1870 and has long established itself as a common inhabitant of undisturbed lowland habitats in southern British Columbia (as well as in backyard gardens), it doesn't seem to have reduced the native ground beetle diversity in a serious way.

A European Ground Beetle scuttles through a Vancouver Island garden.

Coastal Forests

The temperate forests around Vancouver and Victoria have a climate much like that of Europe, and so are particularly vulnerable to invasion by species from the Old Country. Familiar plants like English Ivy, English Holly, Himalayan Blackberry, Scotch Broom, and Spurge-laurel have all become abundant members of the coastal Douglas-fir forests and meadows.

English Ivy is an amazing vine that sprawls over the ground and can clamber over trees and buildings, completely shading out native plants. Despite its aggressive nature, it remains a much sought-after ornamental plant. English Holly can dominate the shrub zone in the forest and is very efficient at pulling up whatever water there is in the soil, effectively removing it for native plants. Spurge-laurel is an attractive, evergreen shrub that somewhat resembles rhododendrons, but possesses poisonous berries and toxic sap. It, too, grows rapidly and outcompetes native vegetation in shady forests.

British Columbia naturalists often have a love-hate relationship with Himalayan Blackberry, since they crave the abundant, sweet berries but despair as the vines smother entire forest edges and stream banks. Despite its exotic name, this plant comes from Europe—it was introduced to North America in 1885 and had spread along the West Coast by 1945.

Scotch Broom was introduced to British Columbia in 1850 by the homesick Captain Walter Grant of Sooke. It was a spectacular success there and soon spread throughout southern Vancouver Island, the Gulf Islands and the Lower Mainland. Its dense thickets are now a common sight as far afield as the Haida Gwaii, Terrace and the Kootenays, but its greatest threat is to the many native plants that are restricted to the sunny meadows and rocky outcrops in the Douglas-fir and Garry Oak woodlands of the south coast. The royalists living in the Victoria area might be interested to know that the House of Plantagenet—rulers of England in the Middle Ages—derived its name from its heraldic badge, the planta genista, or Scotch Broom.

Native to eastern North America, the Eastern Gray Squirrel is another attractive species that can become a successful invader. In fact, because of its successes in Great Britain, Italy and other countries, it has been named as one of the top one hundred invasive species in the world. Eight were brought to Vancouver from New York in 1914, and by 1920, their descendents were well established there. In 1966, three escaped from a game farm outside Victoria, and again they spread quickly, helped by pest control companies who live-trapped them and relocated them outside the city. It is now common in some Interior cities such as Kelowna and Kamloops. In both England and in British Columbia, it displaces the native Red Squirrels wherever it goes. On Vancouver Island, it is particularly a concern in the Garry Oak ecosystem, where it consumes great quantities of acorns and strips bark from young trees. Like the Red Squirrel, it eats the eggs and nestlings of birds and competes with cavity-nesting species for tree holes.

Grasslands

Grasslands have been especially vulnerable to foreign species because over-grazing was coincident with the arrival of weed seeds in animal feeds and on the animals themselves. Knapweeds (see page 285), Cheatgrass and other invaders now cover huge areas of formerly productive bunchgrass communities. Cheatgrass, originally from the Mediterranean region, is an annual grass that thrives in open, dry, sandy soil. Its barb-tipped seeds stab through the socks and open shoes of walkers, causing much pain and irritation. There are a number of other introduced, invasive grasses in British Columbia, but the changes wrought by these species often go unseen; to most of us, a grass is just a grass. Leafy spurge, introduced from Europe to North America almost two hundred years ago, is an attractive herb that spreads with an aggressive root system that can extend 4.5 metres horizontally. The roots also extend up to 9 metres below the surface to tap into scarce water resources.

Fresh Water

The threat of introduced species in freshwater ecosystems is especially insidious because its effects are not usually noticed by the average person. The native plant and animal communities of rivers, lakes and marshes may be completely overwhelmed by foreign species while the habitat itself appears superficially normal. In some cases, such as the introduction of exotic fish, the changes may even be welcomed by some people.

In wetlands, Eurasian Water-milfoil is spread by boaters from one lake to another, where it produces masses of thick, weedy growth, replacing native plants and creating an unappealing environment for swimming and boating. First discovered in Okanagan Lake in 1970, it has spread to a number of lakes in the southern Interior and Lower Mainland, and to Vancouver Island.

Another invasive wetland plant is the Purple Loosestrife. With its attractive flowering spikes, this species is often planted in garden ponds, but it soon spreads to local marshes where it can quickly replace a diverse native plant community with a sterile, purplish-pink monoculture.

Of all aquatic creatures, fish are especially loved by humans—and whether they are sport fish or bait fish, we love to take them with us to new lakes and streams. Nineteen species of exotic fish—including Brook Trout, Carp, Largemouth and Smallmouth Bass, and Pumpkinseeds—are living in British Columbia waters today. In the Columbia watershed, sixteen species, a full 37 per cent of the entire fish fauna, are introduced. All of these non-native fish are a potential threat to the native fish fauna—and fifteen of those species are found nowhere else in the world. And within our borders we have moved Rainbow Trout to literally hundreds of lakes that were formerly either fish free or at least trout free, permanently altering the ecology of these systems.

The striking pink plumes of Purple Loosestrife are a sign of death for many native wetland ecosystems.

The Opossum Shrimp story is another cautionary tale of environmental meddling. In 1949 and 1950, Opossum Shrimps were released into Kootenay Lake to enhance the growth of Rainbow Trout. The shrimps didn't help the Rainbow Trout, but in the years following the introduction, they seemed to give the Kokanee a big boost in size. Fisheries managers jumped on the bandwagon of Kokanee enhancement and released Opossum Shrimps into twenty more lakes in British Columbia. But the Kokanee in Kootenay Lake, it seems, had been aided by pollution from sewage and fertilizer in the lake, and when these additions were curtailed in the mid 1980s, the Kokanee declined in size and numbers, and spawning runs in the south arm disappeared. It seems that Opossum Shrimps are fed on only by the very largest Kokanee and allow them to grow even larger. But the shrimps consume great quantities of the zooplankton that the smaller Kokanee depend on for their survival and growth—and now the shrimps are a permanent part of some of British Columbia's finest fishing lakes.

Of all the introduced animals in southern British Columbia's lakes, the Bullfrog has perhaps made one of the biggest impacts. Bullfrogs arrived here as farm animals, their owners planning to serve their legs in fine restaurants, but these ventures all failed and the farmers released their stock into local lakes. Bullfrogs are generalist predators, eating just about anything they can fit into their mouths. Luckily, they are still primarily restricted to lakes and wetlands of eastern Vancouver Island and the Lower Mainland, but where Bullfrogs live, many native species have declined or vanished. Red-legged Frogs and especially Oregon Spotted Frogs have been affected, the latter almost disappearing from this country. Luckily, Bullfrog populations in the South Okanagan remain very small and thus far, control programs seem to be effective in eliminating them.

Marine

As in fresh water, big changes to marine ecosystems can occur without the public being aware of them, either because they cannot be seen or simply because we don't pay attention to invertebrates. Some invasions are the result of intentional introductions, some species have arrived as unintentional hitchhikers, and others have come in the ballast of ships from distant ports.

Perhaps the greatest changes have occurred under the sand or mud of coastal bays. In the late 1990s, I was enjoying building a sand sculpture on Cortes Island when I became increasingly horrified at the number of Varnish Clams that were coming up with each shovelful of sand. I had never heard of them before my friend told me what they were, and the density of these new invaders was truly astonishing. I wondered how much of the plankton of the inshore waters must be filtered through their siphons! Native to Oriental waters, these clams had arrived on the shores of British Columbia only about ten years previously, probably as larvae in the ballast of ships. Now they are common throughout the Salish Sea, the Strait of Juan de Fuca, and the west coast of Vancouver Island. The good news part of this story is that Varnish Clams don't appear to be displacing native clams, and because they live higher in the intertidal zone than other clams, they are more available as food. They are feasted upon by Black Oystercatchers, scoters, gulls, Northwestern Crows, Sea Otters and Raccoons.

In the warmer inlets of the Salish Sea and Barkley Sound, and throughout the warm shores north of the southern Gulf Islands, the large, wavy shells of Pacific Oysters are abundant on rocky substrates in the intertidal and subtidal zones. Pacific Oysters were first brought from Japan to British Columbia in 1913, but were imported in much larger numbers after 1930. Over the years, they spread throughout the inside waters of the south coast, outcompeting the native Olympia Oyster, which is a smaller, slower-growing shellfish. And every time new shipments were brought in, they brought with them hitchhikers. One of these was the Manila Clam, which first showed up with oysters in Ladysmith Harbour in 1936. Now it is common and widespread along the coast—as far north as Bella Bella—and dominates the commercial clam industry. It lives higher in the intertidal zone than the native Butter Clams and Littleneck Clams, and does not burrow as deeply as those species.

Similarly, the Japanese False Cerith came to California with Pacific Oysters in the 1920s, and subsequently found its way to Canada. Their 2- to 3.5-centimetre-long, turret-like shells can be hyper-abundant on the surface of mud flats in the protected waters of the south coast, where they feed on the slimy diatom soup on the surface of the mud. This means that they are in direct competition with the tens of thousands of shorebirds that depend on the nutritious "biofilm" during their stopovers in the Fraser Delta. But it may be that there is plenty of the biofilm to go around; and one can assume that any declines in shorebirds that may have resulted from this competition happened long ago, because the snails have been an abundant part of the ecosystem for many decades. One piece of good news here is that these snails have crawl-away larvae, not ones that are carried great distances in tidal currents. As a result, they are restricted to areas close to present or former oyster farms. The mud flats of Boundary Bay in the Fraser Delta have a particularly rich alien fauna because oysters were imported there from both the Atlantic coast of North America and from Japan. Other foreign snails common there include the Atlantic Mudsnail and the Japanese Nassa. The Nicomekl River still supports a relict population of Eastern Oysters, the only self-sustaining one left on the Pacific coast. On Vancouver Island, the New Zealand Mudsnail has become established in the Somass estuary near Port Alberni.

One of the most recent and worrisome arrivals on British Columbia's Pacific coast is the European Green Crab. The first were noted here in 1998—having moved north from San Francisco in only a decade, they are now ensconced in all sounds and inlets of western Vancouver Island and have established a satellite population near Bella Bella. They come with a reputation; they are efficient, skilled predators and eat crabs, clams, oysters, mussels and snails. On the east coast of North America, they have been blamed for the collapse of the native clam population and the destruction of the soft shell crab fishery. What their impact here will be is still unknown.

Invasives on Islands

Some of the most strikingly direct examples of the effects of introduced species have taken place on the small islands of the Haida Gwaii. Until recently, hundreds of thousands of seabirds nested in relative security on these remote islands, since no land-based predators had managed to colonize them. But in this century, rats found their way from ships to some of the islands and then Raccoons were purposely introduced to Graham Island to contribute to the fur industry.

In 1960, the Ancient Murrelet colony on Langara Island numbered an estimated 200,000 nesting pairs—at that time it was by far the largest colony in the world. In only three decades, rats have reduced this city of murrelets to

only 13,000 pairs. However, a massive eradication program beginning in 1995 eliminated rats from the island, and the Ancient Murrelets responded by almost doubling their numbers to more than 24,000 pairs in less than ten years. At the south end of the Haida Gwaii, rats had also taken over a number of seabird islands in Gwaii Haanas National Park Reserve, but in 2011, Parks Canada, the Haida Nation, Island Conservation, and Coastal Conservation began a major control plan to eliminate them there as well.

The Raccoons released on Graham Island have subsequently spread throughout all the main islands of the Haida Gwaii and have reached many of the smaller islands within a kilometre of them. Hordes of Raccoons now roam island intertidal communities that never knew these predators before, including the spectacularly productive shoals of Burnaby Narrows. If this pattern of colonization continues, Raccoons will threaten the survival of 80 per cent of the nesting colonies and 75 per cent of the seabirds on the archipelago.

Raccoons are an integral part of the ecosystem on the mainland coast of British Columbia, but their introduction to the Haida Gwaii is producing catastrophic changes to wildlife populations there.

CLIMATE CHANGE

Throughout this book, we have tried to highlight climate change and some of the significant effects that it will have on the ecosystems of British Columbia—and the rest of the world. These changes began at the dawn of the industrial revolution, are happening right now and will continue to unfold over the coming decades. The complex interactions of atmospheric temperatures, wind patterns, ocean currents, sea surface temperatures and myriad other variables make it difficult to predict when certain changes will occur and to what magnitude they will change our world. It is clear, however, that our biosphere is rapidly entering a state that humans have never witnessed. The warming of the atmosphere, the acidification of the oceans and other changes wrought by increasing greenhouse gas concentrations are all happening at rates unknown in the past million years. Even if we act decisively and quickly, those changes will persist for centuries to come. Our goal must be to limit the magnitude of the changes as much as possible.

> LOSS OF POPULATIONS WILL LIKELY BE SUDDEN RATHER THAN GRADUAL, PRECIPITATED BY CLIMATIC EXTREMES OR THEIR EFFECTS. IN GENERAL, THIS SUDDENNESS WILL LEAD TO IMPOVERISHMENT OF LOCAL AND REGIONAL FLORAS BEFORE THE RE-ESTABLISHMENT OF NEW SPECIES.
>
> Richard Hebda, in *Biodiversity in British Columbia*, edited by L. Harding and E. McCullum

To accomplish that goal, we will have to move quickly to wean global civilization off its reliance on fossil fuels for power. British Columbia has relied on hydroelectricity for most of its power over the last century—a source of renewable power but one with tremendous local consequences in terms of a direct loss of biodiversity and ecosystem functions. Other renewable power sources such as wind, solar and geothermal are all more expensive than hydro and have their own impacts, but they must be promoted and improved to reduce those impacts and their costs. We also must rethink our transportation infrastructure and its assumption that everyone must have a car to get to work or to travel to the next city. The North American belief that driving a car is a birthright is completely unsustainable over the long term. Transit infrastructure may be expensive up front, but it will save society untold money and ecological impacts over the next few decades. We have only to look to the countries of northern Europe, which have thriving economies despite high fuel costs and massive investments in transit and new, renewable power sources. British Columbia has made some tentative steps in this direction—its leadership in the form of a carbon tax has indeed reduced consumption of fossil fuels—but we need to take bolder strides to tackle climate change.

There are other things we can—and should—do to ensure that our grandchildren and their grandchildren can live in the spectacularly natural British Columbia that we know, but this is surely something we must do.

WHAT WE CAN DO

Parks and Other Protected Areas

One of the obvious things we can do to aid the survival of British Columbia's natural ecosystems is to protect them in a well-planned system of parks and ecological reserves. If we were really serious about sharing this planet with our cohabitants, we would make sure that these protected areas were large and well connected to other, nearby natural areas. This provision would allow species to move easily from one area to another, and even large animals such as Grizzly Bear would have enough room to support sustainable populations. Past development is difficult to reverse, however, and in lowland ecosystems in the south, it is simply impossible to find large, linked areas that can be preserved. In any case, it seems that we will end up protecting less than is necessary for most ecosystems.

If we preserve only 12 per cent of the provincial land base in parks, then it is essential that we manage the other 88 per cent in a manner that is sensitive to the ecological processes vital to the survival of our fellow natural citizens. It is vital to our survival as well, since we depend to such a great degree on the health and productivity of our natural lands.

Protecting Natural Ecosystems without Parks

Because the remnants of the most endangered ecosystems in British Columbia are concentrated in the 6 per cent of the province that is privately owned, and because the land is so expensive that we cannot afford to buy large, representative tracts for conservation, we must use other means to protect their natural communities.

Most owners of natural lands are proud custodians of the ecosystems on their property. Often, however, they need help in understanding the threats to the long-term health of the ecosystems in their care. Habitats are more often degraded or destroyed through ignorance than through malice. Land stewardship programs could help a great deal in private land conservation by providing ecological information to willing landowners, by giving them tax or other monetary incentives to preserve the natural values of their land and by recognizing their efforts publicly.

Protecting Valleys

Although it seems inevitable that humans will continue to proliferate in the temperate lowlands and valleys of British Columbia, there are a number of things that we as individuals or governments can do to minimize or mitigate damage to lowland ecosystems.

Most city or regional parks can be recognized by their playing fields, tennis courts, swing sets, picnic tables and parking lots. But there is no reason why we can't set aside the remaining fragments of natural land within our populated valleys as nature parks, primarily for wildlife. Stanley Park in Vancouver is a prime example of an urban nature park, even though regular urban park development has encroached on its natural features over the last century. Other good examples of natural areas protected within British Columbia cities include Maud Roxbury Marsh and Knox Mountain in Kelowna, the foreshore of Shuswap Lake in Salmon Arm, Scout Island in Williams Lake, Cottonwood Island in Prince George and Uplands Park in Oak Bay. Communities and regional districts throughout the province should be identifying natural spaces within their boundaries and setting them aside now, before they are lost.

But we can't always find large natural areas within our cities, and we should be conscious of smaller areas that are perhaps already significantly altered from their natural state. We could actively create, as best we can, somewhat natural areas from vacant lots or former industrial sites. We should protect and enhance stream corridors and avoid sentencing waterways to become underground storm sewers.

We could also do much more with the parks we already have. If the grass of some city parks or boulevards were allowed to flourish and grow tall, if trimmed horticultural shrubs were replaced by patches of native greenery, if sculpted ponds were allowed to revert to their past marshy ways, or if creeks were given back their protective lining of shrubs and trees, natural diversity in British Columbia's lowlands would be greatly increased.

Much of the land within cities is taken up by residential areas—the backyards where we live. The wildlife diversity in cities could be greatly enhanced if we all made an effort to create wildlife sanctuaries in our backyards.

There are a number of books on the market giving detailed instructions on making your yard a haven for everything from birds to butterflies, but the simplest way to start is to get rid of most—or all—of your green, trimmed lawn and replace it with native trees, shrubs or herbs. Appropriate native plants not only are attractive to native animals but usually thrive without watering. Reducing or eliminating the use of pesticides and herbicides in your garden will also enhance local wildlife by providing a good base for the food chain and eliminating toxic effects on vertebrates.

HOW YOU CAN CONTRIBUTE

One of the most exciting things about being a naturalist in a place like British Columbia is that we can all make exciting discoveries. How can you contribute?

Keep a Record
The easiest way to begin is by keeping a record of your observations. In the past, this meant keeping a natural history journal, whether that was writing bird and flower observations on your wall calendar or keeping detailed

records in a field notebook. This is still an honourable discipline and perhaps the best way of recording your observations before they fade from memory.

> "LET THE COLLECTOR'S MOTTO BE 'TRUST NOTHING
> TO MEMORY'; FOR THE MEMORY BECOMES A FICKLE
> GUARDIAN WHEN ONE INTERESTING OBJECT IS SUCCEEDED
> BY ANOTHER STILL MORE INTERESTING."
>
> C. Darwin, *Journal of Researches*, 1839

Darwin's remark is still valid today, but the twenty-first-century naturalist has a few more options available when it comes to keeping notes. Probably most of us still prefer pencil and a notebook, but you can also transcribe your sightings directly into your smart phone or tablet. The important thing is to get the information out of your brain and into some sort of permanent record before you leave the forest, field or fen. And if you have GPS capabilities with your camera or phone, remember to record your precise position.

The Power of Citizen Science

Individual records of birds or dragonflies or wildflower blooming dates may not seem to mean much, but when a few thousand are put together, fascinating patterns appear. The massive volumes of *The Birds of British Columbia* could not have been written without hundreds of naturalists contributing millions of individual bird sightings written on individual "sight record cards." Now, birders simply enter their daily sightings into eBird and they are compiled automatically, ready for analysis by any number of projects. Similarly, butterfly enthusiasts can record their sightings on eButterfly.

Your digital camera is an invaluable tool in recording anything in the wild: an unusual bird, unfamiliar plant or unknown spider. High-quality photographs can now be sent instantly to the world experts for identification, and for many species, these images can take the place of a voucher specimen. Websites with databases such as bugguide.net not only help naturalists identify the organisms they photograph, but also maintain the photographs as records of the species' distribution, behaviour and ecology.

The Conservation Data Centre, in the provincial Ministry of Environment in Victoria, gathers and records all the information about rare and threatened species and ecosystems in the province. Each species—plant or animal—or ecosystem that is on the provincial Red or Blue List is tracked. Every occurrence is recorded in detail in a computer database and digitally mapped as precisely as possible. This is a big job, especially since the goal is to keep the information as up-to-date as possible—meaning theoretically that thousands of sites must be found and visited every year. Because the staff at the Conservation Data Centre can't possibly do this on its own, naturalists are needed throughout the province to volunteer their time to monitor rare plant, animal and ecosystems sites—one visit a year would be enough. If you can help, please contact them.

Websites

There are an ever-increasing number of websites that collect and display information about the distribution and abundance of animals and plants around British Columbia and the world. Here are a few websites that are most applicable to naturalists in British Columbia:

eBird Canada
http://ebird.org/content/canada/

eButterfly
http://www.e-butterfly.org/contents/?portal=ebutterfly

eFauna BC: Electronic Atlas of the Wildlife of British Columbia
http://www.geog.ubc.ca/biodiversity/efauna/

E-Flora BC: Electronic Atlas of the Flora of British Columbia
http://www.geog.ubc.ca/biodiversity/eflora/

BugGuide.net: Identification, Images, and Information for Insects, Spiders and Their Kin for the United States and Canada
http://bugguide.net/node/view/15740

Canadian Journal of Arthropod Identification
http://www.biology.ualberta.ca/bsc/ejournal/ejournal.html

WildSpecies: The General Status of Species in Canada
http://www.wildspecies.ca/

The Committee on the Status of Endangered Wildlife in Canada (COSEWIC)
http://www.cosewic.gc.ca/eng/sct5/index_e.cfm

Species at Risk Act Public Registry
http://www.sararegistry.gc.ca/default_e.cfm

BC Geology maps
http://www.empr.gov.bc.ca/Mining/Geoscience/Mapplace/pages/default.aspx

Biogeoclimatic Ecosystem Classification Program
http://www.for.gov.bc.ca/hre/becweb/

Join Forces with Your Neighbours

It's always fun to share your interests with others like yourself—and if you and your friends can get together to gather important information about a natural site in your neighbourhood, so much the better! There are an infinite number of valuable projects that naturalist clubs or small groups can do—if you're not sure how you can help, call the nearest office of B.C. Environment or B.C. Parks, the Royal British Columbia Museum or the Federation of British Columbia Naturalists.

Narrow Your Focus

Often the most valuable contribution you can make to increasing our knowledge of natural history occurs when you narrow your focus. Instead of trying to learn as much as you can about everything, decide on a group of organisms that interests you and search them out, watch them closely and make a scientific collection, if possible.

If you try this, you will be surprised how easy it is to learn things that have never been known before. You can discover species that are new to the province—and, if you are looking at invertebrates or fungi, you can easily find species as yet undiscovered anywhere. Even if you choose a group as well known as birds, you can find fascinating ecological or behavioural stories—there simply hasn't been a lot of detailed study in any group in British Columbia.

The other way you can narrow your focus is to limit your observations to a small area or habitat and try to gather as much information as possible on that one site. If done properly, this will be more work than narrowing your focus to one group, but you will probably gain much greater knowledge.

Make Scientific Collections

Most people think of plant or butterfly collecting as something that only slightly odd children or even odder adults do. But making a good collection can be extremely valuable, especially in a province like British Columbia, where we have so much to learn. In fact, scientific collections are the basis for most of what we know about things around us.

To identify a plant or animal, you need a book with illustrations or written identification keys. To write and illustrate such a book, you need a collection of specimens. The reason you can go out and identify birds in flight using only a book and a pair of binoculars is that many people created orderly, scientific collections of bird specimens decades ago. Put simply, without museum and private collections, there would be no bird books, no flower books. Without collections, we wouldn't even be able to put species names on anything, since the formal designations and descriptions of species are necessarily tied to specimens in collections.

Although today we can't (and wouldn't) go out and shoot birds to make a personal collection, specimen collection is still necessary for identification in many other groups. For example, if we want to know the distribution and ecology of a group of insects in which half the species in the province are still unknown to science, it is essential that specimens be collected and preserved for further study. In addition, there are over two thousand plant species in British Columbia—and if you want to make an accurate, useful plant list for your local area, you will have to collect some plants so that experts can confirm your identifications.

If you do make a collection, you must do it properly. Ask an expert at a university or the Royal British Columbia Museum how to go about it before starting. Then make sure that your collection ends up where others can also gain from your work. Scientists from around the world are studying the collections at our universities and museums all the time. Your specimens are only valuable to them if they can see them.

Collections can be valuable long after we are gone. Even if you want to keep a personal collection, make sure that it will not be neglected or destroyed after your death—will it to an institution where it will be cared for and used.

EDUCATION, REVELATION AND FUTURE CHANGE

Let's not kid ourselves. All the things we can do mentioned above aren't going to be enough. If we are serious about the survival of the environment we live in, we have to make big changes. We are losing the valleys of British Columbia subdivision by subdivision, highway by highway, dam by dam, clearcut by clearcut. We have to deal with ever increasing population and with the crazy idea of ever increasing economic growth.

We have to make big changes in our attitudes—we must reconnect our society with its life-giving ecosystems. And the key to changing attitudes is education. If we aren't aware of the natural ecosystems in this province, and if we don't understand the effect that our modern lifestyle has on them, nothing is going to change.

The best way for children (and adults) to learn about nature is through a direct, hands-on experience—the kind only experienced outside the classroom, on a guided trip to the woods or on a visit to a local nature interpretation centre. There, knowledgeable and enthusiastic guides can open up a new world to youngsters who, in turn, will take their enthusiasm home and teach their parents.

Every community should have a nature centre where its children can learn about the local environment and the place they have in it. Programs such as the Lynn Canyon Ecology Centre in North Vancouver and Scout Island Nature Centre in Williams Lake provide excellent models for other communities to follow. But nature centres are only starting points—one or two trips a year to a nature centre or to the woods will not make the difference. We must make environmental education an integral part of the main school curriculum. The problem, however, is greater still, because children will never get the environmental message if the society they are part of continues to feed them with dreams of unfettered consumerism and with expectations of material wealth.

> ANGRY AS ONE MAY BE AT WHAT HEEDLESS MEN HAVE DONE AND STILL DO TO NOBLE HABITAT, ONE CANNOT BE PESSIMISTIC ABOUT THE WEST. THIS IS THE NATIVE HOME OF HOPE.
> Wallace Stegner, *The Sound of Mountain Water*

Education is necessary, but it is only a steppingstone to action—it will only lead to change through a society-wide revelation. We as a society must wake up from the pleasant dream of unlimited growth before we are awakened by an apocalyptic nightmare, before we have destroyed all that is wonderful and special around us.

We have the whole world in our hands. And in our small corner of the globe we hold the future of the kelp forests and eel-grass beds, the big sandy bays filled with clams, the steep-walled fiords draped with great conifer forests, the Grizzlies fishing for salmon, the oak and arbutus woodlands on island sandstone, the eagles and seaducks drawn to spawning herring, the ephemeral flower meadows of the mountains, the fragrant pine and fir forests on the eastern slopes, the hot grasslands awash with the smell of sage, the deep valleys with Moose moving through still waters, the endless plateaus dotted with lakes, and the big northern spruce forests with Lynx and hares galloping through thickets of birch and willow.

Let's not let them go.

APPENDIX: MAP OF BRITISH COLUMBIA

Atlin

YUKON

Cassiar

CASSIAR

Liard River

Fort Nelson R.

NORTHWEST TERRITORIES

Telegraph
Creek

Stikine River

Fort
Nelson

ALASKA

OMINECA

Stewart

Nass River

Williston
Lake

PEACE

Fort
St John

Skeena River

Hazelton

Fort St John

ALBERTA

Prince
Rupert

Skeena

Smithers

Peace River

Masset

Terrace

Babine
Lake

Dixon Entrance

Kitimat

Stuart
Lake

54

Haida
Gwaii

Hecate Strait

Nechako
Reservoir

Vanderhoof

Prince
George

Quesnel

McNaughton
Lake

Bella
Coola

CHILCOTIN

Quesnel
Lake

Queen
Charlotte
Sound

Chilcotin River

Williams
Lake

CARIBOO

Chilko
Lake

Fraser River

North Thompson River

Shuswap
Lake

Columbia River

Port
Hardy

Ashcroft

Vancouver
Island

Lillooet River

Kamloops

Revelstoke

CALGA

Campbell
River

Powell
River

Lytton

OKANAGAN

Arrow
Lakes

Invermere

Comox

Squamish

Okanagan
Lake

KOOTENAY

PACIFIC OCEAN

Port
Alberni

VANCOUVER

Kelowna

Ucluelet

Nanaimo

Hope

Princeton

Penticton

Kootenay
Lake

Nelson

Cranbrook

VICTORIA

WASHINGTON

IDAHO

MONTANA

0   100 kilometres

NATURE ORGANIZATIONS

BC Nature
c/o Parks Heritage Centre
1620 Mount Seymour Road
North Vancouver, BC v7G 2R9
604-985-3057
bcnature.ca
This is the umbrella organization for the fifty or so naturalists' clubs in the province.

Nature Canada
Suite 300, 75 Albert Street
Ottawa, Ontario K1P 5E7
1-800-267-4088
naturecanada.ca

British Columbia Field Ornithologists
P.O. Box 45507
Westside RPO,
Vancouver, BC v6S 2N5
bcfo.ca

FOR FURTHER READING

There are many books—ranging from the detailed and technical to the more general and accessible—that cover certain aspects of British Columbia natural history. Here are a few that would be useful to the naturalist who would like to learn more.

General
Royal British Columbia Museum (formerly British Columbia Provincial Museum) Handbook series
A long series of inexpensive handbooks covering a variety of plant and animal groups, discussing their identification, distribution and ecology in British Columbia. Some are quite technical; others are not so technical. Many are out of print but are still available in libraries throughout the province.

Farley, A. L., 1979. *Atlas of British Columbia: People, environment and resource use.* Vancouver: University of British Columbia Press.

Finlay, J., and C. Finlay. 1992. *Ocean to alpine.* Edmonton: Lone Pine.

Goward, T., and C. Hickson. 1995. *Nature Wells Gray.* 2d ed. Vancouver: Lone Pine.

Hanby, B., and A. Lamb. 2005. Marine life of the Pacific Northwest. Madeira Park: Harbour.

Kozloff, E. N. 1983. *Seashore life of the northern Pacific coast.* Seattle: University of Washington Press.

Nightingale, A., and C. Copley, eds. 2014. Nature guide to the Victoria region. Victoria: Victoria Natural History Society.

Ricketts, E. F., and J. Calvin. 1968. Between Pacific tides. Stanford: Stanford University Press.

Scudder, G. G. E., and N. Gessler, eds. 1989. *The outer shores.* Skidegate, B.C.: Queen Charlotte Islands Museum Press.
An excellent technical overview of the natural history of the Haida Gwaii.

Smith, K. M., N. J. Anderson, and K. I. Beamish, eds. 1988. *Nature west coast.* Rev. ed. Vancouver: Vancouver Natural History Society.

Snively, G. 1978. *Exploring the seashore in British Columbia, Washington and Oregon.* Vancouver: Gordon Soules.

Geology
Armstrong, J. E. 1990. Vancouver geology. Edited by C. Roots and C. Staargaard. Vancouver: Geological Association of Canada, Cordilleran Section. Out of print, but available online at: http://www.gac-cs.ca/publications/VancouverGeology.pdf

Gabrielse, H., and C. J. Yorath, eds. 1991. *Geology of the Cordilleran orogen in Canada.* Ottawa: Geological Survey of Canada.
A thorough but technical summary of the geology of the Canadian Cordillera. A set of large colour maps is included.

Gadd, B. 1995. *Handbook of the Canadian Rockies.* 2d ed. Jasper, Alta.: Corax Press.

Harris, S. L. 1980. *Fire and ice: The Cascade volcanoes.* Rev. ed. Vancouver: Douglas & McIntyre.

Ludvigsen R., and G. Beard. 1994. *West coast fossils: A guide to the ancient life of Vancouver Island.* Vancouver: Whitecap.

Mathews, B., and J. Monger. 2010. Roadside geology of southern British Columbia. Victoria: Heritage House.

Roel, M. 1995. *Geology of the Kelowna area*. Kelowna, B.C.: Kelowna Geology Comm., Okanagan University College.

Yorath, C.J. 1990. *Where terranes collide*. Victoria: Orca.

Climate and Oceanography

Hare, F.K., and M.K. Thomas. 1979. *Climate Canada*. Toronto: Wiley.

Oke, T., and J. Hay. 1994. *The climate of Vancouver*. 2d ed. British Columbia Geographical Series, No. 50. Vancouver: University of British Columbia.

Phillips, D. 1990. *The climates of Canada*. Ottawa: Environment Canada.

Thomson, R.E. 1981. *Oceanography of the British Columbia coast*. Canadian Special Publication of Fisheries and Aquatic Sciences 56. Ottawa: Department of Fisheries and Oceans.

Ecology

Arno, S.F., and R.P. Hammerly. 1984. *Timberline: Mountain and Arctic forest frontiers*. Seattle: The Mountaineers.

Carefoot, T. 1977. *Pacific seashores*. Vancouver: J.J. Douglas.

Gayton, D. 1992. *The wheatgrass mechanism: Science and imagination in the western Canadian landscape*. Saskatoon, Sask.: Fifth House. A well-written and thought-provoking work on the bunchgrass grasslands.

Maser, C. 1989. *Forest primeval: The natural history of an ancient forest*. San Francisco: Sierra Club.

Meidinger, D., and J. Pojar, eds. 1991. *Ecosystems of British Columbia*. Victoria: B.C. Ministry of Forests. A good but somewhat technical summary of the ecological characteristics of all of British Columbia's biogeoclimatic zones.

Pielou, E.C. 1988. *The world of northern evergreens*. Ithaca: Cornell University Press.

———. 1991. *After the ice age: The return of life to glaciated North America*. Chicago: University of Chicago Press.

Botany

Douglas, G.W., G.B. Straley, and D. Meidinger, eds. 1989–1994. *The vascular plants of British Columbia*. 4 vols. Victoria: B.C. Ministry of Forests.

Lyons, C.P., and W. Merilees. 1995. *Trees, shrubs and flowers to know in British Columbia and Washington*. Vancouver: Lone Pine. An updated version of Lyons's classic introduction to the common plants of the region.

MacKinnon, A., J. Pojar, and R. Coupé, eds. 1992. *Plants of northern British Columbia*. Vancouver: B.C. Ministry of Forests and Lone Pine. Like the following book, an excellent guide to the common plants of the region.

Parish, R., R. Coupé, and D. Lloyd, eds. 1996. *Plants of southern interior British Columbia*. Vancouver: B.C. Ministry of Forests and Lone Pine.

Parish, R., and S.M. Thompson. 1994. *The tree book: Learning to recognize trees of British Columbia*. Victoria: B.C. Ministry of Forests and Canadian Forest Service.

Pojar, J., and A. MacKinnon. 2013. Alpine plants of British Columbia, Alberta and northwest North America. Edmonton: Lone Pine.

———. 1994. *Plants of coastal British Columbia*. Vancouver: B.C. Ministry of Forests and Lone Pine.

Vitt, D.H., J.E. Marsh, and R.B. Bovey. 1988. *Mosses, lichens and ferns of northwest North America*. Edmonton: Lone Pine.

Zoology

Campbell, R.W., N.K. Dawe, I. McT. Cowan, J.M. Cooper, G.W. Kaiser, and M.C.E. McNall. 2001. *The birds of British Columbia*. Volumes 1–4. Victoria and Vancouver: Royal British Columbia Museum and University of B.C. Press.

Corkran, C.C., and C. Thoms, eds. 1996. *Amphibians: A complete field identification manual for Oregon, Washington and British Columbia*. Vancouver: Lone Pine.

Edgell, P., and A. Lamb. 2010. Coastal fishes of the Pacific Northwest. 2nd ed. Madeira Park: Harbour.

Groot C., and L. Margolis, eds. 1991. *Pacific salmon life histories*. Vancouver: University of British Columbia Press.

Hart, J.L. 1973. *Pacific fishes of Canada*. Reprinted 1988. Bulletin 180. Ottawa: Fisheries Research Board of Canada.

Kozloff, E.N. 1987. *Marine invertebrates of the Pacific Northwest*. Seattle: University of Washington Press.

Lewis, A. 1994. *Salmon of the Pacific*. Vancouver: Raincoast.

Scott, W.B., and E.J. Crossman. 1973. *Freshwater fishes of Canada*. Bulletin 184. Ottawa: Fisheries Research Board of Canada.

Conservation

Austin, M.A., D.A. Buffett, D.J. Nicolson, G.G.E. Scudder and V. Stevens, eds. 2008. Taking Nature's Pulse: The Status of Biodiversity in British Columbia. Victoria: Biodiversity BC. Available at: www.biodiversitybc.org.

Hammond, H. 1991. *Seeing the forest among the trees: The case for wholistic forest use*. Vancouver: Polestar.

Harding, L.E., and E. McCullum, eds. 1994. *Biodiversity in British Columbia: Our changing environment*. Delta, B.C.: Environment Canada, Canadian Wildlife Service.

Hume, M. 1992. *The run of the river*. Vancouver: New Star.

Leach, B. 1982. *Waterfowl on a Pacific estuary*. Victoria: British Columbia Provincial Museum.

INDEX

Boldface indicates a photograph, figure, illustration or table. Species are listed by Latin name only if this appears in the text. Otherwise, species are listed by their common names.

Graham Island, 93, 344, 345
Grant, Walter, 340
Grassham, R.T., 75
grasslands, 262–85; animals of, 275–81, 284; bunchgrass steppes, 263–72; Bunchgrass zone, 105, 267; cliffs of, 281–3; coastal prairie, 273; communities of, 263, 267, 285; decrease of, 103; expansion, 109, 111; and fire, 175, 250, 285, 328–9; forestation of, 113; and grazing, 283, 284–5, 329; Great Plains, 273; in interglacial period, 108; and introduced species, 341; and larks, 208; mountain, 273; northern, 273; and pine forests, 255; talus slopes of, 281–3; threatened, 273, 328–9; and timberline, 199
Great Bear Rainforest, 121
grosbeaks: Black-headed (*Pheucticus melanocephalus*), 89, 91, 322; Pine (*Pinicola enucleator*), 92; Rose-breasted (*Pheucticus ludovicianus*), 89, 91
ground squirrels, 199, 208; Arctic (*Spermophilus parryii*), 90, 199; Cascade (*Spermophilus saturatus*), **252**; Columbian (*Spermophilus columbianus*), 90; Sharp-tailed (*Tympanuchus phasianellus*), 275
grouse, 238; Blue (*Dendragapus obscurus*), 232; Franklin's (*Dendragapus canadensis franklini*), **231**, 232; Ruffed (*Bonasa umbellus*), 232; Sage (*Centrocercus urophasianus*), 284; Sharp-tailed (*Tympanuchus phasianellus*), 283, 284; Sooty (*Dendragapus fuliginosus*), 191, **191**; Spruce (*Dendragapus canadensis*), **231**, 232
Grouseberry (*Vaccinium scoparium*), 217
Guillemots, Pigeon (*Cepphus columba*), 132
Gulf Islands, 32, 79, 96, 101, 174, 273, 343
gulls, 116, 121, 126, 130, 163, 343; Bonaparte's (*Larus philadelphia*), 69, 124, 130, **130**, 163; California (*Larus californianus*), 130, **130**; Glaucous-winged (*Larus glaucescens*), 130, **130**; Herring (*Larus argentatus*), 130, **130**; Mew (*Larus canus*), **130**; Ring-billed (*Larus delawarensis*), 130, **130**

Gunnels, Penpoint (*Apodichthys flavidus*), 140, **140**
Gwaii Haanas National Park Reserve, 345

Hagfish, Pacific (*Eptatretus stouti*), 133, **133**
Haida Gwaii: and Brants, 140; Canadian Galápagos, 100; and Coastal Mountain-heather Alpine Zone, 201; earthquakes, 39–40; endemic species, 92–3; and glaciation, 53; and introduced species, 344–5; rainfall of, 70; and salmon run, 296; and sea lions, 128; and species evolution, 100–1; and tides, 68; and treeline, 184; warbler genetics, 95
Haig-Brown, Roderick, 289
halibut, 335; Pacific (*Hippoglossus stenolepis*), 295, 334
Hammond, Herb, 330
Handbook of the Canadian Rockies, 53
Harding, I., 346
Hare, F. Kenneth, 71, 79
Harebell, Mountain (*Campanula lasiocarpa*), 90
Hares, Snowshoe (*Lepus americanus*), 100, 199, 212, 233, **237**, 237–40
Harriers, Northern (*Circus cyaneus*), 275
Hawkes, Mike, 334
hawks, 200, 201, 203, 206, 229, 237, 245, 322; Harlan's (*Buteo jamaicensis harlani*), 90; Red-tailed (*Buteo jamaicensis*), 90, 275, 319; Rough-legged (*Buteo lagopus*), 275
Hebda, Richard, 102, 346
Hecate Strait, 68, 93
Hemiptera, 306, 308
hemlock, 164, **165**, 191; Mountain (*Tsuga mertensiana*), 175, **175**, 191; Western (*Tsuga heterophylla*), 75, 102–3, 108, 155, **165**, 166, 175
Herons, Great Blue (*Ardea herodias*), 319
Herpotrichia juniperi, 191
herring, 69, 70; Pacific (*Clupea harengus pallasi*), 124, 127, 128, 334, **334**
Heterosigma akashiro, 120, **121**
Highbush-Cranberry (*Viburnum edule*), 216
Holly, English (*Ilex aquifolium*), 340
Hoodoo Mountain, 38
Hooper Tracy, 329

hot springs, 318, **320–1**
huckleberry: Black (*Vaccinium membranaceum*), 216; Evergreen (*Vaccinium ovatum*), 169; Red (*Vaccinium parvifolium*), 169
Hume, Mark, 296, 335
hummingbirds, 196, 250; Calliope (*Stellula calliope*), 255; Rufous (*Selasphorus rufus*), 167, **196**
Hyalella, 307
hydrothermal vents, 134, **134**
hyrdoid medusae, **125**

Ice Age. *See* Pleistocene Epoch
ice-free refuges, map of, 88
Illecillewaet Glacier, 82
Indian Hellebore (*Veratrum viride*), 196
Indian potato, 194–5
Indian-paintbrush, 192
Indian-pipe (*Monotropa uniflora*), **163**
insects, 158, 163, 204–5, 234, 277, 278, 284, 297, 306, 329–30; water, 308–11
Insular terranes, 15, 21, 28, 56
Intergovernmental Panel on Climate Change, 81
Intermontane terranes, 56
intertidal zone, **114–5**, 118, 141–8
inversions, 78
invertebrates, 7, 96, 143, 149, 158, 234, 270, 298, 308, 323, 330; marine, **124**, 144, 146, 290, 334–5; terrestrial, 337–40
Ivy, English (*Hedera helix*), 340

jackrabbits: White-tailed (*Lepus townsendii*), 267, 283, 284
jays: Gray (*Perisoreus canadensis*), 198, 231; Stellar's (*Cyanocitta stelleri*), 92, 163
jellyfish, 118, 124–5, 335; Stalked (*Haliclystus auricula*), 140
Journal of Researches, 349
Juan de Fuca Plate, **13**, **29**, 32, 38, 40
Juan de Fuca Ridge, 11, **13**
Juan de Fuca Strait, 62, 65, 68, 343
Junegrass (*Koeleria macrantha*), 267, **267**, 284

kelp, 136–9; Bull (*Nereocystis luetkeana*), 136–7, **137**, 292; Giant (*Macrocystis pyrifera*), 119, 136, 137–8
Kingbirds, Western (*Tyrannus verticalis*), 275

kinglets, 229; Golden-crowned (*Regulus satrapa*), 179, **179**, 231–2
Kinnikinnick (*Arctostaphylos uvaursi*), 174, 214, 220
knapweed, 283, 285
Kokanee (*Oncorhynchus nerka*), **299**, 300, 342
Kootenay Mountains, 155, 178, 284
Kootenay River, 300, 331
Krajina, Vladimir, 103, 105
krill. *See* shrimp: Euphausiid
krummholz, 185, **185**, 186, 201
krummholz line, 183, **184**, 186, 187
Kula Plate: 29, **29**, 30, 31, 32, 56, 57

La Pérouse Bank, 116, 118
Lac du Bois, **303**
lacewing, green (*Pseudochrysopa harveyi*), **37**
lakes, 288, 302–14; and climate, 78; eutrophic, 303; evolution of, 93–100; Interior, 304, **304**, 306, 323; limnetic zone, 305, 307–8; littoral zone, 305, 306–7, 308; oliogtrophic, 303; and pollen, 102; post-glaciation, 102; profundal zone, 305, 308; saline, 312, **315**
Land above the Trees, 203
land stewardship programs, 347
Langara Island, 344
Langley Prairie, 273–5
Lanternfish, 126
larch: Alpine (*Larix lyallii*), **180–1**, 196, 197, **197**; golden, 37; Tamarack (*Larix laricina*), 217, **217**; Western (*Larix occidentalis*), 178, 248, **248**
larks: Horned (*Eremophila alpestris*), 203, 206, **208**, 275, 284; Streaked Horned (*Eremophila alpestris strigata*), 275
Larkspur, Nuttall's (*Delphinium nuttallii*), 267
larkspurs, 199
Laurentia, 11–2, 18, 22
laver, red (*Porphyra* sp.), 142
Leach, B., 332
leaf miner: Aspen, 227, **227**; Willow Blotch, 227
lemmings, 199; Brown (*Lemmus sibiricus*), **199**, 199–201
Lepophtheirus salmonis, 336
Liard River Hot Springs, 318, **320–1**
lichen, 156, 157–8; Common Witch's Hair (*Alectoria sarmentosa*), 215, **215**; horsehair, 215–6; Lettuce Lung (*Lobaria oregana*), 158, **158**; Reindeer (*Cladina* sp.), 220; Rock Orange

PHOTO AND ILLUSTRATION CREDITS

Photos

Steve Cannings: pp. ii, viii-ix, 32, 34, 62, 92 (right), 107, 185, 210-11, 221, 240, 242-43, 254, 256, 260-61, 272, 276, 282, 292 (top), 332, 345
Ian Routley: pp. iv-v, vi-vii
Richard Cannings: pp. x-1, 3, 5, 47, 50-51, 55, 66-67, 74, 89, 143, 146, 160, 194, 195, 196, 200, 208 (top), 215, 222, 228, 231, 246, 251, 257, 292 (bottom), 303, 342
Al Grass: pp. 6, 163, 167, 168
Chris Harris: pp. 8-9, 27, 98-99, 152-53, 286-87
Sydney Cannings: pp. 22, 24, 58-59, 76-77, 87, 90, 227, 233, 237, 241, 315, 320-21
Trudy Chatwin: pp. 26 (top), 129, 145, 249
Carlo Giovanella, pp. 26 (bottom), 39
Douglas Leighton: pp. 33, 84-85, 156, 180-81, 198, 203, 209, 224-25, 229, 230, 235, 236, 241, 268-69, 299, 307, 316, 328
Robert Cannings: pp. 36, 150, 207, 216, 252, 265, 279, 281, 314, 319, 322
Mark Wilson: p. 37 (top)
James Basinger, et al.: p. 37 (bottom right)
Ruth Stockey and Wesley Wehr: p. 37 (bottom left)
Deanna McLeod: p. 38
Mark Hobson: pp. 92 (left), 93, 139, 144, 149, 159, 161, 165, 178, 179, 193, 330
Richard Hebda: p. 102
Graham Osborne: pp. 114-115, 173, 188-89
John Ford: p. 117
F. J. R. Taylor: pp. 120 (left and middle), 121, 122
Elaine Humphrey: pp. 120 (right), 124
James Cosgrove: p. 125
Verena Tunnicliffe: p. 134
Leah Ramsay: pp. 135, 274
Jim Ginns: p. 162
Dave Fraser: pp. 170, 171, 197
Jeff and Sue Turner: p. 176
Len Jellicoe: p. 191

Clair Israelson: p. 239
Andy Valadka: p. 271
Bill Leonard: pp. 291, 311
George Doerksen: pp. 294, 313
Robert Cannings and Brent Cooke, Royal British Columbia Museum: p. 309
Tyler Boyes/Shutterstock: pp. 324-25
David Reesor: p. 331
Joaquim Alves Gaspar: p. 338
Dave Ingram: p. 340

Illustrations

David Budgen: p. 21
Donald Gunn: pp. 42, 43, 48, 91, 96, 127, 130, 132, 133 (bottom), 135, 136 (bottom), 137 (bottom), 140, 141, 172, 184 (Figure 6.1), 195, 197 (bottom), 199, 202, 205, 214 (in box), 226, 258, 259, 267, 289, 290 (middle), 293, 295, 297, 301, 309, 310, 311, 312, 334, 335
Briony Penn: p. 95
Illustration by R. G. Carveth for J. D. McPhail, *Canadian Journal of Zoology* 62: 1402-8, Fig. 3: p. 97
Royal British Columbia Museum: pp. 126, 290 (bottom), 307
Reprinted from Richard Lydekker (ed.), *Royal Natural History*: p. 133 (top), 147
Reprinted from T. H. Carefoot, *Pacific Seashores*: pp. 136 (top), 137 (top), 142
Nola Johnston, B.C. Parks: p.158 (margin)
Hannah Nadel: pp. 158 (bottom), 318 (bottom)
Canadian Forest Service: pp.162, 223
B.C. Parks: pp. 165, 166, 174 (top), 175, 197 (top and centre), 214 (top and centre), 219, 245, 248, 253
G. B. Straley and R. P. Harrison, *An Illustrated Flora of the University Endowment Lands*, University of British Columbia Technical Bulletin No. 12 (Vancouver: The Botanical Garden, University of British Columbia, 1987): pp. 169, 306 (top), 318 (top three)
T. C. Brayshaw, *Trees and Shrubs of British Columbia* (Vancouver and Victoria: University of British Columbia Press and Royal British Columbia Museum, 1996): pp. 174 (bottom), 217 (bottom three)

Patricia Drukker-Brammall in W. B. Schofield, *Some Common Mosses of British Columbia* (Victoria: Royal British Columbia Museum, 1992): pp. 217 (top), 290 (top), 315, 317
Ralph Idema, *Manual of Nearctic Diptera*, Vols. 1 and 2, Figs. 25.1, 27.1 and 31.3, 108.1, and 110.1, based on information from Agriculture and Agri-Food, reproduced with the permission of the Minister of Supply and Services Canada, 1981, 1992: pp. 204, 218
Robert Cannings: pp. 234, 304
C. L. Hitchcock, A. Cronquist, M. Ownbey and J. W. Thompson, *Vascular Plants of the Pacific Northwest* (Seattle: University of Washington Press): pp. 271, 306 (bottom)

The following sources have given permission for quoted material:

From "maggie and milly and molly and may" in *Complete Poems: 1904-1962* by e. e. cummings, edited by George J. Firmage. Copyright © 1956, 1984, 1991 by the Trustees for the e. e. cummings Trust. Reprinted by permission of Liveright Publishing Corporation. From "Out Past the Timberline" by Murray McLauchlan. Copyright © 1983 by Gullwing Music/Sold For A Song/MCA Music Canada. Reprinted by permission. All rights reserved. From "Mon Pays" by Gilles Vigneault. Used by permission. From "Where the Coho Flash Silver" by Lloyd Arntzen. Copyright © by SOCAN. Reprinted by permission. All rights reserved.

RICHARD CANNINGS works as a consulting biologist assessing endangered species and organizing broad-scale bird population surveys. He is the author of *Birdfinding in British Columbia*, with Russell Cannings, *An Enchantment of Birds*, *The Rockies: A Natural History*, and, with Sydney Cannings, *The New B.C. Roadside Naturalist*.

SYDNEY CANNINGS is a biologist working on species at risk for Environment Canada in Whitehorse, Yukon. He has also worked as an endangered species specialist for the British Columbia government.